UPRISING OF THE HUMAN SPIRIT

UPRISING OF THE HUMAN SPIRIT

Eric Williams Towle, PhD

Integral Publishers
Tucson, Arizona

© 2014 Integral Publishers, LLC. All Rights Reserved.

Integral Publishers
1418 N. Jefferson Ave.
Tucson, AZ 85712

No part of this book may be reproduced in any manner whatsoever without written permission of the author and the publisher, except in the case of brief quotations in critical articles and reviews. For information, address Integral Publishers.

Cover design by Jeannie Carlisle.

ISBN: 978-0-9896827-1-8

For Ginger and Denise,
for all your love and support

Table of Contents

Introduction ix

Chapter 1: The Basic Situation 1

Chapter 2: The Inside and the Outside of Life 55

Chapter 3: Egocentric Materialism 93

Chapter 4: Civilization of Side Effects 137

Chapter 5: Society of Manipulation 177

Chapter 6: Orchestrating History 273

Chapter 7: The Integral Structure 313

Appendix: Suggestions for an Integral Uprising 383

Bibliography 385

Index 393

Introduction

The Uprising of the Human Spirit

There is a world crashing out there. It is the end of a good idea that had its day. There are grand eras of civilization built on a notion, an idea, a way of seeing things, and this has its run through time, growing to prominence and then fading slowly from focus as a new idea, a new way of knowing things arises. We have come to recognize these new ways of knowing as the result of an evolution of consciousness that has pulled us toward an ever expanding horizon from the earliest days of our awakening as human beings on earth.

History is a wave that travels across vast oceans to break on the shore of a new world. History's wave is now breaking again. The eternal force behind Nature rises within every human life, call it the human spirit, it moves each of us to our own unique destiny. Through this genius entire civilizations rise. What is explored within these pages is the relationship between this rising current of life energy that has pushed conscious evolution along for untold eons and the socio-economic world this human spirit creates and inhabits. It is a particular moment in this relationship that interests us now, that place in time where the growth of the human spirit seems to outpace the established structures of society that stagnate in their growth so as to maintain an entrenched authority. The difference between what people are feeling in the yearnings of their spirit for a better world and the deficient reality of what is before them causes a profound friction that has punctuated critical junctures in history since the beginning of human society. This friction has been the source of profound works of art and bold new social formations like Athenian philosophy, the Roman Republic, the Renaissance, and the Constitution of the United States of America.

That feeling that our lives have meaning is a call to discovery and a road to the future we travel together. There is a great struggle going on in our time because every life that reaches for a brightening future faces another that clings anxiously to the darkening past. We have reached the edge of history and now we must face our fear and move through the blockade to our expanding potential as human beings, within ourselves and within our civilization. What we give up is the ever accelerating freight train of competition towards a mirage that is the ultimate ego gratification and materialist nirvana, where, as Henry David Thoreau once said, "All our inventions are but improved means to an unimproved end." What we gain is nothing less than the reestablishing of our true calling as human beings working towards a world of cooperative creativity on a multi-dimensional scale as we discover whole regions of experience neglected within ourselves and the world. In the knowledge offered here routes towards joy and meaning are established as the productions of a new mind capable of seeing and feeling a life previously known only to an enlightened few. Just as Leonardo Da Vinci demonstrated an engineering genius rare in his time but common now, we are seeing an evolution of consciousness that is rendering an old genius commonplace and so opening an opportunity for anyone to free themselves from the frustration and fear of a declining civilization. The explanation for this will unfold in the pages ahead but before this task is approached it is essential to understand the dynamic of time and change we are caught in.

If history were a landscape stretched out so that we could survey the long view in a single glance we would see societies rising from small villages of natural construction, bark and timber and clay, people in animal skins and then crude woven fabrics, then the skyline would gradually rise as stone architecture becomes prominent first low and stout but then reaching ever higher into the air as civilizations of monumental accomplishment rise from the landscape. We would see them thrive for a time, their bannered towers shining in the sun, and the squares filled with colorful festivals and lavish markets. Then something would seem to shift in the activity of the city, celebrations halt, things grow shabby and fall into disrepair, people drift away at first and then leave in masses as outside forces overrun the area. The once great nation falls into ruin, the stone structures now serving as crumbling backdrop to the shanty town of a simpler people living in its shadow. Elsewhere down the line another great society is building. It will rise to its glory and then the greatness will fade, and these contours of human aspiration will roll up and down out across the field of time for as far as we can see.

What happens? Why does the long view of history show us these hills and valleys, up and down, over and over, as civilizations rise and fall across time and all across the globe? The answers may be found in a complex formula of politics and environment, every discipline from ecological science to epidemiology has their pet theory but always at the center of it all, no matter what the material factors, what we find are people. People have demonstrated a tremendous capacity for overcoming any obstacle, for adapting and outsmarting any limitation. When the ancient Romans found the local water sources to be inadequate in keeping up with the tasks of their imagination as their city expanded they constructed great aqua ducts, an engineering marvel of the age, to bring water in abundance form nearby mountains. Centuries later they made an equally fateful decision not to maximize local grain harvests in preference of expanding imperial holdings abroad; a decision that benefited a powerful elite minority over the welfare of the broader population, leading eventually to food shortages and hastening collapse.

Ultimately it is the evolution of the human mind, the imaginations and, in the end, simply the decisions *of people* that bring great societies up from the dust and the lack of imagination and the wrong decisions that return them there, surely without intent but just as surely their light goes out, with a bang or a whimper.[1]

This book is about the wave of history, about the energy within that wave, what is essentially the evolution of the consciousness of humanity. It is about those fateful decisions. It is about power and the path of our civilization. You are in a revolution, whether you know it or not. The festivals are in full swing even as the fractures grow ever wider beneath our feet. The band plays on but the wave of history ceaselessly rolls forward, cresting to crash on the shores of a new world. The sort of world this will be is what we are now deciding as life faces off against death once again.

In understanding where we are now, it is essential to understand two major forces at work in the history of human civilization: the first is the force of the evolving mind of the individual; the second is the force of political power that gathers around the institutions that run a society. In the development of civilization the first force of the expanding mind creates the second force as new fields of knowledge and power come into being in response to new ideas but in time, although the human mind and therefore society continue to evolve, institutions do not, they harden into stagnate forms that change only so as to extend the profit and influence of those who benefit most from their established centers of power.

History shows extended periods where the evolving human mind seems to plateau and sudden flowerings where human thought explodes into new dimensions fecund with vital new insights. When this occurs the public will at some juncture come into conflict with the established institutions. Fractures begin to appear in the society. Voices rise in protest as the deficiencies of the power centers cause increasing difficulties for the people. The institutions then defend themselves against the call for change so as to retain their power and the degree to which they are successful in doing so is the degree to which the society will veer towards its own eventual destruction.

There is a way of looking at the history of the human race and lifting from the great eras of developing societies an outline describing phases in the evolution of consciousness. These great eras of thought are based on what can be understood as emerging "structures of consciousness." Ways of understanding the world flowing from a certain mode of meeting life, a predominance of certain senses over others, and a philosophy of interpretation emerging from those senses and their circumspect view. In each bygone era a specific structure of consciousness dominated, with other structures being latent or marginal in their role in life, so that, for instance, sound and hearing were dominant along with raw emotion in one era, to be replaced by vision, imagery, and heroic passion in the next. In the first era sight was used, of course, just not in a dominant way so as to create the visual language, as in writing and symbols, which occurred in the second era, when an oral culture gave way to a written one. In just this fashion human history displays for us a gathering of greater and greater perceptive capacity evidenced in the appearance of larger domains of thought.

In the ancient world between the years 800 BCE and 200 BCE a great shift in human consciousness occurred. A new way of knowing life worked its way into existence within the mind of humanity all over the planet. This great shift was dubbed: the "Axil Age" by the German philosopher Karl Jaspers because it seemed to pivot the entire course of world culture. During this period major new philosophies emerged typified by an expanding intellectualism. The Greek thinker Socrates arrived at the height of the period and contributed to the spirit of the age with nothing less than a new way of knowing truth, questioning everything that had come before. "I am the wisest man alive, for I know one thing, and that is that I know nothing." Along with the work of Socrates' contemporaries, foremost among them the philosopher Plato, the Greek achievement went on to profoundly affect Roman culture, the growth of Christianity and on, to become a major influence on the Renaissance, to remain a vital inspiration today. In the East there was the arrival of Buddhism in India and Confucianism in China, two ancient traditions still very much alive. In the Middle East Zoroastrianism appeared with its doctrine of eternal opposition between light and darkness forming the foundations of all Western dualistic philosophy to come.

Jaspers believed the message of the revolutionary minds arising at that time represented a shift from group to individual values. Essentially, consciousness intensified within the individual so that people began to see themselves as independent operators in the world and with this shift in perspective came the realization that wisdom could emerge from a single person rather than simply being divined from celestial or earthly indicators or from ritualistic practices looking to reveal the will of the gods.

This axial shift is understood in the study of the evolution of consciousness as the emergence of the first glimmers of the "mental" structure of consciousness, at a time when the "mythical" structure was still very dominant. The evolution of consciousness constitutes a process within the individual of an experience of greater *awareness* through the development of larger dimensions of thought. The French theologian and evolutionary philosopher, Tellhard de Chardin, referred to this as "complexification," a pattern discernible in cultural history that demonstrates more and more complex ways of understanding things. This evolving consciousness has created expansions of culture that mark great shifting points in history. The entire system describing these great periods of thought will be presented in some detail in the following chapter. The basic outline is made up of four historical structures: the "archaic," "magic," "mythic," and "mental/rational." A fifth structure, the "integral" is the new structure of consciousness emerging in our time. Each of the historical structures was punctuated by a unique focus. In the archaic period humans were ensconced in nature, responding to instinct. In the magic period humans were primarily focused on emotion, sound and the word in emerging language. In the mythic period imagery, symbols, and a written language were the primary focus, giving rise to mythic stories explaining reality. In the mental/rational period a mechanical logic came to prominence, a measuring and calculating approach was applied to the world.

These developments are understood to have occurred very early in the human story so that by 500 BCE it is thought that all structures had appeared up to the mental, even though the mental structure of consciousness would not fully come into its own until the Enlightenment period of the 17th Century.[2]

There is at first a mixing of structures, the new with the old ways of understanding life are blended, one on top of another. Then the new eventually becomes dominant pushing the old mode of thought out of mainstream practice considering it primitive or for the simple minded. Often previous structure practices like ritual dancing or chanting are retained outside normal daily practice as entertainments. The new structure of thought dominates all the elder ways of life and those outside the new society still focused on the earlier structure will be looked down on and considered, "savages." In a certain sense, then, we can say that during this process of dis-identification with earlier structures human beings were losing older abilities just as much as they were gaining new ones; essentially making progress at the expense of more primary skills that grew progressively dull or dormant. Progress was accompanied by a retrograde development. This could very well account for our current confusion as to the origin of many mysterious ancient productions like pyramids and elaborate astronomical systems without telescopes, as well as metallurgic wonders where the more complex processes like bronze production came earlier than the simpler iron. Like alchemy, these were likely magic/mythic structure practices that under the pressure of an evolving consciousness became incomprehensible to the rational mind. The "sharpness" of earlier capacities were lost to make way for the exclusive focus necessary to bring to fruition the next emerging structure.

When the mythic minded Viking explorers reached North America they encountered magic structure Native Americans they referred to as "Skraelings," a derogatory term they used for all indigenous people that meant something like, "wretches," or "screechers." This is the typical pattern: those demonstrating an historically earlier worldview are denigrated. In this case the earlier magic consciousness dominated by sound in an oral tradition produced the behavior of a myriad of calls in imitation of animals. The Norse experienced this as simply "screeching" even though they themselves still used war cries derived from the very same behavior but by then well subsumed into their mythic view. The Viking culture even though having progressed to the dominance of runic writing and symbols as a conveyor of power emanating in the mythic mind from imagery rather than sound, still held onto deep magic structure consciousness in the form of warrior rituals such as the "berserker." To "go berserk," in the mythic mind meant "putting on the bear shirt," language symbolic of a regression to the early magic structure mind where a shamanic identification with the fierceness of the raging bear allowed warriors to defy pain and fear and garner a kind of psychotic strength making them very hard to stop. The Norse ritualized and thereby contained this and other vestiges of magic consciousness practice within a larger mythic consciousness that dominated their worldview. In time the "bear shirt" would be found only in children's games. This is the pattern present throughout history: the old ways are first reimagined and contained then reduced by the broadening structures of the new mind. From guiding lights the old sacred stories become legends and folk tales, the old practices become party games, the old rituals become theater.

In time consciousness always opens again to yet a larger field of consideration. The great scholar of the evolution of consciousness, Jean Gebser, said that, in essence, consciousness continues to *intensify*. Think of consciousness like the proverbial light bulb above the head of the person with a *bright idea*. We'll say the person is sitting in the dark and as consciousness increases the bulb gets brighter, thus illuminating a broader circle around the person so they can see farther into the landscape they inhabit. This must be understood as a limited metaphor because *seeing*, as in the appreciation of imagery, is the dominate mode of the mythic structure. Whereas within the overall progress of evolving consciousness it's really a matter of differing *domains of sense impression* emerging with new intensity in each era that broadens the circle of illumination as time goes on, thus allowing more of what's in the universe to be perceived on *multiple levels of perception*. For instance, in the magic period the aural sense is primary in decoding the sounds of the world. In the mythic image, symbol and scene become primary and refined in appreciation. In the mental, a reasoning logic is developed. Each of these turns up the light in their respective domain and in addition to the whole the overall light is brightened. (In addition to this is the proviso offered by generations of finger wagging philosophers, that we never really perceive what's in the world in a completely objective way because every impression is coming through our human physical sensing apparatus so that we are wrapped up in the world and the world in us.) With the entrance of the mental sphere of development is the illumination of the interior of the mind itself, the possibility of thinking about thinking, so that new ways of using information about the outside world come to light in the form of abstractions and formula.

In the present era we are transitioning again so that one structure of consciousness that has dominated our lives, the "mental/rational structure," typified by measuring and calculating leading to abstract analysis, is giving way to what is being termed the "integral structure." The previous structures all seemed to dominate their eras, largely rejecting conclusions from previous modes of consciousness as they struggled to overcome the limitations of the older ideas. Along this path each era in consciousness became strongly dominated by a single structure. The integral structure's purpose seems to be to integrate all the former structures into a more cohesive, healthy and functional whole, so that all the previous structures can be freely utilized by people in appropriate ways. In so doing it offers a balanced, "multi-valiant," way of knowing the world and experiencing life. Each structure can be understood to have its own specialty within a multi-valiant consciousness so that specific types of experience should be "read" with the proper structure. For instance: the archaic animal sense is still good, among other things, for sensing danger, whereas a purely mental/rational assessment of the situation might miss the danger altogether. Additionally, the integration of the structures into a conscious whole have been found to provide the platform for yet another step in the evolution of consciousness.

The integral opens the mind to a new freedom that sees beyond the surface, beyond the simple divisions of the material to detect greater patterns of connection and beyond this toward what the esoteric doctrines call a "non-duel" consciousness that begins to intuit the dynamics of the universal energies that are both matter and light simultaneously and so offer new ways of understanding both time and space. All this will be explored in some depth in the final chapter.

The first task is the freeing of each structure within its own proper domain. This allows each previously denigrated and reduced structure of consciousness to be reinvested with attention and further developed. As the original eras of prime development for each structure were surpassed by the next emerging structure the potential of the previous structure as a channel of experience and understanding was curtailed. By reinvesting each historically previous structure with attention we can open these avenues once again for maturation. In this way the contact with nature in the archaic structure, the passionate intensity of emotional life in the magic structure, the existential journey of the hero in the mythic structure, and the rational appraisal of the mental structure come together in a coordinated fashion to create an experience of wholeness and multidimensional contact with life that is ever renewed. This description pales before the actual experience, which is really what this integration process is about—not *thinking* about these other structures, which is a *mental* act, but delving deeply into each on their own terms.

As an example of magic structure development we can look at the experience of musicians. It is recognized that it isn't enough to be simply *technically precise* in the playing of an instrument (a mental and physical training task). One must be able to transmit *passion* through the music, linking sound and emotion in a way not associated with mental constructs—*you've got to feel it*. The musician's practice leads them into the depths of their own emotion which is the feeling response to life at its core and when they are doing it best we can meet them there. The poet expresses another contact with the magic/mythic depth we share when the ear and mind are properly attuned. We recognize the impoverishment of those who have none of this. Some of this is what was once called, "refinement" but it was unfortunately associated with oppressive class structures that made the idea ultimately unpalatable for many. What we're doing now is something that escapes those former prejudices while it seeks to lead the soul back into communion with abandoned practices that are essentially *sources of life*.

Consider each structure of consciousness as being a separate interface with reality with its own unique validity. For instance, the magic structure is the avenue through which our emotional sensors read the tenor of life energy around us. We can feel anger, tension, deceit, there is an energetic signature of each that an aware human being can pick up on. Now this sort of suggestion sounds to the mind dominated by the scientific materialist doctrine of the age like "airy-fairy nonsense," because when one structure attempts to judge the experience of another structure it can't understand its perceptive terms. The mind controlled by the dominate structure then attempts to understand the issue through its own mode of comprehension. In the example above the mental structure may attempt to detect the emotional energy through a device in the form of an electro-magnetic reading, perhaps a needle on a dial. If it can't pick it up then it declares the perception an error or phantasy. This is a self-deluding game humanity in the West has been playing with itself for a few centuries now. At present, although we slip into these other structures of consciousness from time to time, our lives are overly dominated by the last structure to arise: the mental. While the previous structures are generally considered inferior leading to a cutting off of their sense of the world thereby impoverishing the individual's experience of life.

The central idea, the mode of comprehension, within the era that is passing, what's been called the "mental/rational structure," was built almost exclusively on the breakthrough insights of the scientific revolution. This was that first attempt at science based on the art of ascertaining knowledge through empirical experimentation that sought to establish exacting measurements of material mechanisms in nature. This early science was born in opposition to the authority of religion which had wielded power in the West since the first civilizations to the final centuries of Roman dominance in the form of the Catholic Church. Theirs was an authority based on the invisible hand of God, and science, having been condemned by the Church for the heresy of finding truth outside their authority and finally having escaped the fiery wrath of the Pope, broke loose in rebellion against all things spiritual. Although the foundational thinker Sir Isaac Newton himself was a very spiritual person and a practicing alchemist, as science grew in dominance it purged from its thinking all resort to the invisible hand of deity. Science would become a purely materialist inquiry. It demanded that everything sought as explanation of the myriad displays of nature be material, something that could be measured by an "objective" standard. No invisible forces, intelligence behind the scenes, or any such intentionality would be tolerated. This earth was a machine made by no one for no purpose, and this would be the controlling ethos of generations of scientists.

This idea was largely based on Newton's mechanics that demonstrated that the motion of objects could all be determined by mathematical formula. If position, course, and speed were known then the complete future and past of the object could be hypothetically known and since it was believed that the whole world was nothing but objects in motion then everything could be determined. Everything was just running down from original causes, like a big clock that had been wound up a long time ago. The great philosopher of science at its birth, Rene Descartes, had God winding up the clock but those who followed couldn't stand for that so "random events" was inserted in every slot where "God" had served before.

Newton's objects were understood as separated by time and space and transferring force through brute physical contact alone. This was understood as the basic facts of all things on earth and so when Darwin came along it was clear to him that the separate objects in his study that were the flora and fauna of the world were themselves in a situation of the transfer of brute force from one to the other in a sublime competition for survival. No underlying invisible connections, no larger mind at work in nature, nothing but mechanics, the big fish eat the little fish, nothing more to it. Nature was shaped the way it was because some creatures had "triumphed" over others. There were "kings" of the jungle, and "dominant" species and all of this was simply the outcome of original factors. Like rolling balls bouncing from one random event to the next, everything worked out its path set in motion and therefore determined a long time ago at the very first random event.

From this beginning Western Civilization threw itself into two centuries of materialist, mechanistic interpretation and analysis that spawned an utterly amazing explosion of ever more powerful and complicated machines that have dominated our society as they have our minds. If the plains Indians were the people of the buffalo then we are the people of the machine. "In machine we trust."

You wouldn't know it unless you looked into it but all this is in question now. All this--the lifeless mechanics of Western thought--is reaching a kind of "apocalypse of materialism" in our time. The problem that has become apparent is simply that human experience and, indeed, the universe itself, simply isn't confined to the material world of "objective" things. There is an "inside" to consciousness that turns out to be part of reality, as well; just as there are non-material forces in the universe that form the foundations of reality itself. We have been transitioning into a new stage in the evolution of our consciousness for some time now, perhaps since the nineteenth century. It is typical that as the elder stage wears down the old ways of thinking start to overreach the limits of their usefulness and begin to blind rather than reveal and with this they lead to devastation. Ironically, pure or "radical" materialism has taken over as the basis of all mainstream culture even as its scientific foundation disappears. Consumerism as the economic expression of materialism as a way of life and the over consumption it promotes has produced numbers of toxic side-effects. From bursting garbage dumps leaching toxins into the water table and oceans to pervasive credit card debt, to mental disorders such as hording and compulsive shopping, to corporate strategies for maximizing profit by sending manufacturing overseas, to simple moral decline evidenced by the growing preponderance of greed. If the whole world consumed like North Americans it would poison the whole planet in a few short years, report environmental scientists in increasing urgency with few bothering to listen.

At its height scientific materialism combined with the fresh ideas of a new, unbounded and well-funded American society to create an explosion of innovation unprecedented in world history. The scientific materialist worldview within the milieu of a democratic republic worked extraordinarily well for a time. It unleashed a vast technological abundance but like all great guiding doctrines applied to the exclusion of other values, it showed itself to contain a terrible poison when taken in too large a dose.

In a society dominated by values inspired by orthodox science and its strict materialist belief system, money becomes more than a medium of exchange. It becomes the whole point of existence. This condition has led to a clear decline in the human values that were once the sacred inspiration for the hard fought creation of the American Republic itself. Every major institution of American society is now more interested in serving itself and making money than effectively serving the purpose for which it was originally created. The insurance business, for instance, is less interested in insuring your health and property than in insuring the incomes of their major stock holders. What was once the primary purpose of the institution is overcome by the financial incentive, thus subordinating people to profit. This dynamic has insinuated itself into all institutions and is evidence of a crisis in values and the hegemony of Wall Street into all sectors of American life. This corruption of institutions, typical of failing civilizations, is then protected from reform by the elite groups that own them so as to continue profits now at public expense.

When societies begin to run their course and the old ways begin to produce more problems than benefits then individuals are motivated to create alternatives. This has been going on for some time. People in the know have simply abandoned the decaying system and taken up an alternative. We see this clearly in the rise of the "health food" industry that is really just offering food with the nutrition once available to our ancestors before chemical farming and heavy processing filled the grocery stores with hollow food missing many nutrients, fibers, vitamins, and other things essential for our health. Once people find out they may develop Alzheimer's due to a lack of essential minerals because their food has been grown in burnt out soil, or their tooth paste or shampoo may be slowly poisoning them due to toxic additives they'll find an alternative, its self-preservation.

The alternatives spring from the rising new consciousness, a consciousness that has stimulated the growth of new lines of scientific inquiry revealing a structure to nature and the universe much different than the old Newtonian picture. One of the initial experiences of the new stage in consciousness now dawning is a recognition of a larger system connecting all life; a "web of life" where living things are intimately connected to their environment and all things exchange information in a myriad of ways including at subatomic levels where distance, as we perceive it, is not a factor. Nothing is really separate in this new understanding. Once people see this and begin to understand the ramifications they start to develop alternatives to everything created from the old disconnected Newtonian view. More than just a philosophical shift, people put this new found worldview to work in their lives from toxic free mattresses to psychological treatments for physical ailments. They also begin changing their behavior, recycling being the most mundane and common example created by the realization that throwing things away is stupid from a resource systems management view while it constitutes an assault on a larger ecosystem we are dependent on.

There is a new civilization rising up to offer something better than the products produced by a system that sees the world as a collection of disconnected objects whose primary concern is making money with the ultimate health and safety of end users and the environment being entirely secondary in concern. It is now the money mindset that runs the hospitals and the food corporations and it is this who the doctors, engineers, and all those concerned with ultimate quality must answer to. We have created a civilization which has put wealth at the top of our list of concerns and so everything follows behind the dollar. This is an instructive observation because in seeing this truth we must wonder what is behind it, why money? Why not health, truth, justice, or the pursuit of an economic system which benefits all while constraining the creativity of no one?

The answer to this question leads us back to the understanding that our history is a reflection of our evolving consciousness and that in the current era we have been occupied with what we've been calling the "mental/rational stage" of development, where a particular focus on the material has been the primary, indeed *exclusive*, concern. During this stage the major mode of understanding the world and universe we live in has come through a belief system controlled by scientific materialism. A view that has delved into the mechanisms of nature, the material side of the way things work. This has afforded humanity a great advance in creative utility. Because this purely material approach has been so successful a tendency has arisen to believe that the universe in its entirety is simply a material construct. This has led our society into a basic belief that only material things have value and so an unconscious worship of material objects has ruled the modern age. This is what was once called, "idolatry," an erroneous belief that the *god* really does live in the statue we carve.

Instead of spiritual or "non-material" forces giving rise to the material forms of this world, with those nonmaterial forces being *primary*, as older cultures believe--matter being simply the transient form that lives and dies and pass away in time--the mental structure of consciousness focuses exclusively on the material *as the only reality*. In moving into the mental stage of development and the modern materialist culture it engendered we confused our obsessive focus on matter with an absolute truth. Everything we have not focused on, all the forces behind matter—creation itself--have been declared false, a fantasy, a superstition; simply the product of an earlier age which "didn't have our smarts." This is the error of our obsession we are slowly overcoming in the West.

As we move into this next stage in the evolution of our consciousness that has opened a new era in physics where non-material forces are again rising in empirical stature, many people have been drawn to reassess traditional cultures and earlier ways of interacting with the powers of the world looking for hints as to how to achieve a relationship with that which is beyond our material senses. Such things as shamanism, eastern meditative arts, prayer, gnostic Christianity, and physical energy practices developed from ancient times are again being studied. Spirituality in general has become a greater fascination in a society now looking beyond the stilted confines of traditional religions toward a simple understanding of the basic dynamics of the invisible forces and dimensions of existence outside and intersecting material life. It is not a return to old ways of thinking but, among other things, simply reincorporating some approaches that allow us to know the world in ways different from the sciences measurement of material objects, ways we "moderns" left behind long ago, now reimagined from the vantage point of a broader, conscious appreciation. This reclaiming of the entirety of human sense and knowing then allows the individual to step into a more intense, vibrant mode of meeting life. Passion returns to an existence made boring by an over rationalized perspective. This idea will be explored in the next chapter.

As science has followed its materialist obsession reaching farther and farther into the depths of matter, looking for the smallest building blocks of the material world, it has broken into the very entrance hall of creation itself and found, to its great consternation, *nothing*. That is to say, energy without form which escapes the all mighty measuring instrument of conventional science. Like some kind of subatomic phantom, the eternal force that gives rise to all matter evades the too narrow philosophy of the scientific materialists because at that smallest place where matter forms there are no objects at all. What is found there is only a kind of "cloud of probabilities."

Current revelations in that mystical subatomic world are taking our scientific society in another direction entirely, toward a non-material basis, but before it does we will face the political resistance of the last throws of the dying institutions conceived by the logic of the strict materialist past. Our current stage in the evolution of consciousness has been expanding for some time now bringing forth the vision of a multidimensional universe. As the awakening of the next stage takes greater and greater hold of the common mind, a rebellious dynamic evidenced in the rise of an alternative culture grows more apparent and with it a counter reaction--the old culture and the status-quo it supports take increasingly forceful measures to combat the rising alternative society and its progressive views. This effort constitutes a literal attack on the expansion of consciousness. This subject will fill a major part of the pages ahead.

So, this brings us to the question of exactly what the new stage of consciousness rewriting the sacred texts of our civilization is all about.

In brief, where the old Newtonian science saw everything as separate in time and space, the new view sees everything connected beneath time and space, a view well demonstrated by the new physics. As discussed above the old "disconnected universe" theory gave impetus to ideas of everything acting in a kind of war of all against all, whereas the new understanding sees larger systems of communication and coordination dominating what seem on the surface to be competitive processes. The "survival of the fittest" becomes, on second view, an ordered system of ecological balance where no "king of the jungle" exists and survival rises and falls on the health of the *entire system*. From another view the new stage provides a kind of "seeing through" of the material world. A view that penetrates the surface; meaning is seen in all its connectedness; order is found emerging from chaos; the random is located within invisible webs of influence. In human affairs material objects as carriers of ultimate value and materialism as a way of life loses its grip on the mind due to the realization that the most dominant forces in our lives are non-material, that material objects are little more than props for human endeavor and not the goal of existence at all. The egotistic flaunting of ostentatious objects as symbols of superiority, an age old practice, is finally defeated within a mind opening to the notion that who I AM and what I *choose to do with my life* is more important than what I have. The old ethic is all on the surface, whereas the new is in the depth, the old is entirely material and the new uses the material for a deeper purpose. And just as the new physics suggests a myriad of multi-dimensional invisible forces at work in the dynamics of the universe and life itself, the new consciousness draws inspiration and knowledge of meaning and healing from internal intuitive sources unknown to the mechanical logic of the traditional scientific mind.

The new mind reveals this fully connected systems view and beyond this to a wholeness that transcends the individual and the material world, a realization of the truth that you can't do something to one part without affecting the whole. This really puts a kink in the old world industrial model wherein only the input and direct output is considered--in goes coal and out comes power, that is all they needed to know. In the new view we must consider the effects of removing coal from the ground, what is added to the air in burning it, and how the power is distributed. These considerations get in the way of profit seeking and so campaigns are mounted to dissuade the public from looking into them. This is but one example of how the expanding mind stimulates culture that runs headlong into the establishment of the old view. This is the age we live in--a time where new truths are in conflict with established power, both vying for the allegiance of the public, a dynamic manifesting in what some have called the "information wars."

As this battle ensued the new mind continued to rise, its alternatives in tow, and as it has gotten stronger the status-quo has reacted by progressively attempting to control more and more of the debate by simply buying up the organs of information distribution themselves. So that now corporate power, four companies for the most part, has a virtual monopoly on television news and programing, most radio, and nearly all major print media in the United States. The barons of materialism believe they can simply stop evolution from moving forward, much as the Church of Rome once thought it could stop the heliocentric structure of the solar system from being known, (and all that would follow in its path). The masters of money from the citadels of their church of materialism believe most assuredly that they can control this process as well.

And this is where the old systems of thought always falter. They literally can't conceive of how people could come to know things that they themselves are incapable of realizing. It is a mystery how these expansions of thought are triggered but as the dark ages moved into the Renaissance it was the rising humanism that moved society forward, the facts of planets in orbit becoming merely new observations available to the expanded view. This was a vision that brought with it the notion that human beings could be important as individuals rather than simply trash heaped at the door of God humbly minding their place in the order of things as they awaited their reward in heaven. It was this rising of the mind that sought and drew back into Europe the classical knowledge preserved in what had become of the old Eastern Empire of Rome and turned it for new purposes in the likes of a Shakespeare and a culture exploding beyond the boundaries of the old narrow Medieval worldview.

It isn't in the evening news that we find the stuff of conscious evolution. It is a process that is *noetic* in nature, meaning that it comes from within. Development in children demonstrates the pattern. When a child reaches the threshold of a new stage of psychological development they will start to lose interest in their old toys. The same old stories no longer hold their fascination; they strike out on adventures seeking something more, a new story, more complex toys better suited to their expanding sophistication. Nothing outside the child precipitates this dynamic. Neglect may produce developmental delays but, barring extreme abuse, you can no more prevent this development from eventually happening than you can stop the seasons. It is a natural inevitability and in like manner when a civilization hits the limit of its current stage it will develop. Even the mighty edifice of the Roman Empire couldn't hold back the tide of nature. No man denies life its destiny forever. At most it can be frustrated in the average person for a time by limiting their education and feeding them misleading information but extraordinary people exist in all eras that damn the odds and, not to be held back in their quest, *they get on their horse and ride into the frontier*, to invoke a sacred American archetype. These heroes seek out the knowledge that will rewrite the sacred texts of the evolving truth and from this the meek are tutored, thus whole societies slowly transcend the old view. Power structures don't seem to be able to stop this influx of truth once it begins. Even Stalin's Russian totalitarian complex of mental domination couldn't put a lid on it, and the propaganda and "infotainment" that passes itself off as "news" in the United States won't do it either.

It is equally true that dark ages often seem to follow at the functional end of a stage in the evolution of consciousness but they are only "dark" in that the mainstream is stagnant due to oppressive forces maintaining an order that should have fallen and been replaced. Beneath the surfaces a hidden intelligentsia continue to move awareness and knowledge forward just waiting for the dam to break, and break it always does, Pope or no Pope, media monopoly or not.

As a force of Nature evolution erodes all impediments over time. As the old saying goes, you can't keep a good man down, or woman, for that matter. A man named Viktor Frankl had a liberating revelation in a Nazi death camp by which he created an entire body of breakthrough psychological theory.[3] This goes to show that sometimes no amount of physical and psychological domination will stop the mind from evolving. Some evidence suggests hardship may even act as an accelerator of psychological growth.[4] I believe the bottom line is this: if the individual has reached the end of his or her old stage of consciousness then *they're leaving the farm*, and nobody in this world is going to stop them.[5]

Many people mistakenly assume that human beings have always had the same brain capacity and we've just been "figuring it out" over time. What's important to understand is that people have been incapable of figuring anything out that lies beyond the capacity of their minds, until that is, their minds develop. It is development that allows for greater insight and creativity. As the opening occurs it is the challenges the new vision affords that moves the mind forward in completing the work of the new stage. This is to say that, you can't just sit there and wait for it to happen. When the world gets dull and the old explanations seem way too thin and you look around and feel that "there has to be more to life than this..." then the individual must step out beyond their comfort zone, beyond their old prejudices, beyond their experience and follow their intuition, rather than their "reason" because reason has been defined by the old materialist logic that simply ties a person down to the same old tired possibilities.

If you are deciding what to do with your life reason dictates that if you want to be successful then you should get into a career that offers upward mobility, the chance to make a substantial salary, to distinguish yourself in some manner. This may point a person toward law or some position in a rising industry like computer technology but even though this may be "perfectly reasonable" it may also be completely contrary to what your own personal authentic being is really asking for. Inside every person is an evolutionary imperative that if encouraged to awaken will carry that individual to a transcendence of the old system of logic based on materialist values toward a new horizon where the material is not rejected but carried into a higher order of relationship.

In order to understand the changes underway on the leading edge of consciousness we have to reassess our value system that has been tuned to the purposes of a worldview grown deficient in its capacity to speak to the human spirit. For those not comfortable with spiritual theories and language think of the spirit as not just some ghostly presence within the body but representing a deeper nature in the human system directly connected, and following from, that central energetic component within each person that is part and parcel of that which gave rise to the universe. That primordial energy that burst into existence literally creating three dimensional space and fostering the growth of planets and on them life—this is also the source of the individual spirit, of life. It is the origin of all things and its thrust into this dimension in the big bang(s) resides in us. We are driven in its creative mission by that spark of life that is not lost in the remote past having started the ball rolling and faded away but continues in each of us and in everything that is.

We can argue about the nature of that creative energy but we cannot deny its existence in us. We are made from it and it demonstrates directionality, it grows from the simple to the complex, from atomic particles, to matter, to one celled organisms, to fish, to fowl, to the most complex creature of all, and all of this is written in the book of time within the layers of history quite clearly. [6]

For those sensitive to the notion of human origins being related to lower species such as apes let us pay respect to this position by simply putting evolution in God's hands. Whatever your definition of God let the almighty simply use evolution as a tool for creating a body in which to endow a spirit because without a doubt the vehicle of animate life is organic and the fossil record strongly suggests that organic forms develop and change over time. We may argue about the mechanisms of evolution but to argue about evolution itself must constitute an immense denial. Just the same, what happens in the space between one stage and the next is not discernible from the biology alone. Further, that which gave rise to the universe, recognized from science or religion, is an invisible force that resides still within the heart of atoms that make up all that is. Cutting edge biology now tells us that as organic life evolves in complexity of form it allows the emergence of higher orders of being. [7] A frog is a collection of biological processes that were once individual creatures at large in the primordial soup which through the process of evolution have become bound together by a symbiosis that provided the possibility of a creature that we know as the frog but that frog can't be found in any of the parts. It is that which emerges from the synergy of the parts. In like manner a person is a collection of organic processes working in concert to form a platform for that emergent order of being we call humanity. This emergence is where one may rightfully insert "the creation of human beings." The physical form seems to have arisen from the biology of the Earth over time, let's not quibble about that, but that which makes us human, *the spirit of humanity*, has come directly from the originating force of creation. Having developed the world to the point where a higher order of being was possible, that being emerged. Human beings carry with them the imprint of the past but each emerging structure of consciousness contains something new, something not there before.

How exactly evolution occurs, how the "new parts" arrive is still very much a mystery, despite what the Neo-Darwinists might say in their ever-so-late materialist ranting. Although human beings share

99+ percent plus of their DNA with apes and even 97.5% with mice, humanity is neither a variety of mouse nor a "smart ape." The world and history demonstrates the striking difference. Humanity represents truly the awakening of a kind of *terrestrial god*; a powerful being who *creates* that is the prodigy of the universe. In a universe that is all about creation, humanity has emerged as an instrument of creation itself. We can view this reality through a spiritual lens or through a scientific lens. The pages ahead will discuss the value and appropriate scope of both views and ultimately show they are each two encounters with the same elephant.

And so life is moving forward through this mysterious creative impulse from the most remote origins of creation itself and although certain large scale parameters may be given for life in this three dimensional oxygenated space humanity represents that point at which the creation becomes self-reflective in consciousness and so a growing portion of the creative endeavor becomes subject to our free will. So there are boundaries for creation where order is given and within this the creative space where choices can be made. In this project there is the original impulse as it manifests in the depths of each human being which carries with it an order for life, health, and an impetus for growth now taking the form of human creativity. This allows for new combinations and unique interpretations that drive the myriad forms spewing from the mouth of time like the cornucopia of ancient myth. If the universe is anything, I think we can agree, it is a system for bringing into being ultimate variety. If it has a mind as we understand it, then it is the mind of an explorer of possibility.

Our Dilemma

So we are all trapped in the predicament of our age that is this running down of the materialist civilization inspired by the previous stage in the evolution of our consciousness, and the rising up of the new civilization inspired by the next evolutionary stage of consciousness. Here we are in the middle of it all, either straining to hold onto that which is passing or pushing forward the slow ascendance of the new vision. Many people live entirely in the old world and some entirely in the new but a growing number have one foot in both. *That portion of the individual that is aligned with the declining old world will be drug down with it and that part aligned with the new will be elevated as it rises up.* This is the task before us: to weed out that part of our mind controlled by the exclusive devotion to the old mental stage of consciousness and all the products and habits that go with it. The mental/rational structure has its appropriate uses and we must return it to those fields and get it out of all the other areas of our minds it has invaded inappropriately. There are a number of "master programs," to risk a computer metaphor that literally "run" us. These values, or active ideas, "memes" as some have come to call them, have taken over Western and especially American culture through historical circumstance and deliberate strategy. This is where the story gets interesting, this shaping of the culture to meet the needs of the "moneyed interests," as Thomas Jefferson referred to them.

It was the development of mass production machinery in the late 19th C. that democratized "shopping" for the masses but it was planned obsolescence and ever accelerating business cycles that drove the consumer dynamic from providing useful goods for all to the "throw away" society of ever growing garbage dumps, accelerating pollution and, most recently, massive trade deficits.

The old mental stage of development that spawned the first scientific revolution in believing everything to be separate objects disconnected in open fields of material forces could not understand how their actions would set entire ecosystems out of balance careening toward collapse. Nor could they envision how their methods would reduce food to nutrition vacant pulp. Nor how their ideas about the world would fill it with products full of "side effects," for the human body, *indeed the human spirit*, and the planet itself—but that is exactly what they did.

Of course many excellent advances were made through these early scientific reductionist philosophies and methods but the down side has been catching up with us and it is time for science to update its central theories. Unfortunately science has become politicized and massively coopted by industry, so like everything else in our materialist society it is money that calls the tune that science dances to, the search for truth be damned. As consciousness intensifies it opens new avenues of research, the new physics, the new biology but industry seeks to maintain its investments in the old technology that was the brainchild of an earlier, smaller phase in the expansion of consciousness regardless of the emergence of better, safer ways. Big science has been largely stuck in a paradigm holding pattern because it is in thrall to industry that forms the power base for a self-elected elite class of rulers who are served by the maintenance of obsolete ideas, (in everything from fossil fuels to chemotherapy).

This has come about through the concentration of wealth in a society that has become increasingly rigged to maintain the powerful few positioned at the top of the finance and corporate industrial pyramids. The heads of family fortunes once labeled, *the robber barons*, who to this day through their descendants control powerful "foundations," along with those of the new generation of super-rich, guide through their strategic endowments the course of much of American progress. Historians and educators, sociologists and scholars of political science, have all noted the use of the monumental financial leverage of the major tax exempt foundations in the shaping of trends in American academia and theory promotion. Through pouring funding into the support of an ideology encouraging "improvement" while never questioning the inevitability of the negative social conditions generated by their ruthless form of capitalism, philanthropy has served the central political imperative of reinforcing the power of the status quo. Observant scholars tell us that big foundations have, "a corrosive influence on a democratic society: they represent relatively unregulated and unaccountable concentrations of wealth which buy talent, promote causes, and, in effect, establish an agenda of what merits a societies attention. They serve as 'cooling out' agencies delaying and preventing more radical structural change. They help maintain an economic and political order international in scope which benefits the ruling-class interests of the philanthropists..." [8]

This influence has produced the general adoption of approaches to "social progress" which always locate the nexus of change in the individual and never in the system. Workers and the public in general are seen to be in need of "adjustment" to the "realities" of whatever measures this undemocratic power finds "necessary." (That is to say, that which insures the concentration of wealth and the disempowerment of the working populace.) Along with the big corporate conglomerates they control, these elite forces have bought the university research labs through the strings attached to large donations thus elevating research that supports their investments while killing that which might lead to competitive breakthroughs. The same process has been implemented in the socio-political arena where foundation money supports agreeable doctrine through academic stipends and grants to congenial professors. [9] Thus, research in the mainstream of technical and social science is herded along paths acceptable to the big money and with their control of the big "think tanks," political campaigns and direct ties to candidates there is little left in the way of genuine "pure" science or democracy, for that matter.

This is all part of the calcification of the institutions found in failing civilizations, avoiding the very changes that would revitalize and insure their continuation. This is why mainstream psychiatry concentrates on adjusting the individual by manipulating brain chemistry while religiously avoiding any examination of the social and economic environment the troubled patient inhabits, (even denying it is implicated in mental health at all). This is why we listen to music and watch video from mirrored disks read by lasers and hard drives containing libraries the size of a finger, yet we drive around in cars powered by engines essentially the same as that which Henry Ford put into his model T over a hundred years ago. The reason is that in the first case of electronics there's money to be made and no powerful interest to stop the progress, and in the second case, there's money to be made but plenty to be lost by huge and powerful interests who maintain their power through the control of a primary energy source.

The problem for these people in terms of much of the new energy technology is the same as that for the new consciousness in general: they both tend to be decentralizing to power structures. Just as the new consciousness encourages self-awareness and values arising from personal sources of wisdom rather than those dictated from above, the new energy technologies tend toward "point of use" structures. With devices like solar panels, wind mills, and the suppressed technology we've never seen, it's possible for each person to control their own energy which takes the power out of the hands of some central provider, dolling out gas and electricity from gas stations and big power plants. (This is why the oil companies are one of the largest holders of patents in solar technology controlling the direction of the market since the 1970's and the power companies offer subsidies for house holders to install solar systems that are hooked into the grid rather than stand-alone systems.)

This is the issue with much of the transition to the new stage of consciousness. Where the old system centralized power in an elite class of "experts," and owners of industry and finance, along with their contrived commercial culture, the new consciousness puts much of the authority over individual lives back in the hands of individuals themselves. This is accomplished by the expanded consciousness not only through the scientific investigations that reveal the profound depths of the mind itself and the deeper connection of the individual to transpersonal fields of information but through its relocation of the source of health, happiness, and higher values, from egotistic achievements and conspicuous consumption to an expanded experience within the individual and the empowered social groups they inhabit. The true power of the human mind and heart is revealed in the new consciousness so that happiness becomes a quality in life negotiated within the individual completely apart from any possession or awarded praise stipulated by the old culture of rivalry and reward. The individual discovers within themselves a source of healing and guidance that allows for a life of genuine psychological and emotional ease, dignity, and purpose that is not dependent on making a certain amount of money or preforming according to functional standards attuned to the needs of a centralized system of production and authority.

Most American's are completely unaware as to how their value system has been structured to accommodate commercial industrial processes so that they are conditioned to work and buy as needed for purposes other than their own welfare and the health of their community. This is achieved through a doctrine that fosters an insecure identity in the average person through the manipulations of the commercial culture so as to compel *striving and buying behavior*. Essentially, what were once considered basic human attributes, things like dignity and beauty could now be sold to people by convincing them that they are bereft of these things. That they are to be acquired as they are centered, not in humanity itself, but in the new car, clothes, jewelry, proper address, job title, etc. As the new consciousness dawns through this darkness, the ploy is revealed, and so your life can't be ransomed back to you as it is in the egocentric materialist world that defined the 20th century. To move into the new stage of consciousness requires a careful process of discernment and reassessment in review of all that has colored one's worldview. This is the task I am undertaking here. Not to be complete in one book, of course, a task which can only be completed in the hearts and minds of each individual but just to offer a beginning for those who have never deeply explored the issue but who are feeling the pressures of our age and want to do something about it besides take a pill.

To begin this process is to open a door and once that door is open it cannot be shut. No sane person goes back to previous stages in childhood.

No one returns to ignorance. Nobody shuts their mind off to their own spirit once it is in rebellion. This is what it really comes down to—*an uprising of the human spirit*. That force that gives us life and substance itself, that sustains our material form and drives the evolution of all life and the universe, call it by whatever name suits your personal philosophy. It will not be stopped. It offers us a range of choice but choose you must because all things that stop and become stagnant are dying. Observers of nature from the very earliest civilizations have noticed that life is in a continual state of becoming. Such has been the observation of Heraclitus, to Lao Tsu, to Frederick Nietzche. The growth of societies can plateau for a period but when consciousness breaks open and starts another stage of ascent then curiosity and adventurous thinking will challenge the status-quo and if apposed this *rising up* of the human spirit will turn to an *uprising*. This is our current condition, we are in rebellion against ourselves, both within the mind of the individual and within the body politic. We are working through the transition to the higher stage of consciousness calling us to transform our world as we transform our lives.

THE STRUCTURE OF THE BOOK

The chapters ahead are arranged to deliver a basic overview of the factors behind the pressures felt by individuals pressed between their own rising consciousness and the old deficient culture of runaway materialism and its declining institutions they are forced to contend with. An exploration of the political science of Dr. Carol Quigley explaining the forces within the rise and fall of civilizations is presented in juxtaposition to the cultural psychology of the evolution of consciousness as described by the German/Swiss scholar, Jean Gebser, with a goal of illuminating the experience of the individual caught in the colliding forces of personal evolution and political power. [10]

With this mission in mind the book proceeds with the historical evolutionary unfolding of the structures of consciousness and the present indicators of the awakening integral structure. Then goes on to describe in detail the forces arrayed against the present development as part of the sociopolitical maneuvering of the status-quo to maintain their power in the face of an expanding public mind, changing value system, and evolving society. The turning of American traditions toward the service of the elite power structures is shown in contrast to the evolving desire of the people for a progressively decentralized government and a return to the original path of American democracy as represented by those who first conceived of a government "of the people, for the people, and by the people."

The three branches of government, the criminal justice system, and all major institutions from medicine to academia have all been pulled into the orbit of the corporate financial power which has distorted every industry and social institution so as to better serve the central goal of the elevation of an increasingly steep hierarchy of wealth and power. The evolving consciousness of humanity is pitted against this regressive, "dark age" dynamic that rises throughout history just at the time when human beings are attempting to move beyond the limitations of a faltering system and expand into a broader appreciation of the human spirit. This condition is examined in some basic detail as to the psychology that promotes it within the mind of the average person. To this end the book moves into an historical review revealing the various methods employed to facilitate a gradual control of the public mind through education, media, "public relations," direct mind control techniques, and staged "events," perpetrated for the purposes of producing public support for both domestic and foreign policy.

Due to the deteriorating condition of any accurate historical memory in the American public, a condition purposely induced, a short history of major manufactured events over the past century is included so as to make clear in the mind of the reader that, although there have been conspiracies at work here, there are no "conspiracy theories" promoted within these pages only the actual facts of American history. This history lesson is needed and relevant to the major thesis of this work because the central methods of gaining public support for an elitist agenda have been largely psychologically coercive and a matter of misinformation that remains embedded in the American mind to an extent largely unrecognized . A condition which frustrates the true potential of the people by promoting fear, narcissism, and an egocentric materialist identity based on a manufactured culture useful to power but a hindrance to the expansion of consciousness.

In a society based on democratic principles the public cannot be herded about at the point of a bayonet as in more traditionally autocratic nations; here stealth must be employed. To this end what was once called "propaganda" now known as "public relations," has become key to allowing the big money to have its way while it convinces Americans that it's all in their best interest. Americans have been subjected to so much of this manipulation that most simply have never actually oriented themselves historically or in relation to world events in anything approaching an accurate accounting of the facts.

The intent within these pages is to draw back the surface of this illusion. A psychologically coercive ploy developed as cover for a massive program of imperial manipulation abroad, political disempowerment of the citizenry at home, and a drawing up of the prosperity of the nation and much of the world into the hands of a small but powerful group now coming to light as the .01%. These people are essentially *supranational* elites a portion of which seem to pose as Americans but fail to demonstrate any concern for the health of American society, or for that matter, of any people in the world other than themselves. [11]

Although this is not really a book about the history of Anglo-American geopolitical strategy, per sey, it has been necessary to draw out a simple outline of the program of empire so as to illustrate the conditions in which everything from simple propaganda in the schools and media, to incredibly sophisticated forms of mind control have been employed. The age old struggle between management and labor is now a struggle between a new aristocracy and the rest of the population. "Management" long ago stopped trying to convert specific worker populations to their needs and broadened their scope to American society as a whole through influencing the course of education and the culture industry. Most people have very little understanding as to how far this agenda for control has gone. Some readers may be familiar with bits and pieces of this history others will be surprised and appalled.

Although there are megalomaniacs involved and certainly pathological antisocial personalities, there is no "James Bond style" mastermind villain at the center of it all orchestrating events from his hidden lair. It is simply the natural outcome of a certain socio-political philosophy, a value system derived from a structure of consciousness inappropriately applied and followed to its absolute dead end. The point in placing this situation before the reader is simply to allow he or she to understand the forces arrayed against their expanding consciousness. To help the individual identify the programing that has been fed into their minds with the purpose of hijacking their life and subverting their potential as a human being in the service of an elitist economics very much allied with an antidemocratic power and its imperial goals.

Obsolete regimes extend their life during eras of change by preventing human development. By essentially thwarting the individual's natural tendency to expand the range of their thinking afforded by an evolving consciousness and replacing it with more of the false values and mythology of the old order, often disguised as something new. Dressed up in a new uniform with a new slogan the age of aristocratic nationalist empires is replaced by the age of superstar corporate globalists. The props and the costumes have changed but the story remains the same, like Shakespeare's Macbeth done in high-tech modern.

America has been taken off its natural course as the "great experiment in democracy" so many poets and historians have rhapsodized, essentially commandeered by a rising financial elite who through the 20th century progressively took control of the country through the power of concentrated wealth and by simply manipulating the public's fears and desires. The United States being the *last empire* has tremendous influence on the rest of the world and so as the U.S. goes, so goes much of the world. The key to the liberation of humanity at this time, therefore, is in the humane transformation of American power. This, then, is the grand drama of our age: the struggle between the rising consciousness of the human spirit reaching for new regions of freedom and the forces of oppression behind the cold steel of imperial power seeking to extend its dominion once again.

It is this essential insight at the cliff of history we stand on: that we must now consciously chose between an increasingly inhuman doctrine in the exclusive application of a narrow consciousness that is condemning the majority of life on the planet, including most human beings, or embrace our expanding minds and move swiftly into a new world of possibilities.

The great experiment in the genius of a liberated humanity that America once was can be reactivated and the country returned to the service of the human spirit. The evolution of consciousness supports the cause but awareness and action is required. It is a major revelation of our time that human psychology, personal spirituality, true freedom, politics and economics cannot be separated. They are integral to one another and understanding this is crucial at this moment in time. Every individual stands at the nexus of these domains and wields an unknown power therein.

At last, after clearly delineating the forces poised against the evolving mind and spirit of humanity, in the last chapter the discussion returns to the liberating of the integral consciousness that is rising to prominence to open the way to a better future. The confining feeling of a worldview too small stirs inside and each spirit that rebels against their disempowerment becomes a great power for change. The force of life and creation that made the universe and gave rise to human populations moves us still toward health and beauty and creative wonder but that force can be blocked so as to maintain crude material powers, at least for a time. This is the history of the world: this flowering and slowing and decaying and bursting forth again in life. A process we can learn to move through with grace rather than fury. And so, in the end, we come to realize that the uprising is life itself and we are its insurgents. The uprising is eternal and the uprising has just begun.

Notes

1. T.S. Eliot, *The Hollow Men*, (1925), "This is the way the world ends. Not with a bang but a whimper."
2. Jean Gebser, *The Ever Present Origin* (University of Ohio Press, 1985). Georg Feuerstein, Structures of Consciousness (Santa Rosa: Integral Publishing, 1987).
3. Viktor E. Frankl, *Man's search For Meaning*,(New York: Washing Square Books, [1946] 1984).
4. See: *The 2007& 2008 Shift Reports* (Petaluma: The Institute of Noetic Sciences, 2007 and 2008).
5. This author's own dissertation research confirms this assertion. Eric W. Towle, *An Exploration of the Experience of Paradigm Change in the Individual* (Ann Arbor: ProQuest LLC, 2010).
6. Ken Wilber makes this point repeatedly. See: *Sex, Ecology, Spirituality* (Boston: Shambhala, 1995).
7. Stuart A. Kauffman, *Reinventing the Sacred, A New Vision of Science, Reason, and Religion* (New York: Basic Books, 2008).
8. Robert F Arnove, editor, *Philanthropy and Cultural Imperialism, The foundations at Home and Abroad* (Bloomington: Indiana University Press, 1980), p. 1.
9. Jennifer Washburn, University Inc., *The Corporate Corruption Of Higher Education* (New York: Basic Books, 2005).

10. Please note: this book is not an attempt at a full exploration of Jean Geber's integral philosophy but only an elementary approach which necessarily simplifies complex ideas by way of introduction. This work is interpretive of Gebser while it expands his basic outline with the work of other scholars.
11. Chrystia Freeland, *Plutocrats, The Rise of the New Global Superrich and the Fall of Everyone Else* (New York: Penguin Books, 2012).

Chapter 1

The Basic Situation

So many are searching for a better life. So much of what was once thought certain about how to get there now seems in question.

Here's what is essential to understand: first, everything evolves. Now, regardless of one's personal philosophical feelings about where the human race came from, we all can agree that things change through time. The fossil record shows us that the earth began with simple organisms and over time, through one mysterious force or another, developed more and more sophisticated life. This much is evident from abundant sources. Whether you believe that human beings where created by some omnipotent organizing intelligence you wish to call "God" or whether you believe that they evolved from lower organisms by accident, or that life or humanity itself was seeded here by some advanced space faring people, doesn't really matter in order to understanding that just as organisms have become more complex over time so too has the human mind and hence civilization became more sophisticated as it has developed through history. Evolution, development, change over time is the order of things. The earth seems to be a vast experiment in unceasing movement.

There are ancient theories about the progress of humanity on Earth wherein a cyclical pattern is proposed, so that the human condition rises and falls with iron, bronze, silver, and gold ages, or "yugas" as the Hindu tradition calls them. Whether this is indeed the case – that the human mind is affected by some cosmic force which amplifies human attributes up and down through time – is rather hard to nail down as these cycles are said to be many thousands of years long and the historical record simply doesn't accommodate that kind of analysis. We do know this much, that the development or evolution of the mind has been at the basis of the expanding human experience evidenced within that historical record available. That the mind develops and then the art and technology follow. Simple stick figures on cave walls become the ceiling of the Sistine Chapel. The digging stick becomes the plow, becomes the tractor. Monarchy gives way to democracy and minstrels are replaced by symphonies. Just as children find certain toys fascinating at specific levels of development and loose interest as they move into the next expansion of their consciousness when they discover a more complex fascination, so too has the human race demonstrated over time this developmental evolution of consciousness. [1]

The development of human consciousness will be understood within these pages in more poetic language as the *rising of the human spirit*. The notion of a rising of spirit, *the will* of the human spirit, is the way people have understood this story for millennia. One doesn't have to have any particular religious beliefs at all to speak of "the plight of the human spirit." That driving force of life that seems to have been moving men and women to great feats and leaps of effort beyond all the obstacles of history; a creative exuberance and will to survival, progress, and glory that has been with us since the beginning of time.

So, we have both the path of the human spirit driving a broader and deeper vision of the world through time as the evolution of consciousness, with social structures and culture evolving in response to this development. Of course, all people don't develop at the same pace and culture and civilization itself doesn't keep pace with the development of the population as a whole. What happens with societies over time is that they are born from grand new openings in human consciousness. They are cultural responses to new ways of seeing the world and they flourish and develop based on the playing out of those original inspirations arising from a new psychological "space." Those first humans who looked at the edible plants they sought growing along the river and decided they could make those plants grow in great abundance anywhere they wished if the water could be diverted took a monumental step forward in human civilization, a step that had taken thousands upon thousands of years to reach. It certainly wasn't a matter of "just figuring it out," as some may think. They could figure out nothing until their minds where capable of such novel creative visions. When a person examines the archeological record it becomes clear there is no gradual improvement in tools found that would be consistent with a "figuring it out" process. What we do find is that about 50,000 years ago a sudden leap in human ingenuity took place known as the *Upper Paleolithic Revolution*. People went from making only simple hand axes or "knives," nothing more than a sharpened rock, a tool that was the only durable object produced for literally millions of years, to an explosion of crafts from an array of stone tools and jewelry, including musical instruments and needles, in a blink of the evolutionary eye. Some scholars attribute this change to a sudden advancement in language skills which is always the mark of a development in consciousness. What happened is that the mind of humanity took an evolutionary leap, a major transition opening a new dimension of possibilities where creativity took over with great enthusiasm. This is the pattern we find in the historical record: a development of the mind occurs, followed by a long period of filling in the possibilities of that new mode of comprehension. This happened when hunter/gatherers turned to cultivation and the raising of livestock, when the tribal reverence for the spirits of weather and game gave way to the heroes, gods and goddesses of mythology, when megalithic stone cities began to be built and a stratified social order was instituted, when the Greek civilization of Socrates and Plato began asking all kinds of new questions, and when the logic of Aristotle gave way to the measuring, mechanical perspective of Galileo. All these advances spring from the opening of new psychological dimensions. For instance, when the power figures in the culture of humanity moved from spirits of weather phenomena such as rain, wind, thunder, and sunshine, to a level beyond to describe *gods* who were manipulating these forces, then humanity had opened a larger dimension of thought in which the earlier conception was subsumed. When Galileo started to play around with rolling balls and wonder about the mechanics of the universe, then he was venturing into an even larger mental domain where he sought to learn the mind and methods of the God from the previous expansion.

> The Divine intellect indeed knows infinitely more propositions [than we can ever know]. But with regard to those few which the human intellect does understand, I believe that its knowledge equals the Divine in objective certainty.
> – Galileo Galilei

What underlies these evolutionary advances in human consciousness is a matter of debate but what we do know is that societies grow from the broadening structures of the mind, reaching a pinnacle of function, a "high civilization," and then over time those same societies decline. Becoming less innovative and supportive of broad prosperity and creativity they stagnate as social institutions become calcified into bureaucratic monoliths increasingly unresponsive to the needs of the populations they were created to serve. This doesn't happen because people's minds stop developing but because as material conditions change institutions within a civilization have tended to protect their own power, position, and ability to generate wealth, at the expense of people outside those institutions.

The lauded historian of civilizations, Carroll Quigley, who was said to have taught a "legendary" course in the history of civilizations at the Georgetown School of Foreign Service for 30 years, as well as teaching previously at Harvard and Princeton, was considered an expert on the comparative history of civilizations. He was a consultant to the Smithsonian Institution and a fellow of the American Anthropological association. Professor Quigley's analysis of the factors involved in the rise and fall of civilizations will be used here as a lens through which to understand the current economic and socio-political dynamics at work in America and Western Civilization in general.

Professor Quigley used the term "instrument" to characterize the phase of growth in civic structures in which they are healthy supports to the growth of civilization, and the term "institutions," for the same structures when they cease to operate for the good of the society as a whole and begin to operate merely for their own preservation and aggrandizement. Banks for instance, can be said to be instruments of civilization when they are lending money to open new businesses, providing funding for seed grain for local farmers, and allowing for the building and purchasing of homes by average citizens, but turn into "institutions," in Quigley's terms, when they turn toward their own growth and profits as their major purpose through, for instance, predatory lending and foreclosing on property whenever possible in order to enrich the owners of the bank. "When instruments become institutions, as they all do," wrote Quigley, "the organization achieves its function or purpose in society with decreasing effectiveness, and discontent with its performance begins to rise." [2]

An example of this can be seen in the middle ages when monetary systems of payment began to replace the exchange of commodities such as grain, thus effecting a change in the relationship of feudal lords to their peasants. The lords responded to their need for cash by enlisting the military forces under their command in regular mercenary wars that became a constant threat to life and limb throughout the late middle ages. A once reciprocal system of protection and provision between the people and their lord, if not fair, certainly functional and supportive of life, broke down as the people were asked to give more and suffer more so that the lords could retain their positions. Eventually, it all fell apart and the land and people were organized into larger domains of more powerful dukes and kings, ending the feudal period but not before huge numbers died fighting or simply starved to death in the wake of the destruction that comes with war.

Another example of the "institutionalization" of civilization is found in the simple exclusion of innovation in order to preserve a system based on an establishment of vested interests. Quigley sites the point at which Rome became unable to feed its people due to the ineffectiveness of their farming system that could only be reformed by abolishing slavery and dividing up the big estates. The big landowners simply murdered the innovators, sometimes on the senate floor, and kept the old system in place to the detriment of the people and eventual downfall of the entire civilization.

When institutions resist the efforts to return them to effective supporters of a healthy society, Quigley pointed to three possible outcomes. The first is when the opposition is able to exert enough pressure that the institution is reformed and returns to some level of healthy operation. The second occurs when the institution is simply circumvented and its power shifted to a new instrument of civilization. Such as what happened when the crown in Britain was preserved but power was transferred to the parliament. And three: when the institution successfully defends itself remaining intact, as in the example of Roman social order above.

> In the third possible outcome...the vested interests triumph in the struggle, and the people of that society are doomed to ineffective achievement of their needs on that level for an indefinite period.[3]

Those at the top of institutions, fearing the introduction of innovations like that which beset "king coal" when oil came around, while at the same time wishing to restrict the ability of an exploited public to politically restrain their empire building, have tended over time to put their considerable financial resources to work politically and privately to shut down any populist interference that would curtail their plans. Thus over time, institutions tend toward greater and greater control of society so as to avoid the first and second of Quigley's outcomes and to insure the third that will maintain their power positions no matter how difficult it gets for the public.

Nowhere in the world has this tendency been more evident in the current age than in the United States where corporate power has achieved a nearly complete lock on the political process and the institutions of government itself, including the Supreme Court and the various regulatory agencies meant to police their actions. The "high court" has ruled, since the dubious "Santa Clara decision" of 1886 that gave corporations "personhood" and thereby the same rights as any citizen, to increase a long list of "constitutional" rights for corporations so as to create super human entities of them. If corporations are a form of "person," as the Supreme Court insists, then they are like giant monster mutant persons out of a vintage Sci Fi film who stomp about the land overwhelming anything in their way with the mammoth blasting light and sound created by their dominance of the media, their ability to control political campaigns with the towering stacks of money needed to win elections, and their countless snapping appendages of lawyers ready to crush any person or group attempting to defend themselves against their hegemony. [4] The corporate business structure is the preeminent tool through which institutions – health care, banking, petro-chemical, etc. – defend themselves against the reform that would return them to healthy instruments of a just civilization. Corporations have produced many wonderful products and employed millions. It isn't business that's the problem. It is something peculiar to the human tendency for empire building at any cost. This too, is a facet of the expanding dimensions of the human ego; "the human spirit gone tyrannical," one might say.

Innovations such as a monetary system or things like the plow have had tremendous effects on the course of civilization and are themselves the result of an expanding consciousness. They are the products of mental development that rock the boat of the older established system. So as a rule institutions as they age have tended to clamp down on innovation in order to forestall the changes that would threaten their investments. The Pope simply put Galileo under house arrest and forbid him under penalty of torture and death to disseminate his ideas. Nowadays, inventions are suppressed by buying up research, shutting it down, and shelving the potential breakthroughs in an attempt to control when they might be used, if at all, or by offering a university a lot of money to pursue research favorable to an industry's interests while demanding that they shut down that which isn't. Some industries are allowed to run full speed, like the personal computing market, and some are kept at the same level of technology they have been at for a century, like the automobile industry and its internal combustion engine. Personal computing was a new market that did not threaten established interests, while auto and oil companies like things as they are and have the power to ensure that nothing happens to their profit streams. This political dynamic leaves medicine in America being controlled by the pharmaceutical and insurance industries, transportation and power by oil and gas interests, economics by banking and finance interests, etc. etc. All at the growing expense of the general public.

Over time the institutions of a society: the financial, business, political, legal, medical, scientific, etc. all become insulated, self-serving, bureaucracies led by groups of individuals who have bowed to the power interests and in doing so have made their way to the top of their professions and having arrived intend to stay there. They accomplish this by promoting their ways of thinking and those that support them over competing theories and reformers who are quickly shuffled to the margins. In the sciences this is done by the control of peer review boards at major journals who simply refuse to publish any research that challenges the major theories on which the "giants" of the field have built their authority. Science is the starting place for much innovation and so science is carefully shepherded by the major corporate interests. Much control is asserted in keeping things just as they are. Great amounts of money have been put into a certain way of doing things, whether it be a way of lending money, a way of treating disease, or a way of creating energy. Those who have invested great fortunes in building and maintaining these systems do not want to see them change any more than those whose expertise runs them. To change in any major way would mean the end of careers and the end of sources of wealth and the influence that come with these positions. A myriad of superficial changes and innovations may offer the public a false appearance of progress and some response to their needs but the central structure of the institution is never allowed to be questioned and so no real, truly meaningful change ever occurs.

Besides the odd lack of progress in automobiles one need only look at what happened with the 2008 financial meltdown caused by the unscrupulous activities of the financial industry for confirmation. Simon Johnson , an M.I.T. professor of economics and management, with the business consultant, James Kwak, wrote of how this came about. "The Wall Street banks are the new American oligarchy – a group that gains political power because of its economic power, and then uses the political power for its own benefit." [5] The U.S. and consequently Europe were brought to the brink of economic collapse, the waves reached countries all over the world. You would think in such circumstances a return to sensible regulation to control the sort of dishonesty that caused the disaster would rationally follow – no such luck. An array of superficial changes were made without touching the toxic behavior of the central institution one, little bit. "They did little to address the problem at the heart of the financial system: the enormous growth of top-tier financial institutions and the corresponding increase in their economic and political power. In place of bold measures, the administration preferred technical solutions...regulatory deck-chair-shuffling." [6]

Much of the way power stagnates a society is through limiting public control but perhaps the more important method is through limiting cultural change. The church of the Middle Ages kept a very tight hold of culture, dictating the details of belief and informing the value system with an uncompromising totality. The Inquisition and a person's own neighbors ensured compliance. The method used in the modern world in the so called "free" nations is to simply dominate the organs of culture: film, television, radio, and major print media, with a message that encourages cultural traditions and attitudes toward support for the status-quo while simply denying honest coverage and depiction in fictional shows to any attitudes and beliefs that are counter to the needs of industry and the elite. Holidays have been twisted into opportunities for increased sales: the "traditions" most Americans associate with Christmas and Thanksgiving, for instance, like shopping and turkey, have no place in the original traditions observed by America prior to the twentieth century. These "traditions" have been entirely concocted by industry.

American society has been essentially derailed from its true traditional culture, being led from Jefferson's America of thrifty, fiercely independent families and communities more impressed with contribution and good character, to a society of acquisition, impressed with fame and "conspicuous consumption."

Reputation was worth more than all the money in the world because without it, without being seen as a person of hard work and contribution, you were nothing, not taken seriously and at worst ostracized completely. But all of that changed when Americans began to shop. There's a difference between going to buy something you need to live and "shopping" in the sense of its current meaning. Shopping has become an immersion in the land of fantasy, an entrance into a dream of glamour, luxury, even adventure and power. The department store was born in 1876 in Philadelphia where a guy named John Wanamaker converted an abandoned train depot into a new kind of giant "shop of everything." Before long the salesman learned that displays could greatly increase sales. People like L. Frank Baum, who later penned the children's classic The *Wizard of Oz* combined a background in the theater with sales to revolutionize window dressing, quickly spinning it into a fine art. Windows became magical productions passers-by could project themselves into. The idea was to create in the mind of the unsuspecting public a fantasy of plenty and luxury, status and pride no longer confined to some isolated upper class but now through the march of democracy a right offered to all. Necessity gave way to desire as Americans were enticed into a mindset of consumption as a way of life. [7]

The old values were twisted to the needs of commerce. The older mythology of America as "earthly paradise and land of plenty," cherished by the old pioneer culture was transformed to a mercantile dream of *plenty of goods and a paradise of personal comfort*. It had been the freedom from the poverty of serfdom in Europe where all the land was owned by the aristocracy and all labored under that oppressive rule that made the personal ownership of property in America such a paradise. A family could live and prosper by their own labors, owing nothing to ancestral barons and dukes and it was this wonderful new freedom, truly a spiritual freedom, not based on titles and fancy clothes and carriages, but the wide open glory of being the captain of your own destiny.

After the civil war rapid industrialization created a huge growth in wage earners that did not make their own lives with their own hands but sold their labor to manufacturing and a myriad of fields supporting commerce. Slowly through the twentieth century Americans progressively substituted their myth of a spiritual freedom for the commercial myth of material comfort, "status," and luxury. Prosperity had meant land and freedom from exploiting overlords. Now people moved from control of one's own work to an almost total lack of control. From autonomy to dependency and for the exchange they were offered a new definition of prosperity – a house full of stuff.

This very eventuality had been warned against by Thomas Jefferson at the opening of the nation. He had feared that wage earners, dependent on another man's largesse, were not totally free to voice their opinions and vote as they please, that democracy would fail if such a condition prevailed. A significant populist and union opposition to the trend of commercialization did rise up in the face of this bastardization of democracy and freedom but the freight train of commerce and the desire of people for novelty crushed the dying cry of the old American non-material values.

The "new" was common parlance in America in the early days. It was the land of new things, a new prosperity, a new Eden, of new social institutions, a new land of spiritual abundance. Mark Twain had once remarked about the country that, "we early get and permanently retain the impression that there is nothing old about it." As the historian William Leach put it, "It was hard under these circumstances to defend any tradition, any inherited custom or belief, when the past itself was hostage to the new." [8] American authors Emerson and Whitman both encouraged people to dive into the new as a spiritual exercise in opening the mind and heart. The entire age was a celebration of the distinctly American democratic idea of an expanding education for all, a bursting of provincialism outward to the great promise of the new land of limitless possibilities for discovery and experience.

Commerce took up this torch and simply diverted the stream away from the new as a broadening "spiritual" freedom, a feeling of limitlessness, toward a broadening desire for possessions. This is where the great fantasy makers had their chance, as Americans became increasingly tied to humdrum repetitive labor and anxious about their status in a mass society they fell under the spell of theatrical manipulations that played on their lost possibilities for true meaning. Now the public could play at crafting their off work identities as reduced aristocrats in posh attire in parlors decorated as diminutive estate drawing rooms, while their children were catered to with an incredible explosion of toy worlds, recreating the great exploits of history or circus extravaganzas in miniature.

But it wasn't just possessions people traded their spirits for, soon experience itself became a commodity. As women became enthralled by artificial fashion "seasons," lifted from Parisian society, mass produced, and accelerated for maximum profit, working men less interested in the middle class preoccupation with emulating the aristocracy immersed themselves in heroic fantasies. As the frontier grew dim in the American psyche men could see it all at Wild Bill Cody's Wild West Show, where real Native Americans fresh from their defeats in the West would die all over again for an increasingly bored, pacified and restless wage earning masculinity. Aggressive team sports and boxing became more and more important in male culture, as legions of pyramid builders no longer finding an outlet for heroic action in their own lives became watchers of a new elite class of professional heroes. Men would pour out of factories and into beer halls and saloons to medicate themselves with alcohol after a day of soul-numbing labor, wagering and arguing on the upcoming game or match where somebody would win and somebody would lose and if they were on the winning side then they could pretend that they had won a little too. Maybe they'd make a buck on the friendly bet but any way it went they would witness the champion emerge from the fray and they could imagine the victory their own for just a moment, they could maintain the fantasy, the grueling bloody charge over the top defeating some vague darkness inside them, if for only a day.

This is how the great American fantasy began. This is how we slowly traded real life for an imitation we could watch, real clothes for costumes, personal authenticity for an "image." Film and then television really cemented the deal. Modern people everywhere and Americans in a big way became enamored with material possessions and canned "experiences" as a substitute for a truly meaningful life of personal engagement in the challenges of building a better world.

With television becoming the main mode of cultural transmission after WWII, American culture has become easier to "guide" and so more and more a product of powerful institutions that seek to both stagnate innovation in established industries and pour forth a never ending array of consumer products in ever accelerating cycles of the new in industries that are set up for innovation, like televisions and cell phones, while all else receives a *style* make-over. This culture of acquisition, the "shopping center as paradise" mentality, has been thoroughly engineered and supported by a program of cultural manipulation in advertising and the subtle brain washing of television shows and movies so that over the years American society, for all the supposed "advancements" has really just been spinning in an ever accelerating whirlpool of ego driven consumerism; achievement measured in buying power as the single goal in life. As the actual value of average wages in the U.S. has continually sunk since the early 1970's and deficit fueling cheap Asian goods and proliferating credit cards have kept the buying sprees going America is now reaching both an economic and existential meltdown. The bank is busted and the soul is desolate, although the majority don't quite understand why and, in testament to the narrowing of human comprehension, still hold out the hope that new technology and a better paying job is all that's necessary to save them.

What happens to people when they are led to believe that money is everything because dignity, respect, and indeed, even happiness itself is represented as a commodity to be purchased? Depression and anxiety run rampant and even the winners can't seem to get enough to stop the feeling that they haven't quite arrived. A respondent to a recent study at Boston College concerning the lives of the rich stated that *he wouldn't feel completely comfortable in life until he had at least a billion in the bank.* [9] Few people of any financial status stop to ask exactly where they are going on their road to riches – a personal amusement park, a technological nirvana? And yet, through it all, people do continue to evolve and as they do they find the society around them reflecting less and less of their expanding consciousness. A gulf begins to widen between the continuing development of the people and the deficient, whirling merry-go-round civilization frenetically trying to sell them the same old promises in a new package.

This is how civilizations rise and fall. They are alive and responsive to the human spirit in their early years and then they become ridged and unresponsive as they age. So they eventually crumble and fall as the self-serving, ineffective institutions undermine the very minds of the people and so the stability of the society itself. When this deterioration reaches a critical mass the society will simply fall apart of its own bad weight, such as what happened to the Soviet Union, or more often as history demonstrates they will be easily overrun by stronger civilizations outside their borders. The hoard that overran the Soviets was an oligarchic capitalism. (The United States will not be literally overrun, as were the Romans, but the barbarians are indeed at the gates in a world where the ability to properly provide for the rise of the human spirit eventually pushes some countries down while pushing others up.)

So we have two conflicting dynamics: an ever evolving humanity moving toward greater vistas of human potential and so pushing toward a better environment for the advancement of the human spirit, and an ever more rigid civilization made up of institutions that are being run for the aggrandizement of those inside them and their investors rather than for the continued progress of the society they are meant to serve. The leading intellects supporting the moneyed factions make up the elite in society who begin quite early on to see their own needs in a different light than those of the "common people." The cohesive tribal family is broken open to accommodate a new class structure in the rise of the mythological consciousness that soon creates the *lesser than* disposable human. It is a peculiar condition of human beings from the beginning of the age of empires onward that when an individual leaves the masses behind and begins his or her climb up the socio-economic ladder that they quickly begin to entertain rationales in which they see themselves as a "superior" grade of human being. With this as their truth these people find all kinds of reasons why the beings beneath them deserve little to none of the consideration they would give themselves. This egocentric status psychology is, not always but often, then compounded in the following generations who grow up in wealth thus estranging them from "the masses" even further and thereby increasing their lack of empathy for the circumstances of "the people" whose lives their powerful positions will come to effect.

These self-serving psychologies who create self-serving institutions, whether political structures or energy systems, are then faced with a growing resentment in the populace and respond by whatever means at their disposal for quelling this agitation. As the economics of the Roman Empire became more uncertain over time the elite began to call for "bread and circuses" to distract and placate and thereby forestall any revolt by the people. The Romans used a combination of pure authoritarian muscle, distraction in games, races, and gladiatorial matches, as well as welfare in passing out food, to accomplish the end of keeping the common people in line as the Empire grew more dysfunctional and conditions for the average person more difficult.

In Western democracies with images of themselves as "free societies" authoritarian means for putting down public resentment certainly are used but are problematic at best and for the most part simply serve to increase agitation. Strong arm police tactics have often been the match that ignited all-out rioting. Welfare, too, has been used successfully by the status quo to buy off oppressed populations and keep them out of the hair of the elite. The Johnson administration in the sixties, for instance, helped to quell a growing agitation in the African-American population pushing back against continuing oppression with new welfare and housing projects that didn't offer any real assistance into the mainstream but served to take the edge off growing black militancy.

But beyond strong arm tactics and public bribes the most potent and well honed, tried and true, method of keeping the discontented public in line in the United States is to be found in the many forms of manipulation that stream from the media. Just as the old guard in each scientific field control the major journals that vet new work and so keep out challenges to their dominance, so too have the major corporate interests brought under their control the entirety of the mainstream press. Virtually all the major television, movie making, print and radio in the United States is now controlled by a handful of major corporations: CBS, Viacom, Disney, Clear Channel, Time Warner, News Corp.; and what appears through those many venues is, if not mostly in support of the status-quo, certainly without any major opposition to it. The unvarnished reporting still survives in the independent press and some internet sites but these sources attract a tiny portion of the overall media consuming public. People have come to expect that if something "is really true" they'll see it on the evening news or it will be in the paper or on the cover of their favorite magazine, in print or online. Unfortunately, what story they may see in their favorite source is likely to be twisted to the advantage of the owners of the corporate megaliths that control those sources. More usually, stories that may cause unwanted interest in corporate affairs simply don't appear at all. [10] This systematic ignorance is aided by people plugging themselves into internet sites that are designed to confirm all their prejudices without challenging any of their misconceptions with other views and contradictory evidence. The integral scholar, William Irwin Thomson, calls this the "ideological feed stall," that has encouraged narrow mindedness and a breakdown of healthy public debate. [11] For all its information delivering power, the internet offers no broad public forum for discussions challenging misconceptions and allowing the head-on discussion of ideas. The old life of the small town had one public square, one or two local papers, and all views were aired, argued, defended, and considered. Now there are thousands of public squares to choose from and people tend to gravitate to the one that makes them comfortable. This inability to consider information that doesn't suit a person's prejudices even extends to the U.S. Congress where members routinely don't show up to the speeches of those they are at odds with.

As the major structures of American power continue to resist change, public relations firms have been massively deployed by corporate power and government alike to keep people from the certain knowledge that the institutions of their society no longer care about their wellbeing. Indeed, the mounting evidence indicates a growing exploitation of common people as a means of increasing profits and power amongst an elite minority of stock holders, executives, owners, their lawyers, and the "knowledge brokers," who attempt to keep the critique and innovations involving ruling institutions within "acceptable" boundaries. [12] From credit cards distributed by specific strategy to ensnare people into long term debt, to drugs that are disguised versions of older marginally effective and largely toxic products sold with fan-fare and TV hoopla as new miracle cures, to tax laws that dump the burden on the middle class while the wealthy and the corporate powers pay little to nothing, "the people" so lovingly spoken of in the Bill of Rights and the Gettysburg Address, have become a source of food for vampires at the top of the pyramids of American power.

As business has become consolidated under fewer and fewer giant corporations the relationship between major corporate interests and the people is one that places the value of the common person in basically two essentially "instrumental" roles. First: as workers in maintaining the status-quo institutions and corporations and second: as buyers of products and services; fulfilling the second role as supporter of consumer capitalism at the other end of the system. The average citizen of the West has become nothing more to the systems of accounting at the highest levels of power under which they live than a "worker/buyer unit." As long as they are performing these two functions when needed the system has no concern whatsoever for the average person's health or welfare. In point of fact, if the citizen's health and welfare stand in the way of profit they will be sacrificed. The introduction of genetically modified organisms into the American diet, despite the horrible results for test animals, is perhaps the most glaring out of many possible examples.[13] The government bodies that have traditionally been tasked with upholding the rights of the lone, otherwise powerless, individual in the face of organized power interests in places like the United States have been largely coopted by corporate power so that the three branches of government: the executive, the judicial, and the legislature, have all been seriously compromised through the financial leverage of the corporate and financial sectors.

This has created an increasingly poisonous and dysfunctional world for average people as, for instance, chemicals are used in the processing and preserving of foods that are meant solely for increasing profits while they have been proven to decrease nutrition as they introduce toxins into the human body. At the same time the chemical methods for accelerating growth in food crops damages the land and pollutes the rivers and oceans. The use of "confinement feeding" in livestock production, where animals spend their entire lives in a cage only big enough for their standing bodies, has converted ranching into an inhuman torture factory that produces "sick food" and monumental pollution but the agribusiness profits are booming.[14] The FDA, being run by individuals who have come from the agribusiness and food processing corporations themselves, has nothing to say about the situation. The companies involved in these processes having dismantled and prevented regulation through buying politicians and having infiltrated government oversight agencies but still fearing an assault on their profits from direct public agitation respond with political action to limit the power of the people and through massive propaganda efforts to misinform the public regarding the dangers.

As an example: Dairy products that contain bovine growth hormone are banned in Europe due to the research linking cancer and other dangers to their consumption but the Wisconsin dairy industry pushed a law through that makes it illegal in their state for dairy companies not using it to say so on their packaging. This kind of political blockade of information the public has a right to is added to an ever increasing array of "public relations" techniques to make sure people have no idea what's being done to them. These forces work to create an experience for the average worker/buyer unit – that is you – that allows for the least amount of recognition that conditions have changed. The surface is left unruffled as the core of an ethical democratic republic is quietly hollowed out so as to not spook the work/buyer units who might get upset about being slowly poisoned, politically and economically disenfranchised, while having their email and internet traffic analyzed by powerful computers at the NSA. The grocery stores are still full of brightly colored packages and the new fall line-up on the television networks will be funnier and more exciting than ever, the news will be earnest and yet reassuring, and it all will look just the way it always has, only bigger and faster and more "modern."

Regardless, many people simply look around and realize, intuitively, that something is amiss, not just in the obvious fact that institutions such as medical insurance are raping them financially but the sense that the overall culture itself has grown more and more exploitive while it seems to lack some vital element that supports their own healthy progress as a human being. There is a growing agitation in the public evidenced in the soaring rates of depression and anxiety that is both the product of living with the negative effects of declining institutions and this building longing for a meaningful way of life that the mainstream culture seems incapable of delivering. Many people are waking up to the reality that they can't buy their way to contentment or a life that seems to matter by following the clues within the dominant culture and are looking around for something more.

The postwar period brought on a growing critique of many of the assumptions that underlie the guiding mythology of the West. What came to be known as "postmodernism" pulled the rug out on the modernist assumption that the scheming of the mental/rational mind would provide all the answers for a fabulous future. A list of doubts regarding old "truths," began to appear in the minds of the intellectual public. Things like technology as savior, scientific empiricism as provider of every truth, speed as a measure of progress. All these things and more came into question and a great philosophical reassessment gripped the sophisticated populace. These doubts and questions have grown over the years to enter the mind-set of a broader and broader population and at this time moves American culture, person by person, in a broad arch turning toward a new society. Some things are being restored by this change of course. The community, for instance, that our ancestors had enjoyed, seriously eroded by the trends of modernism, is now looking to be rejuvenated. Old trends such as that of the use of power and domination as a method for solving conflicts is hoped to be left behind as the progressive public increasingly looks through dialog and understanding to find the "win/win" answer.

Unfortunately, the status-quo, as described above, holds on tooth and nail to the old stories that brought them to prominence. It is all of one piece: the traditional cultural mythos with its fighting hero tales and landed values having been turned to the uses of an industrial growth economy with all its attendant militarism and runaway consumerism, and the decaying institutions themselves, represented as "the only way to do things" in the mythological culture that flows from the television and cinema. Many of the values represented in these stories have been quite bent from their starting places in early America and in a more pure light wouldn't support the fraying institutions, even as they furiously paint themselves in red, white, and blue. For instance, the framers of American liberty saw the rejection of a large standing army as foundational to that liberty, hence the tradition of the "citizen soldier." After WWII the military didn't scale way back as they always had in the past but, instead, finding one enemy after another, put the nation on a "permanent war economy" as described by President Eisenhower. Thus creating exactly the condition the forefathers wanted to prevent. History had demonstrated to the framers of the constitution that large military institutions, if allowed to grow, always produced an insulated culture of power that, in the context of an American republic, would pose a threat to democratic control. Half of all discretionary spending by U.S. administrations since WWII has gone to the military and the various arms of the national security state. Billions upon billions of dollars every year, since 1947 have poured into "black budget" military programs completely beyond any civilian oversight or control giving the Pentagon a massive authority that has in many ways eclipsed the power of the presidency. [15] You wouldn't know any of this from the current mythological image of the military in popular culture that continues to portray military power in the vein of Revolutionary era "sacred duty and honor in the service of liberty." The average person, being completely ignorant of the wisdom that gave birth to American liberty, hasn't a clue that the switch has been made. Washington and Jefferson would be aghast. Military personnel themselves are the most betrayed by this switch as their lives have been offered up not for the protection of liberty but for the advancement of corporate interests abroad. This is evidenced in the unnoticed change in political rhetoric that makes little reference to the cause of human rights and now baldly refers to our military challenges abroad as, "defending our interests."

At the close of the American frontier wealthy industrialists and financiers dreamed of pushing American enterprise beyond the boundaries of the continent. To this end they began promoting empire on the model of classic European imperialism. "I wish to see the United States the dominant power on the shores of the Pacific Ocean," declared Teddy Roosevelt in 1898 and threw all his political energies into making it happen. Americans were encouraged to believe that they were the cutting edge of civilization and the very progress of humanity itself. There were Imperialist advocates that took up the banner of empire with enthusiasm and an "Anti-Imperialist League" that denigrated the idea. "We hold that the policy known as imperialism is hostile to liberty and tends toward militarism, an evil from which it has been our glory to be free," began their platform statement. [16] Regardless of the "march of civilization," it quickly became apparent that the general public was not interested in any such grand adventure abroad, so the tactics for pushing the reluctant masses into action called for the mounting of a monumental subterfuge. The plan necessitated the clothing of an economic imperialist agenda in patriotic garb and in the act of carrying it out a split in the mind of American citizens came into being.

On the one side, a national identity derived from a largely manufactured worldview supported a belief in "American exceptionalism." This was a philosophy portraying Americas as leaders in the great march of human progress and so playing a special role in the world as emissaries of freedom and democracy. On the other side has lived a political and economic reality at home and abroad that has often been something other than the humanitarian crusade it has been billed as. This schism has produced a tendency in Americans to retreat from the many reports that give the lie to the sacred mythos into an increasingly impregnable and self-contained fantasy. From the very opening of the American imperialist agenda abroad in the Spanish American War when soldiers returned from the Philippine Islands with stories of wide spread rape and massacre the big money forces in America have simply struck up the band to drown out the truth each time reality has had the impertinence to intrude on their myth making. Upon his retirement Marine General Smedley Butler, trying his best to break through the fantasy and alert Americans as to what the real agenda was, went around the country in the 1930's giving a lecture entitled *War is a Racket*, published as a small book in 1936.

> I helped make Mexico, especially Tampico, safe for American oil interests in 1914. I helped make Haiti and Cuba a decent place for the National City Bank boys to collect revenues in. I helped in the raping of half a dozen Central American republics for the benefits of Wall Street. The record of racketeering is long. I helped purify Nicaragua for the international banking house of Brown Brothers in 1909-1912. I brought light to the Dominican Republic for American sugar interests in 1916. In China I helped to see to it that Standard Oil went its way unmolested. [17]

In our time no one recognizes General Butler's name despite the fact that he was the most decorated soldier in American history in his day, winning the Congressional Medal of Honor *twice*. His name appears in no high school history text. His legacy and his warning has been forgotten by all who do not deliberately dig it out from beneath the carpet of American fantasy it has been conveniently swept under. After WWII this sort of *business at the point of a gun* became institutionalized as the U.S. banking and corporate interests capitalized on the power position of America as the last man standing after the smoke cleared. With the world's biggest navy and industrial might unparalleled anywhere in the world empire building was kicked into high gear.

America has been sold to its citizens as a special country whose mission has been to bring democracy and "superior American knowhow," to a benighted world, *whether they want it or not*. A vision promoted by the corporate elite who have profited immensely from this heroic ideal. After President Franklin D. Roosevelt's "new deal" finally brought some fairness to the lives of working people many ordinary Americans began to share in the benefits making the fantasy so much easier to swallow. But all the while, outside this happy vision of Americans leading the way to freedom, remains the other side of the story; the actual conditions and bitter course of events in the world often out of sync with this fantasy narrative. Most Americans look to their country's role in liberating Europe from the Nazis as the most glorious proof of their heroic position but few have ever looked under the surface of that much mythologized event to find the finger prints of Wall Street all over the rise of the Nazi party in Germany that reveal how the war got started to begin with. [18] Just as foreign aid is another area where Americans fail to find the strings attached to all the money and relief supplies. This and other aspects of the split between the American heroic fantasy and the geopolitical realities of empire will be explored in a later chapter.

The terrible irony is that America *is* a special country in that it was the first true democracy that included *all* the people; a republic that proclaimed the rights of every citizen regardless of wealth or status and provided an open country to play out the liberated imagination of its people. There were victims of this freedom of course; Africans and Native Americans getting the worst of it but America even in its rough beginnings represented the manifestation of a great hope for humanity, a true expression of the evolution of consciousness planting new political ideals that in time would grow to include all its people, if imperfectly. This condition did for so long hold out the hope of true freedom for people all over the world who endured great sacrifices to land on America's shores and become a part of this great experiment in human freedom. Unfortunately, the ongoing project of freedom has been largely compromised and the ideals of America, "the land of opportunity," rather than allowed to grow, have been hollowed out and turned into stage props used in a nonstop advertising campaign. What is a grand illusion covering a shift back to the old system of elite control the U.S. Constitution and Bill of Rights were supposed to defeat. America is no longer what it started out to be, a nation built for common people but is now run for the ultimate benefit of a financial aristocracy whose manipulations provide a patriotic cover for the business of war, the impoverishing of American workers, and what has been too often a rapacious exploitation of foreign resources and labor in support of what is essentially empire by any other name, call it "globalism," or whatever you like. This is a far reach from what the fathers of the nation had in mind for the course of their United States of America.

From the late 19th Century on the founding father's vision came to be clandestinely replaced by the growing rule of manipulation by a new moneyed aristocracy completely at odds with the ethos of a democratic republic. Much of American tradition has been twisted for the purposes of institutionalized power. This decay of the major institutions of the United States has precipitated a growing sophistication in control methods employed by the power elite to stave off the challenge to their power arising from reaction to the deteriorating conditions. The authority of this elite group stems from their control, on the one hand of energy industries, primarily oil, and on the other hand, of the banking and financial system which sits at the center of power over key industries that have consolidated into an interlocking mass of transnational corporations. In the fall of 2011 a group of complex systems analysts at the Swiss Federal Institute of Technology released their findings from applying some sophisticated software to better understand the relationships between 43,000 transnational corporations. What they discovered was 147 key corporations at the center of it all that virtually control the rest. At the center of these key companies was an even more elite group that exert massive influence over the key players and they were all – surprise – banking and financial firms. These top corporate groups turned out to be quite incestuous in that all the central players seem to be sitting on each other's boards of directors constituting a cabal of top managers with their fingers in all the leading pies. [19]

The final reality of centralized power lies in the fact that world banking is centered in New York and the petro-dollar system that demands Middle East oil be paid for in U.S. dollars makes the American banks the most powerful in the world, placing them at the center of the whole world of international trade. Oil and world credit markets, the dollar as reserve world currency, and a massive military establishment are the central pillars of what has become an American empire at the service of an elite that imagines its position as having surpassed the "quaint loyalties" of nation states in their socioeconomic rebranding as *corporate globalists*. [20]

In other words, the United States is now run for the benefit of an oligarchic in-group that has no interest in the welfare of the American people as anything other than laborers and consumers. Any shared sense of an American destiny and responsibility to the values of a democratic republic have been lost. Nothing else could be expected in a society that has given itself over to free market capitalism as the guiding force of life itself. The godfather of the Neo-Liberal faith, Milton Freidman, spelled it out quite clearly in his 1962 book, *Capitalism and Freedom*: "Few trends could so thoroughly undermine the very foundations of our free society as the acceptance by corporate officials of a social responsibility other than to make as much money for their stockholders as possible." Freedom as a concept for free marketers is exclusively about the freedom of the moneyed class to tilt the economy in their favor without ethical consideration for others. This economic doctrine has been an unmitigated disaster for the world, from Latin America, to Europe and Russia, to the United States itself and although most economists have pronounced it dead,[21] it seems the bankers haven't gotten the message yet as they try to wring "austerities" out of Europe to squeeze the last dine out of the people before the game is up. Iceland seems to be the only place where the people had the power to actually put the bankers in jail. In the U.S. Wall Street and their accomplices in the military establishment are still sweeping the wealth of the nation into their own corners as the poverty rate climbs at an increasing pace. "The fact that politically organized interest groups with vast resources operate continuously, that they are coordinated with congressional procedures and calendars, that they occupy strategic points in the political process, is indicative of how the meaning of "representative" government has radically changed." [22] Once the corporate infiltration of the American government was complete then no moral authority was left to stand up for the people and so this philosophy has set the tone for a new despotism that is at this time strangling the life out of the promise of a country founded on respect for common people.

People occupying this society are then faced with this cultural environment that is out of tune with the original tenor of the democratic republic and the human potential it is supposed to support. Although many are unaware of the history and the manipulations of tradition they still feel a sense of estrangement from the current culture as it attempts to bolster institutions that have ceased to support the material, spiritual, and psychological wellbeing of those within the nation. As this estrangement grows it leads the person to search for the authentic life they are missing and so they begin to turn away from the mass culture. This is the rise of the integral structure of consciousness breaking through the mass manipulation. There are several indicators of the evolution of consciousness this trend indicates and so in our time we are witnessing the rise of the human spirit even as the forces of slavery redouble their efforts.

The eminent sociologist, Dr. Paul Ray, has studied an emerging social formation for decades that he has termed: the "cultural creatives," the attributes of which he describes as:

> spiritually motivated and committed to personal growth but are not dogmatically religious; embrace technology and

economic development but only within a deep affirmation of the environment and community; tend to view the world from the perspective of holistic systems; pay attention to world events and global trends; can be characterized as both inner-directed and socially concerned; have spiritual and psychological depth as well as the maturity needed for a new culture; are also intensely entrepreneurial and creative: founders and leaders of most of the green and socially responsible businesses; involved in many of the most socially active NGO's and non-profit organizations; etc. [23]

Dr. Ray and other sociologists believe that this emerging trend that started in the post WWII period reached about 26 percent of the adult American population in 1999 and growing at about 1 to 2 percent a year had reached about 30 percent in 2008. The European population was thought to be at about 35 percent at that time. This trend is considered as profound a shift in the consciousness of the Western world as the Renaissance in 16th century Italy was to the culture of that time. This ongoing research is offering ample evidence of an emerging new structure in the evolution of consciousness moving toward prominence at this time.

Additional evidence of the evolution of consciousness can be found in the work of the paleoanthropologist, John Hawks, at the University of Wisconsin. His research has identified genes that seem to be responsible for increasing brain size over evolutionary eons. Hawks has posited that these genes change or adapt causing leaps in intelligence and ability in 30,000 year cycles as evidenced by the fossil record. He also has stated that rapid evolution has gone on during the last 40,000 years and that during the last 5,000 years humanity has experienced "supercharged evolutionary change." Hawks declares that so much evolution has gone on in the last five millennia that a person from 3,000 BCE would have more in common genetically with a Paleolithic cave dweller than with any person from our present era. [24]

Another interesting clue that consciousness continues to evolve is suggested by what has been called, "the Flynn effect." The political scientist, James Flynn, during research in the 1980's discovered that I.Q. has been rising all over the world for the past century at about 2 points per decade.

These indicators help us to substantiate the historical analysis of Jean Gebser and others that strongly suggest an evolution of consciousness spurring cultural change over the period of recorded history and to realize that such evolutionary effects are active in us today. With this movement of consciousness there arises a "dimensioning" effect spoken of by Gebser as a way of understanding development as adding new "dimensions" of thought. This can be seen when a child begins to move from a purely concrete way of thinking to the broader dimension of abstractions, literally intensifying consciousness through additional dimensions of consideration. In this sense we have an intensification of nonmaterial values in the *cultural creative*. Where the old view was materialistic centered on profit and position, the new view centers on experience and human value.

This is what happens when people outgrow a social order. Their minds are literally too big for the old way of living. Individuals within the late medieval populations of Europe must have felt something similar as they began to chafe against the church's worldview that cast earthly life as nothing more than a "waiting area" for a heaven the priests carried the keys to. Now the human spirit wants to move on again while the exploitive society it is trapped in does everything it can to prevent this from happening. Many will look for answers within the given culture but a growing minority will break free. Still largely unconscious of new movements and not fully aware of all the strategies being used against their freedom, many people will regardless realize with great conviction that something has taken over their lives that feels like an anchor on their soul, that the given culture does not hold the answer in a tropical vacation or a new car, that the given culture is the source of their dilemma. All those in the population not entertained or distracted or bribed or drugged into submission have recognized a growing sense of loss as the growth of the human spirit has been progressively shut out of mainstream society.

This is the condition of so many people who are feeling the impulse in the evolution of their consciousness to put down the childish toys of conflict, status seeking, and materialism of our egocentric culture and pick up something for the building of a new world based on the belief in the possibilities of a human spirit unfettered by petty preoccupations and thereby released into its full potential. This conflict is the head-on confrontation of two profoundly different world views. One is the belief in a centralized power run by the "best of the best" the "cream of the crop," the "best and brightest" of society who have demonstrated their ability (or their ancestors did and the current generation is still riding on their accomplishment). This elite society sees the average person as simply a being whose sole worth is in how much they can contribute to the execution of the ideas of the "best" people at the top. The average person is seen as nothing special, not very smart by elite standards and can be easily replaced. They are not so much individuals as they are types, like livestock that are good for certain uses, one chicken is as good as another. These lower types of human beings are thought to have no "potential" other than having a certain amount of work value, like an engine with so much "horse power."

The opposing philosophy suggests that each individual human being has at their core a unique genius and therefore value. It may be a very subtle talent in some cases, perhaps more pronounced in others. It may only show itself in times of great need or may be confined to some particular situation. It may be something as mundane as the ability to make another person smile or be concerned with a job that they themselves will invent. This philosophy believes that out of a crowd of kids standing on a corner in the worst neighborhood in the bombed out inner city slums of an American wasteland there is one that might invent a new way to save lives, one that might write a song that could stop a person from hating others, one that might work two jobs to send their sister to a private school, one that might start a business in one of the broken store fronts that would send hope out like a beacon in a storm, one might just love another so much that that that person would feel empowered in such a way that everyone they meet feels filled with a simple joy that makes them glad they're alive. These are not all "important" things by elite standards but they are essential things by the standards of the human spirit. These people that the former philosophy simply deems as "excess population," or potential workers if they can be broken of their bad habits, or possibly soldiers to secure access to foreign resources, as essentially "instruments" for the corporate goals of the state, the opposing philosophy sees as unique beings with something important to offer if they can be connected with that core of authentic genius within themselves. [25]

The philosophy of elite society of the "quality" people leading the faceless masses of ordinary folk is very old and is on the verge of being replaced in the evolution of human consciousness on earth. This was the whole idea motivating the American and French revolutions and should have come into the light much earlier if not for the monumental oppression of the Roman church. Although a new aristocracy arose in America to manipulate and divert the course of individual human freedom to build new pyramids of corporatism this diversion is now breaking down. What is happening is that a new stage in the development of the human mind is becoming more and more common among people everywhere and as this opening of the mind continues it brings into possibility a renewed opportunity for this new kind of society where each individual is valued and supported in finding and expressing that unique talent that every human life contains. Each person is seen as a piece of a new social organism that will come into being naturally when we learn to get out of the way of a diverse and defuse human genius.

The elite philosophy believes that nature is something to be dominated and controlled, that human populations are full of tendencies that must be subdued and shaped from the top down. The philosophy of independent human genius believes that Nature knows exactly what it's doing and that although the young must of course be socialized, some amount of custom is critical, at the same time at the core of each person is a healthy impulse to live with love and creative vigor that only needs to be nurtured for the person to offer society their best in whatever way they're highest nature moves them to contribute. (It will be found that it is the denying of this nature and economic abuse that creates most of the bad behavior the rulers feel they need to control.)

The society that follows from this way of releasing the potential of people is far different than the top down elite control version most of the world has experienced to date. It has been the "pyramid building" sort-a-speak, of the rulers that has necessitated all the top-down control in the first place. This is what made early America different. Western people were for the first time released to their own devices. Many of the accomplishments of America came through a belief in the unique genius of ordinary people but that time has largely passed as the institutions and power elite have calcified the nation into ridged forms resistant to any change that doesn't support their investments. When Thomas Edison's work on an efficient battery that would have made electric cars a viable alternative to gasoline driven models was sabotaged in 1903 it marked the end of the time when individual genius would lead America. After that the big money would decide what genius would be allowed to do. [26]

Nature through evolution has created amazingly complicated systems of organization that have given rise to an incredible abundance of life all working in interdependent precision. As nature has become self-reflective in the creative consciousness of humanity it has released its children from the constant restraint of instinct into a play land of open possibilities. Mistakes are made, sometimes of horrifying proportions but beneath the wild chaos of freedom remains the basic genius of Nature that has the power to create a higher order organization through the limitless possibilities of human imagination. Just as cells linking together for mutual benefit evolve into a higher order organism in evolutionary process, so do human beings come together to create higher order civilizations. "A more perfect union," as the U.S. constitution says is an example of that process. Freedom from instinct creates opportunity for novel human organizations to allow for a greater range of creative possibility in the advancement of the human spirit. This is possible, despite negative human weaknesses for selfishness and brutality, through an organization of human effort linked to a basic morality that is a rudimentary aspect of the human spirit; the morality which seeks to preserve and promote human dignity and life itself. This basic instinct for nurturing life may have been lost and buried at times beneath an avalanche of competitive culture but it has remained active beneath it all pushing civilization toward a more fair and just end. Fairness and justice is how human sophistication interprets this natural instinct for giving greater autonomy to *individual human value*. The elite have often missed this fact and so the elite have been overthrown throughout history when they have attempted to suppress this nature for too long. What is pushing forward through this human history has been called "God," "Nature," and "the human spirit," these terms all, ultimately, converge on the same definition.

There is a genius behind the creation of the world that can be understood in a scientific way as "higher order organizing forces beyond the range of our theory and knowledge," or in a spiritual way as God, which is simply the name people have given since the beginning of time to that guiding force they feel resides behind the material surface of life. The first definition is that of the mental/rational mind, the second is that of the mythological mind, both have their virtues within an integral comprehension of reality. The sense the scientist has that something amazing and revolutionary is waiting to be discovered is the same thing the person of faith feels in his or her conviction that some great power beyond their senses made the world and continues to inform it. Both feel a great order and wisdom outside their present understanding but close.

Historically science in its desire to completely usurp the power religion held in the former civilization could not admit any higher order organizing forces for fear of the clergymen co-opting their theories to shore up the church's failing power over the people. The great philosopher Rene' Descartes divided existence in two giving the understanding of all earthly activities to the methods of science, leaving the priests with the non-material matters of souls and heavens. Although Descartes never intended it, as his philosophy came to be applied all order on earth was interpreted as the result of accident or blind chance and necessity in order to kick the clergy out of the discussion once and for all but as science has progressed it has become more and more clear that something more than chance is involved with the ordering of Nature. Random chance simply doesn't cut it.

The co-discoverer of the human genome, Francis Crick, remarked to the effect that the amazingly functional intricacy of the DNA double helix had about as much chance of being created by random mutation as a hurricane blowing through a junk yard had of assembling a 707 airliner. Even the math doesn't work out for random chance as a possibility for creating the amazing productions of nature. You would need many, many times the earth's current age just to get life started by chance, little lone create a primate of any sort. This has been a little problem for the old theory that has been conveniently overlooked because it suggests the necessity of higher order organizing forces of an "invisible" nature that is just the sort of thing that materialists loath. Although no longer necessary science continues to reject "invisible forces" as a matter of habit. It is no longer necessary due to the fact that physics and cutting edge biology have both demonstrated evidence which give credence to invisible forces in the form of energy fields of one sort or another that inform nature and matter but you'd never know it from the "popular" face of science that remains quite materialistic. [27]

Unknown to the casual observer, science ceased to be an open experimental discipline a long time ago, and as such, the orthodoxy of science is now better described as "scientism," a belief system characterized by an irrational belief in a purely material universe. Like the fundamentalist in any religion, they simply won't allow themselves to consider any contrary evidence, labeling "fringe," or "pseudo-science," the empirical findings of the "outlaw" researchers they fear and deplore. This is all perfectly in line with the needs of industry that has successfully co-opted the majority of science done in America. Through a deluge of money poured into the university research system the strict materialism that underlies the socioeconomic system is maintained in science so that all human endeavor and progress is narrowed to technological products that center power in electric plants, gas stations, and in objects that can be sold. This is how the status-quo strengthens itself against the evolution of consciousness and culture by attempting to control the very definitions of "reality" itself. The reform that would follow from the increasing revelations of outlaw science – that life is more than just material forces and stuff – would return corporate power to a business structure that is healthy for the person as a whole by taking the obsessive emphasis off material gain alone. Those at the top of the pyramids of power defend against this possibility in America thereby multiplying the anxiety of its citizens who feel increasingly harrowed by the accelerating pace of "labor for less" and their inability to capture this material nirvana held out to them as the ultimate goal for their existence. Each product promises a better life and centralizes power in the producers. The evolving mind is thereby trapped in a world that seems terribly out of touch with the deeper currents of life he or she feels moving through the world and themselves.

Essentially, orthodox science in its devotion to materialism has become a form of worship whose idol is a robot, the universe as an automatic construction they insist was built entirely by accident, whereas the evolving mind is inclined to believe that the power which gave rise to its own sentience must itself be sentient and alive like themselves but with a consciousness that contains all things, infinite and incomprehensible as a whole. The irony is that at every turn the more orthodox science has sought to discover how their robot god works the more they have come to understand that the robot may not be made of dead rocks and chemicals and senseless particles spinning in a meaningless void at all but may actually be better described as a vast field of energetic information. The great astronomer, James Jeans, once said:

> Fifty years ago the universe was generally looked upon as a machine...When we pass to extremes of size in either direction – whether to the cosmos as a whole, or to the inner recesses of the atom – the mechanical interpretation of Nature fails. We come to entities and phenomena which are in no sense mechanical. To me, they seem less suggestive of mechanical than of mental

processes; the universe seems to be nearer to a great thought than to a great machine.[28]

All this underlies the principle of this work that there is an ordering nature in the universe that creates and structures at the same time it has room for the random, chaos, (that which is not prescribed) which allows for the field of choice in human consciousness. In other words, the "great thought" has some basic structuring influence but allows for human beings to take over more and more of the creative structuring of their own lives as they evolve but if this creative work interferes with the most basic structure itself a conflict arises. This is to say that humanity has many choices available but you cannot get in the way of the basic rise of the human spirit through the individual – that basic program is inviolable. In coming to terms with this imperative the evolving mind sees itself departing from both older mythological stories of how this "great thought" operates, now understood as religions corrupted by power, as well as from the far too mechanical and materialistic, i.e.: *dead*, models of conventional science, looking for an approach that combines the logic of science and the deeper focus of religion to offer answers more commensurate with their maturing consciousness. [29]

The plight of the individual then is increasingly one of being caught between a commercial culture that seeks to titillate their senses – to distract and blind to any progress not to the liking of the elite run commerce machine – and their own interior psychological development which asks for a life in a different world. Any person who has had children, or anyone at all who remembers what it was like to be an adolescent, understands what happens to teenagers when their consciousness expands beyond the joy of simple games and activities of the home and they begin to seek bigger, broader experiences. *The backyard and the old toys are simply not enough and the world beckons.* If that child is trapped by an oppressive or fearful, overly protective parent, then they will grow sullen and their personality will be stunted until the child finds a way out of the too narrow confines their spirit is trapped in. In a like manner many people in the world are waking up to this developmental evolutionary push inside them to find a way out of the old backyard of the stale societies and "official" cultures they find have tied them to a wheel that drains their life energy and gives so little in return.

The Evolution of the Structures of Consciousness

Scholars have tracked this gradual awakening and have proposed different systems for labeling the historical progression but, as stated earlier, I will here use Jean Gebser's terminology which delineates a path toward a growing *intensification* of consciousness. Gebser was very careful to separate his theory from biological definitions of evolution. Evolutionary biology sees organisms as evolving to fit the changing conditions of ecosystems, whereas the evolution of consciousness is doing the exact opposite. Humanity evolves by expanding beyond its niche and then altering conditions to meet its developing vision by reworking the land and natural materials and eventually gaining control of ecological processes, as in agriculture and animal husbandry. Geber's system is basically broken down into four major periods demonstrating the evolution of human consciousness since the beginning of self-awareness. A fifth, the integral, is presented as the new structure now awakening. Let us now expand on the description of this system begun in the introduction.

The Archaic Structure

The "archaic" is the label given to the first "structure of consciousness," attained in a period when human beings were essentially still part of nature with minds that showed little or no creative capacity beyond the strict dictates of instinct and survival. This was a mind that was moved by unconscious feeling alone, that was a member of an ecosystem and responded to the subtle pressures and currents of nature with animal spontaneity. Their community was that of the troop, as displayed by all higher primates.

This structure represents capacities still latent in the human system today that allow for a deep participation in Nature and natural environments; it is the structure of consciousness that allows for the profound empathy that human beings have for animals, the subtle forms of communication with dogs and other pets. Just as animals are able to interpret the energy fields of Nature in what seem a "psychic" fashion, humanity too retains this capacity. We are not broken off from Nature but trail behind us a lifeline connecting our root feeling structure to the world from which our ancestors emerged so that moments in the wilderness can feel like a return to a long lost home.

The Magic Structure

The "magic" or what is sometimes called the "tribal" period, is the name given to the second great eon where, still greatly ensconced in nature, human minds had expanded to allow for an array of tool and structure making and had produced culture in the form of personal adornment and funeral practices while living in clan relational groupings, expanding later to large village tribal configurations with chieftains or counsels of elders. This was a culture based on the expansion of mind that allowed for language, so that aural aspects of life in sound and word were most important. "Magic," was their theory of how things around them came to be, it was the "causal factor" in their worldview.

This structure of consciousness carried on a spirituality that drew its connection to the ecosystem into a more deliberate and interpreted form so that the energetic elements of nature formerly responded to as forces working on instinct now become consciously encountered as Nature Spirits. These forces inhabit a realm visited by returning to the previous structure – now with a measure of consciousness – through the use of trance states. This trance capacity was at first not hard to achieve since consciousness itself was a barely established experience. As time went on it became necessary to use rituals of repetitive drumming or chanting and at some point hallucinogens derived from mushrooms in the northern latitudes and vines and other plants in the equatorial regions, as still demonstrated today by the use of ayahuasca, "the vine of souls" in South American shamanistic ritual.

What this structure of consciousness encounters in this formerly unconscious realm, what Eastern Yogic philosophy terms the "subtle" realm, is a level of existence where natural forces out of sync with visible light wave forms (to speak of the physics) have their natural zone of activity. The "face" given these phenomena is, strangely, not entirely projected from the cultural mind but has been shown to have some continuity in form from one tradition to another in shamanic practices all over the world. [30]

So that "giant lizard creatures" are part of the shamanic lore in Siberia as well as in Native American and Amazonian lore, suggesting a phenomenological interpretation and that some basic archetypal consciousness is at work here along the lines of that suggested by the psychologist Carl Jung. What was part of Nature only *sensed* by the animal mind in the archaic past becomes "spirits" when exposed to the magic structure of consciousness. What these natural forces are, in themselves, is impossible to say beyond what can be derived from the various traditions that have recorded their attributes but it does seem reasonable given the experience of contemporary investigations into shamanic "journeying" that these forces are more than simply blind mechanisms. [31]

THE MYTHOLOGICAL STRUCTURE

Next is the "Mythological" mind which had moved from the tribal worship of the forces of nature and the animal spirits to a story about those forces that became personified in the form of gods and goddesses. At this level in the evolution of consciousness the mind was capable of looking beyond the rudimentary forces of vegetation and animal life to what commanded these things from a "higher" realm. Here was found *The Gods*, the will behind the wind and thunder and all the creatures of the earth. Through a new type of spiritual activity: *worship*, humanity sought to stay on good terms with these *super beings*. In the Yogic system this level of spiritual practice seeks to negotiate the *causal realm*, just above the subtle. Here, ritualistic practice allowed priests to *read the will of the gods*. It was probably at this time that meditation practice introduced a new, more refined, form of self-induced trance state meant to move the mind into communion with the divine powers.

This was the age of the rise of the heroic ego that acted independently from nature to lead human populations to construct stone cities and develop agriculture. These were societies based on a growth of consciousness that allowed for imagery to become important. The birth of complex symbols and written language followed this development and so vision and heroic experience were the important avenues of progress introduced with the mythological mind. The central power of the mythological structure of consciousness is in the use of story to form explanatory models so as to give form and direction to life. Not just any story "I went to the river to jump in the water," is a story but is not the sort suggested by mythology. The mythological mind creates symbol systems in story form that allow for an interface for the mediation of powers between the psyche and the world, what Carl Jung termed, the "psychoid." [32] The mythological mind also creates *patterning stories* which offer maps to locate oneself in the universe and so give parameters for action. This is a fantastic creative ability and leap forward into autonomy because ultimately it will be found that the gods don't entirely control the myths.

The Mental/Rational Structure

The "mental/rational" mind is the term given to the next eon from which we are just emerging. This structure of consciousness presents a deepening of thought that allows for a much more systematic speculation regarding the material phenomenon of life. This intellectual consideration moves away from image and symbol as the representation of numinous forces in the world toward a direct study of the mechanics of nature that can then be abstracted to use in developing technology. Although the Greeks began this speculation the "mental/rational period" really didn't come into full power until the Enlightenment in the 17th Century at which time the scientific revolution came by way of this direct, analytic, materialistic and mechanical way of interpreting the universe. It then slowly took over the Western mind and culture almost totally as the major mode of understanding life. This rational view gave rise to the modern nation state and provided the basis for the development of democratic principles. This is literally a "way of seeing things" that is based on a linear perspective where the observer stands apart from what is observed, dispassionately, without resort to tradition. Jean Gebser describes the mental/rational consciousness as a mode in which the world is "spatialized and quantified." The phenomena surrounding humanity are believed to be best apprehended through measuring the object in a three dimensional space in various ways: dimension, weight, movement, etc., so as to describe the object's action within a mechanistic framework. This is the era of abstract intellect and schematic overview and planning. The causal element in the mental/rational worldview is sought in a reductionist manner that is looking backward through time and the internal sequence of events to find the "first thing" that triggers the phenomenon.

The Integral Structure

Now we come to what is perhaps the most intriguing part in the introduction of what evidence suggests is the next stage in the evolution of human consciousness. It is believed that this structure has been stimulating a new culture since the late 19th Century. This awakening consciousness has been termed the "integral," because it seems that at this point in human development we are being moved to *integrate* everything we have experienced through all the previous structures of consciousness.

> The integral knowledge admits the valid truths of all views of existence, valid in their own field, but it seeks to get rid of their limitations and negations and to harmonize and reconcile these partial truths in a larger truth which fulfills all the many sides of our being in the one omnipresent Existence.

These are the words of the great Western educated Indian sage, Sri Aurobindo, [33] whose writings became a bridge between Western and Eastern philosophy. He saw that many of the prejudices of the modern Western viewpoint were simply based in errors of comprehension in judging Eastern thought by the wrong criteria. He demonstrated through deft argument and deep scholarship that different worldviews must be understood by their own terms and that these so called, "primitive" views were connected to vital necessities for the health of the human mind and body. Aurobindo was the first to use the term "integral" to refer to this task of pulling together, "the many sides of our being," into an integrated whole, with a goal of transcending this whole in what he termed the "superconscient." A term describing an expansion of mind by way of the inculcation of a "higher" field of consciousness. Aurobindo explained that it was truly impossible to describe this state, one simply had to experience it but he did say this: "In the supermind all is self-known self-luminously, there are no divisions, oppositions or separated aspects in the Mind whose principle is division of Knowledge into parts and setting each part against another." [34] This is a final stage of integration where the wholeness underlying our reality is "luminously" revealed. This Jean Gebser understood as a kind of "seeing through" of materiality in what he described as the "diaphanous," nature of the world open to the discernment of the truly initiated integral mind.

All of these terms seem a bit absurd to our mental/rational mind conditioned to judge the world on spatial measurements but that is the very point: *that the world is more than this and we are now learning to perceive what was previously unperceived with an evolving intensified consciousness*. The absurdity of the terms comes by way of using a language developed for describing a different order of consciousness; we are aware of its failure. This is what led Jean Gebser to make-up some of his own terms in an effort to create new language that was equal to the task of describing elements in a way of thinking outside habitual patterns.

One of the first reactions people often have when confronting the idea of an evolving mental progress comes from the feeling that people are just as much the mean, murderous, cheating, dishonest, creatures they have always been and so notions of any sort of continuing human evolution seem specious. It must be understood that moral or ethical development is something apart from the growing sophistication of the mind evidenced by the expansion of larger domains of thought found in the historical record. The psychologist Lawrence Kohlberg studied the development of moral concern in people and found that it could often lag behind other forms of development. Kohlberg discovered that people developed moral schemes based on their intelligence and developmental progress while growing up, so that the more sophisticated the mind, the more complex the schemes to justify actions. Ideally, in healthy development a person moves from rule based forms of morality in childhood, to empathy based forms of morality in adulthood. Ultimately, morality then rests on the development of empathy for larger and larger groups of people and life in general. [35]

Unfortunately this expanding empathy is limited in the previous stages in the evolution of consciousness, so that empathy tends to be confined to the tribe, then to those of the same culture or mythic affiliation in the next stage, then to the same nation state. As civilization has grown larger it has become a more complex issue and certainly within a cosmopolitan society morality based on empathy becomes much more problematic. These developmental limitations and pitfalls have all led to the continuing brutality in our time but it is one thesis of this work that as we transition as a people into the next structure of consciousness on our evolutionary journey a basic morality affixed to the reviving of the efficient mode of all the structures of consciousness required for the integral stage will bring forth a new moral capacity across the face of humanity. This will be explained in some detail in the pages ahead.

This integration process we are now involved in has been rejected in the past. The tendency was to dismiss the earlier stage when a culture began to move into a new consciousness structure with its unique way of understanding the world. The old culture comes to be seen as evil or primitive. So as societies moved away from the magic stage into the mythological they tended to put aside the spiritual ways of the tribal peoples where every dream and vision was important, in favor of a specialized priest class where the leader was himself a "priest king" and intermediary between the people and the spiritual powers. In time the surviving cultures where the old shamans and healers still operated were not just regarded as primitives but came to be feared as "evil sorcerers and witches" and were persecuted. This was due to the belief that the powers they invoked were lower demonic forces that had been properly conquered by the gods. Eventually in the latter mythological period, the one "true" monotheistic god cast the old gods as well in the same evil light.

When Western humanity moved into the mechanical and entirely materialistic approach to understanding the powers of existence the denigration and marginalization of the previous mythological view became the constant subplot of scientific culture. This has often been understood as science's war against religion. As the integral structure really began to rock society the feeling arrived that each of the previous stages may of had something important to offer a complete comprehension of life on earth and that too much haste had perhaps thrown out with the "outgrown" elements something vital from the life history of each step in human experience. When Sigmund Freud wrote of *Civilization and its Discontents* he was acknowledging the experience of all that this "civilizing" progress and his upbringing in a very up-tight Victorian society had denied in the body of humanity. Freud believed that this repression of instinct was absolutely necessary for the progress of civilization and so man was condemned, in his view, to a never ending frustration of his deeper feelings. The German social critic, Herbert Marcuse, later proposed in *Eros and Civilization* that this was not necessarily so, that Freud's scheme produced *a certain kind of civilization* and that a healthier relationship with "instinct" could create a better civilization altogether. Indeed, this better more free society has been rising to the surface for some time, if we may broaden this notion of instinct to include all structures of consciousness prior to the current mental/rational. A certain romanticism and ennui, a longing, shall we say, for something within the embodied human spirit repressed and denied has been pressing itself on consciousness since the 19th Century, asking for integration and the culture of the West has been responding in progressive movements ever since.

When the impressionists began to attempt depiction of another dimension in paint they were trying to infuse the canvas with a recovered vitality from the archaic age. When the poets Keats and Shelly began to lament a more passionate past obscured by industrialism, they were responding to the tribal/magic mind's lusting embrace of life and using the mythological mind to conger the dream. When Jazz took hold of America against all "proper" standards and despite its "dark" origins the people were again responding to the magical mind let out of its *white bread* box.

The great scholar of the evolution of consciousness, Jean Gebser, proposed in his magnum opus, *The Ever Present Origin*, (a work that serves as a primary source for this book), that within human evolution there has been a process wherein the origin of all things, which gave rise to the earth itself, has been revealing its nature in greater and greater expressions though the building sophistication of the human mind. Simply put, what came into the universe at the beginning of time, as we understand it: the subatomic information pouring into this dimension at the big bang and coalescing as planets and stars, that was completely unconscious in its earlier manifestations in the flora and fauna that emerged as living organic structures, became aware of itself in humanity and through the continued evolution of the species is revealing *consciously* what was contained in that original energetic force. We are becoming more and more aware of the universe that we were born from and through which its origin lives in us. Another way of putting this idea is that, what caused the big bang, the creation of the universe, must be a force so profound and expansive it is beyond our conception and so it is to the world and us as parents are to children. As the child grows it partakes in the greater expression of the intelligence it inherited from the parents. We are like orphan children transported to a new land who do not know our parents but as we grow we discover more and more what those parents endowed within us. If the life span of that which gave rise to the human race is infinite and homo sapiens are said to be only 150,000 years old then we see as that which created us would see at our stage of development. Indeed, in a sense, *we are the thing which created us* growing up through a biological construct and discovering our deep heritage as the foundation of an awakening creativity.

Defenders of the old "wind-up-toy" universe type of science respond to the above sort of thinking with accusations of "creationism!" and its newest manifestation "intelligent design!" as a strategy for branding any proposition that suggests higher order ordering forces as a new assault on reason and progress. What is being suggested here has no relation to the sort of concept promoted by fundamentalist religious factions that have simply taken their god of the mountain top and moved him a little higher up into the cosmos. What is proposed within these pages is not the ministrations of a god form like Jehovah, Zeus, or Athena moving humans around like pons on their chess board but rather an energetic force *that must contain within itself the structuring forces of that which springs from it.* This is a proposition that contains a very strong logic whereas the orthodox evolutionary theory is based on a very weak logic that suggests that nothing gave rise to something and that dead matter gave rise to life. The original scientific ideas of Galileo and Newton had the old God at the basis of creation but in time the leaders of the scientific doctrine threw God out and replaced him with nothing. All this more progressive science is proposing to do is replace "nothing," and "accident" with "something" and "structure." There is no desire among progressive thinkers to bring back the old god of the mountain top only to suggest that "random accident" and "nothing" is inadequate to the task of explaining our existence.

If this sounds like a religious idea then this is only because at a certain limit of the known universe science begins to take on a spiritual hue. If by *science* we mean the systematic search for truth. Any physicist will tell you energy is information and the information of the big bang continues to flow into this dimension within the atomic structure of our very being. We are supported by the infinite at the center of every atom. Even the very elements our bodies are constructed from were forged in the center of stars, as the popular astronomer, Carl Sagan, was fond of pointing out. Astrobiologists have discovered transformations of these elements reordering themselves to create the basic foundations of life within interstellar gas clouds and the peculiar conditions surrounding comets. The more we find out about how life has developed in the universe the more it supports the conclusion that the universe is finely tuned for creation. These galactic compounds constitute evidence of *order*, if you will, emerging from the non-material dimensions which support matter and life; an order that was foundational in a construction which emerged from outside the space/time continuum. A translation has occurred of something less dense in its makeup into the density of matter where biology provides the platform for complex life forms and consciousness.

The structures of consciousness that have developed in the human mind since the dawning of self-awareness are therefore expressions of our heritage from eternity and the stars as it has come into being here on Earth. It is not the intention of this work to fill many pages with the story of how that emerging consciousness expressed itself through the entire historical evolution of culture and civilization. For this I refer readers to Jean Gebser himself who carried out an exhaustive study of how evolving consciousness is reflected in the products of culture through time. Each eon of thought has expressed what Gebser referred to as a "structure of consciousness," these are essentially the "mind" of each emerging life space, moving from the world of pure physicality to cultural ecosystems of a growing complexity. What this approach to human experience attempts is to alert the many individuals who are experiencing an alienation from mainstream culture and beliefs, possibly successful in many aspects of life but still lost in some essential rejoin of their being, that by recovering something of what has been rejected from our past structures of consciousness and by using this to create a platform for an expanded awareness a person can make a leap of consciousness out of the alienation so common today.

This "integral" development, so termed for its "integrating" function, is understood to be emerging at this time to move humanity beyond the exclusive claim to superiority of the mental/rational structure which has reached a point where clear deficiencies have become obvious. Two major effects being a "deadening" of life and an egocentric competition that results in an emotional isolation from others – but that's just the beginning – the repression of the previous structures of consciousness create the grounds for a myriad of neurotic tendencies. The exclusive use of the mental/rational structure of mind tends to promote a kind of "disembodied" intellect which rejects all other ways of experiencing the world in favor of a calculating, cerebral abstraction, which is to say: numbers and labels in the place of visceral experience, esthetic impression and connected intuition. The world and its contents – animal, vegetable and mineral – is measured and classified, given designations and ratings, and treated thereafter in a formulaic manner which cuts the person off from the actual experience of life in a body and leads to decisions, personal and public, that drastically narrow the individual and the community along with the subjects of their work. People experience this all the time in situations where they have been reduced to a number and treated as such by government offices and insurance companies. A distinct lack of humanity is felt; the cheerful recording on the phone seems a thin lie masking a cold hearted machine. This is but one dimension of a much larger problem the integral is meant to address.

The passion for living that so many are missing is a direct result of an imbalance in the appropriate use of the available structures of consciousness that any human being can experience. To touch on the matter briefly: something of the healing connectedness within an ecosystem felt by the archaic human mind and body is still available to us in our deep emotional bodies. The vivid tribal experience of bonded community, the voice as resonator of deep truth, sound as the emotional language of nature continues to offer essential knowledge. The power of symbol and image and story as a route into the psyche where meaning and purpose have their nexus is a place where so many have lost the keys to the mythological realities of their lives. Our current focus on the mental/rational structure must be pushed back into its proper sphere so as to allow a complete and harmonious experience of life in this multidimensional universe our physics is telling us we live in and into which we are maturing with greater awareness.

What this integration leads to is a reappraisal of the objects of human experience and contemplation and thus the experience of life and the world itself. The resulting reordering of experience has a tendency to shift a person's value structure away from materialism, finding a proper place for the material in a larger framework for a life in balance with the values that emerge from each of the revitalized structures of consciousness. From this place the integral awareness opens up as an emergent structure based on the other four but beyond them. This is to say, a whole new way of seeing things, of experience comes forward into awareness. The mind itself is an emergent form in that it arrives via the "platform" of the biological structure in all its coordinated and cooperative functions. Children develop from one psychological stage to another, not dispensing with earlier stage awareness but incorporating and building on it. The later stages of development would not be possible without the earlier, each stage resting on the past but achieving something novel and so goes the evolution of human consciousness through history. The integral structure of consciousness is yet another emergent form based on the integrated structures of the archaic, tribal/magical, mythological, and mental. When they are properly invested with awareness, developed and harmonized then a new order of experience and understanding arrive and with it a deep sense of being at home on earth.

This may all sound somewhat mystical or complicated to those first encountering this material but in reality many people are on this path in many little ways already. People naturally respond to a walk in the forest or along the beach with a calm clearing of the mind; this is a dip into the archaic structure of consciousness. People listen to music and are carried away into a variety of hypnotic trance as they find themselves moved to the rhythm or swept away into vast fields of emotion while listening to a symphony; this is a dip into the tribal/magic structure. People are moved by images in art and film all the time and vicariously take part in the tales, stories that influence the person's behavior in the real world, they may be encouraged to take bold steps out of their comfort zone and learn something vital for their lives in the process; this is a dip into the mythological mind. The mental/rational being the primary mode of our age is used all the time in calculating every element of existence in an attempt to control outcomes. From timing the cooking of a roast, to planning how to get a job done, people are constantly calculating things in their minds throughout the day. The modern mind is full of never ending judgments based on rational observation, in essence: measurements.

Here in lies the problem: the mental /rational structure of consciousness due to its success in the technological realm has been over applied to all areas of life, thus pushing out the appropriate sense of things in those realms of human experience where another structure is the only actual mode of accurate understanding. An example of this can be found in the strange world of computer dating. A person puts into the program all of the attributes they are looking for in a potential spouse and then goes about interviewing the candidates one after another. Most people find that none of the persons actually work out for them, a few find someone but for reasons other than what was on the form. The reason for this is due to the fact that picking potential mates has little to nothing to do with the rationally derived criteria asked for in the program. In fact, it is impossible to find a mate without dispensing with rational ego motivations and allowing a deeper sense to take over.

People find they end up marrying individuals for reasons that are often hard to put into words. This is because finding a mate is not a mental/rational task, it is a magical structure task completely in the realm of feeling and emotion. People often speak of just feeling at ease with the other, feeling a deep connection and empathy, "like I've known them all my life." This is a harmony that occurs when deep emotional structures resonate through a compatibility unknown to mental constructs and dating programs. The philosopher Blasé Pascal said "the heart has a logic the mind will never know." Unfortunately most people in Western society have absorbed the message from the scientific orthodoxy that everything can be rationally understood and formulated for control. This idea can be found time and again in movies and television when, in the midst of mysterious occurrences, the hero always exclaims, "there has to be a rational explanation for all of this!" By the end of the show one is always discovered. There may very well be a rational explanation when investigating criminal activity but as an exclusive way of approaching every area of life the mental/rational constitutes a profound error in philosophy our society has been trying to dig their way out of for the last two centuries or so.

Another example of the confusion of structures can be found in the popular cinema. What action films actually depict is what can most accurately be understood as mythological in nature. No actual person can do what James Bond does without being killed instantly. The same goes for the Mission Impossible team, the heroes of war films, and most police sagas. These types of stories are set in a manner meant to depict real life but they show people doing things which in actuality would require super-human abilities, in short – the abilities of mythological heroes. These movie and television stories are depicting the modern age's version of Hercules and Achilles only unconsciously in an age where everything has to be rationalized and so, what were once demigods are made into "real people."

The problem comes when the public believes that humans are actually capable of such things or that they too would react just as the hero does to similar circumstances. Many young men have met the folly of such a judgment after joining the military and coming face to face with an environment where heroes are not bullet proof. A place where glory is absent and instead the air is rife with a tragedy they cannot so easily blow off with the smoke from their gun barrels like the cocky movie gunfighters they grew up with. The most common refrain of the new soldier is "this is not what I expected." John Wayne never had trouble sleeping but Audie Murphy, the infantry hero of WWII turned movie star, slept with the lights on and a gun under his pillow, became addicted to sleeping pills, and had chronic nightmares. "To become an executioner, someone cold and analytical, to be trained to kill, and then to come back into civilian life and be alone in the crowd – it takes an awful long time to get over it," Murphy confessed to the journalist Thomas Morgan in 1967. "Fear and depression come over you." [36]

Mythology drives recruitment; reality drives the exodus from the ranks, the suicides, the sick hearts and thousand yard stares, and the post-traumatic stress disorder. Modern warfare is a mental/rational conception, a technological enterprise calculated for maximum destruction without concern for pity and the limits of the human psyche. The title of a book by an Army officer concerning the plight of the modern soldier sums it all up: *No More Heroes*.[37] To confuse the heroic mythological conception of "meeting the enemy boldly on the field of battle" to determine the better man, the stronger spirit, or the will of the gods, with the technological system of slaughter that controls warfare in the modern age is to set oneself up for tragedy and mental illness.

There are many areas where a confusion of consciousness structures lead to terrible errors in the lives of people everywhere in the technologically minded world. The mental/rational order has subsumed all other fields of human thought and experience under its control. It has done so largely by mislabeling and reducing experience and phenomena to spatial measurements and descriptions, as if describing the size, mechanical function, and surface of a thing is all there is to it. For things like love which defy spatial quantification the reality of their unique power is simply denied by reduction to glandular responses and brain chemicals. Everything has to be physical and mechanical to the mental/rational mind of the orthodox scientist and so the whole world and all of life is understood as simply a machine.

The failure in all this consists of the inability to understand that the world appears mechanical because the philosophy of orthodox science, the exclusive application of the mental/rational structure of consciousness, places a kind of mental "template" over the world which highlights the mechanical causal structures in a linear time sequence and simply blocks out everything else that is going on. "What we observe is not nature itself," informed the celebrated physicist, Werner Heisenberg, "but nature exposed to our method of understanding." Unfortunately, this astute observation has been generally lost on most of the scientific community who prefer to believe they are really plumbing the depths of the universe. Not discovering a *version* of reality selected by their method but *reality itself*.

This is a great and terrible illusion. Human beings can only understand as much of the universe as the development of their consciousness will allow them to understand. There are infinite fields of knowledge beyond the framework of our current method of understanding. That is the inescapable truth those locked within a mental/rational mindset simply refuse to confront. This refusal is bolstered by an economy and professional power structure that springs from the limited worldview of scientific materialism and through the self-reinforcing dynamics basic to all political systems. The good news is that any individual can make another choice. Some measure of true freedom of thought and action still exists in some areas of the world and so it is possible to pull away from the myopathy of the exclusive rational vision and open life to a full allowance of all the avenues of knowledge humanity possesses. What has been comprehended as one note then becomes a chord and that chord within the individual becomes a symphony in community, hence, a new society emerges.

The issue dealt with in this book is really that of human freedom. Growing up and living in a technologically oriented consumer culture conditions the individual to understand the world in a very narrow sense. The way the mind is shaped by such a culture actually contains its own method of repressing all possible challenges to its dominance. The individual is placated and soothed by the constant application and promise of more gadgets, "the new model," and "the latest thing," and so any sense that the life created by this system is deficient in some way, the boredom and monotony of the "rat race" that suggests that the system is a new form of tyranny is reflected back to the individual as a need for more stuff, more achievement, more money. All searching for *Life* and freedom is directed by consumer society back to the market place because the unenlightened materialist cannot conceive of any answer that does not involve a new thing, a vacation, a promotion, thereby suggesting a reinvestment of efforts in the very system that is the never ending source of their angst and longing.

Media productions, "shows" of every variety, channel human emotion into prescribed dramas that support the status-quo system of competition and material opulence as a sole indicator of prestige and so *true being*. The relationships to the larger connections of life, that of Nature outside as well as that within, are managed by the conditions of life imposed by the technological order. Some cutoff completely and others channeled along lines always compatible with an expanding consumer economy. In response to a feeling of being trapped in the rat race people are extolled to "experience the great outdoors," for instance, and to do so the individual is directed to the sporting goods store, the RV and SUV dealership, perhaps a boat or firearm of some sort is suggested. When the person arrives in the "great outdoors," they set about experiencing the place in the same way they watch their television screens, believing that just being in a "beautiful place" and engaging in "fun" is what it's all about.

In contrast to this approach, a person could experience more of what nature is really about without buying anything but by simply walking into whatever natural environment they have in their area, a bit of forest or beach, untended and unchanged by human hands, and sitting still for a number of hours simply watching in quiet contemplation. In this way they would begin to see and feel beyond the surface of nature and so this person would very likely begin to experience a positive effect unknown to their previous concepts of fun or beauty. Unfortunately, this is not commensurate with the materialist mental/rational order and so it is not offered on television. Everyone is taught to "color between the lines," you can choose the color but the system provides the lines. So many choices are offered, an endless array of styles and flavors and products are set before the individual encouraging material desires while ignoring the non-material – *those human needs that can't be turned into commodities*. This environment produces a kind of self-supporting tyranny where people feel a vague sense of deprivation brought on by the lack of attention to the true sources of happiness but are encouraged to interpret this feeling as stemming from a lack of belongings and/or one of the manufactured varieties of "prestige" offered through advancement in the system. When people are starved for food and out in the cold they know what's wrong and can fight for better conditions without being sidetracked but when those primary needs are met, the "higher order" needs, as the psychologist Abraham Maslow called them, can be lost or misdirected through cultural manipulation. Higher order needs include such things as: companionship, love, community, creative activity, meaningful work, and personal knowledge, deep communion with the source of life, things that have nothing to do with the constant competition and product acquisition of mainstream commercial culture.

This culture, which is itself artificial and manufactured is not a natural outgrowth of human nature but is rather a perverting of human nature so as to create a subtle form of economic enslavement. It is a culture of designed addiction and dependency that subverts satisfaction, true healing and peace, seeking always to keep people coming back for more. "The media have not only filtered into our experience of external realities, they have also entered into our experience of our own selves," wrote the sociologist, C. Wright Mills, of America in the mid 1950's when the strategists behind the artificial culture were in the process of shifting into high gear.

"More than that: (1) the media tell the man in the mass who he is – they give him identity; (2) they tell him what he wants to be – they give him aspirations; (3) they tell him how to get that way – they give him technique; and (4) they tell him how to feel that he is that way even when he is not – they give him escape. The gaps between the identity and the aspiration lead to technique and/or to escape. That is probably the basic psychological formula of the mass media today. But, as a formula, it is not attuned to the development of the human being. It is the formula of a pseudo-world which the media invent and sustain." [38]

Underlying these totalitarian trends is the continued march of modernism and it's never ending sales job for *technology as savior*. As technology expands its power and range into people's lives it seems to suggest that all problems will be solved through this expanding technical control. Few actually ask where technology is taking us or if life is really enhanced by turning the world into a remote control device. This notion contains the largely unexamined assumption that what is missing in life can always be found in a new "breakthrough" product of some sort and so, "the good life" is pursued through the acquisition of wealth and objects of one sort or another. This is the social and economic manifestation of orthodox science's insistence that only matter exists.

In the multi-dimensional world we truly live in thoughts and feelings have reality. The fabric of culture itself is more "informational" and "energetic" than material. Things exist in more than simply width and depth and height, and movement in time but these other dimensions where emotion and thought and the other "non-material forces" of life have their home are completely invisible to the materialism of the mental/rational structure of consciousness. All good things are thought to emanate from material products, like planets creating gravity. Consumer culture persists in the belief that fun and joy and even dignity and attractiveness are the byproducts of material things, the clothing makes the man, or woman, as has been said. This man or woman, now properly clad, need only access the proper toys to have fun or create excitement. What is created by this method is a life like a bad movie full of glitz and action but lacking a coherent story line.

The mental/rational is a highly useful way of creating infrastructure, like roads and bridges and buildings and such, but it has no place in the actual experience of life. When it is inappropriately applied it brings with it a force that kills, in that it removes the focus from what really matters. You need the talents of the mental/rational mind to build the house but if what goes in it is approached only rationally then the person will find themselves living in a machine, quite efficient but wholly without life. Life dances on any kind of floor. Life laughs in any room. Life loves, debates passionately, and savors friendship and beautiful moments under any sort of roof, regardless of interior design or opulent appointments. That which creates *life* is lost on the mental/rational ego and so life is often lost in favor of cerebral considerations of rank and style. This lifelessness is then responded to through the pursuit of entertainment and more possessions.

These controlling features of the current phase of Western civilization tend to hem in the possibilities for a person's life found in the formula: work = money = happiness. Thus the individual is driven to support an ever accelerating economy in which the carrot is forever tied to a stick just out of reach. Because this represents a huge confusion of orders of consciousness where material novelty is mistaken for a living vitality that can only be achieved through attending to all the structures of consciousness, the complete person, the individual is continually seeking that vitality in a manner that is forever destine to disappoint. Many never figure out that material things alone cannot provide true vitality and meaning in life. The belief is unshakeable that the experience they yearn for is contained in the object: the cure for loneliness is a matter of driving the right car or getting breast implants. When things disappoint as usual, when the gleam wares off the new car and the person sees the same old tired face staring back at them in the mirror, an inevitable error is made in the thought that suggests the problem can be solved by yet another application of money, inappropriate "achievement," and *things*. So, the cycle repeats generating escalating levels of exhaustion and depression.

What this book attempts, among other things, is to open the door in the reader's mind to another way of understanding how to approach success in life. There is a value system in this work that flows from the realization that each structure of consciousness offers its own type of power and joy and "sustenance for the soul." What is suggested here is that by coming to understand the root experiences of the multi-dimensional nature of the particular reality formed from the archaic, magic, mythic, and mental structures of human consciousness, a person comes to fully embrace the experience of being human and in doing so discovers an "integral" consciousness that offers a world of riches without price.

Before beginning the trek into this new world of thought and life it must be realized that what is presented here is not presumed to represent some final truth on the growth of the human mind on earth but is simply offered as another map among many created in an attempt to better understand the deep roots of human existence. This map is meant to support a realization of everything we have brought to this moment and what this knowledge may tell us about how to proceed with the building of a better life and society. No map is actually the territory it proposes to represent and this one is not the territory either. It simply marks a trail through the wilderness of ourselves. We interpret our past in order to find a route into the future, to avoid repeating errors, opening ourselves to the new present emerging. History shows us that human civilizations run down at certain junctures in time and in those moments great opportunities abound in reevaluating the journey and setting off in a new direction. We are unquestionably at one of those junctures and the opportunities are springing up everywhere.

Human beings are crucibles of fantastic potential. As the human race has grown out of its primitive civilizations where only small numbers at the top of societies had the possibility to really live their potential while seething masses of laborers, scribes and soldiers made their contemplations possible, today many more human beings through the advancement of fairness and freedom have found greater and greater opportunities to offer their communities the products of their emancipated genius. There is a great power contained within each person and the goal of an enlightened civilization should be to work always to further new ways of releasing that power. America was conceived on such a model but unfortunately, just as the forefathers had warned, this broad prosperity of human possibility has fallen victim, not to a foreign born despotism but to one that has grown out of the very success of the nation itself. Those at the top of the power game have sought to pull up the ladders and stop the creative progress so that they may armor and enshrine their dominance but this is but a passing moment in the history of civilization that has come and gone a thousand times before. The walls come tumbling down, sooner or later, one way or another, because trying to stop the human spirit on its way to a place we cannot yet conceive is like trying to stop the rotation of the planet or any other natural force in the universe.

The human spirit is again in rebellion against that which presumes to dominate and contain it. This vision of the next step in human civilization offers a model wherein all the world's people will have something to contribute. In this world wide uprising representatives of all the structures of consciousness in all the cultures of the world are asking for respect and liberation. Those still living in the tribal structure are the caretakers of a great lost wisdom, those in the mythological world of tradition and powerful doctrine have another piece of the truth to tell, and of course, the mental power of the industrial world must be brought into harmony with the whole to glean its technique while preserving all life. One of the profound truths being uncovered by the progressive new science is that everything is connected at multiple levels. In liberating the individual, everything connected to that single life is affected. Each life radiates outward like ripples from a stone dropped in a pond. Herein lies an invitation to join the revolution, create some ripples and involve yourself in the greatest adventure on earth; the uprising is eternal and the uprising has just begun.

Before describing the outline of an integral life it will be necessary to place before the reader the current state of affairs in Western Civilization with emphasis on America in order to make plain that which seeks to prevent and frustrate the evolution of consciousness. There is no slavery more binding than that practiced against the human mind but it is also true that such methods as mind control can be easier than steel chains for the individual to escape once they discover the locks and the keys within themselves that fit them. The light of truth and consciousness scatters all shadows.

Notes

1. Jean Gebser (1985). Duane Elgin, *Awakening Earth, Exploring the Evolution of Human Culture and Consciousness* (New York: William Morrow and Company, Inc., 1993).
2. Carroll Quigley, *The Evolution of Civilizations, An Introduction To Historical Analysis* (Indianapolis: Liberty Fund, 1979), p. 115.
3. Ibid., p. 117.
4. Joel Bakan, *The Corporation, The Pathological Pursuit of Profit and Power*. (New York: Free Press, 2004).
5. Simon Johnson and James Kwak, *13 Bankers, The Wall Street Takeover and the Next Financial Meltdown*. (New York: Vintage Books, 2011), p. 6.
6. Ibid., p. 191.
7. William Leach, *Land of Desire, Merchants, Power and the Rise of a New American Culture*. (New York: Vintage Books, 1994).
8. Ibid., p. 4.
9. Chrystia Freeland, "The Rise of the New Ruling Class, How the Global Elite is Leaving You Behind," *The Atlantic*, (January/February, vol. 307, No. 1, 2011).
10. See: www.fair.org for regular reporting on media manipulation.
11. William Irwin Thompson, *Self and Society, Studies in the Evolution of Culture*. (Charlotttesville: Imprint Academic, 2009).
12. Charles H. Ferguson, Predator Nation: *Corporate Criminals, Political Corruption, and the Hijacking of America*. (New York: Crown Business, 2013).
13. F. William Engdahl, *Seeds of Destruction, The Hidden Agenda of Genetic Manipulation* (Montreal: Global Research, 2007).
14. Ibid.
15. Chalmers Johnson, *The Sorrows of Empire: Militarism, Secrecy, and the End of the Republic* (New York: Metropolitan Books, 2004).
16. www.Wikipedia.com, Anti-Imperialist League.
17. Smedley Butler, *War is a Racket* (Los Angeles: Feral House, 1936, 2012), p. 10.
18. Antony C. Sutton, *Wall Street and the Rise of Hitler* (San Pedro, CA: GSG & Associates, 2002).
19. www.newscientist.com, Revealed: The Capitalist Network that Runs the World.
20. Sheldon S Wolin, *Democracy Inc. Managed Democracy and the Spector of Inverted Totalitarianism* (Princeton: Princeton University Press, 2008). F. William Engdal, *Gods of Money, Wall Street and the Death of the American Century* (Joshua Tree: Progressive Press, 2009). Johnson (2004).
21. John Ralston Saul, *The Collapse of Globalism and the Reinvention of the World*. (New York: Penguin, 2006).
22. Wolin (2008), p.59.
23. www.worldforum.org/creatives-overview.htm
24. www.johnhawks.net
25. Those writing on this idea have been referred to as the "alternate

tradition," in American letters which is that literature that has held spiritual development above crass materialism. People like Lewis Mumford, C. Wright Mills, David Riesman, John Kenneth Galbraith, Vance Packard, and more recently, people like Morris Berman and Ken Wilber, among many others. (The mainstream elitist ideology comes through Thomas Hobbs, Hegel, and the latter day champion of corporate elitism, Leo Strauss, followed by Milton Friedman and represented by the film character, Gordon Gecko.) Morris Berman has written about the popularity and yet ineffectiveness of the alternative literature: "Americans read, nodded in agreement, and then went out and bought a second car and a truck load of appliances." *Why America Failed* (Hoboken: John Wiley & Sons, Inc. 2012), p. 26. My analysis is simply that it was effective in a minority and that this minority is now expanding into a major movement at the same time crass materialism is driving the old system into failure.

26. Edwin Black, *Internal Combustion* (New York: St. Martin's Griffin, 2006). Richard Milton, *Alternative Science, Challenging the Myths of the Scientific Establishment* (Rochester: Park Street Press,1996). Jonathan Eisen, *Suppressed Inventions & Other Discoveries* (New York: Avery Publishing Group, 1999).

27. Rupert Sheldrake, *Science Set Free, 10 Paths to New Discovery* (New York: Crown Publishing, 2012).

28. As quoted in: Michio Kaku, *Parallel Worlds*, (New York: Anchor Books, 2005), P. 350.

29. Ken Wilber, *The Marriage of Sense and Soul*. (New York: Broadway Books, 1998).

30. Mircea Eliade, *Shamanism, Archaic Techniques of Ecstasy* (New York: Penguin Arkana, 1964). Carl Jung also noted this phenomenon in the mythological accounts.

31. In this regard see the work of: Terence McKenna, Hank Wesselman, Michael Harner, Sandra Ingerman, and Alberto Villoldo.

32. Carl Jung, *The Structure and Dynamics of the Psyche. (Princeton: Bollingen*, Princeton University Press, 1960).

33. A. S. Dalal, *An Introduction to the Psychological Thought of Sri Aurobindo* (New York: Tarcher/Putnam, 2001).

34. Sri Aurobindo, *Letters on Yoga* (Pondicherry: Lotus Press, 1995), pp. 59-60.

35. Michael Green, *Theories of Human Development, A Comparative Approach*. (Englewood Cliffs: Prentice Hall, 1989).

36. Tom Huntington, at: americanwwii.com/stories/audiemurphy.

37. Richard Gabriel, *No More Heroes, Madness and Psychiatry in War* (New York: Hill & Wang, 1988).

38. C. Wright Mills, T*he Power Elite*, (New York: Oxford, 1956, 2000), p. 314.

Chapter 2

The Inside and the Outside of Life

Life is a strange puzzle where hints to the answers are all around us but we don't have the vision to see them. Why it is that so many esoteric systems consider the outside of our minds, the world, as a reflection of the inside of our minds? Sometime around 800 BCE the sages of India began to record the discoveries from their meditative researches. "We should consider that in the inner world Brahman is consciousness; and we should consider that in the outer world Brahman is space. These are the two meditations."[1] The Hermetic wisdom from Egypt that underlies much of Western esotericism states the matter quite succinctly, "All is mind."[2] This link from the inside to the outside is the basis of what has been in some places called "karma" and in other places, "fate."

There is a landscape of our interior world, our subjective personal space, where our contemplations range about and all the little markers and monuments to our history act like bumpers in a pin ball game for our thoughts. Each triumph or misery of our past pushes our appraisal of the outside world in particular directions. In a sense, we make our daily lives out of our experience, in that we come to expect from the world exactly what it has delivered to us in the past, while forgetting that circumstances have changed. We make up our minds about the world very early and then we go about living as if we have it all figured out. Of course, the great tragedy is that we have nothing figured out at all.

What we have is a series of experiences that were almost completely dependent on the unique circumstances in which they arose, the particular personalities involved, the unique moment in time with all of the variables of mood and momentary stressors. We then take this experience and we make it into a template for judging the future, then give up allowing the future to show us its unique possibilities. The inside becomes the outside. But it may be more than simply a psychological process. The inside may be connected to the outside in causal ways we can barely comprehend. More than simply serving as a screen for our mental projections the world may be responding to our minds in subtle ways over time so that our attitudes and beliefs actually effect the arrival of possibilities in our daily experience.

If it was just the mystical systems, the esoteric philosophies that made claims for the inside being connected to the outside, then we might just dismiss the whole idea, thinking it perhaps a peculiar mythological delusion from another age. As it turns out, these old mystical books are not the only thing telling us to check out the possibility of connection between the inside and the outside.

Science is hiding a skeleton in its closet, thought the physicist, J. M. Jauch. It is the ghost of the "observer effect." In short, the observer effect is a phenomenon of quantum physics, a branch of physics which deals with the behavior of subatomic particles. The effect takes place when all the probable locations for the position of a particle are reduced to a single reality. The mystical moment occurs when a person observes, looks at, or makes a measurement of the system in which the experiment is taking place. What quantum physics tells us is that each moment is like one of these experiments. It contains a range of probable futures where the atomic particles that make up the matter of the world, our reality, are suspended in a kind of cloud of possibilities and that it appears to be our minds, our consciousness, that affects this "super position" of all the probabilities in such a manner as to suddenly reduce the cloud to the one reality we find.

Believe it or not, this is actually how it is. As strange to contemplate as this may be, it is the observable truth. The physicist John Bell, who would come to create one of the most startling demonstrations of the quantum reality, came to believe that "the new way of seeing things will create an imaginative leap that will astonish us."[3] He believed that what we are finding in quantum physics is simply the edge of our belief system. At this cliff our minds fall off into something else. Essentially, what the quantum world shows us is that our old way of understanding reality is deficient; our mental/rational materialism is not the whole story. The evidence suggests that not only do our minds interact with the world around us but with places far, far away.

The physics community is split on this issue; most stopped at the edge of the cliff and refused to go further, simply putting the skeleton of quantum realities in a closet and turning right around and continuing with their work as if they never saw the truth. Others have been bold enough to say it outright. "The new physics presents prima facie evidence that our human thoughts are linked to nature by nonlocal connections: What a person chooses to do in one region seems to immediately effect what is true elsewhere in the universe," wrote the eminent physicist, Henry P. Stapp, of the University of California at Berkeley.[4]

It was first argued by those wishing to save the old paradigm that these weird effects are limited to the tiniest of worlds, but now it has been discovered that quantum realities can be demonstrated for larger and larger systems. They are at work in things as basic as photosynthesis and now whole molecules are put into superpositions where they are shown to be in two places at once.

Reality is much stranger than we have conceived in the past, but this is what is to be expected from an evolving consciousness. The mental/rational structure of consciousness can't hold all that is being revealed as greater dimensions of experience open to expanding human capacities. It seems that what we find in quantum physics is the externalized proof that the inside and the outside, our subjective mental/emotional life and what appears to be an external reality, are all wrapped up in one another. This is the discovery on the outside of what was obvious on the inside when humanity was at the magic stage historically when the average person felt fully connected to nature as a being first emerging from full immersion in an ecosystem. Now we are integrating this past structure from a position of individualized development where the greater fields of information available from this deep connection can be utilized at a more conscious level.

What we are discovering on more than one level, scientific and personal, is that whatever consciousness is in its entirety, in our experience it may actually be a facet of the energy on which the material universe is built, indicating that atomic particles are simply "consciousness stuff." Biologists have speculated as much with regard to the behavior of even the most primitive organisms. They seem to demonstrate a kind of simple decision making autonomy, such as when organisms make specific genetic changes in response to environmental stressors or when the primitive organisms called "prokaryotes," build themselves into cooperative communities known as "eukaryotes." The observation of even the tiniest organisms reveals their purposive movements away from toxins like fish swimming away from predators.[5]

So we have new theories about consciousness being with us from the beginning and each stage in the evolution of biological life here on earth as simply allowing this consciousness to have a more sophisticated range of decisions. A one celled organism shows volition in going one way or another but a bird can express consciousness in a myriad of ways unknown to the smaller creature and so on to humans who have the largest and ever growing domain in which to express decisions, and so the creative utility of the universe.

It may be that what this energy does – of which consciousness is a facet – is push itself out so as to create new areas and dimensions of space, as in the big bang, and then develops within some particular structural mechanics until it evolves a platform suitable for full self-aware consciousness. As the author and consciousness researcher, Duane Elgin, has suggested, following the philosopher Georg Hegel who saw humans as vehicles for the universe to become conscious of itself, the energy of consciousness that created the world has been slowly "waking-up" in us.[6] So now we can look around and begin to understand that what the world is made of is another part of us, just more of the original energy released at the Big Bang(s). As such consciousness divides and exerts an influence on itself, each part connected beneath time and space and humanity is the raw edge of the evolving whole.

When consciousness evolves at the brink of a new level we leave the past behind in adventures of thought that open the possibilities for understanding a more sophisticated view of life and the universe. These new ideas are nearly always demonized by the old guard, the status-quo still heavily invested in the old ways. This happens because the new theories that lead to new research and understanding do so by bashing through the boundaries of the old theories. Those that lived within the old boundaries had convinced themselves that these were not self-imposed but actual edges to the universe. A classic example is found in the reaction of the experts to the first flights of the Wright Brothers. The big aeronautical minds of the age were all boxed up within the belief that objects heavier than air could not fly. Their technology was the hot air balloon. Instead of looking at birds, weighing a few, and discovering their theory was inadequate, they stuck to their guns, after all, they were the "experts." The great minds did what science has always been prone to do when the world doesn't fit the theory. Instead of adjusting the theory to suit the world they adjusted the world to suit their theory and so they solved the bird problem by speculating that bird bones were full of some gas like helium that allowed them to float in the air. When news of the Wright Brothers achievement reached the experts they screamed fraud, everyone knew it was a "law of nature" that heavier than air objects could not fly.

The old school of science is very fond of these legal metaphors. If they want to nail down the lid to prevent any new research challenging their decisions about reality then the experts usually employ a legal metaphor. They declare they have discovered a "law," and we all know you can't go around breaking laws. Of course, the history of science is all about the making and breaking of "laws." When electromagnetism was investigated then the laws of materialism began to be torn down when Einstein used this data to help build his relativity theory. Once the quantum world arrived it accelerated the tearing down exponentially, Newton's mechanics being the big one, thermodynamics being another, conservation of energy – forget it – not in the quantum world. So, this has been a very traumatic time for science that has largely looked over the edge of the quantum revolution and been struck by vertigo. So there's little wonder that when faced with things like research demonstrating the power of the mind such as telepathy, mind to mind communication, or the mental interaction with matter we call "telekinesis," or precognition, the foretelling of future events, that the old materialist science, still quoting from their obsolete Newtonian law book, has screamed fraud.

There is no greater proof that the inside is mixed up with the outside than the vast library of data amassed by over a hundred years of parapsychology research. As the evidence has piled up over the years at some of the most prestigious institutions in the country and worldwide, places like Princeton University, Duke University, The Stanford Research Institute, and others, including a massive effort by the old Soviet Union that continues in Russia to this day, the expert defenders of the materialist paradigm have gone from accusations of fraud, to accusations of "bad science," to ridicule and dismissal, to absolute silence. It has made little difference. Opinion polls taken by the American Psychological Association have shown a gradual and significant increase in its members' acceptance of parapsychological phenomena to the current tune of some two thirds of its membership.[7] The numbers for the general population show even higher levels of acceptance, urging old school scientists to write books with titles like, *Why do Smart Folks Believe Crazy Things?* In this case, people believe in telepathy and other "psi" phenomena because as a genuine human capacity it is not that unusual that a person may have experienced some psychic phenomena themselves or have knowledge of a friend or family member who has well demonstrated such capacities. After having direct experience of these things, having an "expert" pronounce that all things psychic are delusions is a little like having someone tell you that your feet don't reach the ground. We can all look down and know that they do. In most of the world psychic capacities are taken for granted and, if you were to tell the average citizen of the Middle East, India, Africa, or China that psi doesn't exist, they would simply laugh in your face.

Changes of levels of consciousness are always hardest on the former experts. Peter A. Sturrock is professor emeritus of applied physics and director of the Center for Space Science and Astrophysics at Stanford University. Dr. Sturrock has confessed to living a duel identity as a mainstream scientist in one part of his life, while researching "unconventional" science, including psi phenomenon and anomalous healing, in another part of his life. Through his researches he discovered a firm reality to a number of topics unfairly dismissed by mainstream science due to simple prejudice and errors in reasoning, but most of all to politics. "To the orthodox scientific community, "real science" is "PC" (politically correct) while topics such as those mentioned above, are "Non-PC," stated Dr. Sturrock, in his 2009 book, *A tale of Two Sciences*.

Unfortunately, the typical reaction is negative to the incoming knowledge and avenues of research pioneered by those whose minds are expanding beyond the old guard. The response is usually dismissive and then hostile. The famous example of this is, of course, the case of Galileo, when he asked the church fathers to look through his telescope in order to prove his assertions, he was met with the response that they didn't need to look at something they already knew to be wrong. When this didn't slow the rebel astronomer down the next step was arrest and threats of extreme consequences for his continued blasphemy in daring to assert the reality of a new truth.

Now psi phenomenon is definitely not a new truth, but in the progress of the West is certainly a truth whose time has come once again and now must be reintegrated at a higher level of sophistication. In doing so we then begin to recognize and utilize the strange correspondences between the inside and the outside for our mutual improvement and the greater mastery of our lives. What parapsychology, or simply "psi," has thoroughly demonstrated, in literally hundreds of carefully controlled experiments is that the mind can effect matter outside the body, can be privy to future events, (or rather those of highest probability, since nothing is set in stone) and can exchange mental content with other human beings, as well as pick up impressions of distant locations in the past and present.[8] There is really no use denying this revelation, it is a simple fact for anyone willing to look into the data with unbiased eyes. Even one of the most famous skeptics of our time, astronomer Carl Sagan, who for years refused to accept the findings of parapsychology as anything other than a popular delusion, after finally giving the data a fair hearing, admitted in a book published before his death that after consideration of the evidence, he believed that the "ESP field" contained findings that deserved "serious study." He went on to name telekinesis, telepathy, and evidence of reincarnation in children, as three areas where the findings had impressed him.[9]

Anyone willing to look into the meticulous work done by this field of bold scientists will be forced to admit that the human mind is not a closed system. The work of such notables as J.B. Rhine, who did psi research at Duke University for 25 years; Robert Jahn and Brenda Dun, who proved psi at Princeton for some 30 years; the physicist Claude Swanson at M.I.T. a champion of the validity of psi who said, "our present scientific theories are badly broken."[10] William Braud, demonstrated the mind's effect on blood cells and other physiology, work that led to important advances in mind/body medical practice.[11] And the many other unsung heroes such as William Tiller and his colleagues whose 2001 book, *Conscious Acts of Creation: The Emergence of a New Physics*, laid out the evidence for what they called, "the power of human intention to robustly influence physical reality," and in the process took on the difficult job of attempting to integrate these findings with theories of subatomic physics, a job assiduously avoided by the majority in the field. What this growing mountain of data amounts to is the clear indication that, *like it or not*, the human mind – the subjective field, *the inside* – is connected to the objective field – *the outside*. The integral structure in consciousness makes this connection central to its evolutionary shift and so the future demands that humanity wake up to this reality. The status quo continue to fight off the evidence, because it presages a revolution in science that literally changes everything.

One of the great studies of these correspondences was undertaken by Carl Jung, a father of the field of Western psychology, who coined the term "synchronicity" to describe moments when the inside perfectly aligns with the outside in some specific detail. Among many examples he gave, one stands out in which during an analysis session a patient was describing a dream that included a certain potent symbol in the form of an Egyptian scarab beetle. Jung heard a kind of tapping at the window as a bug was flying into it. Upon examination he discovered a very scarab-like beetle on the window sill. Jung continued to observe these synchronicities in clinical work, sometimes items in the room even breaking at intense moments.[12]

This synchronizing of the inside and the outside in such immediate striking fashion, Jung described as the result of an "a-causal connecting principle." A-causal, means that there was no direct perceivable cause as the conventional mind understands a cause, but this was before the revelations of quantum mechanics where all the probabilities are present in the next moment until some mysterious conjunction of mind and the universe coalesces them into one reality. In the case of synchronicity what appears to be an event that is on the far edge of the field of probabilities with strong enough feeling pops into reality as the one event selected for the next moment. The question arises as to whose consciousness is selecting the next "reality" within a group experience? Is a group connection carrying everyone along in some democratic fashion; the most votes win? This is one of many important questions we face in this new world.

Of course, as previously stated, all these theories and ideas concerning the workings beneath the three-dimensional world of matter we live in are simply our mind's attempts to make maps of places and forces that are impossible for us to comprehend in their actualities due to the simple fact that all our maps and metaphors are constructed from the known likenesses of our current reality. That is, we are attempting to explain something beyond this world using the terms of this world and the best anyone can get doing this is a nebulous metaphor. It's all a kind of rational myth-making and as such we must avoid the error of mistaking the map for the territory. So, we don't need to get hung-up on any particular story we're weaving to explain this thing. The point is to get a feel for it, to simply begin to take into our appreciation of the world a deeper perspective that opens the possibilities for a multidimensional understanding. Jean Gebser related this to the notion of an "aperspectival" view. Meaning: *not from one perspective* but from many simultaneously, to include none at all.

As the new level of consciousness unfolds we have begun mapping the new terrain using the terms we are familiar with, but as the era matures we will come to more appropriate understandings. One of the issues in this regard is that we are moving from a primarily visual worldview to a multi-dimensional worldview. The current stage in the evolution of our consciousness, the "mental/rational" stage, was very much entranced by the visual appearances of things. It was the beginning of the materialist scientific obsession with external measurements. For anything to be "real" we had to be able to put some kind of ruler on it. This left all those things associated with mind and heart immeasurable and therefore ultimately declared "unreal" by the dons of materialist science. With the new "integral" stage of consciousness upon us we are beginning to understand that the visual (i.e. materialist) sense is only one way of perceiving and recognizing what is real.

In order to comprehend a broader sense of the world we have to begin to entertain the possibility of what transpersonal psychology calls, "alternative ways of knowing."[13] The fact that we live in a universe that is mostly invisible to our ordinary senses should tell us that much of what is associated with material objects is not going to be understood by measuring its material parts alone. Fortunately, human beings are equipped with other senses that allow us to perceive at more subtle levels so that immediate feelings, hunches, intuitions, esthetic impressions and deep emotional responses now can be understood as providing potentially valuable information on everything from new acquaintances to life's challenges and their creative solutions. Of course, this is the way many people have always naturally operated at an unconscious level. We often have a feeling about something that we act on without thinking much about it to find our way in the world. This is a common experience even in the hyper-rational world of scientific research, but we have traditionally downplayed this element. As our consciousness matures it is now time to revise those beliefs. The integral is reviving very old traits and creating new abilities through the maturation of these forgotten capacities while consciously bringing together multiple paths of perception. The trick is in learning to tell the difference between legitimate intuitive information about the situation in front of us or the future and those early decisions about the world we carry around with ourselves as our template for judgment often seriously disconnected from the immediate reality. These hardened opinions and feelings cut us off from the true exchange of information between the inside and the outside through these alternative ways of knowing.

When we look at the idea of the correspondences between the inside and the outside we understand that we are permeated with the deeper "tones" of the world, the energetic "information" that exists all around us outside the visual field, energy that we can interpret and so give meaning to. Temperature, for instance, is a field that we relate to our experience as hot or cold. Temperature in itself doesn't exist except as a feeling relative to an individual organism, what's cold to a chimp is not cold to a polar bear. We've known for some time that intense emotions can change the nature of the field energy in a room at the "feeling" level so that the old saying, "You could cut the tension with a knife!" should now be understood as more than a mere metaphoric homily. We do seem to have the capacity to feel and affect changes in the energy fields we live in.[14] The universe seems to be teeming with fields of various sorts and they move through us and around us constantly. Our bodies are at a very deep level simply another energy field, a coherent one, which is to say it is a field of energy that is coordinated within itself and continuous over time and space. At the subatomic level that coherence simply blends into larger fields so that we are at one level separate but on another not discontinuous with the primary fields that give rise to us in the first place. We are, in a manner of speaking common to physics, simply a "distortion" of that field.

When we think about the outside, the world, being affected by our thoughts and emotions, we can consider what physics calls "entanglement," a phenomenon named by one of the fathers of quantum mechanics, Erwin Schrodinger. He recognized as one of the primary attributes of quantum physics this strange ability of the subatomic universe to pass information instantly across vast distances. The whole notion of "space" as we understand it seems to disappear in the quantum world. Distance is not a factor, so that what we experience as the spaces between objects in our three-dimensional world is simply not part of the subatomic, "quantum," universe outside our primary experience. There, in that dimensionless dimension, everything is connected to everything. Even the idea of "connection" is misplaced in that it is taken from our culturally derived interpretation of the world formalized by Sir Isaac Newton in his "billiard ball universe" where objects are isolated in time and space unless physically contacting one another. One has to make a "connection" between these separate objects in order for information to pass in the form of energy, whether kinetic or energetic, but in the universe revealed by quantum physics this connecting of separate objects is unnecessary, because there is no space to speak of, let alone to cross. Entanglement is simply our crude way of trying to explain to ourselves how what we perceive as discrete objects with boundaries can be in communion with other discrete bounded objects, seemingly in other places. Our common senses are capable of seeing what appear to be separate objects, but are not capable of seeing the ground from which they rose and are still embedded.

What we have been discovering here are the limits of our old stage of consciousness: the "mental/rational" structure of comprehension. Children are always confused by the information existing at higher levels of comprehension. Small children cannot fathom a metaphor or any abstraction; they are completely literal. If a person says, "I have to fly." as they go out the door, then the young child will expect them to leap into the sky and may run outside to watch it happen. We find these events terribly amusing as parents and relay them to friends and relatives to pass on the laugh, but now we are the ones running outside to watch. What is happening in contradiction to our expectations is that this time the man is flying and we're simply dumbstruck. Albert Einstein called it "spooky action at a distance," and others have simply called it "weird," but what is actually happening is that our former stage of consciousness has not prepared us for what we're smart enough to find, but not yet smart enough to completely understand. This is how it works; this is the mind opening to new vistas of reality. This is the bridge to a new world where our primitive beliefs about time and space are revealed to be the product of a former, smaller, too limited way of understanding. In this new world to speak of an "inside" to our subjective selves, and an "outside" as a world separate from us, is really to speak only relatively regarding a certain level of perception. Beyond this level of our common material dimensional experience there isn't an inside and outside. These things are strangely parts of a whole in which the parts are like sparkling light off a windswept ocean. Each glimmer seems separate, but is really just a play of light on a single body of water. The highly respected British physicist, David Bohm, posited that consciousness and matter were parts of the same thing, a unified structure, in a manner of speaking, "previous to and underlying," the appearance of matter and events in the world he termed the "implicate order." Bohm wrote in response to the evidence of quantum uncertainty where the world is held in a suspension of probabilities until being realized as one thing in the moment of observation, or measurement:

> Thus, one can no longer maintain the division between the observer and the observed (which is implicit in the atomistic view that regards each of these as separate aggregates of atoms). Rather, both observer and observed are merging and interpenetrating aspects of one whole reality, which is indivisible and unanalyzable.[15]

When Eastern mystics through using meditative techniques entered this "non-dual" world from which all arises and in which all is connected, mind and body, they found the universe to be all one thing and were perhaps a bit too quick to dismiss the world of daily experience as an illusion. This is demonstrably ridiculous, of course, because this material world of objects is no less a realm of genuine experience than the non-dual world from which it arises. The opposite of this mistake is that made by old school materialist science where all that's seen is the house while the ground from which it rose is ignored. Beyond both these partial views is the dual reality that matter continues to take part in the ground from which it rose so that simultaneously it is both separate and always and forever just a facet of the one continuum.

Everything in our experience has an inside and an outside; that seems to be the "game plan" of the physical world we live in. Living systems such as human beings and perhaps many creatures experience their sense "data" in an "interior field" of comparative judgment that forms another thing entirely that is a sense of individuality or what philosophers call "ontology" or simply a sense of "being." That interior zone in people has a personal level containing one's own history, all that's been learned emotionally and intellectually through a life, and at the same time deeper levels which connect into broader rejoins fading off into the all in descending levels of increasing inclusiveness. So that "being" is both a sense of individuality and one of belonging, a kind of locating oneself within circles of life from the family, to the ancestors, to humanity itself, and further still to the animal kingdom from which we emerged, to greater circles of Nature on Earth, and on to the limitless subatomic sea of the eternal universe where it all started. We have come through it all and remain connected to it all. This is the continual condition of our evolutionary history that is not apart from us in succeeding "yesterdays," but is always with us today and tomorrow as systems of being within us. So that each of the previous structures of consciousness – archaic, magic, mythic, and mental/rational – all relate to various physical structures, "ways of knowing," and particular abilities necessary for a balanced, complete life. Each evolutionary step has created another layer of order not negating previous structures of consciousness but organizing them within a more complex whole.

The old science of the purely material would like to get rid of the inside of things, this "being" that is the subjectivity of living experience, by reducing subjective experience to a physical action, like the firing of a neuron in the brain, a chemical reaction, or a concert of purely mechanical activities in biology that renders free will an illusion. The problem with this intellectual maneuver is that it, first, represents an error in logic in that it confuses orders of reality. An electric impulse in a neuron in the brain is not a thought; it is a species of object that has material characteristics found in electrical phenomena and nothing more. The thought emerges as a higher order creation in what math and physics calls a "phase space," a term denoting a bounded rejoin of activity where all the possibilities associated with the given dynamic can actualize, in other words, a place where all the possible movements can be plotted. Think of it like a game on a field. The ball is the situation and all the inputs from the senses and memory are the players who are arrayed on the phase space of the field. Consciousness, reflective thought, is like the game they are playing. The game is not the ball. The game is not the players. The game is not the field. *The game is not a material thing at all.* It is that which emerges from the combination of all of them – a personal region of an eternal limitless consciousness.

This is what throws old scientific-materialists so much; they can't bring themselves to give the stamp of "reality" to something that is not a material object, even though physics has been doing this for over a century. Although the game metaphor is helpful, as is the phase space idea, it doesn't really explain the most amazing thing about consciousness, which is that it is there to begin with. The capacity for consciousness lies behind all the games we entertain in our minds. Beyond all objects of contemplation lies "the watcher." It is this entity that watches the play on the field of the phase space that is really the core of the great mystery of what we are. It is this watcher that seems to hold the secrets of evolution as the structures of consciousness expand its view and it brings forth the realizations as to exactly what the great game of life is all about.

What the new emerging level of consciousness is revealing to us is that we are living in a multidimensional universe, invisible and visible, and that we are multidimensional beings integrated with it. *The goal is to make this fact conscious*. In making this realization our task is to revisit the various structures of being within ourselves and in so doing learn to express each structure in the "efficient" or healthy mode integrated within a single life. Any person who takes on this task will come to understand the utility of the subtle connectedness of the inside and the outside. They will come to sense the functional "wholeness" of the universe they inhabit and so live in open awareness of the seamless connectedness beneath the world of separation while they move through the spatial reality of the physical world each day. It is a view of life and the universe where eternity shines through the present, where multiple perspectives are held at once. Those perceptions are somewhere between the inside, subjective, and outside, objective, they have no "perspective" at all which leaves you outside the frame looking in; *the world is now a subject with you in it*. Empathy is an experience that has you feeling another's feelings. This is but an open door leading to sensing an entire room of feelings, an entire society, a forest, an ocean, a cry through eternity in moments of epiphany, that are not "objective" but are transpersonal in that it is *you as the crowd, you as the ocean*, etc. This is a conscious recognition of a "communion" that has always been there.

We have come through stages of evolution we are calling the archaic, the magical, the mythical, and the mental/rational. Each of these structures has always been with us, some literally in the world represented in various societies and all within us as aspects of our (un)consciousness and being. Just as the physical brain itself is a layered structure from the instinctual "reptilian" part in the brain stem, to the later development of the emotional sector in the "paleo-mammalian brain," to the reflective thinking more complex part in the frontal lobes in the "neo-mammalian brain," so too our perceptive, "experiential" structures are layered within us. Just as you wouldn't want to get rid of your brain stem because it still does something for you very important, you wouldn't either get rid of those areas of your life dominated by the archaic structure, like sex, or the mythic structure, like discernment of polarities and their relationships illustrated in myth (story and theory making) drama and poetry, or the mental structure that allows us to engineer processes and products through an understanding of mechanical causality. Unfortunately, we have had a tendency to try to discard earlier structures as outmoded when moving into the succeeding structure. This seems to be a the result of the way old structures burn out or become "deficient" as the controlling ethos of existence and the conflict that arises as new stages are rising up to replace them. As scientific materialism and the egocentrism and consumerism it inspires is burning out as the central ethos of Western culture, in our own time it continues to disparage the previous structures as "primitive" and irrelevant as it offers good reason for us to discard the mental/rational virtues with its decadence. This is not to be done. The integral does not call for anti-materialism, or anti-egoism, or a disparagement of technology, but it simply brings these things into balance so as to express them, along with the past structures, in an "efficient" manner, which is to say—healthy for the evolving organism of the entire biosphere.

Although some believe it possible and even preferred to simply stress the mental/rational capacity above all others (seeing themselves as quite superior in the process), ultimately it makes for a lopsided personality. The classic "nerd" is an example of such a person, where the analytical mental/rational mind has been developed in exclusion to the mythic mind of experience in the world and relationships and the magic mind of understanding feelings so as to create a very smart technical ability, but lacking a capacity for functional human interaction. Having thus cut themselves off from humanity, such personalities find it all too easy to create weapons of mass destruction and all manner of toxic inventions seeing humanitarian concerns as someone else's department. This is a perfect example of the civilizational disease that forms when a structure of consciousness has become unbalanced. (In a healthy personality humanity is always your department.)

William Shakespeare told us that "All the world's a stage, and all the men and women merely players..."[16] In a certain sense this seems very much the case as we write the plays of our lives from all the forces that appear to come at us from outside the actual theater. The theater where we act out our dramas and comedies in this three-dimensional world of light density is the smaller part of the universe we inhabit. As we grow and mature as creatures on this planet in the never ending parade of evolution and change, we come to recognize more and more of what creates the context for our plays and what surrounds us awaiting our wisdom. Like children growing up to finally understand the conversations of the adults around us, we are beginning to grasp the language of this earthly experience, not once and for all, but in an elementary way, perhaps finally bringing the basic pieces together for the first time. The pieces are all those experiential realms that have unfolded over time as our evolutionary heritage forming the stages of our gradual awakening and that have provided the inspiration for the great dramas of life throughout history.

Moving out of the total emersion with nature that was the archaic structure, our "Eden," we entered the magic structure where the human mind in its first glimmers of self-reflective consciousness realized relationships to the powers of life and death in a kind of comparative unity of the contents of the mind to the contents of the world so that drawing a picture on a cave wall made a direct connection between the image and the actual animal. This "magic mind" is still with us and as the evidence now shows the feeling for the connections between mind and nature are not entirely erroneous. In our animal state we surely enjoyed a more freely instinctual response to quantum information arriving on the "energetic winds" within our ecosystem. Just as animals have been shown to predict earthquakes and dogs know when their owners are coming home, our hominid ancestors probably could tell where their dinner was waiting to be hunted. As we grew out of our Eden we became more conscious and less instinctual as consciousness draws choices in life away from the patterned responses of instinct. The price we have paid for our "awake-ness" is probably in a distancing of our minds from our natural psychic capacities. That capacity became specialized and ritualized in the magic structure so that shamans would go into trance to find the herd for the next day's hunt, even donning the animal headdress and skin so as to make the connection to the now deified creature they then knew consciously was the source of their survival. Modern day anthropologists have observed and even taken part in exactly this kind of shamanic hunting "magic" where visions foretold the exact location of game on the following days hunt.[17]

With the arrival of the mythic structure the polarities of life that became apparent and formed the grand narrative of this age of Titans and heroes, light and dark, good and evil was the stuff of legends as humanity played out their new found awareness in stark relief and for the first time recognizing an interior space and formalizing it as a "soul." So the inside and the outside draw apart somewhat more as consciousness rises to create high culture and megalithic architecture looking back at nature as a model, but less as a master. Now a formalized priesthood takes over for the village shaman and in the latter stages of the mythic mind the three great religions of the West – Judaism, Christianity, and Islam – would completely disavow Nature, turning her into a demon witch and finding their god in the pure, clean air of a celestial heaven. This was an attempt to finally break from all instinct and embrace pure consciousness in the origin of all things as it was before creation and "the fall." It was a way of trying to "get right by God" so as to win the game of existence by falling on the right side of the good and evil tug of war.

Certainly this level of mind is still with us today spurring much religious conflict while at the same time remaining an important part of any just civilization where there will always remain a need to discriminate between right and wrong. (Our current era seems to have lost the focus of this particular structure when it comes to economic conditions where justice and fairness seem to have faded from the concerns of power.) Where the magic structure may have been about raw feeling, the mythic structure is the realm of personalized emotion and empathy, which is feeling inspired by judgment. The mythic informs our sense and sexuality. It glorifies our strain and strength, our deep breathing action and the good pain of gain, our victory and defeat and all the fear and longing that dogs our path as well. It is the realm of love where the heart leads the head. It is not a lesser, less reliable source of knowledge but another form of knowing just as important as that of the mind. [18]

When we entered the mental/rational stage humanity's focus narrowed to the material world and its most superficial mechanical processes. We learned to manipulate matter so as to create a myriad of machines that continue to make our lives easier and in some ways more interesting. However, with all the advantages the mastery of mechanical processes delivered a shadow also crept in with the utility. Over time we have been negligent in understanding the needs of the less dominant but still very much active previous structures in our evolutionary endowment. The average individual in the West has largely lost touch with the healthy expression of the magic and mythic structures within themselves. So it seems we are called to not simply "entertain" these structures within our lives in walks in the woods and evenings at the symphony or, more often, movie theater where the mythic dramas of good and evil explode across the screen (too often in support of the sociopolitical agenda of the elite) but, more to the point, actually delve into the depth of these structures within our minds and hearts. We are thus providing from the vantage point of our current individuated consciousness a new power for personal development. This development represents a kind of evolution under the control of the individual, a "self-evolution," where all our deep values as human beings can be reintegrated into a new society. Rather than increase the narcissism and alienation of individuals with more of the self-aggrandizing, ego oriented, activity our current society inspires, the integral stage of development we are in the midst of entering seeks to reorient individuals to the nonmaterial source of their true power as human beings on earth. In this way we will begin the process of truly harmonizing the inside and the outside of our being with the world we live in.

In order to achieve this it will be essential to break free from the influence of the old crumbling world of the exploitive systems of corporate power that have overtaken the republic and its democratic intentions. A new culture has to be created in reintegrating healthy human relationships to all that human beings have been and are becoming. Otherwise, the process simply gets hijacked by the same old power structure that seeks to keep everyone supporting a system that subordinates the healthy development of the individual and the integrity of ecosystems to the needs of the ownership class who seek to prolong the pyramidal institutions they control long past their functional life. As laid out previously, this creates rising levels of dissatisfaction in the general public who find that their needs are being neglected and their lives slowly impoverished as the institutions gradually increase profits at the expense of the actual function of the services they were created to perform.

In order to maintain this increasing exploitation it became necessary for the status quo to capture the apparatus of culture making, "the media," so as to make sure that the information people are getting remains something other than the truth, which would foment rebellion and demands for reform. In the place of truth is a manufactured culture that seeks to assure people that all is well and that any problem they may be experiencing should be blamed on the government, momentary fluctuations in the economy, or in particular situations, *foreigners* or *enemies* like Middle-Eastern terrorists.

The outcome of this culture control is to colonize the interior of human beings, that is, to control the mental space inside of people so as to insure that the outside world continues to conform to the needs of the power elite. This is the crucial realization that the interior, the subjective realm, within the individual must be liberated as a key element in the struggle to reform the outside, socio-political world. The inside is connected, or is another aspect of the outside – not only in the obvious behaviors of people in the world as they follow their beliefs, but also in that inexplicable "action at a distance" within the subatomic world that connects our strongest beliefs and feelings with the stream of probabilities that will actualize in the future.

As long as people are fixated on the outside world, on materialism, and cannot make contact with the freeing knowledge that the inside and the outside are intimately interwoven and thereby utilize this realization to reshape their existence on the terms of the deep evolutionary imperative that drives the expansion of consciousness, then they are lost to the addictions of the world and their lives will be consumed by those who control the materialist machine through money and position.

For a person to truly own their own life they must control their interior realm. Any individual who cannot accomplish this turns his or her life over to the powers who do and it is they who will use the person's life energies for their own purposes. Most people at this time devote many of their life energies to supporting a system that is designed to ensnare their minds with addictions and beliefs inauthentic to themselves so as to compel them to put their shoulder to the wheel of another's empire building project. This condition leads to a kind of chronic dissatisfaction with life, a feeling that no matter how much is achieved something vital remains missing. The vital thing is the life most authentic to their unique human spirit, their deep character structure, their soul, if you will. It is only when an individual is able to clear out the control programs from their minds and open a calm space for personal contemplation that the authentic human spirit clearly emerges. When it does, it brings with it "inspiration" that will put the individual's life energies to work for a "higher" purpose, that is to say – that which combines the creative impulse of the universe (God, if you prefer) with the material medium, which is life on earth, in a manner that is unique to the individual. This doesn't have to mean that people end up doing their own thing in isolation but more often in cooperative communities of interest that have the potential to form the basis of a new economy.

There is no other task more important to shifting our civilization onto a healthier track, one in cooperation with the human spirit, then reclaiming one's inner world. It is here that the control resides. This is precisely why large societies since the late mythological stage in the history of human consciousness have all sought to control the thought, belief, and identity of their people.

The Ancient Repression of Consciousness

The Roman Empire was in power in the Western world when the evolution of consciousness reached a point where large portions of the population became interested in developing an individualized spirituality. Previously, group worship was the norm in community rituals and offerings to the gods or a particular patron deity, like Jupiter or Athena. Sometime in the late fifth century BCE the cult of Osiris, the living and dying god of Egypt and a predecessor to Christ, came to the Greek world and inspired a reformation of the cult of Dionysus so that he too became a god form that dies and is resurrected in a higher form. This idea, spread all over the Roman world, in what were called "mystery cults," that simply reworked the mythology of whatever local deity had a biography that would lend itself to this new interpretation. In Rome proper his name was Bacchus, in Syria, Adonis, in Asia Minor, Attis, in Persia, Mithras.

The story was always the same: born of a virgin under a star, wise men came baring gifts, he is the bringer of a new truth, and he is killed by hanging on a tree or cross and is resurrected in a higher form. All of the elements now understood as the Jesus story have their original source in these earlier mythologies.[19] Jesus, which is the Greek for the name Joshua, was the name from Hebrew scripture for the messiah, or redeemer, who would someday come and lead the Jews to the Promised Land. When Hebrew people became involved in mystery cults and their minds opened to the revelation of the deeper consciousness the practice revealed they quickly moved to create a fully Jewish version of the mystery. Thus was born Christianity. It seems the reason why this mystery "religion" could so easily skip from one mythological system to the next was simply because at the highest revelation, the earlier mythology that formed the most simplistic entrance to the revelation simply didn't matter. The enlightened state afforded by the experience of the "inner mystery" was (and is) truly pan cultural, or *beyond culture*.

The mystery cult was one that allowed for an emerging structure in consciousness to be understood and utilized by the people. This required initiation into "the mysteries," a mystical system of revelation that involved many different teachings and practices but which can be most simply understood as comprised of three levels. The first was simply the "outer mystery" which was basically the story itself, the literal story of the "god/man's activities in the world; the second was an "inner mystery," which was the allegorical interpretation of the story as mythic symbol for a larger truth that involved everyone, not just the hero of the story. Each individual initiate was to see themselves as on the same road as the hero, struggling as he did to achieve sacred wisdom. The third level of mystery initiation was the actual illumination of the initiate's mind in achievement of direct gnosis. In this moment the initiate transcended the need for "literal" stories as a teaching aid and realized their identity as the "Christ." This "higher self" Gnostics believed was emerging from a "lower self," that had to die, or be "crucified," so that a second birth, or "resurrection," could give rise to the enlightened mind. Through little known forms of contemplation, practice and ritual within the mysteries initiates were led to the experience of contact with their own inner connection to the ground of being, deity, or the source of existence. In words that come down to us from a surviving Greek source, the initiate, Theon of Smyrna, tells us that the mysteries lead to, "friendship and interior communion with God." [20] The initiates in the mysteries spoke of direct contact with "the Logos," which was understood as the "thought of God," and which was said to reveal the "idea of ideas," the higher logic on which reality is built. This is why the Gnostics referred to their initiations as revealing *the true way of things*, and did not produce a dogmatic religion but rather nurtured the continuing revelations of their practitioners. No man or woman became a high priest among them. Rather, the leadership was rotated and all individual interpretations sought. What they were looking for was gnosis, which is simply the Greek word for knowledge.

Here we clearly find a broadening mind beginning to grasp a higher logic beyond mere forms towards the unity within complexity that explains the acceptance within the Gnostic ranks of realizations that transcend cultural variation. The outer mysteries may have differed but the inner were transpersonal. "This is why Heraclitus sets out to find himself, but discovers a 'Logos shared by all,' because the Logos is our essential common identity."[21] Yet the key to this deeper reality that informs every spirit was to be found through the individual; "know thy self" was the entrance into gnosis and so the individual realization was within each person.

This was a huge leap forward for the consciousness of the average citizen of the ancient world. The idea that truth could be realized from within by any person, regardless of rank or position, was revolutionary as only high priests were thought to have the ability to interpret the ways and will of the gods. Certainly not every initiate would reach the highest revelation that seems to be a form of what the Hindu tradition calls, "samadhi," and the Zen Buddhist practice calls, "satori," but the leap from the literal story of the heroic "god/man" or demigod (little god) to the universalizing revelation of the allegorical interpretation, which made every man and woman a player in the story, was itself a great expansion of consciousness. For instance, in each of the various cultural versions of the mystery there is a story where the hero rides a donkey. Christians are familiar with this motif from the tale of Jesus riding a donkey into Jerusalem. At the second level of initiation it was taught that this symbolized the "higher self" mastering the "lower self," represented in the animal aspect. The Zen tradition has a similar, if more involved, tale where the protagonist rides an ox. It is a universal theme in spiritual development within the evolution of consciousness that is descriptive of the further movement of consciousness away from its original immersion in nature and instinct towards an independent intellect capable of comprehending larger domains and responding to their more complex possibilities.

At a certain point in evolution humanity breaks free of the purely mythological or "religious" attempts to map the unseen world of the "Gods," as outside forces acting upon humanity and moves into actual experience of larger dimensions of psychological life. This allowed, first, for understanding the mythology symbolically as describing forces running through the individual and, second, for direct revelation. What was conceptual in mythological symbolism in the first revelation is now gnosis, knowledge, knowing, in the second. In the same way that early scientists observed processes through the microscope that before were known only by secondary effect and went from theory to empirical understanding, the Gnostic path looked within and went from philosophy to realization.

One need not have been a philosopher or member of the elite, but only join a mystery cult open to all, invest some effort and faith was replaced by certainty. In this realization is the birth of a profoundly larger world, opening a space within the individual mind, which understands that the inside is very much a part of the outside. Mind is in the world and in a sense animates the world, "anima mundi," the soul of the world, but in this realization lies a challenge to the power of the old gods and the state religion on which the power of the emperor rested. As long as this idea was just a fanciful thought of philosophers it did not pose a problem for power, but by the late 3rd C. vast numbers of common citizens were getting the idea. As the mystery cults grew in popularity, the Roman government routinely purged them from the capital and issued edicts against their practices in many cities. In time they became so popular, a popularity that eventually invaded the ranks of the military and Roman hierarchy itself, that tolerance became common.

Eventually, by the fourth century the Romans are beginning to really lose control of the vast empire they have built by conquest, but cannot hold by military power alone. The Emperor Constantine and his advisors conclude they must unite the empire under a common faith with its center in Rome. To do this the evolution of consciousness represented in the mystery cults must be suppressed. The need for an imperial religion of the old sort where the priest/king rules by mandate from the gods makes it necessary to crush the mystery cults which offer a personal experience of God and his Logos without need of priests or kings.

It is not the original mystery Christianity that Constantine settles on for his new state religion, but an offshoot of the Jewish messianic movement that has taken a particularly literal form. This "alternative" Christianity had been growing for over a century and been in conflict with the original, better respected, symbolic understanding represented in what has been called the "Gnostic" tradition. This is a point missed by earlier scholars who took the doctored church histories at face value where the Gnostics were portrayed as a late digression from the literalist camp. We now know the opposite is true: the Gnostics were the original Christians. The literalists were thought by the majority Gnostics to be ridiculous simpletons that simply *didn't get* the higher philosophy and who were taken advantage of by unscrupulous leaders wanting to empower and enrich themselves through holding office above the masses. Many literalist bishops were known for their materialist greed and power mongering, enriching themselves at their follower's expense and maintaining their power through strict control over the doctrine from which only they dispensed "truth." In the Gnostic churches there was no hierarchy, because all who achieved the realization of the inner mystery were thought to be equally in contact with the truth.[22]

The literalist Christianity is the natural choice for the Emperor Constantine. Not only does he win over the slaves, many of whom have joined the literalist camp, but the literalists have essentially taken a mystic realization of the inner workings of the human place in the universe and reduced it to a materialist history that happened once long ago in the form of a special person – that is not you, but the one and only *son of God*. (Directly the opposite of the realization of the Logos as the one spiritual reality reflected in every person.) The literalist camp had appeared, conveniently for the Romans, as an alternative to the troublesome messianic cult that drove the Jewish rebellion, turning it into a peaceful, cooperative group that "gave unto Caesar what is Caesar's." Roman imperial power had long made a habit of modifying religious cults for just such political purposes. Literalist Christianity offered a readymade throwback to the old pagan belief in the "super hero" gods that legitimized the power of the emperor as the representative of the gods on earth and so became a perfect state religion centralizing power.

This religion is a return to the old pagan belief in the "super hero" gods that legitimized the power of the emperor as the representative of the gods on earth. With literal Christianity you have all the outer mystery and none of the inner mystery and it is the latter that empowers individuals. The literalists created their own rigid hierarchy of priests and bishops that policed the doctrine for heresies that challenged their interpretation, schooling their parishioners on what they will believe, not from their own experience of God but from "faith," something that was not necessary in the original Christian mysteries. The whole idea of faith is antithetical to the evolution of consciousness represented in the inner mysteries where a personal experience afforded the individual direct knowledge, or *gnosis*. "Faith," is what you get as a replacement for knowing, when knowing is dangerous to power.

This adoption of literalist Christianity required the suppression of consciousness. The deepening and expansion, the "intensification" of consciousness, as Jean Gebser would call it, that had been evidenced in the arrival of the mysteries was furiously put back in the bottle by a vicious centuries long campaign of murder and destruction. Once Constantine had nationalized the literalist church, tolerance for other cults was soon replaced by persecution. Fifty years later the Emperor Theodosius outlawed entirely all other religions and the "Christians," then set about methodically killing everybody who dared to seek gnosis, putting to the torch library after library of spiritual wisdom and metaphysics, along with a whole lot of ancient science. "In 415 Archbishop Cyril of Alexandria had his monks incite a Christian mob to murder the last Pagan scientist of the Alexandrian library, a remarkable woman called Hypatia. She was torn limb from limb and Cyril was made a saint." [23] The most remarkable storehouse of ancient knowledge in the Western world was ransacked and its contents burned, a scene repeated in centers of learning all over the empire. In 529 the Emperor Justinian shut down Plato's Academy that had been in continuous existence outside Athens for 9 centuries because he found its teaching unacceptable to Christian doctrine. Thus, the Roman strategy of power through mind control plunged the Western world into the thousand year dark ages.

This was the great turning point for Western Civilization, the moment when another road briefly opened for the evolution of human society towards a higher plane of existence. A place where the individual human being was respected and allowed to seek their own potential through contact with a higher wisdom within themselves but this was not to be. Power ruthlessly cut short this flowering of consciousness so as to retain a highly centralized authority and political structure. This is the main point in keeping people away from the inner mysteries, or that which contemplatively focuses the mind on its own depths – that which leads to personal revelation of individual purpose and deeper understanding of what life on earth can be. It offers a competing source of information that rivals centralized power and its claim to authority through its mediating position between heaven and humanity. Once people start searching their own depths for what is right and wrong then outside authority fades.

The Roman church jealously kept the entrance to higher wisdom barred from the public. Then they set about over the centuries to kill anyone practicing any last vestige of the old gnosis, or any mystical approach to the inner mysteries that would lead to truth. All pagan shamans and gnostic practitioners that flourished in the lands of the former barbarians in Germania and what would be France and the rest of Europe had to be branded as devils and exterminated. This was a crusade, or series of crusades, that were literally trying to stop people from evolving.

Once the Roman church's power began to falter and the Reformation began then it became all about which king or prince would control the minds of the people and so then different versions of Christianity sprang up all over Europe. King James in England didn't like many of the passages referring to the power of kings in the Bible of the Reformation, now called the Geneva Bible. So he put his own priests to work editing in order to clean things up for his purposes of power over the Church of England. (This "King James version" is the book raved about so fervently by American evangelists as the *word of God*.) Similar doctoring went on in many places continuing a practice the Roman Catholic Church had been at since the inception of the institution. Scholars now have revealed vast areas of forgery and rewriting of earlier mythology in the scriptures.[24] It has always been about controlling populations. Knowledge equals power and ultimate knowledge equals ultimate power. The human connection with the source within is the key to it all.

Once the Enlightenment began to wrench the power of control over people's minds from the churches then a new power took over, one that simply either left these ultimate questions in the hands of the disempowered theologians or denied that there was anything in the depths of humanity whatsoever. Under early science, human beings become biological machines with no higher purpose and no deep connection to creation because only that which is material could be real. This is the ultimate control story; it sets people free from the church but continues their control agenda in a new form. Before people were asked to believe that they had no connection to a higher source except that offered by the story of a hero god/man who had lived and died in the First Century CE. A demigod on the order of Hercules, but gentler, had died for their sins, a sacrifice to a mean spirited god who didn't like them because they were descended from a woman who was tricked by a talking snake. She ate an apple from the tree of good and evil, the tree of knowledge. This is exactly, not what God, but *earthly* power forbids. The people are to stay ignorant and easy to control.

When the scientific materialist philosophy slowly replaces religion as the controlling doctrine in the West, then this story goes away and a new one replaces it that allows for apples but only of a certain kind, a materialist, mechanistic, and particularly product oriented sort. All apples, knowledge, that might again seek wisdom within the depths of the human mind and spirit are simply said to be a primitive myth that leads to nothing. This system creates another disempowering structure for the individuals who are again cut off from their own source and told to pay strict attention to the experts. This is the politics of knowledge that erects a new power structure that will dictate again "acceptable" knowledge from "unacceptable," unauthorized knowledge.

We need experts, of course, and science has been worthwhile despite the atomic weapons and toxic side effects, but the questions most important to the meaning of an individual human life cannot be answered by experts of a materialist science at all. The big questions: how should we live? Why am I here? What am I truly capable of? These sorts of questions can only be answered through self-knowledge, and this is precisely the source that centralized power works towards concealing. Centralized authority does this by colonizing the self, the interior space of the individual, because in order to produce the sort of outside world power wants it knows it must first produce this vision inside the populace. In a sense, it is a kind of "frequency control" in that in order to produce the outside world preferred by the status quo the majority of the population must be *tuned to that channel* and so projecting the specified choices.

The Romans understood this, not in the terms of particle physics but in the experience of the Logos afforded by the inner mysteries revealing to them this correspondence of the inside to the outside. This was a correspondence formerly the province of a specially trained priest class selected from a small population of individuals of extraordinary talents. Now, due to the evolution of consciousness, what was rare was becoming common. With the help of a little special training now common as well through the explosion of mystery cults all over the ancient world the link with gnosis and the true system of the universe could be revealed.

This is the secret that had to be kept and the Emperor Constantine and his cronies devised a plan to put this revelation back in its hiding place through the drawing up into Rome the reigns of religious authority.

When science became the new religion of the educated masses in the West the same process occurred in the late 19th, early 20th Centuries when the scientific method was itself used as a lens for peering into the inner world of humanity.

THE MODERN REPRESSION

The American philosopher, William James, is considered one of America's first psychologists. The religious experience became a major focus of his work. James met other prominent researchers, like F.W.H. Myers, looking into the depths of the psyche at the Society for Psychical Research started in London in 1882, which applied the scientific method to all manner of paranormal phenomena including telekinesis and higher states of consciousness. Myers's work looking into the capacity of the unconscious mind, what he called the *supraliminal self*, to access information and effect matter outside the body was highly respected in the scientific world of the time. James became the first president of the American Society for Psychical Research and psychology in America was in its early years strongly associated with this search for the non-material roots of consciousness. By the early 20th Century this strange connection between mind and matter became a paramount concern of research across the country at a number of universities that began focusing on the deep mind in hypnotic states and in parapsychological abilities.

At the same time, the depth psychology of Sigmund Freud had given way to the work of C. G. Jung, who left Freud's more mundane drive theories behind to make a deep study of spiritual systems and mythology in their relationship to the profound capacities of the human mind. Jung produced his theory of the "collective unconscious" wherein the mind fades into transpersonal depths in connection with greater layers of consciousness beyond the experience of the individual life. Jung became convinced that the mind was, indeed, strangely connected to the course of events in the world and hypothesized exactly how in his *theory of synchronicity*.

Then, a very telling thing happened. The big foundations run by the American ultra-wealthy elite like the Rockefeller and Carnegie Foundations, began pouring financial support into the work of the American followers of a German psychologist by the name of Wilhelm Wundt. An official state psychologist funded by the Prussian military and political establishment, Wundt believed that human beings have no "soul," or meaningful deep interior world of any kind but are simply biological robots that could, and should, be conditioned to serve the purposes of the state. This theory must have strongly appealed to the elite in America struggling with "labor problems" and all manner of pesky democratic tendencies in the body politic. The massive financial support given this mechanistic theory of human life gave rise to what came to be called "behaviorism" and influenced quite strongly educational psychology as it developed in the United States.

This new way of understanding human psychology caught on as a more "scientific" view and rode the rising wave of popularity for technical innovation through the early 20th Century. It was a psychology more amenable to the methods of the mental/rational obsession with measurement than that offered by depth psychology with its mysteries of the human psyche. Those at the top of powerful American industries and institutions took advantage of this trend to promote the idea that human beings were simply another sort of machine that can be technically modified for higher performance. Through grants and financial support of all kinds this model was guided into every corner of American social science and its efforts to "improve" society.[25] Whether as a conspiracy to subvert human autonomy and democracy for the purposes of creating a new social order and cementing in place a new ruling class at its apex or simply out of the desire alone of industrialists to manipulate society's ability to produce the sort of workers they wanted, really doesn't matter. Either way you end up in the same place.

The continuing desire on the part of a centralized power to shape human life from the top down continues to this day to subvert the striving of the human spirit. To suggest that human beings do not have a psyche, a unique character, that they are not connected with the source of life itself that informs their existence, is simply a denial and therefore a subversion of the natural evolution of consciousness and *the human spirit* on Earth, and as such, a philosophical trap door into human slavery.

The Romans knew exactly what they were doing when they stuffed the "inner mysteries" back down into the human mind and locked it inside of churches controlled by a centralized authority under the new emperor who was the Pontifex Maximus, the top priest of the church. It is interesting to note that Gnostic belief and practice persisted in

Europe regardless of the Roman efforts to remain in charge after the fall of the Empire proper. The medieval religious movement of the Cathars, who were natural descendants to the original Christian Gnostics, resurfaced and flourished in open defiance of the Catholic Church in the Languedoc in the 12th and 13th Centuries of what would one day be southern France. Interestingly enough, it was southern France where the "black Madonna's" were venerated that modern scholarship has discovered are actually Egyptian stone statues of Isis and the baby Osiris on her lap that survived from the ancient period when Gnostic cults were popular in the area. The Cathar movement represented a true upsurge of higher consciousness in its humanitarian and libertarian tendencies evidenced in their insistence on individual rights, even in the face of royal whim, and their lack of gender prejudice that gave equal respect and position to both men and women within their society. This was a miraculous leap forward for Western humanity and so, of course, had to be wiped-out by the Roman Catholic Church who could not allow any such independent progress to threaten its claim to ultimate authority. The Albegensian Crusade that the Catholics mounted to meet the challenge stands as one of the most horrendous examples of a crime against humanity ever recorded in world history. The "crusaders" burned masses of people alive, murdered and tortured men, women, and children in the most gruesome ways and even killed in like manner great numbers of the Catholic population that lived with and respected the Cathars. How, one wonders, was this ever justified as "Christian" behavior? It is no wonder that the Cathars, like the Gnostic Christians before them, considered the Pope the anti-Christ and the Roman Church to be a false Christianity.

It is also quite significant that this understanding that true Christianity, known to have been usurped and twisted to the purposes of the Roman Empire, maintained itself in something of its original form in secret all the way up to the French revolution in the late 18th Century. Even after the Popes crushed the Cathars, the powerful Italian ruler, Cosimo de'Medici developed a curiosity for knowledge forbidden by the Church and so sent a man on a mission to the old Eastern empire, now in the hands of the Moslem sultans, to retrieve lost books of Hermetic wisdom. Hermetic philosophy was another strain of the same Egyptian metaphysics that formed the basis of the mystery religions that spawned the original Christianity. These works of Hermetic thought became the basis of a quiet revolution in Europe inspiring important figures like Giordano Bruno and Tommaso Campanella, who influenced Kings and powerful figures and helped to bring on the Renaissance, despite Bruno's death and Campanella's long imprisonment and torture at the hands of the Inquisition. The egalitarian influences that developed from Gnostic thought, the equality of women and the basic civil and human rights of all people, were also a part of the Hermetic tradition and as its wisdom permeated the intellectual fabric of European thought these ideas became the basis of the political and philosophical assertions of the leading lights of the French Revolution, Voltaire and Jean-Jacques Rousseau. [26]

It is a forgotten bit of history that as the revolution succeeded the Catholic Church was unceremoniously booted out of France and replaced with the veneration of what the leaders of the revolution called the "Supreme Being." France literally underwent a "de-Christianization" process as the revolutionary government took charge. Masses of Catholic clergy abdicated and cathedrals all over France were converted to temples of the new cult of freedom exemplified under the Supreme Being, which was none other than the high god of the Gnostics. It was believed inside the ancient mystery cults that the literalist Christians and after them the Roman Catholics had made a lower "god" their supreme deity. "Jehovah," was known as a primitive Hebrew tribal idol of war and revenge. Also known as "Yahweh the Destroyer," this idol was known as a spiteful, jealous figure and was despised from the higher consciousness of the inner mysteries who understood the true supreme being of the universe to be a genius beyond all childish human passions residing in the Logos.

It appears the French revolution attempted to reinstall the Logos as the Supreme Being of the new Republic believing, after Rousseau, that the true power of creation favored all life and liberty in the sanctity of every human soul regardless of station at birth. "...the idea of the Supreme being and the immortality of the soul is a perpetual reminder of justice. It is thus social and republican," wrote Robespierre in his report to the Convention of the revolution.[27]

The revolutionaries went so far as to install a statue of Isis flanked by two lions in the plaza where the infamous Bastille prison once stood, having been ripped down by the fervor of the liberated citizenry as an intolerable symbol of the former tyranny. The statue was erected as part of a celebration of the guillotining of King Louis XVI and the upcoming execution of Marie-Antoinette. The statue was called the "fountain of regeneration," as it was designed for a massive ceremony in which citizens passed before Isis taking a drink from water flowing from her breasts. This act was said to symbolize the regeneration of life as the people reconnected with the intent of the true Supreme Being after having been suppressed by the church's phony deified power and the despotic French emperors whose reigns the church sanctified. This Egyptian symbolism was thought to speak to the original source of higher wisdom that informed the Gnostics and all the secret societies that kept the inner mysteries alive since the days of the Roman suppression.

One of those secret societies was the Masonic order that informed both the leadership of the American and French revolutions. The Masons were guided by this belief in the sanctity of the individual as carrier of the mind of God or the Logos speaking within the heart of every person. The American revolution was an attempt to create a country where that spark of sacred life within each citizen could live free to express the creative potential of the Logos on Earth, or what the Masons referred to as "the master architect." They thought this could be accomplished by providing freedom and encouraging education for all citizens that would create the space and opportunity for that potential to be realized. The Hermetic philosophy that informs Freemasonry tells of a spirit that is of a higher realm of light that has been locked within darkened matter for the purposes of bringing to fruition a higher purpose on earth, a transformation carried out by those who awaken to this spark of light within. The great scholar of the esoteric, Manly P. Hall, in his 1923 book, *The Lost Keys to Freemasonry*, puts it like this: "The true Masonic Lodge is a Mystery School, a place where candidates are taken out of the follies and foibles of the world and instructed in the mysteries of life, relationships and the identity of that germ of spiritual essence within, which is, in truth, the Son of God, beloved of His Father." Here we find traces of that original Gnostic Christianity that found its highest revelation in the discovery of *the Christ within*. Hall explains in another passage: "Man must realize that all the powers which his many years of need have earned for him have come in order that through them he may liberate more fully the prisoner within his own being." The point of releasing this inner being was to allow for the individual life to help build a society based on this higher influence. This was accomplished through the Masonic initiations in degrees that led inward to the ultimate source of knowledge while finding and expanding their concomitant expressions in the world. Again, we find the inside being connected to the outside.

It has become more broadly known of late through novels and movies (Dan Brown's *The Lost Symbol*, and the film: *National Treasure*) how the founding fathers laid out the streets, buildings, and monuments of Washington, D.C. in a manner keeping with the sacred geometry of the *Master Architect* himself, so as to evoke the powers of heaven on earth in support of their sacred mission. Any visitor to Washington, D.C. will find overwhelming evidence of Masonic symbols and philosophy in the art and architecture of the city. There is no doubt as to the Masonic influences in the creation of the new American state and there is no doubt that the insistence on freedom of religion was meant to allow for the evolution of spiritual thought that had been thwarted in Europe. Once human beings stepped out of *the garden*, then that impetus to evolve becomes a starting place for a higher order civilization. This is what the Masons were trying to help along, knowing that at each stage in the rising of human civilization certain stumbling blocks arise: power mongering and despotism that seeks to hold back that evolution. It was the plight of their progenitors, the Knights Templer, along with other such organizations, to smuggle past the Inquisition the knowledge of maintaining contact with this *higher source within* that challenged the authority of emperors and popes alike.

Although beyond the scope of this work, it now appears that Freemasonry largely lost their earlier spiritual mission over time as materialist science overcame the esoteric in the minds of the common members, reducing the organization to another service group, like the Lions Club, or the Rotary. In the upper regions of the organization, 33 degree, the big lodges are now widely thought to have been taken over by big money elites who use the brotherhood as an insider's business and political networking cooperative. In other words, they seem to have lost the key to the true path and confused their own financial potential with the potential of humanity itself, leaving that to a few charitable causes, and so the great experiment in human freedom on the North American Continent no longer seems to be tended by the Masons.

Unfortunately, a veiled despotism in the form of the concentration of wealth and power in the hands of a new aristocracy in America has crushed much of what that great experiment in human freedom once offered. The exterior forms are still standing—elections, the press, the courts—but it's all been hollowed out and filled with corporate power. The spirit remains alive and consciousness moves forward beneath the weight of history, nothing can stop that, but too many Americans have been so diverted from their potential as human beings, so wrapped up in lies and distractions, so mentally conditioned to support the very thing that suppresses their freedom, that a titanic pressure is again building to eruption within the populace. Tyranny, even a "wide screen," candy coated, drug assisted one, cannot be sustained because the human spirit cannot be ultimately defeated and so we find ourselves again entering a revolutionary period.

The evolution of consciousness that should have moved forward from the time of the rising popularity of the mystery cults, including the Christian version, was partially redeemed, first in the recovery of ancient wisdom in the Renaissance and then in the Enlightenment that allowed for the expansion of the mind into a mental, empirical quarter. This expansion in the rational sphere drove the determination to release human potential that fired the American and French revolutions and led to the slow defeat or circumvention of royal privilege throughout Europe and much of the world.

Unfortunately, the other sector of developing consciousness in the area of spiritual, or "non-material" science of the larger influences of life, saw nothing recovered in the Protestant Reformation. This revolution largely transferred the same superficial Catholic literalist interpretation of Christianity away from Rome and into the hands of the various kings and lords who started their own churches to better control the populace themselves, King James, in England being one of the better examples. This being true it seems to be also true that left on its own in the open country of America Christianity began later to find its way beyond the "priest as middleman" concept and people began to speak of a "personal relationship to Jesus." This is essentially a Gnostic realization. Unfortunately, this positive turn in religious experience has been overshadowed by the regressive influence of a post-puritanical, sexually repressive, and politically hyper-conservative, even *proto-fascist*, far right wing ideology that continues to mix up Roman despotism and extreme elements of Manichean "devil hunting" with Christian love and forgiveness, often sacrificing the later to the former. Thus, the attempt of the human spirit to break free once again is often thwarted by television evangelists and hometown preachers who divert their flock's spiritual aspirations away from any further travel into the inner mysteries that would free them, knowing nothing of it themselves, into oppressive socio-political crusades full of ill judgment and hate. [28]

This left the esoteric wisdom in the form of Christian mysticism, Hermetic philosophy, alchemy, and Eastern thought to work a path beneath the surface of Western culture as the mainstream was diverted decidedly to materialist science to map the universe and the workings of nature as the quest for non-material knowledge was stranded in the leaden churches of "faith." As stated above, when science itself began to probe the depths of the human mind and its connection with larger fields of information and the "inside/outside," paranormal effects demonstrated in "psychical" research, then science was diverted away from this study and such topics were thoroughly denigrated and put on a taboo list of subjects to be ignored.

Regardless, the work went on, just as the march of consciousness has gone on. Now we stand at another juncture where the walls limiting the progress of the human spirit are once again beginning to show major stress fractures. As the "cultural creative" and other such research and indicators demonstrate the rebellion of the human spirit is underway once again and nothing can stop it, no concentration of wealth and power can block it. The human race is developing a new structure of consciousness that literally outflanks the materialism, fear, and egomaniacal, centralized power that underlies the old philosophy of human potential as isolated in an exceptional elite. The genius of human potential is becoming diffuse in populations where not only are more individuals capable of what was considered exceptional in the past but genius now emerges from the potential of cooperative groups much more than the singular achievements of heroic leaders. This, combined with the movement of "human values" away from the collecting of objects, wealth and status, as the goal in life, towards the expression of a deep character, "true self" life style and creative career, makes the possibility of controlling people through the old "labor for reward," system ineffective. This is key to human freedom, this stepping beyond the primitive ego and its needs, because it is here that the chains of modern slavery are forged.

Notes

1. Chandogya Upanishad, 3. 18. 1.
2. Three Initiates, The Kybalion, Hermetic Philosophy (Chicago: Yoga Publications, 1912, 1940), p. 26.
3. Bruce Rosenblum and Fred Kuttner, , Quantum Enigma, (New York: Oxford, 2006) p. 87.
4. As quoted in: William Braud, Distant Mental Influence (Charlottesville: Hampton Roads, 2003), p. xii.
5. Willis W. Harman and Elisabet Sahtouris, Biology Revisioned (Berkeley: North Atlantic Books, 1998).
6. Elgin (1993).
7. Etzel Cardena, Steven Jay Lynn, & Stanley Krippner, editors, Varieties of Anomalous Experience, Examining the Scientific Evidence (Washington: American Psychological Assoc., 2001).
8. Dean Radin, The Conscious Universe (San Francisco: Harper Edge, 1997); Entangled Minds (New York: Paraview Pocket Books, 2006).
9. Radin (1997), p. 3.
10. Claude Swanson, The Synchronized Universe, New Science of the Paranormal (Tucson: Poseidia Press, 2003), p. 3.
11. Braud (2003).
12. Jung (1960).
13. Tobin Hart, Peter L. Nelson, & Kaisa Puhakka, Transpersonal Knowing, Exploring the Horizon of Consciousness (Albany: Suny, 2000).
14. Arnold Mindell, Dream Body (Boston: Sigo Press, 1982); Quantum Mind (Portland: Lao Tse Press, 2000).
15. David Bohm, Wholeness and the Implicate Order (New York: Routledge, 1995) p. 9.
16. William Shakespeare, As You Like It.
17. Michael Harner, The Way of the Shaman (San Francisco: Harper, 1980).
18. See the research of the Heart Math Institute.
19. Timothy Freke & Peter Gandy, The Jesus Mysteries (New York: Three Rivers Press, 1999).
20. Ibid., p. 22.
21. Ibid., p. 84.
22. Ibid.
23. Ibid., p. 246
24. Freke & Gandy (1999); Jesus and the Lost Goddess (New York: Three Rivers Press, 2001). Elaine Pagels, The Gnostic Gospels (New York: Vintage Books,

1989); Beyond Belief, The Secret Gospel of Thomas. (New York: Random House, 2003).
25. Rebecca Lemov, World as Laboratory, Experiments with Mice, Mazes, and Men (New York: Hill & Wang, 2005).
26. Graham Handcock & Robert Bauval, The Master Game (New York: The Disinformation Company, Ltd., 2011).
27. As quoted in: Hancock and Bauval (2011), p. 27.
28. Chris Hedges, American Fascists (New York: Free Press, 2007).

Chapter 3
Egocentric Materialism
The Insatiable Love of Our Stuff

When all things that cannot be seen by the eye and are therefore invisible, and so "spiritual," have been rendered "unreal" then all non-material values like integrity, compassion, and justice are subordinated or completely obscured by profit and material gain. When all humanity has left to idealize is found in objects of luxury, celebrity, and power, then we produce just what we've got: a world where people strive by any and all means to be "rich and famous," or rich and powerful, or even rich and infamous, but always rich. As consumer capitalism has risen to become the main theme of American life we have seen a decline of those older American values that once saw reputation and personal integrity within a community as the highest virtue. Now most look only at what a person has acquired and not at all how they got there. There's no such thing as "blood money," anymore and the only shame is in being poor.

Prosperity is a good thing, we need a roof over our heads, food on the table and a warm place to sit at night and read or commune with our families and friends. Our ancestors paid dearly for this privilege, but we take all this for granted now. Americans have long departed from the hard won basic comfort of their pioneer past and in doing so adopted the values of the European bourgeoisie, whose main interest was in emulating the aristocracy. As the merchant class of Europe became wealthy through the windfall profits that came with the opening of the New World they had no model of what to do with their new found wealth but that of the royals above them, and so they became imitation dukes and duchesses themselves. When the industrial revolution created the means to manufacture what were once considered "luxury" items at a high pace and a low cost, the ownership of "stuff" became "democratized" in the American sense of things. That dynamic has accelerated over the years to the point to which we are drowning in our stuff and our garbage, the one becoming the other sometimes almost instantly. Storage lockers are a booming business and "hording" has become a rising pathology among the masses. The environmental impacts are downplayed, but many feel them looming darkly over their shoulder as the weather grows more unpredictable and extreme each year, their health more uncertain, and entire regions are despoiled by oil spills, chemical runoff, and just plain trash.

We have a society based on materialism as the ultimate value in life. People like to convince themselves in the United States that love and family and all the other concerns of traditional American values come first. But the fact is that divorce is more common now than intact families, that children are abandoned to day care, media and the streets, because careers demand it, that movement has become the norm as people chase the promotion from company to company all over the country, making cohesive communities impossible, that schools are crumbling and colleges are having their budgets cut annually while shopping malls have sprung up across the landscape like weeds in the spring rain, a trend only abated of late by the increase of internet shopping. This and the soaring credit card debt in the country clearly tell us that our true values are material regardless of the traditional mythology that's constantly trumpeted from television shows and the mouths of politicians. The truth is what you do, not what you say; the truth is where your feet take you.

Why? What is it we're chasing? If it's true that materialists find their heaven in luxury and status then we must admit that we have, if not to a person but as a people, found this heaven long ago. No one in the history of the world has enjoyed such wide spread material prosperity as Americans. We have wallowed in it. We're not all millionaires but almost everyone, except what was once a small underclass that is unfortunately now expanding rapidly, has experienced material abundance in some fashion. The average suburban home in America is a veritable palace of riches and luxuries beyond all expectations for the random citizen of the world. In 2001 PBS aired a special called, *Affluenza*, meant to educate the viewer as to the diseased nature of over consumption. To illustrate the difference between the average North American's relationship to stuff and those of an average family from Ahraura, India, they asked each to pull all the possessions they had out onto the front lawn, (or dirt patch, as it was). The Americans have yards and yards of appliances, furniture, sports gear, and assorted stuff that spills out far into the street. The Indian's have a small pile of pots and pans, a bed, a bicycle, sacks of rice, and the clothes on their backs. The average size home for Americans after WWII was 750 square feet, the average home now is 2400 square feet and families have gotten smaller. The Indian family's home looked about the size of a single car garage and there were two generations of six people living there. The majority of people on this earth will be born into little and die with little, at least by our standards. Many of these people enjoy spiritual riches we do not understand and they carry on through life without the mountains of stuff, quite happily, all over the world – a phenomenon that seems quite incomprehensible to Americans. Westerners have been involved in a grand experiment in materialism for two centuries or more, one that is part of the expansion and natural progress of the mental/rational stage in the evolution of our consciousness.

We have taken this worldview as far as it will go, exploring our exclusive focus on everything the material of this earth can deliver in the most intellectually intense regime imaginable, scientifically boring into the material until it has disappeared into the subatomic infinity from which it comes. In equal fashion, sensually immersing ourselves in the material to decadent extremes in vast displays of luxury far exceeding what the Romans or Louis XIV were able to muster. We've made money king and that which it can buy our central goal, and yet the ultimate experience of value and satisfaction we have sought in our material paradise has eluded us. Not that there haven't been moments of joy. We have reveled in our accomplishments as a people, in the grandeur of our architecture, the beauty of our landscapes, and the power of our technology in endless innovations, but most have found in the midst of it all that it's not the answer to everything that it pretends to be. After having recognized the true worthiness of pride and adulation these accomplishments deserve, that which drives our evolution, speaks in the heart for something the material is, in the end, incapable of delivering.

If there was anything more to be learned from luxury and material indulgence we would have found it by now. The truth is that the rich are no happier than anybody else, sometimes less so. The research is very clear on this: once a person rises to the level of material security with a place to live and enough food and clothing, all the essentials covered, the amount of true happiness that can be accrued through the acquisition of increasing amounts of possessions diminishes rapidly. In fact, those who were found to be most motivated by materialist values turned out to be the least happy. Higher levels of dissatisfaction in life and poor relationships predominate in their experience. This was found to be true across all affluent Western nations.[1] Addiction is what has taken hold of these people, The "thrill" of acquiring and using a material thing, like every other "high" humans chase, can easily become an addiction and like all addictions it ends in decay, sometimes physical, sometimes moral, sometimes spiritual, but most of the time with all of them.

When we look deeply into the nature of each addiction we find behind it a transcendent desire, so that the cocaine or meth addict feels themselves propelled with a sublime speed through the surface of life toward some ultimate light where all goals are reached and their destiny fulfilled. The plans that race through their minds all end in that perfection and they feel as if all obstacles have vanished. It's all possible and all happening in the glorious now they are racing toward. Of course, this is a delusion, an artificial enlightenment that is a false stimulation of the biochemical responses that are the physical aspect of what would normally be reactions to actual events or genuine realization. These capacities of feeling, the "highs," are ultimately structures of life connected to some greater depth of existence and in the right circumstance these feelings would be triggered in a way appropriate to their evolutionary function. That is, in signaling the arrival of a realization of deep truth that renders worry and dread inconceivable. When artificially stimulated in an extreme form the person gets the feeling without the realization, which is a way of cheating nature.

Drugs of addiction are a phenomenon of our scientific reductionist culture that reduces all the meaning of our feelings to nothing more than a physical response in the nervous system and brain. In that classic materialist maneuver of identifying as "real" only the physical we are offered the stimulation of what it believes is the "only real thing," (i.e. our body), via the drug, as an enhancement to "normal" experience. People pick it up as a way of breaking their boredom with the endless surfaces of things that is all the materialist vision can offer. Sensing some greater depth, a person will "enhance" their experience with this drug or that, a drink, a desert, a new object for their cluttered home, not understanding that there is some greater force at work behind their drive to buy, to ingest, to stimulate or sooth themselves. That force moves life forward, creates development in children and adults. What it suggests in this example is that there is more than what lies on the surface of the world. Unfortunately most are caught in the materialist web wherein they simply attempt to cure their hunger for something deeper through a higher dose of the same material fix, whether it be another drink, another donut, another pair of shoes, or another hour on the video game. This is addiction and the cure lies beyond the material that forms the substance of their prison and the source of the inadequacy they are trying to escape through the endless enhancements, be they stimulants, soothing substances, possessions, or entertainments. Ultimately, those who do not perish while chasing their high or who do not fall for the false promises of the pharmaceutical fixers drifting into the purgatory of empty, glassy eyed smiles, will simply grow more disillusioned with the surfaces of the techno-consumer worldview and in time will be moved in their angst and desperation to throw off the materialist blinders and seek that which is behind it all. In essence, they will begin looking for a way out of the machine.

The machine civilization we have created as a rendering in space of our rational, linear causal and mechanistic belief system forms a template for our senses that we have placed over the complex phenomena of the greater reality around us and in doing so we are led to a selection of data, a "puzzle of parts," if you will. This thing leaves no room for the human spirit in attempting to understand its purpose. If we can think of the spirit as not something religious or occult with all the accompanying rational doubt of its existence, and simply understand it as the non-material part of the human structure, that part that is beyond our senses and "below" the material form as the subatomic foundation is to matter, then we can begin to understand that just as our material structure has requirements for its health and wellbeing, so too does our non-material aspect have requirements. First, let's be clear about how the ego operates, then go on to the needs of the non-material self.

Egocentrism

The body needs food and water and air and protection from the elements. It is our egos, that part of human psychology which recognizes ourselves as independent beings separate from others, that is tasked with the job of being on the lookout for both food and danger. Now, animals do this quite well but as the human animal evolved beyond their embedded place in Nature and began to form complex communities the ego took on more complex functions within the new human made social and physical environments. Now the ego had to be concerned with its place in the social structure and its worth to the community and all the judgments that come with a burgeoning reflective consciousness. In this place "staying safe" and finding "food" took on larger meanings to include safety as a function of reputation and nourishment that went beyond food to include all sorts of comfort and emotional support from family, clan, and community. As human consciousness has evolved and inspired different ways of living, the human ego has expanded its original instinctive role to allow the individual to protect itself and acquire what it needs by the expanding terms of any new culture it finds itself in.

The human ego is naturally, then, "egocentric" in the sense that it instinctively watches out for number one. Just as the nervous system is set up to alert the individual to injury through pain or attract to proper temperature ranges through relief and comfort, the ego senses injury or enticement of a different sort and moves the individual to take action within the values of any given culture. In the massively materialistic culture of America, such that it has retained religion at all, religions are themselves materialistic in the sense that they amount to lists of rules for material life. The ego then, not moderated by any truly spiritual consideration, tends to perform in the service of material acquisition, comfort building, and status seeking with an obsessive focus. When your society has expanded to the level of a world empire and wealth and status have taken on monumental proportions, then the agenda of the ego becomes grandiose and in most cases impossible.

In American society the population lives by the myth of social mobility, a story that tells of individuals who were born poor and grew up to be rich through their own ingenuity, hard work, and a special form of luck that only a place like America can offer (or so the myth goes). Children are told this story in a myriad of forms and the ego gets the message quite young that happiness is all about the stuff you can buy and the fame you can achieve. Playing baseball is fun but being a professional baseball player is "really doing something." Not everyone, of course, has the same dream, but all dreams seem to retain the message of singular achievement and personal forms of glory and reward when the ego is focused on material life.

As the ego has evolved it has moved from a total concern for the individual to an expanded concern for the family and clan in the early magic structure, to the extended ethnic family of the village and to the city state of the early empires in the mythic structure, to the combined peoples of the nationalist countries of the mental/rational structure, so that identification with the group and concern for its status broadens as larger social structures are achieved. Additionally, there is a broadening of self-definition that has gone on where the individual identifies with the larger community that allows for a feeling of solidarity and common cause between them, not always in a way that allows for concern for each other's welfare but always in the background ready to emerge when, for instance, a war or the Olympic Games arrive. Suddenly, the individual identifies as a member of a nationality.

This larger "circle of concern" does not alter the need of the ego for personal achievement due to the Western cultural program. One gains higher status in the circle through the proper achievement and so the broader social arena that arrived with nation states simply creates a need for larger achievements. Most people are happy to achieve anything at all and just make a good living while they are doing it but there is a curious dynamic that takes hold in most where one achievement leads the person to seek the next higher up, just as the attainment of the "right" size house is sometimes followed by a desire for a bigger one. It is a common experience in this cultural game to set goals that the individual believes will satisfy for the rest of their lives, feeling that they will be "set" once they've made it to the dreamed of position, financially or in a sought after job, or winning a certain honor. Curiously, once the goal is achieved and the person lives with the new condition for a while the old longing starts to call again. This tendency has led to a general conclusion that "people are never satisfied." When we look closely at this dynamic what we find is simply the addiction process displaced to an activity instead of a drug or drink. The ego is gratified by the achievement and its rewards but the "high" simply doesn't last. This is how people become addicts who will do anything for their next fix. This is how people go into debt and it is how a runaway greed has become normal behavior in our civilization.

In order to understand what is driving this addictive process we have to return to the question of what the other part of our beings, the spiritual or "non-material" aspect of the human endowment needs. In creating a society based increasingly on materialism, a belief which excludes non-material realities, human beings find themselves in moments of quiet reflection feeling an emptiness, a sense of lack, of something missing and something inside them unattended to. In previous eras this space inside was attended to by spiritual practice and public ritual – people considered themselves embedded within a spiritual world swimming in the current of both nature and the powers of gods and goddesses, the invisible was all around permeating existence itself. On the outside they were embedded in their land, the lineage of the ancestors, and the tribe. In the terms of the evolution of consciousness this longing, this sense of lack, felt so poignantly today whenever the frenetic action stops long enough to allow a person to listen to their own soul, can be understood as a loss of contact with the world and reality that once flowed from the earlier structures of consciousness. Having cut off the archaic, magic, and mythic avenues of perception and having relegated these cognitive structures to a narrow range, people feel the loss but can't understand where it's coming from. This feeling remains mysterious as long as the individual continues to believe that everything has a material, i.e. a *rational* explanation. When the non-material, the spiritual, is considered fallacious then none of the connected nature within the archaic structure, nor the sympathetic resonant emotional bond in the magic structure, or the symbolic poetic meaning of the mythic journey is perceived. The individual has no depth in the world, they simply skate around on the surface of everything in the mental/rational structure with all its quantified three dimensional conceptualizations their only guide. An impoverishment of spirit follows.

Spiritual systems start as mystical revelations that become ritualized and end up over time as religious dogma expressed as rules and philosophy. As the experience of the individual moves away over the ages from the original spiritual revelation of the larger non-material reality, each generation begins to feel a distance grow between the needs of their spiritual self and what their religion is delivering. Religions grow stale over time and occasional recharging of the well is necessary to keep the system relevant to the needs of the people. When spiritual systems are high- jacked by political structures then this reconnecting is not allowed. The great Christian mystics from Hildegard to St. John of the Cross who tried to offer a way back to true connection with the world of spirit were all silenced by the church authorities.

When we entered the age of materialist science in the West, and as it became the all-encompassing explanatory model for life, it pushed all systems attempting to deal with the invisible, non-material aspects of life, out of the picture entirely. Carl Jung suggests that what happened there was a "swallowing whole" of spiritual forces down into the Western psyche to be projected out onto material things. In another way of putting it, the non-material became "concretized" or made concrete. This is to say that what was formerly considered to be an invisible force at times infusing material objects and events became the objects themselves. The mythological mind is made manifest. For example, looking at a sleek new red sports car might bring to mind all kinds of associated feelings and ideas, things like "sexiness," "power," "style," "sophistication," and "cool." Perhaps there will be an almost god-like speed and control of the road, the road itself becoming a symbol of the course of one's life and so the car representing a status and experience far above the average, lifting the driver into a little bit of ego heaven.

All of this has actually no material reality in the car at all, the car being really just a collection of metal parts, leather, plastic, rubber, and synthetic carpeting. All of those associations are purely psychological and in another sense, "spiritual" in that they relate to what are essentially non-material forces. What is sexy, lavish, or powerful? Are they actual forces in the world or simply human judgments? These things exist. We see them. We feel their force. We deal with them, but they exist in a nether world between matter and the mind. They are the substance of culture that drives history once described as aspects of godly power, or simply the gods themselves, understood by modern psychology as "archetypes." The Romans didn't personify the gods in the way the early Greeks had. They knew them as formless forces; the feelings they inspired *were* the gods. The tales of actual "super beings" had become quaint by their day.

When people conceive of their relationships with these forces that inhabit our minds and bodies as actual *things* in the world and not as psychological or simply *life energies*, then they believe they can buy a ray of light, or measure of love, or a cup of glory. This fact is not lost on advertisers, of course, and so the tendency is reinforced and made common through the media environment. Materialism leaves no room for the spirits that move our world and so we pretend without knowing that the sports car is sexy and powerful and as long as everybody conspires together to maintain this fantasy then the culture works as if it is. What the car actually does is act as a kind of "temple" for the ritual enactment of the god's power. Being able to worship at a particular temple requires a material devotion to that god. This god's grace is for sale. In Rome people would come to a temple with coins for the priest or priestess so he or she would perform a bit of magic for them, invoking the power of the gods and goddesses on their behalf. Now, they simply sell you the temple and you preform your own rituals.

Many people lie to themselves about being smarter than this, believing they understand these things and navigate above them, but few actually do. The person who doesn't see the sports car as the object of power often worships at another temple, has simply concretized the force somewhere else more commensurate with the subculture they inhabit. It might be a four-wheel-drive pick-up truck, or a Volvo, or perhaps they've turned their body into the power object in the form of a muscular build and "six pack abs." It's all the result of materialism where everything, even love, has to be a thing and so we are encouraged by the television ads at every holiday, and concocted "occasion" to head to a jewelry store to "show her how much you care," and to "make your love real." No object in the world can make love real or show how much you care, of course. These are spiritual qualities that must be felt in the heart in a form of communion with the other that transcends all materiality completely. You could give someone the Hope diamond and if you didn't feel actual love and know really how to engage in that communion then the gift would be nothing more than a monumental bribe. Unfortunately this is exactly what many relationships are founded on in the contemporary period. They are based not on real love but a kind of narcissistic mirroring where each believes the other desires them for their good qualities, but in actuality each are seeing a projection of their own fantasy of what a lover is supposed to be, of what they've sought as missing pieces of themselves. The other quells their doubts in their value as a human being. In time the projections break down and the individuals are left looking at the real person. This is when their friends will hear the oft spoken phrase, "She changed; she's not the same girl I knew before," or "He fooled me, he was so perfect when we first got together, then he turned into a jerk!" It's not that people don't get hooked up with the wrong person some times. Of course they do, but too often in our materialistic society people go hunting for relationships based on entirely material criteria – bodies, clothes, jobs, cars, even "personality type." Love is blind, they say. Love is mysterious precisely because it cannot be reduced to material criteria or a list of personality attributes.

All of this, the confused love, the concretizing of universal energies in objects one attempts to possess, all the materialistic reductions of human emotion, human purpose and striving to brain chemicals and ego rewards one achieves, all of it is deeply troubling to the human spirit. A person can follow the path of pure materialism only so long then things start to slip. The spirit rebels, the uprising begins.

It happens like this: a person achieves what they think they want – it certainly is what the culture as a whole has advertised as valuable – the prestige job, the cool car, the palatial home or it might be the little cottage in the woods just like the Thomas Kinkaid painting, whatever the dream may be. At first it's all so wonderful, but then one day a strange feeling starts to sink in. It seems to be saying, "Is this it?" Well, of course it's not it. The cottage needs more flowers, the cool apartment needs to be a penthouse, the car just isn't what it used to be – the thrill is gone. Another car, another house, more of this or that, a different paint scheme, a bigger flat screen, a better spouse – let's go shopping! It's out there somewhere, that thing they're searching for, that missing piece, that elusive object of desire that will fill out the picture. But the syndrome goes on. Whatever the next material thing may be, it is never quite the final answer. The whole story starts to descend into the depths of one of those Greek tragedies: "The gods do not live here any longer!" shouts the protagonist at the uncaring sky. More work, more money, just keep working so you can't think about it. The feeling only sneaks in when they stop and the quiet closes in on them then the empty place inside whispers its discontent. Work keeps the devil away, distraction, shopping, television, movies, games, off to the gym to work on the six pack abs or firm up those thighs until she can crush walnuts. Then, in the quiet of the evening when the small voice within tries to speak up with its troubling riddles it's time for some serious drinking, and drinking, or a pill maybe, and then the sweet oblivion of sleep. The dreams are troubling, though, running from something dark and menacing and running after something they come so close to but cannot catch. The uprising has begun.

What does the non-material part of us require? What is this thing so many have termed spirit, or soul? What food does it consume? What activity does it prefer? What is the goal of its revolution? The ancient Greeks personified this goad of their souls in the form of a spirit being they called the "daemon." This daemon was understood as the carrier of the life plan, what Plato referred to as the "lot" in life, who tried through every means available to goad the flesh and blood, being that was their change toward fulfilling their plan. This is much like the Christian idea of a guardian angel but in this case, rather than just protecting, there is an attempt to move the person in life toward some course of experience that will be good for the growth of their soul.

We should not dismiss this idea simply because it was formulated in the mythological language of an earlier time. This theme of the "spirit guide" appears in many spiritual systems and metaphysical philosophies: called the Fetch in Norse and Germanic tribal culture, the Amakua, to the Hawaiians, the Amahlolozi in some African traditions, but also appears in a form more palatable to the scientific mind in the psychological literature as a "higher self," or the "true self." Through the ages humanity seems to have felt the need to explain what feels like a guiding hand that interacts with our psychology at a very deep level. Carl Jung referred to this central guiding nature as simply, the "Self." The Self in Jung's terms is our unique character structure that is much like a germ within a seed that when planted will guide the growth of the plant so as to produce the proper form unique to the individual species. Within an acorn is the mighty oak, as has been said, and so within the human being. Within the non-physical aspect, there exists this "forming principle" that moves the individual to seek the proper ground for the expression of their unique life energy. Jung called this the process of "individuation" and counseled that in order to individuate a person first had to peel away all the layers of social conditioning that did not serve their authentic individual nature.

Materialistic science has attempted to reduce this and everything else about biological existence to some genetic factor, but the fact is that genetics only seem to control very basic substances in the make-up of the physical body, coding for muscle fiber, bone, hair, and such. Genetics has been unable to show even how the development of the physical form is controlled, let alone the psychological form. Unlike the physical material, structural development is simply not in the genes. In other words, the bricks are there but not the blue print for the building, which is probably controlled by some non-material subatomic field force as in Rupert Sheldrake's "morphic resonance" theory. So too, we suspect, do the basic attributes of character and the deeper currents pull a person in life in one direction and not another, the favorite things, the more profound likes and dislikes, the attractions to certain experiences and certain fields of work, certain types of knowledge. These seem quite unique to each individual and can't possibly be the result of some Darwinian imperative built into the "selected" physical attributes of their bodies. If this were so, people would be much more uniform. People would be like breeds of dogs that can be counted on to behave in characteristic ways. But people are not at all like dogs. Their temperaments and characters are incredibly variable across ethnic groups and all human populations. Even people in tribal and traditional cultures that stipulate all manner of dress, behavior, and activity and where children are raised in virtually the identical way in the exact same environment by all, demonstrate unique character traits within individuals.

So, we know that character is a factor of individual nature that transcends simple explanation. This unique personal force that demonstrates itself in each human life is one of the great mysteries and presents each individual as they mature with a personal puzzle of sorts, a riddle of the self that each must solve on their own terms. We give much of ourselves to the world, but there must be a general attendance to what is most vital for the individual, emerging from deep character, or soul, for a person to feel as if their life is truthful and authentic and as such, meaningful and capable of delivering some measure of contentment. It's as if the self is hidden and must be sought out.

The revelation of the emerging integral consciousness is that the self is hidden within all the structures. It can't be located in just one place. The pieces are spread all over the land, like the body of Osiris in the Egyptian mythology. His consort, Isis, had to collect all the pieces of her husband Osiris before the sacred child, Horus, could be born. The feminine principle utilizes not a calculated process, as in the mental structure, but an intuitive one, as if feeling your way in the dark. Horus, the child born from the meeting and transcendence of the masculine and feminine principles is the "anointed one," which is another way of saying the one who has put all the pieces together of what's really going on.

But what happens when the demands of the inner Self are not in any way met? What happens when the standards, fashions, and expectations of the outer world become the sole director of a person's life? What if they pay no attention to the voice of their own unique being, what if they don't even understand that they have this sort of personal guidance system? This is not an idea that is broadly understood in American culture; it does not serve capitalism which generally requires types, not individuals. We make a big deal out of being individuals, but expect people to be one of the accepted types of individuals. When they don't match one of the expected types then the person is said to be "weird," or "eccentric," even crazy. Children have often been raised in such a way that all activities are dictated by the parents in order to prepare the child for "success." Parents sometimes believe their children are simply blank units of life that are waiting to be stamped into the right shape by the hand of experience. Little to zero attention is paid to any personal interests of the child. They are shoved into whatever lessons, sports, and extracurricular activities the parents believe are essential. Sometimes children and adults do it to themselves, finding so little value in their own opinions and interests and feeling a pressing need to be accepted by others they turn themselves over completely to the outside world, making every concession possible to please others in a constant bid for acceptance.

When a person through whatever means is led away from their internal guidance and becomes totally or even generally "outer directed," they will begin to experience symptoms. The true self of the person inhabiting a position in the unconscious region of the mind will send up messages to the conscious mind in the form of a general feeling of discontent. A kind of malaise may set in where the energy starts to drain out of their days. They will experience a dwindling interest in what they are doing and although they may drive themselves through the tasks of their job and daily routines by the ego's desire for recognition or hope for promotion, or simply to meet the demands placed on them, in moments between the frenetic rush to get the job done and the next event of the day they may feel a quiet sadness building under the surface.

There are many unique ways the authentic character of the individual may express itself but the reality is that in most cases it doesn't shout, it whispers and so it is easy to drown out with work and distractions. When the impulse arises from the depths it often feels like a sense of dread, as if something is terribly wrong, but you can't figure out what it is. If given prolonged attention the feeling may express itself in more vivid terms, but at first there is usually just this sense of detached sadness, an ocean of sadness in some cases. It measures the distance between the way the person is living and the way they ought to be living. Because sadness has been turned into a disease in our society, we attempt to race past it, suppress it, drug it and laugh it away, but what it actually requires is our attention. Within that sadness is our true self asking for a little space in our lives, but we must sail across that ocean to find that space. This is what has literally been called, "the night sea journey." St. John of the Cross called it, "the dark night of the soul." When a person recognizes that the world they have invested so much of themselves in is really a façade, its values hollow, certain regret sets in, a sense of tragedy descends and a kind of death is experienced. This is the space between leaving one understanding and finding the next in an evolving life. It can be a dark crossing that takes courage and faith that a new shore will rise on the horizon in time as the self lets go of the superficial view of the ego and opens a space for a more mature vision to come into focus.

But who wants to take such an arduous journey when you can simply turn on the television set and immerse yourself in a drama that will mesmerize your ego for those last few hours before bed? People unaware that a better world is beckoning run away from the sadness, from the feeling something is wrong, and seek relief or distraction by the same old addictions. It's easier to just go shopping then to answer the call but in the end one can only put off the confrontation with the Self for so long. Sooner or later, the life will drain from everything and it will be just you and the sadness. The only way to successfully avoid the Self is to keep ourselves in emergency mode. If a person is literally living on the edge of doom, if they are barely making it in life, then all higher psychological considerations are subordinated to immediate survival needs and the person will simply be glad to be alive and with a roof over their heads and something in their stomach each day. If this isn't actually the case, some people manage to make it the perceived case as a clever strategy to keep the sadness away and in this they usually don't know what they're really up to at all. "I have to keep moving...I like to have something to do all the time," we hear them say. If they sat down for a moment they would risk confronting themselves.

The terms, "inner-directed," vs. "other-directed," and "tradition-directed," first appeared in the insightful landmark work entitled, *The Lonely Crowd*, by the sociologists, David Riesman, Nathan Glazer, and Reuel Denney. First published in 1950, it tells the story of a new kind of American sensibility that grew up as corporate business structures expanded their grip on the rising middleclass after the Industrial Revolution. What the authors learned from their research and explained in detail was that earlier populations had been largely motivated by religious and traditional cultural mores and beliefs that in the open expanses of the new American life, a shift had gone on to a more individualized sense of destiny dependent more on the personal strengths and disposition of the single person then having escaped the bounds of tradition. The conditions of the American frontier bred what became the "inner-directed," person, making decisions based on an introspective view of their own experience and self-image, intuitions, and desires, rather than consulting some external authority on what had come before. They drew from the experience of others but they did it for their own purposes and in their own way. Instead of following strict instructions, as in the traditional way – you will dress like this, eat this on that day, etc. – the individual began to follow general values – be honest, be brave, be faithful, etc. that could be applied in whatever unique circumstances that suited the individual.

This inner-directed sense persisted in American society, but slowly gave way in the 20th Century to the "other-directed" – a sense that grew out of the mass consumption culture of the middleclass where trends, styles, and the "cult of the new" took hold and formed a new culture that became a reference for individuals comparing their progress to others. What a person owned, what they drove, how they lived, even the books they read and discussed became a matter of what was "popular." What Riesman and his collaborators discovered regarding the fate of the other-directed was that because they hold most important this desire to relate to others and be accepted by the group, to "fit in," and "measure up," they have a tendency to become alienated from their own inner selves. Essentially, their ability to "know themselves" is compromised. This is a perfect fit for the demands of corporate work and the disposition necessary for the efficient maintenance of a consumer economy, but it has consequences for the deeper life and mind of the individual.[2]

What we've seen since the publication of, *The Lonely Crowd*, as the main consequence of a society alienated from themselves is that the unique potential of such a society is diminished due to the lack of nourishment of individual genius and creative expression – not in the commercial world of product development, of course, but this is the crucial point. The focus is ever more strongly placed on the surfaces of everything around the person and as such the nature of the cultural products they seek become increasingly intensified and decadent in a futile search for a misplaced fulfillment. Because mass consumer culture becomes a method of self-expression that is not really about the self, but about a social persona, there is a feeling of restlessness and a lack of satisfaction that dogs the efforts of such consumers to reach a point of satiation, of getting what they came for. It's all so uncertain and dependent on a moving target that misses any consideration of the unique personal being. This combination of consumerism and other-directedness underlies the "egocentric-materialism" that is the main driving force of our times. What egocentric-materialism rests on within the minds of individuals is two drives that are, in and of themselves, healthy aspects of human existence.

In the other-directed aspect we find simply the basic human desire to be accepted in a social context. Human beings are social creatures. We are pack animals and we have a basic need for companionship and good relations within a social unit. What we find in the other-directed dynamic as it has manifested in American society is a lack of compromise between what is given to the group in terms of personal behavior and material practice, conventions of dress, speech, living arrangements, etc., and what is kept for the self, in terms of personal taste and development motivated by queues originating from within the personal feeling and intuitive, magic and mythic consciousness structures of the individual alone.

Historically, there has always been a compromise between the needs of the individual and the needs of the state or tribe but it seems that in earlier stages of development within the original magical and mythical eras the needs of the individual may have been much more subtle and an overall conformity was easier to reach. As the consciousness of humanity has emerged from its unconscious immersion within nature it has increasingly differentiated the individual mind so that self-expression became more important to the sense of wellbeing and meaning in life. As the mental/rational structure developed through time it has created the most autonomous individuals yet seen in any previous era. Just as evolution in general has increased the complexity of the biological world over the ages, so too has the individual mind grown in complexity. This development is seen within the maturing integrated structure of each individual. The ego has developed an increasing separation from instinct and "group think" as a function of an evolutionary imperative where within the experience of the individual a need arises for developing a personal potential emerging evolutionarily through the self. This is a revolutionary construct – that evolution now proceeds in human beings through individual creativity as the expression of a universal inspiration.

The mature ego, then, instead of keeping its focus on the external world and issues of safety and material satisfaction, seeks to utilize the material environment as a medium for carrying out the inspirations of the deep self as it is emerging within all the structures of consciousness. Because we now understand that the cultural environment in all of its effects – in family structure, social conditions, material environs and such effect the development of people in profound ways even effecting the expression of their genetic structures, in its ability to modify these conditions – it is clear that humanity has gradually gained more and more control over the direction of its evolution.[3]

In the physical sphere we are faced with what is required of us from the ground of Nature we are built from, its needs as maintenance – which we can understand as: nutrition, protection against the elements, rest and relaxation, exercise, mental stimulation and social interaction, sex – and how far we can take these needs in never ending cultural variations. Basically, we've taken the above list and evolved each category. Nutrition has become "cuisine;" bodily protection has become "architecture" and "fashion;" rest and relaxation have become a search for "tranquility" and a million ways to have "fun;" exercise has become a plethora of technologically extravagant gym machines and a selection of activities fetishized into "life styles," (I'm a runner, mountain biker, tennis player, etc.); mental stimulation has become "science" and "art" in all its myriad forms, dominated in the masses by television and the internet; and the social possibilities have exploded as integrated traditional towns have disintegrated into mass suburbs where individuals make their own social units from work or interest affiliations; sex remains sex although now attended by a culture of "technique," and augmented by drugs.

In all of this we create an environment to live in with expectations of the individual that either push us away from ourselves or further into ourselves. We compromise our own tastes and tendencies in a thousand small ways regularly in meeting others for the various connections we desire. The social, sexual, and collaborative work benefits they offer outweigh the small exceptions to ourselves, but there is a line where the group benefits expire and the more a person goes with what's expected from others beyond that line the more they abandon themselves. In practicing this other-directed approach to life that is normal in adolescence but seems to stretch on into adulthood in so many in the current period, people never really locate themselves as unique beings. Instead, they manufacture a personality and socially constructed life that ultimately leaves them with a sense of hollowness and falseness about their lives. When people do begin to wake-up to the deficiencies of this life, they often have no sense at all of where to begin to find that central seed of their unique existence on Earth.

The confusing thing about the Self is that it is not found in some final form within a dark recess of the mind, like a precious artifact waiting to be discovered. This is an error induced by the materialist frame of reference. The Self is not an object, not genetic material, but a tendency, a formless energetic influence that contains a particular directional quality that either resonates in harmony with a practice, experience, interest, or it doesn't. When it does "resonate," which is an actual description of something physical and a metaphor that seems to feel right by experience, as if a tuning fork inside begins to hum in harmony with an exterior source, then the person has a clue in what direction to take their life, what to investigate further. In doing so it will be as if they are following a trail in the external world that is detected by a series of indications of deep feeling. It is a trail you don't see with your eyes but experience in sparks of interest and feelings of being in the right place. It is a flowing contentment that moves from one subject of interest or experience to another that slowly puts the puzzle of the self together, a picture, an identity one can only see as it forms.

This internal guidance system doesn't seem to be locked into specifics so that an individual may find a way to express and live in harmony with the self by doing a number of different things, it isn't as if there is an inscription on the back of the brain that says, "You must be a sixth grade teacher in a progressive school in Sedona, Arizona." The given individual may, indeed, find themselves right there, but they might have just as well have ended up doing social work or becoming an innovative organization consultant. The Self, or unique character structure doesn't get specific. So, when people feel like they should have been born in another era, riding the range with Buffalo Bill or discussing art and literature in the saloons of Paris in the 20's, what they are really finding in these things is a historic source of resonance, not lost forever in time but another hint for the present. This might very well be the whole point – that something from the past has been lost and it is their task in the providence of our times to help create its new form, to bring it back to life so as to reintegrate the spirit of the thing into a more inclusive now. This is true of each developing person these days as we enter the integral stage in the evolution of our consciousness, we are "integrating." Evolution proceeds through our creativity and the past is as much a medium as the future.

While on this path of self-discovery and creation, a personal authenticity is experienced and that feeling of living in harmony with one's authentic being provides an intensity of experience that is a type of nourishment. This has been understood in a poetic sense as "food for the soul." This is a nonmaterial sustenance that moves through material life, but is not completely of it. It is like music moving from the musician through the instrument to the world. This speaks to a problem in our current "other-directed" corporate and industrial culture – that expression of one's own unique character is rarely seen as a good thing in this environment where consistency and regimentation is the order of the day. This is the consequence of the machine mind. The discontent within these structures is the spur that urges us onward to a better way of doing things. A better way will emerge from the deep evolutionary creative center of individuals who not only "think outside the box," but also think outside the whole corporate commodity culture.

When a person is in their zone of personal harmony in resonance with their work, they gain a quality of being and life experience that transcends the value of material things as compensation for putting up with a boring "soul sucking" job. This is how much of the consumer culture is generated and driven. When people feel this tremendous emptiness and lack of fulfillment in jobs and lives out of harmony with themselves, they become easy prey for advertisers who fill this void with ego dreams and stimulation. What the population sees on television and movie screens are images of people who seem to be leading meaningful, exciting lives where interesting things are happening and great friendships and love affairs are going on, where momentous events are pushing characters to extraordinary feats or ordinary people are rising to take on challenges that seem to elevate them to the status of heroes. All of this is happening while the average Joe and Jane sit quietly in their seats reveling in it, but when the story ends the melancholy seeps in and they wish their lives where exciting and meaningful, too.

So off to the shopping center they go where a person can layer on various clothing items and products of one sort or another that are all meant to propel the individual into their artificially generated identity. A style is a form of communication to the rest of the world that they are "this sort of character" in this sort of story, where the world they build around them is the scene that sends the message. A thin veneer of other-directed substance is plastered over the individual's life in a futile attempt to take on some of the magic of meaning that flows so easily on the screen but seems like a rare commodity in the world of their actual living experience. Advertisers have encouraged this fantasy for so long that it has become its own reality taken for granted as a true road to what life has to offer. This is essentially how military recruiting works.

This syndrome of the false self, the constructed other-directed "story to be purchased" people build around their lives is pervasive throughout American society. From the worker of the lowest strata spending all his hard earned money on an expensive car with payments that will keep him in poverty but allow a different public persona, to the multimillionaire stock trader who surrounds herself with plush grandeur as if she were staring in her own remake of *Gone With the Wind* with Rhett Butler now costumed in Prada about to stride through the door. Many are simply attempting to carry out the fantasy of the "American dream," in their own stucco mini-mansion, style no. 4, on the street of dreams where all the happy families are located on television. Having achieved their own private version of the fantasy they believe will allow them to win the game of egocentric materialist culture and be rewarded with everlasting meaning and fulfillment they are puzzled when the glow wears off and they don't feel any different. In fact they feel even more distant from themselves. All the stuff doesn't seem to be transmitting its magic as advertised. What's wrong?

It's not that any of these things, in and of themselves, can't be part of the plan of some person's truly authentic life. They can. It's just that the things—the suburban home, the SUV—whatever, must be expressions of the inner-direction of the individual to be experienced as right, as part of an authentic life, not the other way around where the person expects the "rightness" to come *from the things themselves*. The ego is always looking to the outside for hints as to how to stay safe and acquire necessities. In this mission there is much concern for what other people think in our complex, mass society where achieving recognition and a place in some social order is often a difficult and uncertain task. Human beings have a strong need to be seen, to be recognized by their fellows as part of the "scene," whatever it may be. When this ego is working with a culture that places material things on the highest pinnacle of ultimate value in life, then people are driven to acquire as the price of membership in their chosen scene and so we have the makings for the egocentric materialism that drives people to get the whole point of their lives up-side-down.

A person cannot derive ultimate satisfaction and fulfillment in life from material objects. This sounds completely counter intuitive in our materialist culture, but this is an unalterable first and final truth. If the material object is part of the expression of the authentic Self in response to the inner-direction, then the object will have meaning, "make sense," and evoke pleasure or significance for the individual. But if the object is acquired because the person believes that "This is what cool, powerful, fashionable, people own and being seen with it makes me cool, powerful, fashionable too," then this person is bound to be disappointed. The object will not make them any of these things. It is an empty prop in a play they have written for themselves. It is not an expression of their true self but simply an attempt to garner acceptance, admiration, love, respect – the list goes on. Others may, indeed, collude with them in this self-deception, taking part in their play as if real, but in the end the glory will all fade away as these productions have no solid foundation within the individual.

The populace has been manipulated into an addictive relationship with materialism as compensation for offering their life energies to enhance the power of others. The deal is simple: deny your authentic life, help build someone else's pyramid and you will be rewarded with stuff. In being convinced that nothing but matter exists in the universe the individual believes that the best strategy is to find employment with the biggest pay check so as to acquire the most stuff. The idea that they might actually be happiest in life being a ski instructor or whatever, regardless of salary, as part of an authentic expression of their deep character providing some true measure of contentment, completely eludes them. So they go into finance or law or get an MBA, or a different sort of person might go into the trades because the union will ensure they are paid well and protected from exploitation, and for their misery they are rewarded. This is the deal with the devil that always burns. You can find these miserable people everywhere, impressed with themselves and surrounded by growing piles of stuff, but feeling empty and tragically sure the feeling is telling them they have yet to acquire enough. In their fantasies they dream of chucking it all and moving to a tropical paradise and becoming a beach bum; this is the urge to health asserting itself but, alas, they have too much invested, too many responsibilities. These are the people who will confess over late night cocktails or pitchers of beer some version of, "I wanted to be a musician...but my father said it was impractical."

And then there are the many who simply took whatever they could get, who never really believed in their own potential, never looked within, never invested in it but simply went with the herd and did what was at hand, filling the schedule at the local grocery store or getting the sales job because they thought they might afford a little more. These are the people who, years later, die in droves on Monday mornings when the most heart attacks occur, not able to face another week in a life that has become like a tomb for their spirits. Again, it's not the grocery store or any other job that's entirely wrong; it's the combination of the person and the life that is out of sync.

Of course life is more than a job, people derive profound levels of contentment and food for their souls through family and friends and weekend projects, walks in the woods and trips to the lake, but it is the relationship to employment, where the majority of one's life energy is spent and the pursuit of the "good life" that has been turned into a commodity to be purchased that is the primary force in so many lives. In another portion of the populace it is often the case that many individuals do follow some portion of their true self in deciding what to do in life. People seem to feel their way along, instinctively heading for some employment they just know they like better and in some cases individuals will actualize their authentic life simply by doing what makes them feel right without respect to other concerns. Many compromise in staying with employment that means nothing to them but a paycheck, try to find sanity and satisfaction in all the other things they do and in this way eek out a life of meaning.

This is the human condition. Most people on earth have no chance to do anything else but just what is possible to survive. Certainly all life on one level simply requires maintenance, as the old Zen saying goes, "Chop wood, carry water." Enlightened or not, living the authentic life or not, everybody must do things sometimes that are just work. The Buddhist way to overcome this problem in life is simply to remove judgment from the ups and downs of existence concentrating on just what's there, without thought. "Work without thought is just empty motion," the Sage tells us. This is certainly helpful in disengaging the ego and its tendency for complaining and longing that can make a person miserable, but one wonders what is lost when this practice takes over a whole life. Some Eastern philosophy says that there is nothing at the center of each human life. The ego is a false construct and beneath that is simply the "All" from which the individual emerged and to which the person will return, the interval in between simply a matter of fate, or "karma," that must be endured. Other Eastern and Western esoteric systems posit that there is, indeed, something at the deep center of each human life beneath the ego, this soul Western psychology has termed the Self. What the other philosophy of denial is missing from this perspective is that the "All" seems to be constituted in each individual in a very unique way. This unique constitution has a kind of "higher" life separate from the ego and as such forms the source from which the authentic life path for each flows. To deny this "higher self" in a total renunciation of the need for individual expression and experience as a complete way of life seems a choice guaranteed to generate a sense of pointlessness, at least for many people in the contemporary world who enjoy a life beyond that of mere survival.

The "All" that is represented in each person is termed the "atman" in Yogic philosophy, but can be understood from a Western scientific perspective as simply the primordial energetic force which gave rise to the Big Bang and continues to support each material thing from its lower architecture at the subatomic level where mater is supported from oscillating waves of energetic renewal from other dimensions. So, we know from our study of the way matter is sustained that nonmaterial forces are informing everything and in the case of individual human beings takes a unique form. The energy that created everything seems to be driving the evolutionary process. That process is in us expressing the latest permutation of physical and psychological development as this force continues to expand in the material world through time. The complexity of the natural world in all its flora and fauna is mirrored in the self as a unique spiritual species emerging through evolution.

It is an odd and miraculous thing to consider that humanity represents a process that is many billions of years old and in fact transcends what we can even understand as time, but this creative process that is evolution seems not to be playing out a set plan. Rather, it sends out myriad lines of development that either adapt or parish as conditions evolve on Earth. Humanity represents the most adaptive creature ever seen on the planet Earth and it is our incredible capacity for creative activity that has allowed us to survive so elegantly in almost every existent environment. It is this ultimate creative capacity, our ability to dream, to imagine things not yet real that is both our greatest talent and our most vulnerable weakness. It allows us to literally make the future from pictures in our minds, but this same tendency can be used to control people by infiltrating imaginations with images that bait the appetites of the base ego with visions of grandiose fame and heroic action, sexual indulgence and a never ending array of plush and "stylish" worlds that continually reinforce a path away from the creative self. This is how centralized power reinforces itself, by pulling people away from the future emerging through individual creative function and enlisting that life energy in an imposed order that services the top. In ignorance something vital, indeed sacred, is traded for costumes and trinkets.

It is this lure to "go for the money" instead of one's own unique life that has formed the terrible trend in American society that keeps the false self, the constructed fantasy materialist self, in charge. It is this that drives the big material addiction that is running Western civilization into the dirt. The greed hounds that precipitated the 2008 financial crisis were after the money, and the money only; ferocious egos of materialism were at work who were willing to gamble the entire economy of the United States in their play to accrue greater and greater levels of extravagant wealth. When greed becomes so destructive its nature as a true cultural sickness leading to the dissipation of all that is best in us becomes clear.

Some may feel that it is possible that these pathologically selfish individuals are simply following their own true and authentic characters and that they, like other swindlers, tyrants and plotting manipulators in history, are really just being themselves. This would suggest that it is dangerous for people to look deeply into their own character and "souls" to find the clues to an authentic life, that being other-directed in some cases is best. This topic is a deep one that has been wrestled over in the history of philosophy for centuries – is man basically good or evil? Are humans selfish bruits, as Thomas Hobbes suggested, or are they naturally noble and loving in their spirits and it is society that bends them toward evil, as Rousseau believed? Certainly, codes of morals are necessary to curb the drives of egos unmoored from a sense of humanity, but to draw out all the relevant points on this issue here would take us off on a tangent not necessary for our current purposes and can be looked into elsewhere by the curious. It is the position set out here that it is precisely the separation from the deeper humanity of the individual that allows them in a egomaniacal manner to seek unwarranted power and or wealth as a substitute for the pleasures of the spirit, or nonmaterial aspect of their being in harmony with creative activity in the world that is a true expression of the force of life itself within the individual. Greed ultimately is about fear that the perpetrator does not have enough and an imagination disconnected from their humanity that allows them to injure others without consideration.

When we look at the animal kingdom we do not find creatures exploiting and destroying others of their own kind as a regular practice, it is humanity alone that carries on such self-destructive behavior. We have evolved beyond the instinctual patterns that held us in place as members of that primordial kingdom, but we have not lost that basic program that moves us toward cooperation and nurturance of our own kind and, indeed, of all life that we sense at deeper levels of awareness we are connected to in the broad sustaining ecosystems we inhabit. It has been the growth of the ego in the first openings of the mythological development of the mind thousands of years BCE that took us along another path where other human beings could be murdered for profit without concern.

Just think of what a tyrannical destructive force a toddler would be as a king in charge of an ancient city state. When the ego awakens in small children the force of it is startling to new parents, the sheer volume and rage of "the highchair tyrant" can be overwhelming in some children when they aren't getting what they want. Such an ego in an adult form is what we might picture in these very early kings who left their stories on stone tablets and standing monuments that read from a contemporary view like the most ridiculous, blow-hard braggadocio: "Sargon, king of Agade," we read from 2350 BCE, "Viceregent of Inanna, King of Kish, pashishu of Anu, King of the land, great ishakku of Enlil: the city of Uruk he smote and its wall he destroyed. With the people of Uruk he battled and he routed them. With Lugal-zaggisi, King of Uruk, he battled and he captured him and in fetters he led him through the gate of Enlil."[4] The tablet goes on to describe the many victories of Sargon who seems to have attacked his neighbors for no other reason but the glorification of this new found ego. The scholar Joseph Campbell referred to this period where organized warfare seemed to spring up everywhere as "*The Great Reversal.*" What was reversing was the attitude of people concerning death found in the record of their mythology. What was before considered a continuation of the mystery of life beyond the physical began to be seen as simply a relief from suffering. The leading rampaging egos of the period were making the rest of the people miserable and death seemed then a final escape. If Sargon were with us today telling his tale we might be inclined to suggest he "lighten up," just a tad but the ego, having struggled out of bondage to nature achieving a sense of independence, once in charge and on a roll, doesn't want to be told such things, doesn't want to be reminded of limits and the needs of others. When fully inflated it will not be thwarted, "Give me a cookie or I'll kill you." The unbridled immature ego would destroy the world in its rage and desire for everything.

This is the tricky task of an awakening self-consciousness, a mind becoming aware of itself. The ego goes from animal interests in food and sex and safety and lounging with the pack, to an acute awareness of existence as a single being with individual possibilities. In the way of all immature beings comes the frustration of will in the feeling that they should have it all.

Those on the upper end of the evolution of consciousness curve found themselves aware of things others were not and must have naturally become leaders. As such great things could be orchestrated through directing the less aware in support of group projects, like large scale agriculture, irrigation canals, stone architecture, and on and on, but the temptations for abuse in these early awakenings must have been great. The feeling for others as extensions of one's life in family and clan and village must have become remote in the larger city-states of early civilizations, especially the fellow feeling for others in other cities. Turning them into slaves to carry out the work of building a bigger city for oneself must have seemed like a grand idea to the inflated immature egos in the seats of power. This was the inception of a new kind of perpetual organized warfare, aggression not just to protect or provision as had previously been the case but now to gain ego stoking reputation. It was conquest for the sake of expanding material grandeur and power – in other words, ego space.

Much progress has been made by humanity over the millennia, but these tendencies of the ego are still with us today. In time, this ridiculous desire for "more" this usurping of the life energy of others for the aggrandizement of the few will seem as silly and absurd as a way of life as we would find enacting the blood sacrifices of ancient peoples today. The fetish for the material that many modern people carry on is a stage of primitive ego development that is now being overcome in the evolution of our consciousness. We are slowly coming to understand that material things are a medium for the expression of our spirits but are not ends in themselves.

Think of houses. A documentary looking at how human beings have chosen to house themselves showed the largest house in the world owned by a Middle-Eastern prince, or Emir, or some such titled person. He was a young man at the time of the filming, showing him with a coterie of body guards, advisers, and personal companions. The entrance hall to his immense home was the size of an aircraft hangar. The whole structure looked from a distance like an airport building or some kind of massive, modern civic structure in which a parliament or other seat of government might be held. In short, it was the most ridiculously large and absurdly ostentatious, "home" ever constructed. Perhaps the prince felt his gigantic palace was needed as a symbol to his impoverished people that the West has nothing on them. After all, they have the biggest house on the planet. Perhaps it was simply the size of structure needed to contain the massively inflated ego of a person raised to believe he is a favorite of God above all others. It's hard to say. In close-ups of the prince one could detect a note of discomfort bleeding through the bland, austere continence. He seemed a little lost, forlorn, walled in by his handlers. Perhaps he thought the house was absurd himself – certainly not an expression of his Bedouin culture, but some sort of Western inspired aberration.

Looking at such a house most people would instantly feel they would not want to live in it, would find the whole idea utterly ridiculous and would feel quite uncomfortable in such a place, completely laughable to even think about. Looking at the great manor houses of the old British aristocracy and the palaces of European monarchs past, we find, again, "homes" most people wouldn't want to live in, simply too ridiculously large and expressing an embarrassing volume of ostentation. Even the American homes of the barons of industry in the "gilded age" such as the Vanderbilt mansion have been turned into museums and historical sights and public gardens. Not even the families who once built them want to live in them anymore.

What this trend demonstrates is a maturing of the ego, a development of consciousness that has withdrawn value from such gargantuan homes. Egos that big just aren't fashionable anymore. People with money still may build big homes, but nothing compared to what used to be the norm. The more mature ego simply doesn't need such things and when we find some young financier living in something bordering on the old grandiose vision of things we are sure to find an immature character, a child in an adult's body. Those who build mammoth structures by today's standards can be counted on to have deficits in their self-image they are attempting to compensate for.

A person who knows their own value doesn't need material proof to show everybody. No one can actually, functionally, use a gigantic house the size of a high school so the only reason to have one would be to create a frame for oneself. A way of packaging a life in the manner of one of the immature fantasies previously discussed: "Welcome to my monumental home. As you can see, I'm a baron in my own mind."

In the earliest ancient city states the elite were actually more evolved than the common people, one structure of consciousness ahead. Forerunners in the evolution of consciousness in agricultural villages created the first cities that grew quickly when the lesser evolved hunter/gatherer peoples were drawn in by the city's food supplies at times when the wild plants and animals the hunting peoples depended on grew scarce. This created a system of laborers that were literally less evolved than the original city builders who formed a higher class of leaders. By the Roman period this situation was changing. Most common people had moved into the higher mythological/rational structure then becoming the norm for proletariat and aristocrat alike. A broader education helped to keep the elite in a superior role but a certain amount of "stage craft" became necessary. The elite had to surround themselves with much grandiose ostentation and personal adornments to maintain the illusion of superiority. This happened all over the planet. As the actual mental superiority of the ruling class faded the palaces and regalia became more elaborate.

The reason for all the ornamentation and the gold crown with the jewels and such in the old monarchies was to take an ordinary human being and transform him or her into a demigod, a very special person, God's special progeny and favorite. The people needed to be suitably impressed for the whole society to function properly; they had to have reason to believe in "the divine right of kings." The people needed to know there was a special person with the inside track with God in the big house getting the word for them all. It was comforting in a world with so much uncertainty. Of course, the guy with the crown just had to fake it. After some time, given enough development people began to figure out that the crown and the ermine robe and all the fancy fashions were just a costume and the guy inside was just another person like everyone else. Now everyone knows the people who live in Windsor Palace are just people, nothing more, playing a role in a play that the citizens of Britain keep wanting to see. It's a very expensive play but they believe it's all in good fun. You can take tours! The royal family members have become living museum pieces to go with the big house and antiques; the most authentic of *living history* display.

If we're not playing this game of *aristocrats* any longer, a game we now know was based on illusion, then why strive for your own palace? The mature ego knows that their butt will feel no different sitting on the thousand dollar chair than sitting on the ten thousand dollar chair, or the twenty-five thousand dollar chair. The chairs may not even look much different; the difference in price will be due to some custom made fabric and an elite designer label somewhere out of sight. The immature ego revels in such things as feeling an invisible crown on their heads. The mature ego just chuckles and stays out of debt or puts the extra money from the chair and all the other "baronial" excesses done without into a startup to train ghetto kids in small business administration, or invests in alternative energy development, or any one of a million things that demonstrate their commitment to the future of humanity and the world their children and grandchildren will live in.

It's also true, of course, that some people are wealthy enough that it doesn't matter what the chair costs they would still have plenty to fund the future of humanity, if they so choose. The point is that it really isn't about the chair. *It's never about the stuff.* It's that so many people are putting their money into "ego decorations" while thinking that the invisible crown is going to make them whole. In fact it does not. It simply chains them to a never ending slavery in one "factory" or another so they can pay for their addiction to materialism while the system created to maintain this society slowly destroys itself without notice. While so many are working so many hours to expand the padding in their little private castles, however that may be defined by individual tastes, they are missing their children growing up, neglecting the responsibilities of a citizen in the maintenance of democracy, and leaving untended the growth of their own potential as unique human beings. They are trading a life of meaning for a selection of objects that gratify their ego and its desire to be continually stimulated, comfortable, fed treats, and admired. At the same time the contribution they might have made to a better society is lost.

This is the crucial point: individuals in touch with their deep, authentic self are also in touch with their humanity. The expansion of mind that allows for authentic expression is rooted in the deep structures of the human instinctual patterns where altruist tendencies arise. In our deep animal sense human beings will behave just as other mammals will toward their own kind, that is with compassion and a natural empathy and fealty. Even wolves will bring food back to feed injured members of the pack unable to hunt. Contrary to popular belief and some philosophic doctrine, human beings have to be taught to be vicious. Those tasked with military training throughout history have understood this. Trying to get men to kill one another is a difficult task, pressed to the point where one's life and the life of one's friends are in danger, men will certainly kill, but what military commanders have always been concerned with is fellow feeling moving troops to see themselves as having more in common with the troops of the other side than with their own officers. This is why "fraternizing with the enemy" has always carried heavy consequences. In the Napoleonic wars officers where armed not to fight the enemy but to ensure their own troops would do so and were given the power to execute men on the line if disobeying orders or demonstrating any reluctance to fight – often interpreted as "cowardice in the face of the enemy." Research done during WWII into better training methods found in a review of history that it was not cowardice that is the worst problem facing military planners but a simple lack of the desire to take another human life. It was found to be common for soldiers to fire over the heads of the enemy rather than aiming to kill. The main psychological tool for getting around this problem has always been to "dehumanize" the enemy, portraying them as vicious animals and playing up cultural and racial differences as much as possible. In traditional wars of tribal peoples it is often the case that where killing is encouraged the enemy tribe has been thought of as something other than human, creatures appearing like humans but not really so, actually demons, monsters. In the contemporary period military training has maximized a myriad of methods for disposing new soldiers to kill without conscience and this training has been made easier due to the constant indoctrination children are exposed to from television and movie violence, and more recently video games. The problem still arises when service men and women are faced with actual combat situations that they are immediately struck with the difference between fantasy violence and the real thing.

The mind experiences and categorizes at a deep level an extreme difference between game or movie violence and actual violent acts in the real world. The two, contrary to much worrying, do not cross over.[5] The second a person enters an actual combat situation all their feelings associated with fantasy violence instantly evaporate. This makes for a horrible contrast in the person's mind; they have been indoctrinated to understand violence in the service of the State as heroic and even fun in an adventurous sort of way, but when faced with actual killing and the witnessing of real death the individual is prone to all the normal human reactions that emerge from their deep humanity that cannot be entirely suppressed. This healthy core of human feeling will serve to haunt those veterans the rest of their lives as they live with the conflict between the fantasy heroic imagery their experience is meant to reflect and the actual damage to their humanity they feel in their hearts, a conflict only half conscious but experienced as a terrible sense of tragedy and confusion. This creates a well-known habit among combat veterans of not wanting to discuss their experiences. They don't talk about it except with other veterans who understand the feeling of being split between cultural legend and reality, something the public can't, and because their feelings don't match the heroic legends they were brought up on they feel a deep sense of shame that must be hidden, acknowledged only in the eyes of other veterans. It is a lie they keep together and that keeps so many young men from getting the help they need as the suicide statistics for the Iraq and Afghanistan wars now far exceed those of the last three wars combined.

In research done after WWII on combat fatigue victims, which had comprised the majority of the men removed from the front, (a fact hidden from the American people), it was concluded by the psychiatrists carrying out the investigation that the conditions of modern warfare were simply of such violent intensity that no normal human being could escape without psychological damage. They found that only a person who was a homicidal psychopath to begin with could come out relatively unharmed. If human beings were basically violent and ruthless creatures at heart then this situation would be entirely different.[6]

If you combine this evidence with the well-known fact that people will assist strangers as if family members when faced with a mutual disaster, as well as the many acts of selfless altruism seen in the countless individuals who have risked their own lives in attempts to save others unknown to them, the picture that emerges is one of a deep humanity that, despite the selfishness of the average alienated individual in our mass society, still comes to the surface when pressed – when the world breaks through the superficial ego barriers that divide us.

The mental/rational stage utilizes an instrumental reason within the machine-mind template that leads to the using of fellow human beings like livestock or machine parts. This view requires a suppression of our humanity through a strategy that convinces us with a sort of cold, mathematical reason that, say, the exploitation of working people in paying less than a living wage must be allowed in order to achieve certain values at higher levels of the organization, like research and development of new products that will make everyone's life better. It is a type of reason that subordinates our humanity to "higher values" it sells us just like a product and, indeed, it is products that are said to perform the "technological fix" that will make everything right in the future.

The future is here. Many things are still wrong. Some are getting worse. The evolving mind has begun to see through the limits of a reason unmitigated by humanity that always makes the present contingent on the future in a egocentric materialist value system that has everyone running for more prestige, more achievement, more stuff. It is a system that tells us that once we've achieved the unspecified goal then we will have bought our humanity. The evolving mind in seeing through the desires of the superficial materialist ego is unmoved by the ploy, because it knows in returning to the deep authentic self within that it was born with humanity and dignity and freedom and only the mirage of these things is what's sold in the market place.

Some contemporary social critics in looking at the growing focus on individual freedom and the search for authenticity since the social revolution of the 1960's have believed that it is the cause of the breakdown in civic responsibility and all kinds of negative, narcissistic trends in our society, seeing the idea of "finding oneself" as an excuse for selfishness and nothing more. What these critics have been reacting to is what egocentric materialism did with the "do your own thing," ethic of the new society. The person ungrounded in the true self beyond the superficial ego and its fears and desires, did indeed, take the new ethic that said *each person has a right to a life of meaning by their own terms* and interpreted this to mean that they had a right to throw off all responsibilities to anything outside themselves and simply see how far their own ambition could take them, completely unharnessed from the health of society, the family, the environment, anything. Of course, this was exactly the philosophy of John D. Rockefeller and his ilk of the Gilded Age. In this maneuver the average person was simply joining in the philosophy that had motivated the upper classes for generations. The difference was that the wealthy could compensate by endowing a museum or opera house, while they engaged in their monumental acts of self-aggrandizement in the same sort of egocentric materialist competition that eschewed responsibility to others and took an interest in politics only in so far as they could manipulate it in support of their power building.

There has appeared a culture of selfishness in America, but this is not a social trend begun by the "culture of authenticity," as it has been labeled by some. Rather, this selfishness began when the mass culture of consumption had built to the point of high prosperity for a broad, rising middleclass who, within the new "other-directed" culture of the mass society after WWII, began to emulate a new social aristocracy in their own drives for riches and fame. The idea of the authentic life championed by the human potential movement that emerged from the 60's social revolution was that of a person involved with the spiritual search. It meant to link the authentic life with a deep spiritual core in rejection of an ego formerly harnessed by the status-quo for their wars and materialist striving antithetical to the 60's sensibility.

The original idea of "finding oneself" was a way of directing people to something original and authentically human within themselves beneath all the conditioning of a society that was thought to be morally bankrupt in the face of the disaster of the Vietnam War and rampant bigotry highlighted by the ongoing liberation struggles within the country. Unfortunately, as the post 60's period ensued and many began to feel a sense of failure of the more grandiose projects for social reform that characterized the 60's, egocentric materialism reasserted itself with a vengeance.

From the ashes of the social rebellion rose a new hip and cool version of the old 1950's consumer. This new progressive American type was called the "Yuppie," an "upwardly mobile young professional." Molded by a dedication to the ethics of "do your own thing," and demonstrating a passing regard for the ideals of the former era in rejecting prejudice and traditional limits, they jettisoned the concerns regarding the down side of capitalism and in so doing espoused a strong materialist drive to inhabit a new kind of elite society of the hip. They wear the latest fashion, eat at the trendy restaurants, and decorate their homes with ethnic art and bohemian chic' seeing themselves as champions of the a new open society while asserting their right to make as much money as they can in following their own private dream to their potential. It is all just materialist striving in a new package, but this time the 60's rejection of the "up tight" traditional culture that threw off support for the old regime was not accompanied by a dedication to build a new just order through political action as had been the ethic in the rebellion years. Now the old order and all its social and political responsibilities were left behind in the mistaken belief that one could build one's own private nirvana and the rest would take care of itself now that Black women were reading the news and warmongering was out of fashion. The result was a supercharged society of selfishness that worked just fine for the old consumer capitalist order that went right along doing all the things it was doing before but now with new "sensitive society" packaging and news control.

The culture changed and the machine changed with it. The materialist order that encourages the idolization of stuff and presents it as the carrot in front of the wheel of labor is a master of coopting any and all shifts in culture. It is like a net that entangles society. Any struggle to relieve itself from the net through social change from grassroots movements result in simply being tangled tighter in the net. The reason for this is simple: as long as people are at the mercy of the ego and its materialist addiction, then all liberation movements will be interpreted as a bid for a greater share of material objects and as such will simply be gobbled up by the machine. Progressive challenges to the system that sought to reformulate the whole order of things were drained out of the labor movement early on so that in the end all that is asked for is simply a bigger share of the profits.[7] It wasn't long after the Beat poets and writers of the 1950's began their campaign against the stifling conformity of the era when "beatnik berets'" appeared for sale in the back of magazines and "Dobie Gillis," a television character, came on the scene portraying the Beat sensibility as a joke.

Everything gets turned into a harmless product to be purchased by the masses and consumed as simply another "style." All the depths of meaning where the power resides are lost to the surface in the materialist doctrine where only that which you can touch really exists. Rap music, in a more recent example, has been completely relieved of its ghetto rebellion heart and reduced to a commodity, like coffee beans or orange juice, to be invested in for speculative profit. When a rapper gets out of a Maserati or custom Bentley with a hundred-thousand dollars' worth of gold around his neck, everything he says after that is only a fiction, posture and form without true content. It's not that there is anything wrong with driving a Maserati. It's got to be a lot of fun, but in the context of questioning the tactics of the status-quo that created the conditions for the oppression from which the artist has emerged, it nullifies the whole rap by presenting material wealth as the target in life, thus reinforcing the status-quo, no matter what the artist intended. This ends in nailing down the impoverishment that the folks in the old neighborhood see all around them and by this, condemning them to the many addictive processes that guarantee their continued oppression. A better message for the poor is in pointing to the non-material core of the human spirit that needs no "thing" to lift itself up and demonstrate its success, which is its own value and its own source of strength. This isn't exclusively a religious attitude at all but is grounded in a greater empirical reality outside the mental/rational structure of consciousness beyond the mere stuff, the cars and jewelry, of the world.

The French Enlightenment philosopher, Jean Jacques Rousseau, articulating the rising spirit of his times, linked morality to a deep connection with the voice of nature within us. He saw the greatest source of joy and contentment as flowing from this personal nature of the individual, the locus of a genuine morality where a person could speak from a truly authentic voice that was essentially non-material in its ethic. Rousseau's name for the experience of this moral connection was, "le sentiment de l'existence;" meaning: *a feeling for life*, or just "being."[8] He saw this feeling as not contingent on anything else in either the approval of others or possessing anything in particular. He believed that pride in the attempt to impress others was what distracted people from this deeper joy for life. This was not simply a vision of personal fulfillment, but also the basis for a theory of morality that suggested people were most sensitive to the rights of others when in contact with this deep personal nature within themselves. Living from this deeper center was the basis of true freedom in Rousseau's thought, giving impetus to a liberation in values that stood in stark relief to the extravagant materialism of the aristocratic powers that tied their happiness to their lust for gold, a substance Voltaire referred to in the spirit of the times as "yellow mud." The conditions in France before the revolution gave people a good look at what happens when material things are valued above all else, an ethic that tends to lead to the concentration of wealth in fewer and fewer hands as the powerful prey on those below them to feed their passion while the suffering of the less fortunate is ignored.

A similar dynamic has been underway in the United States for some time now and if the trend continues to impoverish the many for the benefit of the few it may produce similar reactions in time. The hope is that Americans can move more swiftly into the conscious evolution that allows for this reevaluation of the role of material things in our lives and so reinvest in humanity. When we are experiencing "le sentiment de l'existence," when we are in a state of being in harmony with the love of life at its most basic, then we cannot but feel a sense of kinship with others that does not stand in the way of our own potential but rather forbids us from getting there on somebody else's back. The immature ego divides us with fear, jealousy, and avarice on our way to proving our superiority. What Rousseau came to see in examining the tendencies of the wealthy and aristocratic element, whose conduct led to the French Revolution, was that a person out of touch with this basic human core of life will fall victim to the despotism of "pride," a word that then encompassed much of what we now understand as the attributes of an immature ego.

"Greed is good," declared the arch capitalist villain, Gordon Gekko, in Oliver Stone's film, *Wall Street*, back in 1987, giving voice to a principal acknowledged by Adam Smith in more polite terms now with the cover ripped off. But greed is not the only thing that can drive a nation and a people to great economic accomplishment. Greed is the expression of an underdeveloped, out of balance, addicted ego and the victories it produces are fleeting and counter balanced by the damage that is its ever expanding byproduct. It is for us now to envision a glory based on a different way, one still emerging from human creativity and curiosity, one capable of producing great architecture and space flight, advances in medicine and social justice, capable of expanding the definitions of art and music and everything that makes life worth living, but one anchored in a deep humanity where all people share a common basic morality that springs not from a political ideology but from the simple experience of "being."

In being human we live within "horizons of significance," a term that points to the notion that everything people do is in relationship to social structures, history, and the environment at all its levels in economic and material forms that surround and inform the actions of any person in a dialogical manner. That is to say, we have an ongoing dialogue with the world around us in reacting to it in actions that cause effects it as it affects us. This world surrounds us always to a horizon that forms the edge of our awareness of what has been done. There is no possible way for a person to live in complete separation from the world. We are always part of a larger system of significance. To believe that we can live as if apart from this as if our decisions aren't in reference to this and in some way without effect is a delusion.[9] The tendency common in contemporary society to view personal actions in isolation from everything around them except the individual and their objects of obsession is sometimes seen as a result of the culture of personal fulfillment and authenticity, but as Charles Taylor in his work, *The Ethics of Authenticity*, points out, this is an erroneous notion. Taylor asserts that any attempt to express the unique attributes of the individual in pursuit of the authentic life is always in dialogue with these horizons of significance. This is always so because true authenticity creates works that are given meaning by their being situated within a field of values, structures and ideas that are the times in which the individual is living, i.e., their *society*. If the person produces something in belief they are expressing their authentic self without reference and respect for the world in which they are situated, then what they have done lacks significance to anyone but themselves and speaks not of a healthy human mind but of autism and narcissistic pathology. (Even the wild departures of Salvador Dali are in reference to the world and attempt to open a new view point.) The corporate executive who doesn't care who he has to stab in the back to move up the ladder, what damage the company is doing on its way to raising its stock value, or what negligence of his family this goal will require, believing he is "maximizing his potential" all the while, is practicing what Taylor calls a "deviant" form of authenticity. This superficial, egocentric view of authenticity has broken free of horizons of significance in that individuals act as though they are not embedded in a social, political and biological environment, but are simply free to act without reference or concern for anything outside their own needs. This is a type of social Darwinist view based on competition with the environment, rather than giving back to and seeking to improve the health of the social, political, biological environment that has given birth to the individual in the first place, an act that would benefit themselves as well as others. They act much like a virus that begins killing the host organism in a bid to replace the healthy system with one that favors their dominance. Unfortunately, viruses have no long term plan. If they cannot jump to a new healthy system to prey on they simply die when they succeed in killing the host organism. This is exactly what occurred in the financial crisis of 2008 when financial organizations set up a scheme that sought to cash in on defective investment products and then dump the eventual crash on the taxpayers. These criminal CEO's simply didn't care that they would sink their own firms as well, because they were guaranteed millions to continue doing what they were doing.[10] The head of the Federal Reserve at the time, the much lauded Alan Greenspan, stated before a congressional hearing that he had been completely taken by surprise by these actions, because he didn't believe that big players of this sort would actually do something that would endanger the long term health of the system for short term profits. This is the virus killing the host and what Greenspan didn't understand is that greed has no long term plan. It is a "slash and burn" operation and it simply moves on to another victim.

Deviant authenticity leads to a myopic view of one's life goals cut off from greater context, often ending up in decadent extremes in personal consumption and "achievement," where more and more is necessary to feed the ego dislodged from its natural matrix in a healthy social order. Disconnected from the basic human core of feeling for life that is where the unique character of the individual is actually anchored and from which it is expressed, the "deviant" reacts to this loss of feeling by reaching for greater levels of sensation in excessive sex, violence, drug and alcohol use and other extreme indulgences of the senses, that all too often seem to be the stuff of contemporary television and film, itself clear evidence of a numb society searching for stimulation. The most dangerous "stimulation" of all is the seeking of massive profits at any cost. It constitutes an act which moves from simple greed to evil in its devastating effect on all the lives that are run over in the process.

To return to the larger thesis of this work concerning the evolution of consciousness as it makes its way through the political landscape of rising and falling civilization, we can now connect the idea of bringing the center of life back to the "Self" or authentic deep character structure, with the next step in our collective psychological evolution in the "integral" stage we are now entering.

The evolution of consciousness is in part the story of the evolution of the ego, as the ego is the "awake," conscious, self-reflexive part of our minds, the part that is aware of ourselves as unique, separate beings. It is also the part that is free from instinct to the degree that it is awake and making conscious choices. As the evolution of consciousness has proceeded, besides adding new structures, it has concentrated more "consciousness" in the individual – what is simply a capacity for being awake and able to make creative decisions based on something besides base appetites, gross material fears and desires. As consciousness has intensified in individuals this greater creative capacity has been accompanied by a greater possibility of ego inflation. This leads some into demonstrations of grandiosity in response to the internal sense of expanding horizons, tempting them to exploit those around them on their way to maximum personal profits. The healthy alternative is for ego transformation wherein the individual realizes a higher calling for the ego's new found power. Rather than the "king of the hill" competition seen in the primitive ego, a mature response asks for a deep engagement with humanity that retains the unique creative features of the intensified individuated consciousness, but now in a complete fealty with the entire social order. So, rather than a pulling away and setting oneself up in a special category to be worshiped on a pedestal, *as someone separate*, which is the goal of "conspicuous consumption," individuals remain fully integrated members of the human tribe, even while demonstrating their special talents. This leads to an economic condition where no one is left out, where those in a position to make more money do so within an ethos that requires the health of all sectors of society. The most talented in the system may make more money, as they should, but not as much as they would through the more ruthless form of capitalism that abandons whole sectors of the population in the name of free market flexibility. Changes have to be made as systems evolve but the new ethic does this with responsibility toward those affected. The *slash and burn* form of economy is only necessary for accruing the extravagant personal wealth and empire building required by the primitive ego. The extra money made through the ruthless pursuit of profits is not required by the evolved ego consciousness, because those having achieved the higher view receive their greatest reward through non-material pleasures – the thrill of working through hard problems and finding creative solutions as a team for the benefit of humanity and the health of the entire biosphere and its myriad life forms. This has got to provide an incredible sense of beauty and "Le sentiment de l'existence," for sure. This is not "pie in the sky" humanitarianism, It is simply a recognition that all fates are tied together in a world we now know to be integrated in a massive planet wide system of ecological, and so economic, health. To deny this and continue to persue profits at the expense of the health of the system at this point in the history of the world has got to be symptomatic of a special form of suicidal narcissism.

When a people are living in harmony with their authentic character, they feel deeply alive. They feel like they're right where they're supposed to be without concern for ego rewards. It is simply a feeling of joy for life that is flowing from taking part in an effort that has meaning stemming from its context in a world where their actions are constructive in a bonded society, where they actually care about the destiny of their society and the ecosystem they inhabit. In touch with their humanity, a person will have their higher ego needs met when creating prosperity for all, rather than a select few. Not that everyone ends up with the same thing but everyone is respected.

The fear that population growth always stands in the way of such humanitarian schemes has been proven wrong time and time again. When prosperity and education rise, birth rates decline rather than explode. (This was a theme in early economic theory, that a rising poor would overwhelm the resources of society with an army of hungry mouths, but such fears have never materialized.)

As individuals begin to question the contents of contemporary life in consumer societies and wonder what their lives are really for, they turn back in contemplation to the core of their own beings. There they find a need to simply be without concern for what they own or what they have achieved, but simply a desire to take part in activities and relationships that offer a sense of rightness in the moment, a sense that life is not something to be earned in the future, put off for vacation or retirement, but can be found in the moment, now. The key comes from finding that lasting happiness and contentment don't flow from material things and personal achievements of power but flow from the actualization of an attitude toward existence that penetrates the surface to find a balance point between where you've been and where you're going, in an ultra-alive sense of being. This is a personal puzzle that leads back to the base of humanity within the individual. There a person discovers not only the basis of their own unique spirit but their connection with the human spirit and with this a flow of pure Life. This is not a route to selfishness, because at that depth self and other are finally recognized to be part of a single thing. From this position flows an abiding empathy for the whole system and all the players in it.

The integral stage in thinking often starts with this search for meaning and the authentic self and leads inexorably to the core of humanity. Without this foundation development will be guided by the unrelenting fears and desires of the primitive ego and will lead the person further along the path of material addiction with all its false promises. One cannot find one's true character apart from one's true humanity and one cannot find the basis of integral development apart from either their humanity or their true self. These aspects are all part of one thing; an individuality in communion with the whole. Without this conjunction of true, or authentic self, and humanity there is no basis for integral growth. Without this basis growth becomes deviant or stalls completely.

Integral awareness leads to a reevaluation of one's own ego. In returning to one's humanity the primitive ego becomes dislodged from its place at the center of control and its urgings for competition and constant pampering are recognized as a path that leads nowhere. That which now sees the fearful and complaining ego as if a separate voice is the Self, as Carl Jung put it. Once a person begins to find this place at the center of the psyche, what has been called the "observer" is born. It is the observing self that sits a bit higher on the mountain to look down on and thereby see clearly from this new vantage point the strategies of the primitive ego that once gripped the mind and held sway over actions without the individual being aware they were being run by a set of ideas that manipulated base appetites.

It is the rein of the egocentric materialist that has driven the economy and the technological order and it is here to which we will turn next.

Notes

1. Tim Kasser, The High Price of Materialism (Cambridge: MIT Press, 2002). Robert E. Lane, The Loss of Happiness in Market Democracies (New Haven: Yale University Press, 2000).

2. David Riesman, Nathan Glazer, & Reuel Denney, The Lonely Crowd (New Haven: Yale University Press, 1950, 2001).

3. Bruce H. Lipton & Steve Bhaerman, Spontaneous Evolution, Our Positive Future (New York: Hay House, 2009).
4. Joseph Campbell, Oriental Mythology, The Masks of God (New York: Penguin, 1984), p. 139.
5. Gerard Jones, Killing Monsters, Why Children Need Fantasy, Super Heroes, and Make-Believe Violence (New York: Basic Books, 2002).
6. Gabriel (1988).
7. Priscilla Murolo & A. B. Chitty, From the Folks Who Brought You the Weekend (New York: The New Press, 2001).
8. Jean-Jacques Rousseau, Reveries of the Solitary Walker (New York: Oxford, 1778, 2011). As discovered in Taylor, below.
9. Charles Taylor, The Ethics of Authenticity (Cambridge: Harvard University Press, 1991).
10. Ferguson (2013).

Chapter 4

The Civilization of Side Effects

When we hear the term "side effects" we think of those drug ads where the list of all the terrible things that can happen to you from taking the new wonder drug go on and on, including everything from bleeding from every orifice to *death*. Because the pharmaceutical companies are required by law to disclose the *unintended* effects of any advertised product along with the intended benefits, they usually tag them on the end of the ad, after you've firmly made the connection between the smiling people enjoying their renewed lives and the drug they are suggesting made them new. The negative possibilities are thrown at you all at once in a rush of words that sound as though they taste bad in the announcer's mouth and he is trying desperately to get them out as quickly as he can. The hope is that you will pay no attention to the spewing language and keep your thoughts on the smiling people leaping through the meadow grass, but a part of your mind registers the dissonance between the two, "*Did he say, bleeding?*" And you are left with a subtle but ominous feeling of something lurking in the tall grass behind the smiling family, "*Did he say, death?*" It makes some of us laugh. So many possible negative effects, why would anyone submit themselves to such a gamble?

The answer is simple: those sick and tired of suffering from some malady that has restricted their lives to a sometimes bleak and narrow path are willing to attach their hope to the smiling faces and brush aside the warnings for a chance at being right again. So they do just as the ad instructs. They ask their doctor. In fact, in an article in the *Yale Journal of Medicine and Law* in October of 2010[1] it was reported that some ten million Americans a year requested drugs they had seen advertised and some 80 percent were given those drugs by their doctors. Negative reactions to pharmaceuticals now stand as one of the leading causes of death in the United States. Some 100,000 Americans die each year from "properly" prescribed drugs, killed by the very "medicine" that was meant to help them. Many new drugs have been revealed to have little to no real positive effect on patients. The real tragedy is that most of the maladies being treated by the never ending parade of drugs that have marched across the pages of magazines and the television screen in the last few decades are simply the result of living the typical Western life style.[2]

It is a simple fact that we've known for a long time now that our diet, heavy in refined starches and sugars, low on fresh fruits and vegetables, chock full of artery clogging dairy products, thick with meats raised at lightning speed with the aid of hormones, steroids, and antibiotics, often preserved with carcinogenic chemicals, produces over time a vast array of debilitating conditions that worsen with age. When people move from so called "third world" areas where little of these modern methods are used and where they eat what's grown and raised in the area the old fashioned way, to so called "first world" areas where the modern diet is thrust upon them, these people will often become sick until their systems adjust to the change. When they do adjust, the change leads to a high incidence of obesity, heart disease, and diabetes. There is a name for this malady. It is called "metabolic syndrome" and it is simply what happens to the human body when it stops eating food and starts eating processed "food stuffs." The intention is to eat something that tastes good and doesn't take a lot of work to prepare, but just as with the many new drugs there are a few "side effects" that come along with the instant gratification of the modern Western diet.

The food business itself is an area where the side effects should be most clear to even the passing glance. The obesity problem in America is in large part a direct result of the calorie rich, nutrition poor "super sizing" of fast food places that have exploded in numbers across the landscape of America in recent decades. Due to economies of scale the "food" served is often cheaper than buying food at a grocery store and so, as the economy has worsened, purveyors of fast food have experienced a boom. This, combined with the explosion of processed food products in the grocery stores, frozen and boxed, that are also questionable in their nutritional content and very calorie heavy, produce more obesity and less good health. Water has been replaced at many dining tables across the country with soft drinks purchased at a discount in liter bottles. Being overweight and without proper nutrition the human immune system runs at a less than optimum level and so colds and flus become more common. Another troubling side effect following the American diet is the rise in cancer. The American Institute for Cancer research reported in January of 2011 that America now had the seventh highest rate of cancer in the world. They attributed the rise in cancer rates in the U.S. and other wealthy nations, who form the top of the list, to the rise in obesity, sedentary lifestyles, and higher alcohol use. The truth is that the United States would be at the top of the list if it had the kind of health care systems the European countries do allowing for the same accuracy in reporting. Poorer nations seem to have a healthier diet with less processed and fast foods and more exercise, but as poorer nations have "developed" and Western foods have poured into their countries the cancer rates have begun to climb there, as well.

The way farm animals are raised has also changed as industrialized methods have created giant machines out of what should be natural processes. Factory farms for chicken, pigs, and cattle where animals are dosed with growth hormone and packed into small spaces has the side effect of rising infection levels that are treated with ever rising amounts of antibiotics. This not only has created an ethical issue in the way animals are treated but also has produced an inferior product that carries hormones and antibiotics into human bodies. Studies have shown that higher levels of these drugs present in the human system have contributed to the rise of mutant, antibiotic resistant strains of infectious organisms. Higher hormone levels in milk have been associated with the early onset of puberty in girls sometimes as young as eight years old. Inappropriate levels of hormone are also associated with the accelerated growth of cancers.

It's not just food and drugs, of course. "Side effects" are everywhere. They're in the air we breathe, which contains 112 various elements bad for the human body provided by the burning of fossil fuels and industrial processes. The water we drink contains not only a long list of common contaminants including heavy metals but also a good dose of elements intentionally added for your consumption – specifically chlorine added to kill biological contaminants, but also known to break down the cell wall in human bodies. If you're unlucky enough to live in a community that puts fluoride in their water supply then you are getting an additional dose of a known cancer causing chemical, because the conventional but erroneous wisdom is that it will prevent tooth decay. Even the carpets and the lawns we walk on produce side effects in the form of poisonous gasses emitted from synthetic fibers and from pesticides and fertilizers absorbed through the skin and leaching into creeks and rivers eradicating microorganisms and choking out fish with blooms of oxygen sucking algae.

The economic system is so full of side effects that it periodically breaks down from all the unintended consequences of a system built to make money from speculation without production, a deficit creation machine built for the benefit of the few whose side effects are mounting like a great storm threatening to pound us into the ground from a great hail of economic side effects now gathering over our heads. The narrow approach to global markets now underway has resulted in nearly a third of the U.S. population being chronically underemployed so that they don't show up on the unemployed statistics, but never make enough money to meet their financial necessities and so fall farther and farther into debt each year, as industry and the government claim single digit unemployment.[3]

The legal system has deteriorated in the U.S. as corporate power has found new ways to subvert justice through manipulating the system where the most money, more often than not, wins. We have, in essence, a two tier legal system: one for the wealthy where the law is set aside and one for the rest of us where the full weight of the law is applied.[4] This should be obvious even to the most stalwart conservative from the way the 2008 financial meltdown was handled. Although easily proven fraud was widespread, not one criminal prosecution has been filed by the federal government to date.[5] The U.S. is the only place in the world, including totalitarian dictatorships, where building prisons is a growth industry. In America's zeal for "law and order" and the old time view of punishment for crime as an "eye for an eye" the side effect has been a runaway criminal justice system that has been coopted by industry and turned into a political interest group, itself, who backs tougher and tougher sentencing guidelines that take judgment away from judges and guarantees high rates of incarceration. This leads to higher taxes and more criminals in the end who might have been rehabilitated if sent to treatment programs. American legal systems are seen as draconian by foreign observers who find our system creates more problems than it solves. This is a classic example of how the drive toward "privatization" in transferring government responsibilities to commercial interests has created cascading side effects throughout our society, all stemming from services being run for the purpose of making money rather than performing the task for the highest good most ethically.

Most people don't worry about it. Everything has a down side, we think. You've got to take the bad with the good. We are so used to the situation that we stopped questioning some time ago, even though the cancer rates continue to rise, new diseases and syndromes appear regularly, the economy is fracturing, and even the Earth itself seems to be sick. Without even getting into the climate change issue, which, man-made, or man worsened, threatens to cause cataclysmic damage to our civilization, it should be obvious that the Earth is suffering from its own "metabolic syndrome" with massive species dying off on land and in the ocean where extinctions go on weekly. North Atlantic Cod fisheries have collapsed and with it whole industries and food supplies. There is a veritable caldron of plastic soup in the North Pacific ocean, a sea of garbage and chemical sludge held together by currents, that is larger than the continental United States and an massive algae bloom seven times the size of the state of Rode Island in the gulf of Mexico from the agricultural chemicals flowing down the Mississippi river that has created a total dead zone where nothing can survive. Deforestation in the Amazon basin is actually lowering the oxygen level on the entire planet.

This is just a small selection of the side effects produced by our current civilization. Many more could be listed for many hundreds of pages but I hope the point has been made. What we desperately need to acknowledge here is not every area were side effects are taking place but why they are so abundant in the first place and what possibilities exist for creating a civilization without them. Like everything else in our lives it is our consciousness that produces our way of life, the problems and questions we face, and the answers we can muster to address them. There is a well-worn quote from Albert Einstein that says, "No problem can be solved from the same level of consciousness that created it." If there was ever a time to heed this advice, I think we're there.

When we look for the roots of where we began to create the civilization of side effects we first find ourselves with the opening of the mental/rational structure of consciousness in the 6th century BCE with the Greeks. It was here that philosophers, looking at earthly existence with new eyes no longer constrained by mythological stories, struck on the idea that everything must be made of some universal substance, some basic unit of matter. This is where the term "atom" was born, which simply meant "un-cuttable," implying that this is the first piece that is not made from any smaller pieces, but is itself the indivisible thing that all objects on earth are built up from. This idea that the route to understanding lay in looking inside things to their beginnings was a major feature of the new way of understanding the world that was the early mental/rational mind.

It is an application of both materialism, which points to the main object of the mental structure, and a reductive reasoning that is an application of the new experience of time that the mental/rational structure brought to human consideration. Time had previously been thought of as simply an eternal "now" within the magical consciousness, and an ever repeating cycle, as in the seasons, within the mythological structure. At the opening of the mental/rational consciousness time was reconsidered to be demonstrated by a never repeating series of events beyond the eternal round of the seasons; this greater march of moments flew like an arrow straight into the future.

It's hard for us to imagine how revolutionary the idea of the "future" was to people who were previously convinced that everything went around in circles. The idea that tomorrow could hold something essentially different than what had gone on the same time last year with the usual observances and festivals was absolutely mind blowing. When the future was born at the opening of the mental/rational stage it was simply a matter of logic that if you wanted to understand how something came about you would simply look at what was happening before and so gave rise to it. This reasoning led backward through time to what was thought to be seminal events – what started it all. This was the impetus for the search for atoms that reappeared when the mental/rational structure came into its prime during the 17th century with the scientific revolution.

With this notion of "linear causality," one thing leading to another and literally "caused" by the thing preceding in time, came the method codified by Galileo and Descartes that would become the general operating procedure of science as a whole: reductive analysis. Reductionism, as the philosophical tradition would dub it, became the way science is done. It is an approach to understanding that once wed to Descartes' vision of "life as machine," led directly to our civilization of side effects. Nature is like a multifaceted gem and the more our minds expand and grow the more of the facets we are able to discern. Our science started by allowing the expanding mind to take a good look at Nature and analyze processes with their newly realized "clock-work" mind set and ended up believing the whole of Nature could be described by this tiny facet alone. So a legion of scientists followed looking to uncover all the wheels and cranks they could find. Galileo had rolled some wooden balls down a plank and gave birth to the notion that such things as their path and destination could be determined by formula. Newton got a hold of this and gave us the three laws of motion and universal gravitation. From this a clever Frenchman by the name of Pierre Simon Laplace generalized Newton's laws to the entire world and everything that has gone on since creation. He hypothesized that if some great intelligence could determine the position of all particles in the universe that the entire past and future, of everything that has gone on and will ever go on, could be calculated and known. He famously replied to the Emperor Napoleon, when asked what place God had in his calculations, that he "had no need of that hypothesis." Napoleon might well have asked if there was a place for anyone to make a decision in his system; Laplace would have told him, no. This is where reductionism turns into determinism and free will goes right out the cosmic window. Descartes saw this coming and tried to save free will and the individual spirit by separating mind and body so that the body could be subject to all the mechanical laws while the mind remained the domain of spirit – "I think, therefore I am." This, probably the most repeated philosophical dictum of the Western tradition is generally ignored by traditional science that replies: You think therefore you are an arrangement of chemical reactions and electrical neuro-synaptic activity that is the result of genetic programming based on Darwinian evolutionary imperatives under which lie – let's just skip to the bottom line – *spinning particles.*

But in Descartes' day God was still given a place in creation as the one winding up all the toys he had made. All animals and humanity itself were modeled on the crude machines that were common in the era of early science: everything from hydraulic mechanisms in elaborate fountains, to cuckoo clocks seemed to give hints as to how God had set the world in motion. Descartes hypothesized that animals were simply "automata," just complicated wind-up toys that had no spirit or anything approaching the mind of man that would give them a status of anything greater than a windmill. Although human beings were given special status in this system as God's chosen creatures, it wasn't long before this dispensation was disputed as an antiquated remnant of an outmoded theology and humanity too joined the animals as simply fancy machines without soul or purpose.

Purpose was one of the main victims of the new reductionism. Humanity or the world couldn't possibly have any purpose, because that would imply that the earth and its creatures was created with some goal in mind and this smacked a bit too much of religious mythology for a scientific mind fresh from the battles with Popes and Pastors and their rationally insupportable edicts and mystical explanations. The world was all about what was happening from the bottom up. This was what the mental/rational mind could clearly wrap its attention around. No faith in invisible forces was necessary; the truth could be found right under our noses. As pointed our in Chapter 3, that truth started with elementary particles and ended with elementary biological processes that motivate hunger for food and sex and survival with genes and proteins as the captains of existence at the bottom of it all. Everything thereafter has been scientifically judged to be simply the logical outcome of those underlying activities, all the products of civilization, art and science and all human aspiration, simply the meaningless fireworks whose fuse is lit in the dark biological recesses deep inside of everything and at the primordial beginnings of the earth and beyond.

It's the "beyond" part that's got materialist science stumped. because it basically implies that everything came from nothing in the "Big Bang," just as we see the same phenomenon in miniature at the "Plank length" where particles get so small that they pass over into nothingness. That just shouldn't happen in a totally material world, but it does. The irony is that reductionism in its search for the smallest things ends up defeating materialism which forms the ground of reason for reductionism itself. "Oh, well, to be explained later," say the determined reductionists ever dedicated to their cause and with good reason regardless of the "big invisible" that seems to be lurking all around them.

The reality is that reductionism and materialist mechanistic science keep going strong, because it produces results. One result it produces is all around us in everything from kitchen appliances, to cell phones, to the pain killers in the medicine cabinet; it is this worldview that has produced so much that it produces as well the civilization of side effects. Early scientists focused their investigations of the world on the only thing they had readily at hand – material objects. Where Medieval thinkers had based their conception of the world on speculations guided by the deductive reasoning methods of Aristotle – that could produce such seemingly absurd "facts" as how many angels could dance on the head of a pin, or such stunning errors, as the deduction that since bees are seen emerging from flowers so often it must be the flowers that are creating the bees – early science decided the only sure method was to come at things from the other end using inductive reasoning. Thus, one could look at what comes before that leads to an outcome, rather than looking at the outcome and reasoning what came before. It wasn't as if this was the first time Europeans had used such a method. The Greeks after all had flirted with the idea and it must have been the basis of much of the early machine making of the Romans and after, but in the scientific revolution the idea, through the urgings of Francis Bacon in England and Rene Descartes in France became the premier approach of research and development and remains so to this day.

This whole approach became so ingrained in scientific thought that to question it has been considered a heresy. Despite this a constant stream of objections has arisen, in large part from biologists who have had a hard time finding the link from the dry business of spinning particles to the wet and wild world of biological processes. How do you get there from here? "But if all the explanatory arrows point downward," argues a prominent biologist, "it is something of a quiet scandal that physicists have largely given up trying to reason "upward" from the ultimate physical laws to larger-scale events in the universe. Those downward-pointing explanatory arrows should yield a crop of upward-pointing deductive arrows. Where are they?"[6]

Physicists are completely unable to deduce how particles of any kind "create" higher forms or explain even rudimentary phenomena like the behavior of a liquid. While physics claims to be the basis of everything it has remained totally unable to determine exactly how. You simply can't read the more complex within the less complex, water is an emergent quality whose manifestation is the result of the creation of the right platform for its existence, but water is not to be found in either of its elements, hydrogen or oxygen, nor is either if its elements to be found in spinning particles. The wetness of water, the quality of its unique being in the world, is very real and not at all to be discerned from any quality in hydrogen or oxygen. You can look for it for the rest of eternity and never find it. This is the "unacceptable" reality that mainstream science has yet to come to terms with. Regardless, it is an argument that is made by Nobel Laureate physicist, Robert Laughlin, who has pointed out that particles have no qualities as single entities but only in groups. A single particle of iron, for instance, has no rigidity but only in large groups does the quality we associate with iron emerge in an iron bar. Rigidity is an emergent phenomenon that does not exist within a single iron atom. For this reason, he believes that reductionism alone is inadequate to describe what is going on in the world of physics. Laughlin is not alone. There are a growing number of physicists beginning to doubt reductionism as a stand-alone explanation, including a number of other Nobel laureates.[7]

Stuart Kauffman, a professor of biology and one of the key figures in the burgeoning field of complexity theory, a new understanding of Nature that avoids reductionist errors, has pointed out strenuously and with convincing logic that evolutionary adaptations can never be reduced to the activity of particles, pointing to "agency" as an early emergent factor in living systems and, "the selective historical conditions in the actual evolution of organisms..." as the only way to explain the appearance of new adaptations. Kauffman shows that there are decisions being made at the biological level that cannot be traced to any underlying physics; the agency, that is active volition, that biology creates can't be found in particles. He also points out that recent research into the origin of life on earth has demonstrated the existence of "autocatalytic systems" where the chemical parts are guided and constrained by the overall organization of the whole.[8] Again, it is the "emergent" element that is important in understanding what's driving the thing; like people, even primitive chemical systems, we are coming to realize, are more than the sum of their parts.

Stuart Kauffman goes on to state: "These limitations on reductionism are terribly important for they imply that emergence is real. Biology is really not just physics. Nor are organisms nothing but physics. Organisms are parts of the furniture of the universe, with causal powers of their own that change the actual physical evolution of the universe. Biology is emergent with respect to physics. Life, agency, value, meaning and consciousness have all emerged in the evolution of the biosphere..."[9]

When Kauffman says, "...with causal powers of their own..." he is perpetrating a major revolution in science. He is pointing to the undeniable evidence that says that we, the people, have power of true choice, and are not just the determined outcome of primary processes. Emergence implies a new order of existence that is determined by its own structures and prerogatives; it contains the past but subsumes it into a greater order. With the rise of consciousness, each succeeding intensification leads to a broader understanding and greater choice. The idea that Nature is put together in these chain reactions from remote beginnings that translate from one structure to the next directly, as in – biology equals physics in different terms – turns out to be absolutely, dead wrong. This begs the question: if something new is going on at each level of evolution, if not seeded within the original forces that govern matter, then where is that new thing coming from? The obvious answer is that there has to be nonmaterial forces contributing to existence.

The big problem with looking at the world in this simple, linear causal fashion, where one condition leads to a single effect, like a line of dominoes falling over, is that when humans try to replicate this erroneous, simplistic vision of Nature in their technologies, although it certainly works well in creating an intended effect, it also creates along with that desired outcome a whole host of unintended and often undesired effects. The reason for this is simple: the world is not built on singular causal chains. It is not made up of single, isolated rows of dominoes falling along their own separate lines of effect. On the contrary, the world is made up of complex interactions woven into a broad fabric of interlocking effects, like a web – when one thread is touched the whole structure shakes. All the interconnected lines from the point that is being manipulated then send out their own chains of effect and so out of a single cause a myriad of changes follows. This is what an ecosystem is and ecosystems are not just what the animals and insects live in. The whole world is nothing but ecosystems, inside and outside, within your body and all around you every day – layered and interlocking systems of shared effects.

This is exactly why those crazy drug ads on television go on and on about the other things besides relief a user might "experience" when taking the new drug, like intestinal bleeding or *heart failure*. It is simply because the pharmaceutical researchers isolated a chemical reaction in the body that is a major antecedent to the symptom they were trying to remove through a simple causal chain of effect and they created a chemical compound – a drug – that would knock over those dominoes from the underlying reaction to its consequence – the target symptom. Of course, they also know very well they are going to knock over all the other chains of dominoes standing next to the one they're after, but because the problem is so complex in trying to avoid unintended reactions it lengthens the research time indefinitely. At some point they make an economic decision to simply live with the side effects while hoping they won't kill or injure so many people that it renders the drug unprofitable.

Now, if you understand that the ecosystems of the earth are much like the human body in their interlocking subsystems of growth, decay, and renewal, then you can see quite easily that when we pour carbon into the atmosphere, or kill off certain species, or remove entire forests, it is going to start knocking over dominoes. As those myriad lines of dominoes start falling we come to experience the side effects of our actions, sooner or later. We may have just intended to produce electricity, or transportation, or we maybe just wanted to make our livestock less vulnerable by killing off all the predators, or we just wanted to harvest enough wood to build new neighborhoods, but what happens when these actions grow to major proportions is that we initiate major changes to the system we live within. Without intending it we have created side effects that, just like drugs in the body, can end up being injurious and even deadly.

The "dust bowl" effect of 1930's America is a perfect example. Settlers moved into areas of the Mid-Western plains that were covered with prairie grass, or "sod." This thick layer of interwoven fibrous grass penetrated the soil for up to a foot having evolved to suit the particular conditions of those dry and open rejoins. The settlers, "sod busters" they came to be called, began digging up the sod in order to reveal the soil beneath so they could plant crops. What they didn't know was that the rejoin in which they had chosen to make their new homes was prone to long dry spells and high winds. When they moved in the area happened to be experiencing unusual rain fall and mild weather, but it wasn't long before the sun and the wind returned with a vengeance and the crops failed and the exposed top soil began to blow away. When the rain did come, it came like a hammer, pounding whatever delicate seedlings would grow into the earth. In the end, the would-be farmers were left with an untillable desert, learning too late that Nature doesn't make mistakes. There was a reason something as tough as prairie grass was all that was there before they came.

Some of those sod busters ended up dying right there, thrashing at the dead dirt in stubborn determination to grow enough to eat, killed not by the long vanquished Indians, but by the plains themselves. Many others ended up destitute and moved West to take jobs as migrant farm laborers immortalized by John Steinbeck in his classic *The Grapes of Wrath*. If the

Native American tribal people of the area had been consulted they would have been able to tell the settlers a few things about surviving in that rejoin but, of course, the buffalo had been destroyed and then even the ground itself had been rendered lifeless, so nothing could be done once the dominoes began to fall.

This is one example out of countless others of how things can go terribly wrong when systems are disrupted. It certainly isn't that we can't change things. Many areas of the world have been altered to agriculture to great advantage, but over time as those changes expand effects begin to multiply sometimes with other than local consequences. If the settlers had understood the ecosystem they were moving into and attempted to fit into it instead of trying to force the land to do something it wasn't suited for they might have survived.

This is the tragic tendency of modern humanity, this desire to dominate nature instead of working with it. In early stages of altering the landscape it often looks as though it all works fine but there is always a point at which alterations can go too far. We have decimated the great forests of North America and the world goes on, but if the same is done to South America as well, as is underway this minute, then, as scientists of wide expertise tell us, we will have killed the "lungs of the world," and tremendous consequences will be suffered. We have every reason to believe that there is a limit to how much you can alter the major ecosystems of a planet before it simply doesn't operate in a manner that continues to support human life. The civilization of side effects has grown in its ability to make changes in our bodies and in the body of the world and those changes are degrading much of life everywhere. Ecosystems we depend on all over the planet are showing tremendous stress and the human body itself is carrying a toxic load so burdensome, so laden with heavy metals, chemicals from plastics, preservatives, insecticides – it's a long list – that it's no wonder new diseases and syndromes are popping up regularly. The masses in the middle class and above don't notice it so much. Industry keeps the news regarding toxins to a minimum. Otherwise, the people hear just an occasional news story about polar bears or some frog in a jungle far away. With our climate controlled homes and man-made gardens pumped up with chemical fertilizers we look at the blue sky and can't see the fractures spreading faster and faster all around us. This is the descent that is noticed only too late in historical examples of civilizations that have risen and fallen, having brought on their own demise through continuing bad decisions, unable to see their old ways were slowly killing them they ran themselves into a wall.

The wall we're headed for has been created for us by the limits of the current stage in the evolution of our consciousness, what we have been calling the mental/rational structure that saw its first glimmers in the ancient Greeks circa 500 BCE and came fully into its own as the dominant worldview during the Enlightenment period of the 17th Century. A way of seeing things that has been structured by the mechanical philosophies of Sir Isaac Newton, following Galileo, and the French philosopher and mathematician, Rene Descartes, who said it all with his vision of the universe as a great, big clock, all gears and levers and simple linear causality marching forward through time in singular isolated lines of cause and effect. Neither of these great philosopher mathematicians, who are indeed towering figures in Western civilization with due honors, were able to foresee the civilization of side effects they were initiating. How could they? The perspective they had developed, that set its sights for the first time firmly on the material world alone, could not comprehend all the structures that connected everything in the world in multi-dimensional webs of interaction and exchange. This was the beginning of science, let us not forget. It was enough that they figured out how amazing things could be done with simple mechanical reasoning. This was a monumental step forward. Unfortunately, those who have come after in league with industry have enshrined the Newtonian/Cartesian philosophy and its methods as constituting a final perfection and so have continued to plunge us, now neck deep, into the civilization of side effects even as the vanguard of science left them behind.

This dynamic seems to hold true for any system, far beyond biology, such as economics and the social environment; the connectedness of the world permeates even the systems we create. For instance, when steel became cheaper overseas, the auto industry and others started buying it from the Japanese and this quite quickly decimated the American steel industry of the North East. There is a geographic swath across this region now referred as the "rust belt," due to all the rusting closed steel mills that stand as monuments to the side effect of unrestrained capitalism. The economic devastation of the area has reverberated through the social fabric to create ghost towns where only the retired and welfare families remain, and boarded up downtowns with weeds growing through the untended asphalt. When drastic economic shifts happen like this and people fall into sudden poverty the condition is always accompanied by a rise in family violence, drug and alcohol abuse, and petty criminality; children's lives are disrupted in sometimes brutal ways that send further reverberations through generations yet to come. Often the only viable moneymaker these days is in the manufacture and sale of methamphetamine, a chemical that preys on the destitution of the weak in creating an artificial but instant elation. The side effects will go on for lifetimes all due to the simple desire to increase a profit margin and the total ignorance as to everything that decision was connected to. Because we've been trained by the Newtonian/Cartesian vision to see our actions as only connected to one single line of cause and effect – a massive myopic error – we feel completely justified in suggesting that, as in the above example, the lack of government set tariffs on steel was only responsible for allowing American manufacturers to make more money and compete more successfully. All the other effects that followed are the responsibility of others. Those people should have shut down those towns with the mills, moved elsewhere to find jobs and continued prosperous lives. The fact that a percentage sank into poverty, drug abuse, and violence is entirely their fault.

Where these theoretical jobs are supposed to be we do not know but, regardless, there is some truth to this indictment, of course. Yet, the greater truth is that the move suggested above may look easy on paper, but is extremely difficult on the ground, ground that generations of ancestors are buried in, ground that is the beloved homeland of people who have lived in the rejoin since the founding of the nation. People are connected to the land in yet another of the invisible connections that are denied by the narrow logic of our time. Those people lived in an economic ecosystem and the organism that provided the food supply was killed off without concern for the consequences. There are always consequences in a continuum of connections.

Now, the truth is that it was the ancestors of these very steel workers who originally disrupted the local economy and ecology in displacing the Native American populations from the area, cutting down whole forests and eventually building steel plants that burned coal in their smelters, polluted the area and carried clouds of acid rain to weaken forests sometimes far north of the rejoin.

It is true that human migrations and activities have always disrupted ecosystems and set off chain reactions on many levels of connection –

social, ecological, and more – but as time has gone on humanity has advanced in its methods so that what used to take centuries now takes a few years. What used to take years is now accomplished in a day. When the country was sparsely populated a few trees and a steel smelter or two had little effect on larger systems, but with the increase in population and the scale of our methods we have now reached levels of effect that are catastrophic in magnitude. Maybe those steel mills needed to shut down or change their ways. They might have been converted to some cleaner industry, but it is undeniable that a direct line exists between the damage done to real human beings and the sudden withdrawal of the people's livelihood through the abandoning of American steel by industry and the government. Both were part of a system of shared profit, a kind of blood supply, and one died when the other decided to increase its profit at the expense of its former partner. The problem with this kind of selfish economic maneuver is that it is a little like a person taking blood away from one part of their body so as to increase the muscles of another part of their body. Over time the part deprived of blood will wither and die, causing rot and infection that affects the health of the whole body. This reality escapes the CEO's who believe they have no responsibility whatsoever with any other industry or social condition and the stock exchange certainly encourages this perspective, listing as it does each industry as a separate line of growth or loss. Regardless, the cost to the families that don't make it out of the failing towns, that add to the misery of generations, to the crime and drug abuse that spills over onto others, that spur the growth of gated communities and security systems to keep the abandoned and destitute away from the "winners," results in a kind of "rot" that begins to sicken the body of the whole country. This is the socio-economic side effect that is denied in the calculus of free market capitalism. Everyone is connected; there is no escaping this reality.

The activities of the pharmaceutical industry offer a poignant example of this inescapable interconnectivity. In responding to changes in the general economic and business climate in the early 1990's drug companies began to conceive of ways to expand their profits so as to create better positions for their companies on the stock market. They began to do a number of things differently, generally shifting capital from research and development to marketing. One big change was to begin aggressively advertising drugs while actively seeking to control what would be written about their new products in medical journals. The drug testing trials that would tell the companies whether their product was working as expected had formerly been carried out by university laboratories. In the new era the drug companies would begin to heavily influence those trials by funding universities and even paying doctors directly with huge personal stipends. Through this influence they began to shape the research in such a manner as to inevitably find the drug in question a fabulous success. Then, through understanding that it was doctors in the community that ultimately would have to prescribe their products, the drug companies began aggressive campaigns to gain control of the process of educating physicians. They accomplished this in two major ways. First, they offered high style dinners and luxury vacations for the doctors and their families at resorts where they would be literally paid to listen to a sales pitch disguised as education. Second, at the university level itself, where through major grants to institutions they coerced their way into the class room where young doctors in training could be presented with material provided by the drug companies themselves, in some cases by a direct representative of a particular pharmaceutical company.

The other technique that greatly increased drug company revenues was the strategy of creating diseases. Drug company doctors would scour the medical literature for opportunities to create diseases that did not exist, things like "pre-diabetes" and "restless leg syndrome." By creating their own disease they could have exclusive rights to the only treatment, at least until other companies jumped on. They also began to look for ways to expand their markets into the huge population of children and saw the *Diagnostic Statistical Manual of Mental Disorders* as a great place to start their work. Pharmaceutical industry advocates, essentially doctors working for the companies, began to stress bogus research that indicated that children were widely suffering from what they termed a "chemical imbalance," that provoked hyperactivity and an inability to concentrate in school, taking a basic childhood tendency, especially among boys, and turning it into a brain disease. The chemical imbalance scheme worked so well they expanded it into a catchall explanation for a number of mental disorders so as to promote a greater use of their products over psychotherapy. The fact that medical research had never been able to prove that a chemical imbalance was at all implicated in psychological disorders did not matter. The drug companies simply publicized their products as if they had and hired high profile doctors at places like Harvard to back the idea.[10]

Suddenly, anyone suffering from the slightest sadness brought on by the normal ups and downs of life was being told they needed medication for depression, which the doctors, usually general practitioners not trained in psychiatry, were telling their patients was now known to be a chemical problem easily controlled by new medications. Drug company influence, with its incredible financial power, utilizing a combination of bribery, manipulation, and by controlling university research and training as part of their development strategies, had steered the entire medical institution toward conclusions regarding a wide range of symptoms that allowed them to sell more pills – many, many more pills. Between the early 1990's and the year 2000 prescriptions for drugs in the U.S. exploded. According to the CDC at this time half of all Americans are taking a prescription drug, mostly to counteract the effects of bad diet and lack of exercise. A study in 2004 revealed that Americans were spending more for prescription drugs then they were for gasoline or eating out.

Now the consequences of this situation has far ranging effects that go way beyond the fact that this precipitous rise in prescription use combined with rising prices for drugs created a trend in the health care field of rising prices across the board that has helped to drive up the cost of health insurance to crisis proportions. The connectedness of the world can be clearly seen in how the overuse of pharmaceuticals has created side effects at many levels of our experience. Economically, the damage is clear in people now paying up to a third of their income to cover health insurance, the average being 20%, compared to previous eras where health coverage might have been 2 to 3% of income and usually covered by employers. This huge added cost has driven American firms to pass on increases in their operating costs to consumers resulting in higher prices for everything made in America while it drives corporations out of the country. It has also pushed businesses to drop health coverage altogether or reissue plans that pass the bulk of the cost on to employees. This has lowered the discretionary income that families can spend on everything from college costs to clothing and automobiles, thus impacting the entire economy in profound ways. Rising costs of doing business in the U.S. have added fuel to the trend of moving operations overseas thus adding to the country's rising unemployment woes.

On the actual health front, because many of the medications, even the "blockbuster" meds, like the allergy pill "Claritin," have been found to be, not only largely ineffective but dangerous to some, many of the nation's physical complaints are misdirected and thereby go untreated. Evidence has shown time and again that most common health issues, everything from diabetes to high blood pressure to even sex problems and psychological complaints like depression and anxiety can be addressed through a change in lifestyle – improved diet, more exercise, and stress reduction practices as well as an honest appraisal of what isn't working in a person's life circumstance can lead to miraculous improvements in physical health and outlook. When people are misdirected towards worthless pills their futures are put in jeopardy and families and children suffer the consequences of parent's ill health and early deaths.

The other major effect on families is not from ineffective pills but from the pills that work all too well. In the 1990's drug companies began to push the FDA to approve highly addictive opioid narcotics for a number of common pain issues and then heavily lobbied doctors to ignore the well understood dangers of addiction to foster a much freer use of these potent pain killers. The consequences have been horrendous: the CDC reported in 2006 that a "national epidemic" of deaths due to overdoses of prescription narcotics was underway in America, starting in 1990 and rising an average of 18% a year. Addiction to prescription narcotics has also skyrocketed in those years now becoming, along with ADHD meds like Ritalin and Adderall, the most abused drugs in America, far outracing illegal favorites like, ecstasy, methamphetamine, and cocaine.

How many young people standing on the corner with a cardboard sign got their start when their parents were killed or turned into prescription drug addicts instead of getting real help? How many people are in prisons for acts motivated by prescription drug abuse? The most common cause of incarceration in the United States is found in drug related offenses. This used to mean cocaine but now is more often suggestive of pharmaceutical products, and the character of the offenders has changed from gang members to school teachers and office workers. This shift in criminal behavior represents a major social rift that has tremendous consequences for families and communities. Additionally, the laws concerning driving under the influence of prescription drugs generally are without guidelines that set limits for how much a person can safely take and drive. So the roads are filled with people who are taking substances that impair their driving resulting in untold numbers of highway injuries and deaths.

Volumes could be written on the social costs incurred by the surge in prescription drug use in America, from the deaths to the costs to children's lives, first of which might be the nation-wide experiment in child development that has been going on with the explosion of class two stimulants administered to children. No long term studies exist that tell us what happens to children when their brains are bathed in strong stimulant drugs while they are undergoing profound periods of mental development. It simply is not known what sort of psychological and physical mutations may be underway in this population. This is especially tragic when it is so clear that most children are misdiagnosed with ADHD. When the lives of children are disrupted with emotional impacts like divorce and/or an addicted parent, they will usually begin to disassociate or "space out" as a reaction to emotional overwhelm. Boys, in particular, also tend to act out physically, behaviors that are classically associated with ADHD. The last two decades have seen a precipitous rise in disrupted families and prescription drug abuse and with it has been this rise in the expected symptoms seen by school teachers. Unfortunately the pharmaceutical industry has seen to it that teachers and school nurses have been inundated with their advertising disguised as "education" informing these professionals that what they are seeing is a brain disorder they can cure with a pill. Millions of American children are being drugged daily instead of receiving the proper attention they deserve. Along with all the naturally rambunctious kids whose normal behavior has been pathologized, these children are now part of a vast unmonitored study in long term stimulant use.

In 2005 researchers at Oregon Health & Science University evaluated all the scientific evidence to date regarding drugs prescribed for ADHD and concluded there was no evidence to find any of the stimulant medications were safe to give children for more than 6 months. They also found a total inadequacy in the literature looking into the side effects of the products, including stunted growth.[11]

The effects of the prescription drug boom are not limited to economic, social, or medical, side effects they also go further through the web of connection to the environment. Researchers have discovered that the rivers around metropolitan areas where sewage disposal plants release treated effluent are polluted with chemicals from some of the most highly used prescription drugs. In 2006 a scientist from the U.S. Geological Survey discovered significant amounts of a chemical used in birth control pills in the Potomac River and its tributaries that was resulting in mutations in fish populations causing male fish to produce eggs. Another study from the University of Georgia found fish and frogs living in waters contaminated by chemicals from antidepressants, namely Prozac, found to be associated with slowing growth. [12]

In another field, drugs used for medicating cattle came to light as the answer to a mystery being investigated by researchers at Washington State University. They were wondering what had caused a 95% drop in the population of vultures in Pakistan. What they discovered was that ranchers in the region had begun to use an American anti-inflammatory arthritis drug they could get cheap in an effort to curb lameness in their animals. In Pakistan ranchers rely on the wild vultures to dispose of dead animals and so the birds had begun ingesting the drug in the downed cattle. Unfortunately the effect of the chemicals was fatal to the vultures and so they had begun dying in droves. Without the vultures the numbers of wild dogs increased threatening local populations with rabies, as well as the potential for an explosion in the rat population. Thus, one small insertion of a drug into the ecosystem of South Asia created a multiplying ecological disaster as its effect moved through the web of connection. This example is one of thousands that could be recounted to demonstrate how small actions meant for one thing are not isolated to that one thing but travel outward in often unexpected and dangerous ways. Regardless, the United States does not regulate the levels of pharmaceutical chemicals that can be released into the environment anywhere, including lakes and rivers from which human populations draw their water supplies or that are given to animals raised for human consumption.[13]

So we see that we are living in a world not made of separate parts but of interwoven elements where effects reverberate through systems at all levels: environmentally, economically, etc. Look at any area of life and the effects are bound to get there sooner or later. There are the pending disasters and the disasters we see every day precipitated by the obsolete machine model of life with its nonexistent "isolated effects." The dropping cod populations in the North Atlantic will someday soon create a food crisis as the dropping salmon populations on the West coast of North America is slowly destroying the livelihood of thousands of fisherman and eliminating a rich source of healthy food that once provided for human populations going back thousands of years. The dam projects created in the 20th Century to provide electrical generation were conceived within the narrow view of the old mental/rational consciousness that saw the rivers as only moving water, blind to the multiple connections the rivers have with the world around them all the way to the sea. Now the salmon have been deprived of proper spawning grounds for too long and are dying off and with them the hopes of millions – just another side effect of the machine model. All they wanted was electricity and that they got, but without considering the connections that came with their methods what they also got is a kind of slow motion death, like tumors growing in the landscape.

It is difficult to see the homeless person standing on the corner with the cardboard sign and connect that moment with a steel plant closing thousands of miles and a generation away, but there is a straight line between the economic policy that condemned those rust belt towns and some particular individual you might find on the corner, filthy and drug addicted, living on a handout. We drive past these ghosts, who look as though their spirits have been sucked out through the soles of their feet, and we arrogantly mutter to ourselves something about how young and capable they appear, how they could be working like honest citizens if they chose to, and we do not see the invisible trail of abuse and anguish that goes all the way back to that dead steel town, or some other place like it, and the business choices that damned them. We Americans believe that every person should be a "rugged individual," who pulls him or herself up by the bootstraps when knocked down, who dives once again into the mean world that daunts our progress, but this is a myth that has been twisted into an excuse for a pervasive meanness. Even Daniel Boone had friends who helped him, Native Americans who taught him their ways and a vast in-tact ecosystem full of sustenance to wander in. What the individual faces now is something profoundly different.

As the mind has continued to evolve toward the integral structure, a movement that showed up in earnest in the late 19th Century to great effect that led Monet to paint his impressions and Einstein to his iconoclastic vision of time and space, the underlying connectedness of the world began to become clear. It was the broad awakening of what the integral scholar, Ken Wilber, once termed, "vision logic," the ability to take rationality one more step and find the connections between all the single lines of development it had isolated before, now seen as part of a huge interconnected web, or system. We find this in the birth of the idea of the "space/time continuum" and of ecological science itself; it leads to "nonlinear dynamics," and eventually to "chaos theory," that allows us to begin to understand weather patterns as expressions of interlocking systems from the ground up to the solar system. From that point forward the evidence has piled up that we must consider all the intricate webs of systems, organic and inorganic, that operate within us and all around us on multiple levels – socially, economically, biologically – which operate, not like machines, but like organisms. The difference between a machine and an organism is great and it is a crucial lesson for our time that we clearly understand the difference.

A machine as we have conceived it is an expression of Newton's mechanics that transfers energy through a series of mechanisms – wheels, gears, electronic impulses – in such a way as to create a desired outcome, anything from punching holes in sheet mental, to blending a cocktail, to tabulating numbers, to producing a picture on a screen. All the technology around us is built on such transfers of energy in a singular line of cause and effect. It is not intended to interact with the environment. Of course, the machines do interact with the environments that they are a part of, using electricity, water, fuel of all sorts, and their waste products become pollution, but *the impacts of producing the fuel and the pollution are not considered by the mental conception that created the machines.* Machines are independent devices produced by a mindset that sees the world as a collection of disconnected objects. Machines are simple devices, even super computers, because they work on singular lines of isolated cause and effect; there may be many singular lines working at once, but they are all simply linear causal chains running in parallel.

True "systems" within living organisms work much differently. They are permeated with energetic flows of feeling, sensation, impulse, memory, and forms of consciousness that range from the simple responses of a flower turning toward the sun to the complexities of a human being falling in love. As stated before, matter itself is a multi-dimensional phenomenon existing on non-material levels where energy and information is exchanged just as it is at the material level. The machine mind "template" that has been mistaken for an accurate representation of "reality," is simply an unwitting presumption regarding the world. It represents a crude attempt to understand living systems, but is really a projection of the mental/rational structure of consciousness itself.

The machine way of seeing has been our introductory perspective that is a first opening to understanding how things operate within the material sphere. The trouble is that what this perspective has done in the way of all childhood lessons is grossly oversimplify what's actually going on. It is perfectly understandable that humanity, when first turning our attention to an exclusive analysis of material systems, would tend to pick out the most elementary aspects of the systems under scrutiny and see them within the simplistic linear, causal time conceptions of their era. But we need to get beyond this now. We're way past the point where these simplistic conceptions are viable ways of modeling reality. We need to graduate to the next grade where we can begin to understand the universe in such a manner that incorporates the revelations of our deepest findings, evidence from the new physics that speaks of a universe where time and space can be jumped in and out of like a movie on a DVD, where every tine is a space and space is layered in parallel worlds that form continual selections of every possible future at every point in time, where causality can literally go backwards in time making something that was decided yesterday be decided again to suit the needs of a future we have only now determined. We live in a universe where most of what's going on is completely beyond any extension of our senses, where everything is connected in an unperceivable wholeness, where mind and nature are part of the same thing and mind stretches out into that wholeness to touch the fabric of time where the material aspects of the world are only the ripples on a vast and silent sea.

To continue to carry on in the face of all this as if material things are all that is, as if time is an arrow and the universe is made up of disconnected objects in an empty field, is simply ignorance and denial. So, why do we do it? Part of the answer lies in the truth that so much of what we have learned about the world is in such stark contrast to our previous conceptions that it takes some getting used to, even for most scientists who simply don't know how to proceed. The other reason, the most powerful force at work in this cultural transition, is simply the fact that the majority of people in the West are still primarily focused on life from the mental/rational structure. The mental/rational is definitely a very important adjunct to our conscious appraisal of the world, providing us with helpful tools and techniques. It's great for building bridges and planning transportation systems but the mental/rational, if taken alone, proves to be a trap for the mind, a room with no doors and a sort of trick puzzle where the most important pieces can't be found.

Most people go about their day trying to be "rational" about everything, using "sound logical reasoning" as the basis for making the important decisions they face. Some people go so far as to make lists of desirable attributes for the next person they wish to get intimately involved with. They may even make the mistake of marrying such a person. As the mental/rational grew to its dominance in American society in the 1950's, we conceived whole neighborhoods along rational lines. We created massive grids of streets and tract homes in a repeating pattern that optimized the efficient use of materials and provided for quick entrance and exit for automobiles, centralizing shopping areas away from homes where freeways could bring in large amounts in semi-trucks to supermarkets to efficiently distribute goods to the people. These plans were carried out from above. They were imagined as a kind of machine for people to live in that allowed for efficiency on all levels. It was all very logical, very rational and yet became very uncomfortable.

What was missing was the "on the ground" experience of living in one of these housing machines. People moved in and liked the fact that they shared no walls with others, that they had their own lawn and fenced yard, it seemed to be a fulfillment of the old political promise of "every man in his castle, two cars in every garage, and a chicken in every pot." But in time people began to feel there was something not quite right about these housing machines. The women who were largely banned from careers outside the home were the first to notice it. A new side-effect appeared, a kind of odd malaise seemed to set into the heart of the American house wives who felt listless and bored *out of their minds* in their new rationally designed housing blocks. Doctors started prescribing "mother's little helper," a small, white pill, an amphetamine called Benzedrine, an upper that gave the bored and spiritless women a bit of a kick in the rear to get the housework done. Meanwhile their children were cruising the streets after school not comprehending in their minds but feeling somewhere deep inside that something was missing from this place. They saw repeating houses and lawns, the endless strips of asphalt and the school or the park with sheets of open grass and equipment designed for "play" that quickly lost its appeal and sat mute for all but the very young. The neat straight sidewalks did not lead to adventure or discovery or opportunities for creativity. They led to only more of the same set, planed, geometric, monotonous world.

With all the planning for all the proper needs of the people living in the housing machine the children would strangely end up congregating in the places untouched by the grand plan – in the creeks and little patches of forest on the outskirts of town. They would wander in the remaining orchards or huddle in empty lots where nature had reclaimed the land full of weeds and native trees reasserting themselves. And when the rains came, the little children would gleefully run out to the gutters to float their little home-made boats of wood and paper down the street on the drainage flow as if a miniature Mississippi had suddenly appeared in their fount yards. The planers had never dreamed of these occurences, because the planners never dreamed. They planned on flat, white and blue, bloodless rolls of paper from above it all on their drawing tables as if designing an industrial plant.

The mental/rational structure is not a way to live. It's a way to work and when it has been applied to living it simply creates a place to go crazy in. The men could leave, the poor women just had to deal with it, and having coffee with the girls every day just wasn't enough. So the medical establishment decided, just as they had in a previous era when Freud diagnosed the typical woman as being easily driven into "hysteria" by her peculiar constitution, so too did the doctors of the machine culture decide that the female was in need of adjustment to the rational order. So out came a parade of pills, uppers and downers, valium being the drug of choice for quite a long time. If you're properly sedated even afternoon television can be a fulfilling experience.

Originally, neighborhoods grew in a kind of organic way in ethnic enclaves in the city and towns that housed a people of common culture and background, where the shopping areas were within walking distance and people would gather in local taverns and community centers enjoying a camaraderie and society that made sense on something more than a "rational" level. Having "heart and soul," one might say, which is an expression of the previous evolutionary structures of consciousness still present in modern people. Man does not live by efficiency alone, but the plague of our modern age is the attempt to make us do so through forcing human beings to adjust to the machine rather than the machine adjusting to us. The pharmaceutical approach has only grown in power over the years as the main method of adjusting human beings to live in inhuman circumstances. It works just about as well as the "gin mills" worked in the early industrial revolution in Britain when rural people were forced off the land into squalid cities to provide labor for the new factories. The dynamic seems to be more sophisticated now, the dislocation more subtle, but the fix uses the same principal of erasing the pain instead of what's causing it.

We have learned a few things over the years. Sensing the sterile quality of these places, people stopped building the tract home machines and started moving back to the earlier neighborhoods feeling something more vital there, seeking parks modeled on natural landscapes, intact forests in the area, old unique homes built with more feeling and less efficiency. New developments try to incorporate this lesson if only superficially. Women entered the work force and got to escape the interminable boredom, although working in the corporate machine buildings isn't too much different. Everyone is just kept too busy to notice. It is really the children now, left in their machine schools, designed originally for the specific purpose of training rural farm children with the necessary skills to work in industry, who are feeling the brunt of the mental/rational machine mind bearing down on them. We've abandoned them in the machine world, where we continue to force them into "educational" environments most unnatural, where sitting still in rows facing one direction listening to disconnected "facts" produces the healthy response that yearns to get out of there, move around and seek something of interest and meaning, a natural condition we have created a disease out of that must be suppressed with increasingly potent doses of narcotics. The pharmaceutical industry discovered this child suppression market in a big way in the early 1990's and by 2004 2.5 million American children were prescribed drugs to chemically restrain their natural responses. Instead of looking to the increasingly frenetic pace of modern life, the increase in television watching where the rate of flashing imagery has accelerated over time and the intensity and amount of graphic violence continues to expand, instead of looking at the emotional and physical abandonment more children have been faced with as parents struggle with an economy that is quickly leaving them behind even as they work more hours, instead of looking at a long list of factors implicated in the rise in childhood emotional and behavioral symptoms in our society, doctors and their patients accepted the drug companies explanation: your child has a chemical imbalance.

In fact, the chemical imbalance theory of mental disorders has been time and again rejected by competent doctors and medical researchers reviewing the data. The problem is that this approach is so very welcome by parents who long to be relieved of their fear of shame for something possibly wrong in their family life. Hearing that *it's not your fault, your child has a broken brain*, results in a sigh of relief from many parents and the easy fix that quells children's symptoms seems a profoundly welcome relief to the work involved with keeping up with their children's intense activity. In school these children now sit quietly and do their work, experiencing the same effect that college students cramming for exams have relied on for many years – take some strong stimulants and your ability to concentrate will be amplified. There's no miracle here, of course you can put kids on speed and they study better. The question is: by ignoring the real causes for their behavior or simply understanding in most cases that they are behaving naturally, what will be the eventual costs to our society? This is another example of the machine mind at work. Instead of understanding the systemic problems impacting children, the result of an increasingly frantic and broken economic and social condition, the children are seen as isolated objects, automata with a broken spring, and so they themselves are blamed for what our society is doing to them. They are the canaries in the coal mine of our homes and we silence their call at our own peril. Parents need not be ashamed. They themselves are simply swept along by the same currents and they too are feeling the mounting pressures. They too are taking more drugs than ever, eating more "comfort food," drinking more, moving more, divorcing more, and suffering more.

The conditions of contemporary life have had the singularly tragic and very telling side-effect of increasing the child suicide rate to crisis proportions, although there is an odd silence regarding this issue. According to the CDC suicide is now the third most common cause of death in children ages 10 to 14 years old, and the second most common in the 15 to 24 year old group, and now a new category has been created to accommodate children between the ages of 5 and 9 years old, an occurrence that was literally unheard of a generation ago. These are only the completed suicides, the attempted numbers are much, much higher but also much harder to track due to the fact that most attempts in children are believed never reported. We hear about the increase in depression in children as if it is some kind of new Asian flu that has infected the country, always leading us away from the conclusion that something is wrong with the system we are living in. Instead we are told it's just another "broken brain" problem. Children have good reasons to be sad as the American family structure continues to disintegrate and more and more children live in poverty, but it is equally true that the pharmaceutical industry has corrupted medicine in this country so as to create a system that never asks why children are sad, never looks at what's going on in their lives, but goes directly to the pill, the machine mind having triumphed in medicine. The message from the medical establishment is clear: *the circumstances of your life don't matter. You're just a biochemical robot that is broken.* Take this pill, be calm and go back to work. Like the housewives of the fifties, the kids of today are being diagnosed rather than listened to. They're being given a pill rather than a healthy environment, but unlike the women of the fifties there is no escape.

The civilization of side-effects marches on because it seems to make "sense" which is another way of saying that its "rational." We are simply stuck on the idea of modernity being a place where we've dispensed with all those earlier unreasonable ways of understanding things, ways that include our hearts and souls and a need for beauty and peace and truth, creativity and exploration. We have believed the advertising that suggests all of these virtues can be attained through one material possession or another. The machine mind template that we lay over the world, which shapes our vision so as to believe we're seeing the true workings of things, suggests that the way to fix any problem is simply another application of technology, another machine, electrical or biochemical. But all of these layers of technological fixes, one on top of another, are simply evidence of the deficiency of the mental/rational structure as an exclusive way of approaching life. Instead of realizing the inadequacy of the machine mind approach most simply seek the next "breakthrough" in technology as the answer to the side effect caused by the last breakthrough, never realizing Einstein's warning that we cannot solve a problem by the same level of consciousness that created it. So this is how the machine mind just keeps piling it up over our heads: more side effects followed by more technological machine fixes and so more side effects and then more fixes. We are like the older folks who take handfuls of pills every day, most of which are prescribed to counter the side effects of the pill that is taken to counter the side effects of the one that came before it. If we don't change fast enough this is how our civilization will fall: crushed under a mountain of machines, drowning in literal oceans of unintended poisons and plastic trash that are the inevitable side effects of a civilization based on machine mind reductionism that sees every problem as separate from everything else and the whole world just a collection of parts. The establishment sustains itself through making people adapt to its damage and the technological fix is their method. This ends person by person as we wake up to the alternative, a spirit that's been emerging from outside social controls for quite some time.

CIVILIZATION IN TRANSITION

The shaping of populations to meet the needs of industry has created a number of side effects itself. People are not machines and when they are treated like pieces of machines then they tend to become unhappy, depressed and spiritless. They tend to drink too much, fight too much, and generally live difficult lives. The promotion of standards for laborers fought for and won by union activity through the 19th and 20th Century created, if not a completely healthy condition for workers, at least afforded decent homes and the chance to restore some sanity on the weekends. Regardless, as the years went on the machine model of society was promoted to a point of spontaneous rebellion when large numbers of young people began to survey the ever-more mechanized life laid out before them and say, "I don't think so."

The jazz culture offered a cynical, urban hip critique of the mainstream that came out of the experience of African American people who had largely maneuvered around the machine mind. Working for *the Man* but never completely adopting his mental framework, they found the strict, "straight laced," subdued cultural structures of the white majority ill-suited to the more flamboyant and kinetic energies of Black society. Jazz was cool, a cultural stance that came out of a "feeling state" far outside the emotionless, schematic, hyper-rationality of the technocratic organization man's worldview. It offered a loosening of experience and affect and this change in cultural temperature in the late 1940's and early 1950's was just the relief many younger people were unconsciously starving for. When the Beat poets and writers began to put this subverting, sensual music into words and directly challenge the mainstream dedication to the "up-tight and square" machine mind in the mid to late 1950's and early 1960's it unleashed a steady stream of adherents from all over the country forming the beginnings of a counterculture. Rock and roll then came on the scene and the stream became a raging river.

In this social upheaval we find the breakdown of the exclusive hold of the mental/rational structure of consciousness that had propelled the industrial vision toward a fully mechanized society, people included. It had melded so well with the post-Puritanical Protestant work ethic, but this religious formation in American culture had a lifespan as well. In its suspicion of all things physical, especially sex, the Protestant influence was driving Americans toward a moment of truth when they would soundly rebuke the Pastors and their staid joyless rules and throw the whole thing overboard. The "gray flannel suit" of the organization man and the pious Protestant conservative approach to life that had formed a partnership in previous eras were now jettisoned together. Not that they disappeared entirely, far from it, but they would never again hold exclusive reign over American sensibilities as they had in the period from the depression to the immediate postwar era.

The former magical and mythic structures of consciousness that yearned for a sensual and poetic appreciation for life that began to be reintegrated with the Romantic poets of the 18th C., the American Transcendentalists in the 19th C. and the avant-garde artists of the early 20th, really blew out of the subculture into a major social movement starting in the late 1950's. Even the avid interest in "tiki bars" that came home from the Pacific with the servicemen after the war signaled a growing fascination with non-rational cultural formations, something that appealed to a deeper feeling left out of the purely mental/rational perspective that had become so stifling. The hokey, caricatured images of what were seen as "exotic" cultures featured in films and restaurant culture of the 40's and 50's allowed Americans of the era to render harmless in cautious approach people they once deemed dirty and dangerous "savages" as seen through the narrow lens of their ethnocentric bigotry. This opening to the world was part of the growing internationalism that accompanied America's new role as a world power. The U.S. became the home of the United Nations and Americans began to think of themselves as world citizens in ways they never had before. This too was a sign of the burgeoning integral structure of consciousness that brings with it a "world centric" feeling that starts the breakdown of the tribal nationalism that had previously typified the view of individuals within Western nations who saw themselves as exclusive members of countries pitted against competitors. Although this opening was applauded by the corporate powers that saw this as a move toward the world markets that a later globalism would fully exploit, the down side for the imperial aspirations of American companies was that this new internationalism carried with it a new empathy for people in foreign lands, even "third world" areas. It was no longer possible, as it had been in the early 20th

Century and before, to speak of the people of the developing world as "ignorant savages" in need of the paternal hand of American leadership and control. The old notion of "Anglo-Saxon superiority" that guided America's mission abroad in the early years of imperial reach, that offered a "mandate from God" to dominate "lesser peoples" was an argument that had soured in the American mind after the Third Reich had taken their "master race" ideology to the most dreadful and tragic conclusions.

American imperialism itself is more than a mental/rational construction of expanding territory, being a matter of continuing a progress started in westward expansion across the continent, a kind of unstoppable habitual behavior that sought more than just riches abroad but constituting an addiction to a very literal "pilgrim's progress." In the material literalisms of the mental/rational structure of consciousness the goal (of spiritual redemption, of material success) is sought in the distance of time and space, something one *moves toward*, it dwells beyond the self and must be sought in the distance beyond. America searches for itself in conquest much as the European powers once did but have all now abandoned. When the thing a society seeks can no longer be sought "out there" then it turns toward a cultural and social cultivation within its borders. This America has successfully avoided for a hundred years and more, rendering mainstream culture in America perpetually idiotic and juvenile – nothing but fighting and chasing and heroic rescue and victory over one dimensional "evil doers." A tiny minority carries on the progress of true culture in America while the majority have even stopped reading the mature literature that calls for introspection and evaluation of the American spirit, favoring instead the mindless sensations of Hollywood. It is mainly here, in film and television, that post-war Americans reordered their old identity as strict Protestant tamers of savagery, to a new image for an updated, "postmodern" imperialism, as *friendly teachers bearing gifts*.

Corporate plans for reaping the natural resources of the third world came to be cloaked in the new enthusiasms of world friendship and America as "helper and benefactor" to the poor nations of the world struggling toward modernity. It is true that much helpful assistance has been offered by America to many places on earth, many altruistic Americans have gone abroad to sincerely help people in difficulty in every corner of the world. America helped to rebuild Europe and Japan after the war and has been the largest source of foreign aid in the world since that time. Unfortunately, there is also a dark side to much of this aid, friendship offered often as part of a strategy to thwart a socialistic nationalism inspired by the Soviet Union from taking hold in the third world after WWII so as to leave these areas open for American economic expansion. The Soviet Union was played to Americans as a threat to "freedom" everywhere, but what the Soviets really represented in the world was anti-imperialism, a counter force to the old European colonialists and the new American economic imperialists. The Soviets and socialism of any kind had to be demonized because it sought to inspire rebellion against the old elitist models of government with aristocrats and peasants, whether the "aristocrats" were (post) colonial land barons or corporations. This required that much of that "aid" to the third world had to come with strings attached, pledges to maintain old social structures that condemned major portions of the populace to poverty so as to provide cheap labor and avoid the development programs that required higher prices for the commodities and raw materials the corporations demanded cheap. The usual aid package had conditions that required the money to be paid to U.S. companies working within the country to improve infrastructure that would aid the corporate extraction of resources: port facilities, airports, highways, and such. The price to be paid for these deals became all too obvious when the CIA began to arrange coups displacing leaders pushing back against American control and anyone who even flirted with socialism in countries like Guatemala, Nicaragua, the Dominican Republic, Haiti, and Chile (that's the short list) and in the Middle East, chiefly Iran, the repercussions of which we are still living with today.

Few Americans understand the history of the Middle East and so the troubles there seem incomprehensible to them. They are easily swayed by silly explanations like, *they hate our freedom,* when simply picking up any uncensored modern history of the rejoin and *reading it* would quite easily provide all the context a person would need to understand all too well what the real issue is. Historically, first the British and then the Americans have manipulated the politics of the Arab world since the days of *Lawrence of Arabia*, all in an ongoing drama aimed at insuring the flow of oil to the West. Most Americans look at Iran and see a land of dangerous extremists and are unaware that America stepped into their business in the 1950's through a CIA operation that replaced their democratically elected leader with a tyrant who held power through mass imprisonment, murder, torture, and an abusive secret police apparatus, all because the former leader had the audacity to try to take back their oil fields from British Petroleum.[14]

The growth model of American business and the bankers behind it have encouraged foreign financial incursions since the closing of the Western frontier launched American "manifest destiny" into the Pacific at the end of the 19th Century. The bitter military experience of imperialism in the Philippines during the Spanish American War, in a bloody battle of attrition that plodded on year after year, motivated business interests to pursue their control of foreign resources through other means. They found, as the British had, the old Imperial Roman model of buying off local leaders to suppress any opposition from their own people, replacing those leaders when necessary, a viable alternative to direct military intervention, although it has always been held in reserve. When replacing a leader seemed necessary, as it was deemed in Guatemala in 1954 when President Arbenz sought to make a better deal with the United Fruit Co. by reclaiming land to direct a fair share of profits to his own country, the CIA went into action in support of "American interests." These machinations abroad could always be explained to the American people as part of the fight against "communism," a shadowy enemy that was said to lurk everywhere in the world, plotting against us. There certainly were efforts by the Soviet Union to spread communism as part of their own efforts to secure trading partners abroad and as a function of their ideological mission to aid working people against imperialist exploitation. The irony was that if the people were getting a fair deal there was no place for communism to take hold. It was always in the regions where common people were being exploited, worked too hard and allowed to keep too little that the communists were able to foment revolutions. Cuba was the prime example where the sugar cane trade had devolved to virtual slave labor. When there wasn't an actual communist element at work the CIA would simply invent one, and so they turned the avidly anti-Soviet Arbenz into a "Red" overnight and orchestrated a "revolt" in the streets in the same way Broadway producers put on a show. After all they were only required to produce enough of a revolt to capture on film for the evening news. The scene for American public consumption would be contrived so as to look like a popular uprising, but in reality was nothing more than an army general taking the bait from the CIA to be America's next puppet, a job that pays extremely well. Many years of torture and oppression of the

Guatemalan people followed in order to keep the status-quo favoring American business in place.

These productions were often seen through by the rest of the world and reported for what they were. Thus, what began to look very much like "imperialism" to everyone else in the world was presented to the American people as simply part of the world trade and development efforts, in conjunction with the valiant fight against the "commies." It would not be until the end of the Cold War in the late 1980's that literate Americans would learn that the communist threat had been grossly exaggerated for decades in an effort to keep the military budget high so as to direct a continual flow of tax payer monies into the hands of military contractors on the way to achieving total military supremacy in the world. A capable military has always been one of the necessary ingredients in America's "speak softly and carry a big stick" brand of imperialism. (Some like to believe that Ronald Reagan drove the Soviets into a ditch with his military buildup, but the truth is that their economy simply didn't work and had been declining for years.)

The schism between evolving American integral "world centric" sensibilities that no longer find it acceptable to go overseas and take what you want from "the savages" in exchange for a pat on the head and a three piece suit, and the necessities of exploiting foreign societies to pump up balance sheets, have produced a culture of deception. The imperial machinations of the corporate powers must be constantly disguised as "assistance" or "development" or business in partnership with local people who on closer examination turn out to be despots paid off to threaten or eliminate any opposition to the draining of assets from the country. In a classic example, executives at Chevron Oil in the Niger river delta have been seen meeting with the security chief of the national government, a man known to run death squads. Called by the locals the "kill and go," they race into villages, shoot people, and race away to make an example of individuals complaining about the massive pollution and poverty in the region. Lately oil companies have been running television commercials on PBS extolling the great things they're doing in Africa. Smiling black faces telling Americans, "oil is good for Africa!" If there is something good, there is also something very bad – terrible side effects of oil's presence, like the Nigerian government executing Ken Saro-Wiwa, an author, television producer, and environmental activist, winner of the Right Livelihood Award and the Goldman Environmental

Prize, prosecuted and hanged for the crime of standing up for his people against the massive pollution of Western oil companies destroying his homeland and poisoning his people. The bad things like this rarely reach the American public through any mainstream source of news and when they do the connection to American business is always missing from the report leaving the American public with the misplaced impression that Africans are political primitives who can only be ruled by vicious autocrats and plundering generals, never made aware that most of these types are working for Western business interests within an updated system of proxy colonialism.

As American society began to wake up in big ways in the 1960's when the explosion of counter-culture feeling broke through the machine mind mass society of regimentation, the status-quo launched an ongoing effort to regain control of the society that began slipping away in that revolutionary era. In their efforts to secure control of the population the media has been a central part of their strategy and now a hand full of major corporate powers own and control all the major sources of television, radio, and print media in the United States. This has made it much easier to accelerate the systems of manipulation necessary in order to keep people backing a declining civilization, a civilization that still serves the interest of the elite while it increasingly fails to serve everyone else and as "side effects" of all sorts accumulate toward calamity.

Actions abroad in support of American "interests," (it is never said as "business interests" but that is just what it means) create their own side effects as well and can be often somewhat "messy" as unsightly local oppositions must be dealt with, usually by the installation of a tyrant. This messiness (a polite diplomatic term) at times produces what the CIA calls "blowback." What is *blowing back* is a side effect to the exploitation of a country emerging from elements within its population that resent getting the short end of the deal and act in the form of a revolutionary movement, using all manner of tactics to attack the foreign invaders. These people were portrayed during the early phase of American imperialism as "godless savages," after WWII as communist insurgents, and now as Islamic terrorists.

We are entering an age where the old style imperialist economics is no longer going to be tolerated. First the Europeans stopped trying to push each other around to accrue various advantages, WWII was the end of that, the old European colonial empires have fallen apart, the

Soviet empire has crumbled of its own bad weight, and now America, the "last superpower" is finding it harder to keep its tyrants on the leash and their bad behavior from becoming common knowledge everywhere but at home. (Saddam Hussein was the last attack dog who got away and Mubarak in Egypt was the last to get chased out of power by enraged citizens). American corporate power abroad is faced with having to come to terms with the fact that, although it is much more profitable to control another country's resources by making one despot and his friends rich rather than allowing the country to trade fairly for its resources, the game is up and they are more and more going to be forced to play fair in this new awakening world.

People all over the world are watching America and wondering if we are going to shift our approach to trade to one that truly encourages development and democratic fairness for average people or press our advantage as the last superpower and move into full scale fascist imperialism. The "Bush doctrine," of preemptive military assault against anyone believed to be a threat to "our interests," is a large, troubling, step in that direction. The "communist scare" tactic may have run out of steam but the "weapons of mass destruction scam" can be run anytime a reason is needed to invade. Of course there are so many side effects now building up from the broken economy of greed that before this happens the financial sheet of the American empire will most likely force it to retire from the field.

The manipulation on all fronts orchestrated to counter opposition to the building side effects of the old reductionist, machine model civilization, whether they be industrial, medical, economic, environmental, psychological or political, has historically created a population of Americans who live in their own fantasy world. Americans, unlike Europeans, have always been in something of a bubble, isolated and disinterested in the rest of the world, believing they are living in the *best country on earth!* This may have been true in the past if your criteria for *best country* is based on a thriving consumer economy and large middle class, but even as this, so called "American dream," has become more and more elusive, even as the life span of Americans has shortened and the abundance has become abundant debt, the claims of *best country* continue in a kind of hypnotic mantra based primarily on pure folklore and habit. Many people in the world, of course, have a different definition altogether of what a *good* country is, but this fact has been largely lost on many Americans who have generally viewed other people's cultures as either "primitive," obsolete, or simply *weird*. This childish nationalism has been breaking down for some time in a small but growing portion of the American population, disintegrating under the weight of a maturing consciousness that is waking up from the fantasy of American specialness. This change is driven by both the evolution of consciousness and the breakdown of the old machine model civilization.

As globalism drains the middle-class into a huge under employed class of marginal poverty, as millionaires and billionaires are offered tax breaks and rescued from their own bad deals by tax payer money, many have had the opportunity to reflect. As the manipulations of industry wear thin before their jaded eyes, a deeper value system apart from consumerism and object worship is taking hold in many people, the non-material, or "spiritual values," if you will, are rising in importance. For instance, respected historian and pollster, John Zogby, has revealed that college students have become less materialistic and much more globally aware. "We're not only looking at a transformation of the American dream, but in many ways a transformation of the American character," said Zogby. "Instead of focusing on material wealth and professional status, people in their 20s and 30s are more likely to seek a rewarding and spiritually-fulfilling life." A growing number of Americans are beginning to see themselves as people inhabiting a planet rather than strictly a country, finding value in cultures outside North America and understanding what happens in other places has an impact on them as well. "They are as likely to say they are citizens of the planet Earth as they are to say they are citizens of the United States," reported Zogby.[15]

The communications revolution, especially the Internet, has brought the world together. Young people in the U.S. now play online computer games with others in Europe, the Middle East, Korea, wherever, and chat while they're doing it. Online social networking sites are the new commons of the world and it makes no difference where your home is, not replacing the need for local society but adding a global dimension needed for the expansion of empathy beyond national borders. The democratizing of information afforded by the Internet has made the society of manipulated patriotism and materialism harder to maintain. It is sagging under the weight of truth and a population run ragged on the false promises of consumerism and elitism.

To maintain the civilization of side effects an extensive manipulative apparatus has expanded to manage the reactions and channel the thoughts and desires of American society in continual support of the status-quo throughout the 20th Century and to this day. It is this *society of manipulation* that has overtaken in the mainstream a genuine culture it replaces with artificial constructions. The keys to a new American freedom in an evolved consciousness and to some degree the freedom of souls everywhere the American empire has touched, lies in the dismantling of this multifaceted manipulative system. This begins as each individual wakes up to the falsehoods presented as truths and becomes aware of the many tactics that slide ideas unnoticed into the mind. Just as the power players on Wall Street and in the big banking houses have captured the White House, the Congress, and the Courts, they have also captured popular culture, education, and so history itself. For consciousness to evolve on a broad scale liberation of the mind from this matrix of domination must be first undertaken.

Notes

1. Yale Journal of Medicine and Law, October 2010 (Vol. VII, issue I).
2. Melody Petersen, Our Daily Meds (New York: Picador, 2008).
3. See: www.shadowstats.com
4. Glen Greenwald, With Liberty and Justice For Some (New York: Metropolitan Books, 2011).
5. Ferguson (2013).
6. Kauffman (2008), p.17.
7. Ibid.
8. Ibid., p. 58.
9. Ibid., p.43.
10. Petersen (2008). Eliot S. Valenstein, Blaming the Brain, The Truth About Drugs and Mental Health (New York: Free Press, 1998).
11. Petersen (2008).
12. Ibid.
13. Ibid.
14. See Bill Moyers, The Secret Government, (www.YouTube.com). Engdahl (2011).
15. Katherine Mangan, Today's Students are More Globally Aware, Less Materialistic, Leading Pollster Says (http://chronicle.com/article/Today-s-Students-Are-More/47701 June 7, 2009).

Chapter 5

The Society of Manipulation

This confrontation with the side effects of disconnected materialism with all the dehumanizing machine mind structures we are forced to live within and the ill health, depression, anxiety, loneliness, and just plain confusion that results, has led to an increasing number of questions. This shift in mind and spirit that breaks the dedication to the materialist agenda creates a pause in the consuming frenzy in which to reflect on the deeper meanings of existence. As this pulling back and reflecting pause has spread in growing numbers of people seriously wondering if they're on the right track in life, powerful forces notice and attempt to control and shape this reaction. This has given rise to another feature of American civilization – an intricate and aggressive manipulation of the public mind.

As the alarm bells have been going off in larger numbers of people's minds and bodies, their awakening voice has produced a counter-response to the corporate industrial power base that depends on the public's dedication to the materialist value system and the consumer economy for the continuation of its power. The manipulative response is itself a signal of the decline of the mental/rational materialist worldview, which in the status-quo's struggle to maintain itself demonstrates where the edifice is cracking. What began as a simple desire to control labor populations for the purposes of building a massive industrial capacity became in the latter period of the twentieth century more a matter of controlling consciousness itself, so as to perpetuate the society created by that industrial establishment. When, for instance, chemical fertilizers that have significantly boosted the profit margins of corporate agriculture and the petro-chemical industry have been shown to deplete the soil so that continued use produces vegetables with less and less food value—missing essential micronutrients creating both a kind of "dead dirt" and "hollow food" syndrome, as well as polluting waterways—this provides a bright sign that the underlying science is inadequate. Unfortunately, these businesses are not run by scientists or nutritionists, they are run by business people with their eye on the bottom line to the exclusion of all else. When these problems proliferate throughout society the entire commercial culture is designed as a program for leading people away from questioning the system. So a mind-set is cultivated in the mainstream that sees only the growth and power of a glorious American ingenuity, reacting to any criticism as "liberal bias" or the whining of the lazy welfare class. This being the case the cracks in the system are not fixed, and in true form to Professor Quigley's analysis, instead are covered up with a series of maneuvers meant to obscure and mislead so as to allow profits to continue unabated.

The society of manipulation began in the early 20th Century with wealthy foundations setting the tone of American science and social theory through the backing of preferred lines of research that would accommodate the status-quo, not only endowing select scholars but going so far as to buy whole universities. Beyond this, the tactical plan of manipulation is made up of a series of stop-gap measures and "attitude adjustments" designed to keep the social system from transitioning into something else through a reassessment of realities, which is to say, from moving forward, when moving forward means cutting into profits and questioning established power. It is brought about simply through the desire of those who have power and money to keep the machine going that supplies them with their superior position and authority, even though it is causing increasing levels of damage and failing to provide for the bulk of the population. It also represents the fear and lack of vision within those elite ranks that if the present system ceases to "grow" it will die and chaos will ensue; they simply can't imagine a better way tied as their fate is to the stock market and all forms of speculation. The manipulative dynamic is driven by the foresight of the moneyed interests to shape public opinion to their advantage and even contrive the perfectly "pliable" citizen from the capitalist reformation of the education system and popular culture so that the vision of Thomas Jefferson and the founding fathers is supplanted by that of Henry Ford and the founding bankers.

This vision is a very narrow one that scoffs at the impoverishment and damage that is the side effect of its ambition. This is the way that civilizations crash, by propping up and even accelerating the untenable processes that are stressing the population, economic balances, and the environment to the breaking point. This is what happened to the Romans. It is what happened to the Mayans. It is what happened to countless civilizations throughout time and it is what will happen to America without drastic reform. The barbarians are at the gates and they are not Islamic hoards, (this is yet another side effect and manipulation). In reality, the average individual making up this assault of vandals is an overweight, under employed technician, trained, but never truly educated. He (or she) is an entertainment addict, who knows nothing of the words of Jefferson and Lincoln, Fredrick Douglas, Dickens or Dickinson, Steinbeck or anyone who has ever said anything about real life, but has memorized the latest sports scores and which celebrity is getting a divorce, who believes the environment is indestructible and doesn't know the heavy metals seeping into the water table are developing cancers within him, who is sure if homosexuals are allowed to marry it will ruin the country but knows nothing about the forces that have ruined his health and prevented his making a fair wage. This barbarian arrives in a gas glutton vehicle at the "super store" full of cheap imported goods that have shut down a thousand factories across America. He happily strolls to the door with a fist full of credit cards in one hand and a plastic soda bottle in the other. But this self-destructive tendency is really only the unconscious reaction to conditions thrust upon the public from above.

As the institutions of the society, economic, agricultural, medical – everything – meet the end of their instrumental range their scope of functionality at higher levels of growth deteriorates, which is to say their side effects build up to levels where they seriously compromise their ability to deliver. So as time goes on, the systems effectively work for fewer and fewer people while they cause more and more damage. Those at the bottom of the social pyramid are the first to feel it, but as the deterioration progresses people of higher and higher economic standing farther up the pyramid are affected. All the while those at the top remain untouched, wealth having removed them from the money and value dynamics the average person is subject to. The truly rich get what they want regardless of the economy or what inferior pulp is being purveyed to the masses. They live buffered from problems created by their industries in an environment that encourages a complete lack of empathy for average people.

So, regardless of what everyone else is feeling, the super wealthy and the owners and top managers of corporate groups continue to make money from the old system, sometimes in increasing amounts – the oil companies, the pharmaceutical industry, and the financial sector have all recorded record profits in the last decade, while the environment deteriorates, the cost of living skyrockets, true unemployment figures climb to historical levels, and wage buying power declines. They do everything they can to maintain things as they are regardless of whether these systems are slowly removing value and increasing costs for the average citizen. This requires manipulating the public to prevent people from agitating for change. Through this activity a kind of fake world is promoted, one that creates increasing levels of confusion, depression, and anxiety in the public as their personal feelings and intuitions about the world around them simply don't match what is being promoted.

This manipulation has taken several main forms: the control of the mainstream media, so as to manage public information, to include both "news" programing and the more subtle form of belief shaping accomplished through television shows and popular film. Sports events and other diversions help to keep the public mind preoccupied as another wing of the media manipulation program.

The "dumbing down" of the education system constitutes the complementary component of the overall plan by making Americans more susceptible to influence, so that average people have no basis for the critical thought necessary for understanding the actual causes of the conditions and events that overtake them. Additionally, the status-quo has found the "management" of scientific research to be essential so that new discoveries will not undermine established markets and power bases. This prevents the major side effects of their obsolete systems from being fully recognized and followed back to guilty industries, whether they are connected to financial, environmental, or individual health issues.

Associated with this and ranging beyond the protection of markets into socio-political manipulation is the use of public relations, implicated in the creation of profound misconceptions regarding realities surrounding every major industry in America as well as the government's use of the art to promote a widespread encouragement of blind, "knee jerk," patriotism. Thus creating a social climate that is totally intolerant of questioning those things labeled "American," like "our way of life," which is said to rest on "our interests" (i.e.: investments) overseas. This is an attitude that needs to be maintained through intensive reinforcement in the face of an economic system that has become profoundly unfair for the average citizen.

Perhaps the most disturbing method for manipulating public opinion is found under the heading of "mind control" which constitutes a psychological research effort to improve methods for direct manipulation of the human psyche. This has been achieved through extensive research into the operation of the human mind and nervous system combined with experimentation into behavioral conditioning and hypnotic suggestion, as well as technological devices that accomplish the same. Along this line is the newest modernist enthusiasm: *transhumanism*, which is the name given to the conception of improving humanity through the technological "enhancement" of the human body and mind. Although great things may be done to correct disabilities, transhumanism is fraught with terrifying possibilities for mass psychological control.

The last major method for managing public opinion presented here in its own chapter is that of manufactured "events." These are secretly contrived events that hit the news and sway the public toward adopting the desired belief or backing the desired legislation. This has been a method employed for centuries to manipulate public opinion and often includes "false flag" tactics, a term derived from the old days of naval battles under sail where a ship would fly the flag of its enemy in order to maneuver into a favorable position for attacking before hoisting up their own true colors. Often in more recent times the "true colors" of the enemy are never openly revealed, as when the Nazis burned the Reichstag (parliament) and blamed it on the communists in order to swing public support to their extreme ideology.

The Wealthy Foundations and Cultural Imperialism

Before delving into the details of the main methods of manipulation in America it is necessary to describe the major mechanism that has funded much of the growth and use of these techniques. Charitable foundations were first created by people like John D. Rockefeller in the late 19th Century as a way of improving a poor public image formed from the general distain for the manipulative and strong-arm business practices in use by people like Rockefeller, J.P. Morgan, Andrew Carnegie, Cornelius Vanderbilt, and others of their caliber. In the rough and tumble business world of big money capitalism the use of armed thugs, assassins, pay-offs, trickery and deceit made these "captains of industry" often indistinguishable from organized crime bosses. The foundations became a way for the robber barons of the Gilded Age to avoid taxes while leveraging huge financial forces in support of their power, all while appearing to be philanthropists spreading their wealth around in the public interest.

What the powers of concentrated wealth have really sought to accomplish in America is simply to "guide" progress in such a manner that their power and the means that sustain it would not be challenged, but rather redefined as democracy itself and therefore unquestionable. This came largely as a reaction to early alarm by the people that democracy was under attack by the large trusts that were the cooperative efforts by the robber barons to completely dominate whole industries like steel, railroads, and oil and the political corruption they required. The Ford Foundation emerged in the 20th Century as the leading backer for such manipulations. The sociologist, Peter J. Seybold, explains that the Ford Foundation sought to remake political philosophy in America through the promotion of a behavioral approach that abandoned the study of differentials in wealth and power in favor of an analysis of the individual's ability to adapt to the status-quo system. Continued disturbances in opposition to the big moneyed interests were reframed as the result of "confusion" on the part of the masses to understand the proper definition of democracy. "It was the foundation's task to develop such a definition of democracy in order to cure the confusion of the masses. Those individuals who fail to accept this formula for "democracy from above" and go beyond reasonable disagreement were seen by the study committee as pathological or maladjusted..." [1]

After WWII, the Ford foundation took up the work begun principally by the Rockefeller and Carnegie foundations much earlier to champion a behavioral science perspective across the social sciences as a whole. Behaviorism, as an approach to understanding social problems puts all the stress on the individual and takes it away from a consideration of the context of larger social structures, thus everything from psychology, to medical psychiatry, to sociology, to education theory became dominated by this myopic focus on the individual. "However, this approach was heavily weighted toward the preservation of the status quo for it takes the existing social arrangements as given and then seeks to explain why individuals feel alienated. The stated goal of the program was to reduce social disorder by proposing practical steps to aid personal adjustment rather than fundamentally altering the social structure."[2]

In 1963 at Western Michigan University, Dr. Martin Luther King responded to this program. "Modern psychology has a word that is probably used more than any other world *in* modern psychology. It is the word, "maladjusted," Dr. King declared with ringing conviction.

> But I say to you, my friends, as I move to my conclusion, there are certain things in our nation and in the world which I am proud to be maladjusted and which I hope all men of good-will will be maladjusted until the good societies realize. I say very honestly that I never intend to become adjusted to segregation and discrimination. I never intend to become adjusted to religious bigotry. I never intend to adjust myself to economic conditions that will take necessities from the many to give luxuries to the few. I never intend to adjust myself to the madness of militarism, to the self-defeating effects of physical violence...

These are the words of the uprising of the human spirit and they now should belong to 99 percent of Americans as the power elite move into the final phase of subjugating the masses. The foundations worked throughout the 20th Century to set the direction of any and all scholarly subjects and sciences that could affect their position and utilized those endeavors to increase their power and control of the American people.

> These include the funding of leading individuals and institutions; the identification, recruitment, and training of promising young scholars; the capturing of key journals in a field as well as the leadership of professional associations; and the use of prestigious intermediary agencies, such as the Social Science Research Council and the American Council of Learned Societies.[3]

Scholars are clear that these wealthy foundations do not simply champion the best in the field as it distinguishes itself through the healthy economy of ideas, rather they "first determine the direction a field should take; then, they solicit requests from individuals who are likely to share their interests. In some cases they may even approach researchers and proffer support before a proposal has been submitted to them. "Once the initial funding or 'seeding' period is over (usually a period of 10 to 20 years), foundation-supported institutions and mechanisms are so entrenched as to be self-perpetuating." [4]

The practice continues to this day through the backing of scholarship, trends in academia and science that support status quo power while excluding new avenues in research that would challenge established authority and industries. A whole new cadre of robber barons have joined the ranks next to the old foundations, people like Warren Buffet and Bill Gates now carry on the tradition of tilting the table toward the aggrandizement of what has become a new American aristocracy or what is more often referred to as the "plutocracy." The specific examples of foundation influence and control will be addressed in the various subject areas below.

Media Control

In order to control the populace it has always been essential to control the information they receive. To this end, autocratic societies throughout history have sought to limit what the people know. The Roman Catholic Church during the dark ages restricted Bible ownership to the clergy, keeping it in Latin so as to further cloud in mystery the holy text as something only trusted members of the church could interpret for the people. Joseph Stalin literally wrote the book on shaping public opinion in the modern age believing that the "truth" was not what really happened but what people *believe* really happened. Belief, Stalin understood, is what shapes the future. The communist dictator's method of shaping the news to suit political policy became so blatant in America during the George W. Bush administration that television comedian, Steven Colbert, in his mock conservative news show, defended the practice by calling it "truthiness" suggesting that this was an improved and better way of understanding the truth. The Bush team political strategist, Karl Rove, proved this was more than a joke when he told a *New York Times* reporter in October of 2004 that he didn't understand the Bush administration approach because he was, "part of the reality based community..." Rove continued, "We're an empire now, and when we act, we create our own reality." A bogus reality their friends in the corporate news rooms were more than happy to convey to the public with little respect for the lives lost when the lies led to war. Of course, this was nothing new.[5]

Buying up controlling interest in major papers all over the country was something the big banking interests started doing in the early twentieth century. The congressional record of February 9, 1917 tells us that in 1915 J.P. Morgan interests purchased 25 U.S. newspapers across the country, inserting their own editor in each, with the intent of controlling the news that influenced American opinion. These tactics continued throughout the century but not long after WWII the major corporate powers went into overdrive to bring under their control all the mainstream press, television, and radio in the country. It took several decades and a lot of lobbying to get the pesky laws that once forbid media consolidation out of the way, but by the new millennium the mainstream media was well in the hands of seven corporations: Time-Warner, Viacom, News Corp., Disney, Vevendi, Sony, and BMG. In 1983 there were 50. At the time of this writing the Forbes magazine Fortune 500 list has Disney as the uncontested leader, with News Corp, Time-Warner, Viacom, and CBS Corporation, at the top with Sony trailing just behind. These conglomerates control about 98 percent of what hits the mainstream. They are in turn controlled by an intricate and incestuous meshwork of interrelated boards of directors populated by people from top industry and banking so that the advertisers and money powers are setting policies for what is to be seen and heard by the American people. The major banking interests: the Rockefeller Citibank, J.P. Morgan Chase, Bank of America, and Britain's Rothschild financial empire, Barclays, along with financial houses like Goldman Sachs, not only have seats on the board but also often control major portions of the stock value of the big media companies, as well as controlling who gets financing. Loans to media corporations serve as a strong measure of control. Banking is key to control in film especially in that funding, in the end, is what decides what will be produced and what will not be produced at the big studios.[6]

The media in America has been progressively commercialized so that news programming that didn't provide as much profit has been severely cut back and replaced by "infotainment" with fashion model news casters reading sensational stories in the place of facts usable by the public to form cogent opinions of world and domestic conditions that may come to affect their lives. This is the age of spectacle that recapitulates that of Rome as it maneuvered the masses into a base state of appetite. An updated version of the Coliseum breeds and reinforces base appetites with *ultimate fighting* and blood soaked police dramas. The intent of contemporary culture in the mainstream is to keep the populace in a constant state of primitive, lower emotion – greed, vanity, lust, fear, violence, anger and revenge. The perpetual face-off of devils and angels are the staples of film and television. All the primitive drives make it easier to herd people to the shopping center and toward support for an aggressive foreign policy and a "law and order" society that in the U.S. puts more people in jail than any other nation on earth, half again as much as Russia, and three times the amount as China. It's all about profit and control.

There is an alternative media culture in print, film and on the Internet, but most Americans cannot find their way there, being mesmerized by the tension/relief/tension/relief, content of mainstream dramas that train the mind for constant movement and excitement producing a pervasive condition unsuitable for the calm consideration of stories of higher feeling and intelligence. The sort of culture that seeks to cultivate compassion and insight into the human condition, to penetrate to the deep values beyond fighting and accumulating, a culture that is meant to uplift its citizens is just the sort that is marginalized in favor of that which appeals to the interests of the lowest common denominator. The Internet is a great corrective to media control, but unfortunately is mostly popular with a younger audience raised on lightning attention bites. The net is fed on in a superficial grazing over the surface of a vast wilderness of imagery, text, audio, and video, as if flying low in an attack helicopter snatching leaves from the tree tops and never seeing the horizon or the ground from which their gleanings grow. [7]

The Bush administration's removing the final blocks to media consolidation of markets, so that one company can own all the print, television, and radio in a region, seems to have been part of a deal with the big corporate media interests in exchange for their unquestioning parroting of administration propaganda in the build-up to the 2003 invasion of Iraq. What has since come to be seen as a *terrible failure* of the mainstream media to ask any pertinent questions in that period, to act as a public trust to insure honesty in the government on such a deadly issue, was obviously not a failure at all but the result of a planned policy. No one organization, let alone an entire field, could be that consistently blind and downright negligent by accident.

This was just more of the same by other means as that seen at the beginning of hostilities just after the towers came down when the Pentagon opened its *Office of Strategic Influence* whose job it was to plant false news stories in the foreign media. When the foreign media revealed the plot the Pentagon announced they were closing the office, but it was understood that the tactics continued.

Much of what the media has done to destroy factual news comes in the form of the idea of *balance* in reporting. In the place of the old doctrine of seeking the facts and letting the public make up their own minds is this absurd idea that simply reporting two sides of an argument is all that is necessary. The news has been reduced to a battle of squalling "experts" wherein the truth is left to fend for itself. When Walter Cronkite came back from his fateful review of the situation in Vietnam in 1968 and told the American public that the government's version of events didn't match the truth he saw on the ground, the American public was able to make the right call and withdraw support for the war. Now there is no reporter like Cronkite who is free to make such an assessment in Iraq or Afghanistan. This is by design, because the people who are benefiting from the state of conflict have decreed that the wars are not to be interfered with by democracy. America is to supply its sons to die and to be otherwise maintained in a state of ignorance so that it continues to do so. The so called "embedded press" in the war zones are completely managed by the military for this purpose so that the bloody truth won't reach the people as it did in Vietnam. As the veteran journalist, Studs Terkle, remarked, "embedded" sounds a bit too much like "being in bed with..." Afghanistan has proceeded much as Vietnam did, with troops fighting hard to subdue an area of operations, paying for it in the blood of many, then leaving and having the area return to the same condition it was in before they started, rendering the losses pointless. But none of this is allowed to reach the American public. Releasing pictures of military caskets on their way home carries severe consequences and no casualties lying on Middle Eastern battlefields have ever been seen on American television.

Every American should read the report of Lt. Colonel Daniel Davis published in *Rollingstone* magazine.[8] "Senior ranking American military leaders have so distorted the truth when communicating with the U.S. Congress and American people in regards to conditions on the ground in Afghanistan that the truth has become unrecognizable." This is the opening line of an 84 page report that documents the deceptions of the military in maintaining an image of the war that masks the overall failure to achieve anything of any value whatsoever. "How many more men must die in support of a mission that is not succeeding?" he asks. Lt. Colonel Davis reveals in his article the military's careful attention to what it calls, "information operations." This is their term for controlling the story Americans will see and hear. In this regard, on page 24, Davis cites the report of an officer who in respect to the goals of information operations, stated that, "...if Public Diplomacy and open PSYOP only target foreign audiences, then who besides PA can counter the enemy's or the media's shaping of US domestic opinion?" PA is military "Public Affairs" Officers who handle the release of information to the press. Basically, the officer quoted by Davis above argues for PSYOP (psychological operations) directed at the American people so as to counter what the media might conclude on their own. He states this is essential in order to "safeguard U.S. national will." In other words, if the American people get the straight unadulterated news from the front they might conclude, as they did in Vietnam, that the war was not worth fighting. The military must "safeguard" the public from their own judgments through what Lt. Col. Davis proves by way of much documented evidence arrayed throughout his report, are nothing more than omissions, distortions, and flat out lies regarding the actual state of affairs in Afghanistan. Lt. Col. Davis doesn't let the mainstream media off the hook either, showing that the cozy relationship between reporters and military command creates an environment where information operations are easy to carry out. He dispels the idea that either the so called "liberal media," or right winger, Fox News, type biases were at fault but, "Rather, it was a cumulative failure in our nation's major media in every category: network news, cable news, magazines, and major newspapers." Logic dictates that total and pervasive failures of this sort denote *policy* rather than happenstance.

    The photographs of Mathew Brady of the horrifying results of the battle at Gettysburg are credited with helping to bring the Civil War to a close. The lonely bodies in combat fatigues washed up on the solemn beaches of Tarawa and all those blood soaked Pacific islands are part of the immortal record of sacrifice of WWII. Men weeping in the rain and mud reaching out to the torn bodies of their friends under fire in the delta and highlands of Vietnam moved a generation to ask why? None of this will be afforded the present population in America because it does not suit the needs of the *Military Industrial Complex* that President Dwight

D. Eisenhower warned the American people about in his farewell address to the nation on January 17, 1961.

> This conjunction of an immense military establishment and a large arms industry is new in the American experience. The total influence – economic, political, even spiritual – is felt in every city, every statehouse, every office of the federal government. We recognize the imperative need for this development. Yet we must not fail to comprehend its grave implications. Our toil, resources and livelihood are all involved; so is the very structure of our society. In the councils of government, we must guard against the acquisition of unwarranted influence, whether sought or unsought, by the military-industrial complex. The potential for the disastrous rise of misplaced power exists and will persist.
>
> We must never let the weight of this combination endanger our liberties or democratic processes. We should take nothing for granted. Only an alert and knowledgeable citizenry can compel the proper meshing of the huge industrial and military machinery of defense with our peaceful methods and goals so that security and liberty may prosper together.

The rise of the *Military Industrial Complex* and its media censor parallels the rise of the overlords of media consolidation itself and it all represents a gross violation of the founding philosophies of the United States of America.

> A popular government without popular information or the means of acquiring it is but a prologue to a farce or a tragedy or perhaps both. Knowledge will forever govern ignorance; and a people who mean to be their own governors must arm themselves with the power that knowledge gives.

James Madison said that in 1822 and his words are very much in the vein of what all the founding father's prescribed regarding this central tenant in the preservation of the Republic, that information of all kinds, of the past in education, and in the present in the media, *are crucial to a people that would be free*. Without clear facts – not talking heads debating political position – but basic realities without gloss or spin or omission of pertinent detail, the people are simply not living in the real world, but rather a confused and manufactured one meant to simulate liberty while it shapes the mind to follow the herd.

Essentially, what media control has achieved is the ability to manufacture culture. "Welcome to the desert of the real," said Morpheus to Neo in the insightful film, *The Matrix*, as he revealed the truth behind the simulation Neo had always taken for reality. Culture in the most basic and natural state constitutes a "stylizing" of those behaviors and beliefs that have ensured the survival of the people and is the expression of the human spirit as it reaches for "the good, the true, and the beautiful," in its transcendent role, as Plato put it. When a culture comes under the control of a power group that wishes to utilize it for their own purposes, then the truth of the human spirit is lost and the lush, living, wilderness of genuine human culture is turned to the "desert of the real." Genuine human expression is replaced by a fake monstrosity, a digital simulacra that seem to resemble a culture, but like a Frankenstein's monster or cloned zombie, has no soul. In the place of truth, human passion and wisdom, in the place of the probing of the deepest doubts and questions, what is slipped in under cover is "programming," that's programming as in *software*. It is a container for your mind, a cell of sorts, that tells you what to think while it sets up boundaries that your speculation is not allowed to go beyond. "Only crazy people believe that!" Anything that is off limits is continually presented as grounds for the label of "nut job." Good Americans don't believe in a lot of "mumbo jumbo, airy fairy, egg head, psychobabble, nonsense" – is the message that is rehearsed daily. In this way "dangerous" philosophies and knowledge are rendered invisible. Anything that seeks to direct the individual to a higher order of thought that would examine *the context* of life, the larger, human constructs beneath the economy and politics as it relates to the psychology of the individual is rebuffed, because looking there would reveal the concentration of power and its manipulative networks and the techniques that sustain it. Questioning common beliefs requires courage and independence of mind. It's easier to be "normal." So, *normality* is designed and maintained to support the status quo, while even the "radical" is coopted into the system. Like the girl with the tattoos, funny hair and punk outfits that works in the lab for the Naval Crime Scene Investigation (NCSI) team, one of many patriotic TV shows hunting terrorists and their evil domestic accomplices who, much like Senator McCarthy's "commies" of the 1950's, seem to be lurking behind every door.

The exterior of these characters means nothing, has no relationship to the interior. The punk attire is not an expression of life philosophy any deeper than hair die and tattoo ink. The punk movement in Britain in the seventies and early eighties was an expression of social rebellion against an elitist system that had closed the union factories and was handing out low wage service jobs in their place. The wild attire was meant to make the individual unhireable for what was considered wage slavery. The "radicals" who appear on American TV are only caricatures without soul. They are collections of attitudes presented as archetypal children that refuse to grow up, helping out the adults who dress right, eat meat and potatoes, and accept the system simply as unquestionably right. There is no intelligent questioning by the rebellious on TV. There is only the time it will take for them to grow up and "fly right," in these stories.

Horror is another way that the mind is shut to independent thinking. Horror stories in the contemporary vernacular are not allegories like Mary Shelly's *Frankenstein's Monster*, warning us against a scientific trend that reduces humans to machines, mere collections of parts. The horror stories of today serve much in the way gargoyles on medieval cathedrals served to scare people into thinking that the world outside the holy realm is ringed with demons. The message then as now is one that seeks to possess the interior space of human beings, to order it by a centralized control. The church knew that the route to power and the knowledge of genuine spirituality lies within. As the apocryphal Gospel of Thomas, a remnant of original Christianity, tells us, "The Kingdom is inside you, and outside you...but if you will not know yourselves, then you will live in poverty, and it is you who *are* that poverty." [9]

The Romans, seeking to repair a fracturing empire adopted the most literal of the "Christ" cults, which excluded personal "gnosis" or revelation in order to create a new state religion they hoped would glue the populace back together under the power of a hierarchy of priests who controlled all knowledge on the model of the old "priest king" with Constantine as the first Pope. Going within to find your own private line to God, and thus truth, was something that had to be seriously controlled. By the middle ages the gargoyles had appeared to make sure that when the populace went within they would do it in the only safe place from evil, a sacred zone controlled by the priests. The church building became a patterning model, a program for the interior space of the individual. Thus, the Roman church coopted the personal subjective minds of its followers.

The sacred realm within had to be officiated by the priests. Without their guidance any individual that sought their own private route to God or his angels would be in danger of being set upon by the menagerie of demons that was said to lurk everywhere in the invisible realms of the dark ages.

The common theme of any horror film today where an individual seeks the occult, *the hidden*, through ritual, meditative acts, tarot cards, special radio receivers and recording technology, psychic powers, you name it – what the person inevitably finds is not wisdom but *demons*. Homicidal insanity ensues. Demon possession takes over. Evil aliens steal their children. Devils infest their homes and imprison their friends in abandoned factories ruled by sadistic lunatics under orders from Satan or his minions. These are the new gargoyles informing the audience not to mess with unauthorized routes to wisdom. Stay out of the interior of your mind and the invisible spaces beyond matter. Only demons lurk there, (even Descartes said so).

Keep your mind firmly on the material. That is the modern programing. There is no depth to consciousness, the establishment psychologist B.F. Skinner proclaimed, only "behavior" in the world, only material things we can measure. If you get curious about all those strange myths regarding angels and aliens and treasures deep within, then Hollywood lets you know quite firmly that you had better get your answers from authorized sources, *real* scientists and priests. Doing your own research is *highly discouraged*.

Authoritarian societies always seek to crush any attempt in the populace to go within. Meditation and personal contemplation have always been, as the yogic tradition in India states, the "royal road" to higher knowledge. Not only the great spiritual mystics but also the most talented scientists and artists through the ages have always pointed to the depths of their own minds as the source of inspiration that informed their genius and so the great achievements of human history. Albert Einstein once said that, "In creative work, imagination is more important than knowledge." It is said that creative imagination is fed from "deep springs" of inspiration. To "inspire" is literally to *allow the spirit to come in*. "Fantasy and imagination suggest how the world might be. Knowledge and experience limit the possibilities; melding the two begets understanding. Without the illusions of the mind, a clear grasp on reality is impossible, and vice versa," wrote Robert and Michele Root-Bernstein in their study of creative thought.[10] In accessing this creative imagination the authors point to much from contemplative and meditative traditions, demonstrating the link between creative imagination and the deeper truths accessed by mystics East and West. Horror is meant to regulate access to the deeper levels of this source as one of many controls.

Having "knowledge and experience limit the possibilities" is essential for the maintenance of the status quo, as is thwarting any revelation that might see beyond materialism. They must block this route to independent, inspired thinking that is the very fountainhead of freedom, evolution and human progress. So devils are stationed there to ward off the spiritually intrigued from moving too deeply into their own minds. This effect stands alongside Darwin and Freud's theories of the primitive instinctual "killer ape" that lurks within, concepts designed for the more psychologically inclined person who is warned by these ideas that nothing exists in the depths of their minds but irrational, raw instinct. For those who might investigate the medical data on the deep unconscious they will find the neurological theories that suggest the brain is filled with the random firing of neurons that create loads of imagery in dreams and visions and imaginings, they are told are the chaos of the brain, have no meaning and should be ignored. The status quo culture provides a *shut door* to the deeper mind for all tastes and inclinations, while traditional religious organizations continue the work of the Romans. This is both an outgrowth of the dominance of the mental/rational structure of consciousness and a continuing strategy on the part of culture controllers to thwart independence of mind. There are alternative theories of mind and much data to support the notion that the deep unconscious provides a profound source of personal wisdom, information, and discovery, as discussed in another chapter, but these sources are marginalized in favor of the machine model of human life that is all surface without depth. This ideology has been shaped to conduct thought to one end.

All contact with the source of human genius within must be harnessed to the service of the status quo industries, as must all human effort of any kind – this is the hidden agenda of the artificial culture of mainstream media. Whether its TV shows or TV news, bright glossy magazines or blockbuster movies, it is all in the service of the collective. A population that has been cloned for the service of the elite corporate power base whose materialist doctrine seeks to turn individuals into self-reinforcing "markets," as worker/buyer units. True individuals in the Jeffersonian mold need not apply.

People become individuals with their own agendas through personal contemplation and meditation that sees through the programing of the outside society in search of authentic meaning specific to the individual and their genuine community. This is Carl Jung's *process of individuation*. "Know thyself" was inscribed in the forecourt of the Temple of Apollo at Delphi; "to thine own self be true," William Shakespeare reminded us. And it is this "self" that we must *know* and be *true to* that is counter to our programing as a worker/buyer unit in the service of yet another empire. It is precisely this individuated self that the media seeks to obscure and replace with a sales package.

The once independent media in the United States has suffered increasing attacks from moneyed interests and covert operations alike. In 1948, Frank Wisner, the head of the newly minted *Central Intelligence Agency*, initiated "operation mockingbird," a secret project aimed at influencing the domestic American media. It did so by recruiting influential editors like Phillip Graham of the *Washington Post*, who led the project and was successful in bringing under his influence key people at *The New York Times*, *The New York Herald Tribune*, *Time*, *Newsweek*, *The Miami News*, and a host of publications all over the country.[11] The main point of interest for the operation was American's attitude towards communism and their willingness to devote huge resources to counter it, as well as sending their sons to die in making war on it. Communist movements had sprung up in the third world as a response to continuing Western exploitation and post-colonial elitist governments that sought to maintain their seats on the money train as providers of cheap natural resources to the new American empire and the Europeans. The imperial agenda is always to maintain colonies in a state of poverty and subservience in order to keep the raw materials flowing at a discount back to the imperial nation. This is precisely what the British attempted to do to the Americans that led to the Revolution.

Without going into an extended history lesson what needs to be understood in reference to control of the press under *Mockingbird* was that American power did not want to upset the exploitive economic conditions in the third world that provided the cheap materials that were enriching domestic and European interests, so the colonial exploitation had to be maintained. This profitable situation was also the very generator of the communist uprisings the U.S. government claimed to be protecting the American people from. So, the only thing they could do was fight the ideology on purely political grounds, carefully avoiding discussion of the socio-economic conditions abroad. With this in mind the press had to blind the American people to the obvious contradictions of helping to suppress people around the world who were in exactly the same situation Americans had been in in the 18th century. The American people had to be conditioned to understand these "banana republics" through the proper imperial lens. The media was engaged to provide the story that would obfuscate the duplicity of American power in maintaining the undemocratic and exploitive conditions in the third world for its own advantage while decrying the communist threat that was in those rejoins a response to its own policies. The obvious answer to the communist "menace" was to cultivate democracy in these areas, but this is exactly what couldn't be done at the same time cheap labor and resources were maintained. Leaders elected by the people would always ask the American companies for a bigger piece of the pie, so the CIA went about clandestinely defeating democracy as it did in Guatemala, Nicaragua, El Salvador, Chile, The Dominican Republic, Egypt, Iran, and many other places in order to install strong men who would exploit their own people in favor of maintaining American profits.[12]

This definitely had to be kept out of the papers if Americans were going to be able to maintain their self-image as *defenders of freedom and democracy*, which formed the main rationalization for military service and the public support for American foreign policy. This is the ongoing lie that keeps the machine grinding along over the bones of the conquered – foreign *and domestic*. The general public must be kept in a state of permanent ignorance for this condition to be perpetuated and so as the machinations of American power have advanced over the decades it has been necessary to secure a wider and tighter control of the media so as to foster what Pulitzer prize winning author Chris Hedges, calls "the empire of illusion."

"I spent two decades as a foreign correspondent in Latin America, Africa, the Middle East, and the Balkans. I saw there the crimes and injustices committed in our name and often with our support..." writes Chris Hedges regarding his tenure with the *New York Times*.

> The country I live in today uses the same civic, patriotic, and historical language to describe itself, the same symbols and iconography, the same national myths, but only the shell remains.

The America we celebrate is an illusion...Our nation has been hijacked by oligarchs, corporations and a narrow, selfish political and economic elite, a small and privileged group that governs, and often steals, on behalf of moneyed interests...The government, stripped of any real sovereignty, provides little more than technical expertise for elites and corporations that lack moral restraints and a concept of the common good. America has become a façade. It has become the greatest illusion in a culture of illusion.[13]

If you think of all the information out there as a layer ten inches thick, the top inch is the managed information and artificial culture of the authorized mainstream. Below that is about eight inches of all the other available information. Below that is the last inch which is the suppressed information that elites, governments, and militaries actively work to keep secret. The eight inches below the mainstream is not actively suppressed even though it is dangerous to the maintenance of the status-quo. It doesn't need to be, because video in the form of television and film has largely replaced print as the media of choice and because so many people have had their educations so seriously compromised in the U.S. most people simply don't read anymore. Most of the remaining erudite minority who do don't read below the top inch.

The top inch of the information strata contains everything from what you see on CNN, FOX, MSNBC and PBS (all of TV news) to what is read in the *New York Times*, *Vanity Fair*, *Time*, *Newsweek*, *The Economist*, and the rest of all the glossy print magazines on-line and on the newsstands as well as the well-publicized books of the establishment authors that seek to mythologize American history and events reinforcing the picture of an unquestionable American superiority in the public mind. Occasionally, the more probing journals like *The Atlantic*, the *New Yorker*, *Harpers* and the like might dip into the higher regions just below the authorized one inch, in which case a "furor" erupts in the rest of the status quo outlets in rebuttal, but for the most part the mainstream media stays in safe territory.

Any doubts as to the direct manipulation of the press by the big money in America should consider this statement by David Rockefeller in an address to the Bilderberg society at their annual meeting in Baden-Baden Germany in June of 1991:

We are grateful to the Washington Post, The New York Times, Time Magazine, and other great publications where directors have attended our meetings and respected their promises of discretion for almost forty years. It would have been impossible for us to develop our plan for the world if we had been subject to the bright lights of publicity during those years. But the world is more sophisticated and prepared to march toward a world government. The supranational sovereignty of an intellectual elite and world bankers is surely preferable to the national auto-determination practiced in past centuries.[14]

If the discussions at the Bilderberg meeting had ever appeared in *Time* magazine or on the front page of the *New York Times* then perhaps people at home might have wondered if they really want to be ruled by "an intellectual elite and world bankers." They might have given it a bit of thought and some history professor or clever student might have picked out this quote from Thomas Jefferson: "I believe that banking institutions are more dangerous to our liberties than standing armies. Already they have raised up a moneyed aristocracy that has set the government at defiance..." But, you see, most people have never had the chance to consider the history or David Rockefeller and company's "plan for the world," because the press, the glorious "fourth estate," has ceased to work for the people and democracy. This is why it is essential to probe beneath the top inch of "news."

In the unauthorized but still available eight inches below you find the books and magazines, the occasional on-line interview and documentary that actually seek to reveal the whole story not covered in the top inch. An example is the war in the Middle East that is constantly talked about in the top inch without reference to the history of Western political manipulation and the big elephant in the room – oil. Any individual with an I.Q. greater than a dachshund can read a short history of the region and understand at once why the locals might be a bit *perturbed* with American and British intervention. Their democratically elected leaders have been toppled and despots have been championed and supported by the West who have murdered and imprisoned their people for generations while they fail to develop their economies in a way that provides decent lives for the majority as they do a wonderful job of insuring a generous flow of oil to the West.

If foreign powers came into Texas and installed a proxy government that impoverished most of the people so that the oil could be shipped overseas, then you can bet your bottom dollar that a hurricane of bullets would explode across that land that would make the Iraq war look like a paint ball match. This is precisely why the people of Texas and the rest of the country are not allowed to have anything like a realistic public discussion regarding the true situation in the Middle East. If they did some empathy might be generated and that would not be good for the oil cartels and the big banking interests that are dependent on their massive flow of money.[15]

All kinds of things are floating around in the middle eight inches of information that are not suppressed, but go mostly unread. There are things that would astonish most Americans, like: the fact that many American industrialists supported the Nazis well into the war and received for their largesse commendations and even medals sent by Adolf Hitler himself for their service to the Third Reich. GM built trucks that carried German troops into Poland[16] and IBM tabulating machines helped keep track of the numbers going to the death camps.[17] Forbearer of the Bush presidents, Prescott Bush, was found in violation of the *Trading with the Enemy Act*, as was the DuPont corporation, while the Rockefeller oil interests provided Hitler with specialized additives for aircraft fuel that allowed Nazi bombers to reach England. The Rockefeller Foundation's most morally corrupt contribution to the war was its support for the eugenics race purifying research at the Kaiser Wilhelm Institute.[18] The historian, F. William Engdahl, has written: "Bush, Rockefeller, Harriman, DuPont, and Dillon were all instrumental in providing critical support to the Third Reich in its early years as part of their grand geopolitical game plan – to bring the great European powers, especially Germany and Russia, to ruin by 'bleeding each other to death,' thereby opening the door to the hegemony of the American Century."[19]

The Spanish American War is particularly interesting and virtually unknown to most Americans, but considered a "first Vietnam" by scholars. American forces had kicked out the Spanish and promptly reneged on their promise to allow the Philippines to rule itself. The zeal to rid the countryside of insurgents depopulated entire provinces in some of the most wide spread slaughter the world has ever seen, dragging on year after year as the president promised the American public it would be over at any time. At one point in the war American military doctrine made any male person over the age of 10 a fair target to be shot on sight. Water boarding, far from being a recent invention in the Middle East conflict, was a prime method used on Filipino combatants. *Time* magazine even graced their cover of May 22, 1902 with a scene of American Army troops waterboarding a Filipino prisoner. A story that was meant to chastise the government for resorting to the same kind of human rights abuses they had condemned the European Imperialists for.[20] If this episode in American history had been thoroughly understood and retained in the popular memory, that is taught *in the schools*, then America might have avoided the horrific waste of lives in Vietnam a half century later. One suspects that it is precisely the potent lessons from the war in the Philippines, so discouraging of imperial adventures abroad, that required it to be submerged below the surface of public discourse. (The only thing remembered regarding the Spanish American War is Teddy Roosevelt's charge up San Juan Hill in Cuba, a scene often erroneously depicted with the future president on horseback.)

J.P. Morgan, in league with other banking and industrial interests, was alleged to have conspired to foment a coup against President Franklin D. Roosevelt, as testified to in a 1934 senate hearing on the matter. General Smedley Butler told the inquiry that he had been approached by agents of J.P. Morgan bank and other, at first undisclosed powerful persons, to lead a fascist brigade of veterans against the White House. Wall Street was very unhappy with the president's recent regulatory actions and they wished to engage the general's experience as a military man to plan and carry out the overthrow of the President. Besides shifting major government capital into labor projects for the discarded working class, Roosevelt's leadership had enacted sweeping reforms of the banking and financial field in response to the irresponsible speculating that had led to the great depression. When the bankers threatened to cut off credit to Roosevelt's *New Deal* they thought better when they became very much afraid he would take the further step of injecting into the economy government issued currency that would challenge the monopoly the big banks held in charging interest on the money they printed for the government. Roosevelt probably saved his own life by not taking this further step, much to the detriment of the American people who are saddled with the taxes that are almost entirely dedicated to servicing this debt to the Federal Reserve banking cartel. (An institution which isn't "federal" at all but run by private banking interests.) Prior to their aborted coup attempt, the Morgan group, along with other prominent *robber baron* interests, had been preparing the country for fascism for years through their support of fascist groups recruited from veterans organizations and the Klu Klutz Klan, as well as a number of proto-fascist "citizens defense" organizations hopped up on "red scare" tactics. With names like the *Silver Shirts* and the *Crusaders* they championed a virulent far right militarism that despised labor unions and socialists of every shade, favoring just the sort of militarized capitalism that had taken power in Germany and Italy with the help of American finance. The elite owned press of the era such as the *New York Times* and *Time* magazine belittled the accusations of the General and although the committee concluded that the evidence showed there had been an attempt to *seize control of the United States Government* by Morgan and allied interests, they decided the evidence didn't warrant prosecution and the entire affair has been swept clean from establishment history books.[21]

American history is full of the stories of big money manipulation of the American public; in fact, *it is the story* of the American public as the country matured into an industrial power. The reality is that American elites from the Spanish American war to the present have conspired to promote a clandestine American empire on the model of the old European imperialists, using local proxies for the most part and American troops when necessary. At the same time they were selling it to a reluctant populace as "world trade" and a fight for freedom against "godless communists," recently replaced by Islamic hoards.

An entire genera of historical writing exists on this subject from left to right. Some are for American power using the world's resources as they see fit in a world populated by primitives and despots; others see it as simply old fashioned imperial power mongering slaughtering innocents while carrying out massive acts of piracy, but nobody *in the know* questions the reality of an American empire. Only the rhetoric of politicians and the mainstream American public are allergic to the term eschewing the imperial label in favor of a *Disney* vision of American troops killing "bad guys" and handing out candy bars. Unfortunately, the candy bar rate hasn't kept up with the civilian casualty count in places like Iraq and Afghanistan, and even Pakistan who is supposed to be on our side. A recent 2012 study by the combined efforts of the Stanford University and NYU law schools has determined that only about 2% of those killed by drone aircraft strikes are the intended targets, leaving 98% as people who got the wrong candy bar.

When American troops were handing out chocolate to European kids after sweeping the Nazi war machine out of town, they were heroes and the people loved them, kissed their cheeks and wept tears of joy creating generations of good will thereafter. America has done many great things in the world, but this shouldn't blind its citizens to the fact that in the wars in the Middle East children will mostly remember the Americans as the people who blew-up their house, killed their family and traumatized them for life. This is an image that the majority of the American public just can't accept and when it does reach them it brings up anger towards the source rather than the act itself. Even if the truth were hand delivered to each household with supporting documentation proving that the wars in the Middle East have always been about oil, from Lawrence of Arabia to *Operation Iraqi Freedom*, the average American would simply scoff and think it a conspiracy theory or another lie from the "liberal press." Such is the degree to which the false culture has achieved its end.

No conspiracy theories are necessary. All the facts are well documented on-line and in the libraries and bookstores across the country, but most Americans simply don't look. Intelligent school curriculums have been gutted and the people themselves are way too busy shopping and being entertained to take the time to educate themselves. As the scholar, Rebecca Lemov, stated in her book on the history of mind control in America, "The obscurity attaching to the events here recounted is mainly the result of their having been ignored for some time, and the story of human engineering is in fact available to anyone with a library card" [22]

Unfortunately, most Americans think of books as boring and something they were forced to read in high school or college. Now that they're out they don't care for it and would rather watch TV, see a movie, or surf the net for funny videos. Their reading is confined to short pieces under headlines or on the sports page. The most popular commercial magazine in America is: *Better Homes and Gardens*, the next most popular is a video game magazine. *The Journal of the American Medical Association* has reported that some 46% of Americans can't even read the label on their prescription medication. The NEA reported in 2008 that Americans between the ages of 15 and 24 spent 2 hours a day watching television and 7 minutes a day reading. The National Adult Literacy Survey consistently reports that about half of all Americans can't read at all or are *functionally illiterate*, which simply means they can read but not well enough to actually utilize reading as a way of gaining real knowledge in life. Reading simple instructions, the sports scores, or labels on boxes in the grocery store will allow you to function in the world, but without the ability to read history, commentary of a philosophical nature, and literature of all kinds, you can't really understand the inner workings of the world around you and in such a state become powerless.

The switch from print to video has played into the hands of the manipulators as television and movies are cost heavy industries that can be easily bought up and controlled as opposed to books that can be produced by small presses and distributed through independent shops or mail ordered anywhere in the world quite inexpensively. The Internet too has been an unquestioned boon for the independent thinkers looking to mine the information field beneath the top inch, but the moneyed interests are feverishly at work looking for ways to control it as well.

Those who dwell entirely in the controlled top inch of information in the U.S. are subject to a certain psychological syndrome when they do encounter information such as in the examples above. The average citizen has been conditioned to see the news as a free field that will report whatever is really happening. They think: "If it's true it would be in the news, somewhere; there's always a leak." Used to hearing about congressional scandals and loads of embarrassing trivia they feel that everything makes it into the paper or their favorite show sooner or later. The intrigue and assassination, the secret agents and saboteurs, and the conspiracies and manipulations, that are part of the way the world has worked through history, all happen in the minds of the viewer in the fictional world only seen in TV shows and movies. In the nightly news and their favorite radio talk show this sort of thing almost never appears. It just isn't generally reported in the top inch, so when the truth does break through the barrier on occasion, the public tends to typically respond, "It can't possibly be true – it sounds like a James Bond movie!" and they laugh it off and forget all about it, wondering why people would believe such outrageous things, drifting back into the sleep imposed world of the artificial culture they live in.

In that plebian world everything looks the same every day. No intrigue or "black op" covert military actions are going on in their town except on gaming systems and televisions. These events exclusively inhabit a world of fantasy they see on the "unreal" video screen. It is a typical experience for individuals living through extraordinary events like massive earthquakes or murders to report that they are struck by a feeling of "being in a movie or a TV show." This was an oft heard utterance of those who directly experienced the 911 attack in New York City.²³ This is a direct result of this partitioning of the mind into "extraordinary = unreal video" and "real = boring every day working, driving, shopping." In this way mainstream media has turned the entire country into part of the factory system where the efficient patterns of the populace as worker/buyer units must not be disturbed. Even if they see behind the curtain on occasion the conditioned person has been taught to dismiss the evidence.

Nearly half a century ago Marshal McLuhan told us that "the medium is the message." What he was pointing to is the fact that the way people communicate changes society in profound ways. It's not that content doesn't matter; it's that the way it's delivered formats the mind to understand the world within a certain frame of reference. Radio, television, and now the Internet has brought information to people in an accelerating torrent that surrounds and envelops until what is provided from outside the individual becomes more influential than personal reflection or experience. Media in its evolution has tended to take people away from where they actually live. Everything becomes "mediated" in the sense of an interpretive barrier between the world and the individual. The direct apprehension of the world, just as it is, is lost in favor of a molded, artificial construct shaped by the technology and those who own its content.²⁴

Many scholars and cultural critics have written at length of the influence of Walt Disney, or "Disneyism," on America through the revisionist histories in its film and TV work, its cleansing and reworking of traditional tales, and the actual creating of artificial "lands" in its amusement parks. Disneyland is contrived to offer visitors a kind of midcentury pioneer Protestant vision of an ideal world, the wilderness pacified and turned from itself to a mirror of a child's imagination, history cleansed of massacre and exploitation, and the American future laid out before the viewer as the splendid destiny of a truly blessed people.²⁵ Through Disney's vision Americans are taught how to see themselves in a thoroughly wholesome and flattering way that can be enjoyed by the whole family, but this child's vision of the world is entirely inappropriate for the adults who fall under its spell because it is without honest reflection, without the self-appraisal that would allow for a process of maturity that recognizes past mistakes and urges improvements. Disney is a celebration of a once and never ending American perfection that forms the basis of a mindset that cannot tolerate any critique or questioning of American virtue. Radio and television pundits demonstrate the effect when they regularly label as "America haters," or "traitors," any person who dares to bring up the bad behavior of the corporate state, like exploitation of workers, war profiteering, covert manipulation of markets, or anything from a great list of defects in the institutions that have shifted from supporting society to preying on it. "Patriotism" is equated with upholding the illusion of the perfect America. Any criticism of institutions and American action abroad equates to treason. What better lesson for a people being conditioned to serve an increasingly hegemonic and autocratic corporate oligarchy?

This is the triumph of the managers of the worker/buyer units as they successfully carry out Professor Carol Quigley's "reaction" to the need for reform of a society that no longer serves the average citizen. "We speak of reaction when the privileged vested-interest groups are able to prevent either reform or circumvention."[26] Certainly, information is the essential ingredient for either of these things and information is just what has been so cleverly shaped and edited to prevent suspicion from falling on the guilty parties. All criticism of the financial and corporate powers is deftly diverted to "the government," which now serves as a straw man for the elite buffering them from public outrage and providing corporate cheerleaders with political capital to use for the continued destruction of federal regulation.

The selection of what may seem extraordinary events in American history mentioned above is really quite representative of the sort of deadly subterfuge that has been typical of civilization everywhere from the court intrigues of the ancient empires to the Machiavellian maneuvering of the Middle Ages. Just reading an uncensored history of the papacy would shock and amaze most people. The history of the economic empire of Venice provides a case study in conspiracy, intrigue, strategic assassination and every other dirty trick ever conceived by human beings. The Venetians burned so many people with their constant lies and manipulations that all the powers of Europe rose up together to attempt to smash them forever in the League of Cambrai in 1508.

In the United States during the period of industrialization after the Civil War titanic egos of money and greed set about attempting to capture the biggest shares of economic power in the country through financial warfare. Beneath their feet whole populations of common people were financially ruined in the fallout from their struggles. Farms, ranches, and small businesses everywhere where rendered profitless as exploitive railroad barons jacked the price of shipping through the roof after capturing or destroying the competition. As the entirety of American industry settled into the hands of the strongest players they began to cooperate to thwart competition entirely. They did this by colluding in monopolies of essential railroads and industries through conspiratorial syndicates, variously referred to as "pools," "combines," and "trusts," anything but "monopolies," because monopolies where against the law. Bribing politicians was a regular part of doing business and was simply written off in the books with such terms as "extralegal expenses." By century's close the most powerful man in the country was widely held to be, not the President, but J.P. Morgan, the banker who had deftly gathered up the purse strings of most of the major railroads and industries. John D. Rockefeller was a close second. The game of "Monopoly" Americans all play as children was inspired by the actual economic history of the nation; a history rife with conspiracy.

"People of the same trade seldom meet together, even for merriment and diversion, but the conversation ends in a conspiracy against the public, or in some contrivance to raise prices," stated the hero of American economics himself, Adam Smith, in his "bible," *The Wealth of Nations*, published in 1776. This human tendency to try to secretly contrive things to a person's or group's advantage certainly is not new and certainly not gone, but most Americans have been trained to understand reality as being quite mundane and aboveboard and conspiracy as rare or even ridiculous. Nothing could be of greater pleasure to those elite moneyed interests at the top of the power pyramids than this misunderstanding. The incapacity to see through this gross error is a direct result of the education system both official and unofficial. The official is found in the classroom, while the unofficial is found on the many viewing screens.

Television Shows and Popular Film

Television in general has become the most important weapon in the arsenal of those seeking to manipulate. Although television can provide relaxing entertainment in the evenings after a day at work, some humorous or exciting scenario offering some hours of distraction from the stresses of life, most people don't understand how television programing itself seeks to shape their view of the world. It is commonly thought that television commercials are the things to watch out for as overt attempts to dictate buying habits, but few understand how the shows themselves are designed to move audiences toward desired behaviors while conditioning individuals to carry a warped view of the world outside the limited range of their daily experiences.

Police dramas, for instance, often inform audiences in their promos that they are "authentic" and just like the real thing, with real police veterans advising and reviewing the show assuring people that this show *is as real as it gets!* Each week a new bad guy is tracked down and captured, or more often these days, blown all over a wall with shot guns and assault rifles. The innocent are protected and the evil doers are punished. Sure, there's a few bad cops in there occasionally, there's some short cuts taken, procedures flaunted – but that's what real police work is like. The message is: "It's a dirty world out there but, thank God, we have some real men, and now tough women, who can deal with this scum while out maneuvering the pencil necked bureaucrats and their stupid rules." Folks at home can turn from the equally distorted evening news where crime runs rampant right to the "authentic" police drama where a guy in tight jeans and a designer sport coat lets loose all the pent-up rage the viewer feels from living in a world he or she is convinced has become crowded with evil assholes. Every year there's a new show claiming to be the one that really shows it all, that's *the realist of the real*. And year after year it all gets bloodier and more frenetically insane.

The problem with all this is that if they really put police work on television viewers would yawn and change the channel. Real detective work turns out to be monumentally tedious, spending a lot of time on the phone and meeting people who say very little and writing up reports that usually end in not solving anything. In fact, in reality crimes are hardly ever solved. Bad guys are hardly ever brought to justice, that is, real bad guys not just some poor kid that never had a shot at anything else peddling crack on the corner with a pistol in his pocket. The prisons are full of those kinds of people. They're easy to arrest and convict. That sort of bad guy is simply engaging the economy available to him. The bad guys of profound influence, such as the criminals who defrauded America in the financial disaster of 2008, go generally untouched.

In the U.S. each year way less than half of violent crimes are solved, around 40%; only about 15% of property crimes are solved. The other boring statistic is that, regardless of what the television news may suggest each night, crime in general and murder specifically are way down in the U.S. since their high in the 1980's. Most crime statistics in the U.S. cluster around major urban ghettos in cities like Baltimore, Detroit, and Dallas. Very little in the way of "exciting crime action" goes on anywhere else. Most towns in the U.S. are really quite safe, the biggest crime in years amounting to some kid smashing somebody's mail box. Regardless, from TV news and programming it is easy to get the feeling that the whole society is under siege from street criminals. This serves as a perfect diversion from the actual siege being waged by corporate power against democracy encouraging the public to accept rising police state tactics.

The never ending stream of lawyer shows also seems equally misrepresentative of reality. Although justice is served nightly on the television, it remains ever elusive in actual court rooms where money and politics are more likely determinants of the end result than who may be innocent. In 1978 Harvey Milk, the first openly Gay person to be elected to public office in California as a supervisor in San Francisco was gunned down in cold blood along with the mayor, by Dan White, who was excused for the crime by reason of the now famous, "Twinkie defense." The sentence was reduced to voluntary manslaughter because the court found that the defendant had "diminished capacity" for rational thought due to a diet comprised mostly of Hostess Twinkies. Dan White served a little under five years. It would be nice if this sort of case were rare, but unfortunately justice in the U.S. is incredibly political. At the time of the murders Americans were struggling to accept that gay people had rights too and the jury came up with a verdict reminiscent of earlier times when the murder of Native Americans or African Americans similarly drew light sentences or complete dismissal.

Of course bigotry certainly isn't gone. About 10% of the Black male population of the country is in prison right now, a condition widely believed by researchers to be the product of bigotry that results in stiffer sentences for blacks as opposed to whites for the same crimes. Black men are no longer slaves but are still sold as a commodity in the form of "prisoners," a product of our system that is worth big money to the new private prison industry supported by the tax payers. Lobbyists for the private prison industry regularly work for stiffer sentencing guidelines so as to insure a regular flow of their commodity. If this condition persists black men may soon appear on the commodities market, their value as prisoners will rise and fall like pork bellies or orange juice, providing an investment opportunity the way shares in slave ships once did.

It would be nice if these types of cases were aberrations but unfortunately, the very structure of the modern court system as it is configured in the U.S. is not built to provide justice. It is designed to reward a certain kind of argument and as such is prone to all manner of political and social prejudice. No recent example is more clear on this point than the suits brought against small farmers by the Monsanto Corporation. Monsanto has harassed and sued family farmers when the pollen from their genetically engineered crops blows onto an adjacent property contaminating the neighboring fields. When the patented crop begins to show up in the neighbor's harvest they are sued by Monsanto for patent infringement or for saving seed to plant again, a practice forbidden by contract for those buying the genetically modified product. In a recent ruling by Judge Naomi Reice Buchwald, in the Southern District of New York, at the end of February 2012, small farmers lost their class action suit to prevent Monsanto from suing them for wind borne pollination they could not control and from their agents coming on the famers land to harass them and steal samples of their crops to test. The judge stated in her opinion that because the plaintiffs could only site their 13 cases of Monsanto actually taking these actions that it, "is hardly significant when compared to the number of farms in the United States, approximately two million." [27] In other words, she believed small farmers didn't need to be protected because Monsanto had only perpetrated these acts 13 times. How many times does it take, one wonders, before citizens are worthy of protection from corporate thugs?

Corporate power can punish whistleblowers or anyone getting in their way simply by slapping the person with any kind of suit regardless of merit to force the individual to have to pay the enormous legal fees associated with any court battle. This is one of the main fractures in the American right of access to the courts supposedly guaranteed by the Bill of Rights. It has become impossible for most Americans to actually exercise that right to any satisfactory degree due to the fact that the legal profession has set up a toll both at the door to the court house, charging hundreds of dollars an hour just to have a try at spinning the all too uncertain roulette wheel of justice inside. Law has become one of the most lucrative professions in the United States and as such attracts many individuals to its ranks purely as a means of mining wealth from the litigation landscape.

It is true that there are many fine men and women dedicated to justice fighting tirelessly for the underdogs battered by powerful interests, standing up for the beleaguered environment, and pushing back valiantly against the totalitarian monster now menacing our civil rights, but unfortunately the experience of most Americans with their court system suggests strongly that the system has turned into a *cash cow* of titanic proportions for the legal profession as a whole. This pervasive condition tends to shift the weight of the system behind those with money, thus defeating the whole point of "equal protection under the law" within a democracy.

This, the most important of legal issues today, is never covered in any television legal drama. In fact you will rarely hear anything about fees in these shows. A person can watch a legal drama and come out believing that any person of average income can go to court and, after a bit of touch and go for drama sake, come out with justice served and their bank book intact. This is rarely the case in a country where you are more likely to have to spend the kid's college fund and take out a second mortgage on the house just to get started in court, and what takes an hour on television will more than likely take years in the real world, all the while ruining the person financially while destroying their peace of mind.

When we look at the medical shows we find again that what they portray bears little resemblance to reality. As discussed earlier, the medical profession is in crisis in the United States having been thoroughly corrupted by the pharmaceutical industry. This, as well as their outmoded dedication to reductionist machine-mind approaches to health, has made medical care less safe than stock car racing. On television the genius doctor will root out the cause of the strange and mysterious symptoms by the end of the hour saving the patient in the nick of time, all the while maintaining an affair with the well-built nurse or fellow physician in some passionate subplot scenes full of bare backs and the sides of breasts, only to be interrupted by some equally sweaty squalling argument fought for a patient's sake against a beastly administrator. As a matter of course, like the cop shows, the doctor dramas are always billed as "authentic portrayals."

Except for the affair, the whole show is an elaborate illusion with no similarity to any real hospital where almost all symptoms are never accurately diagnosed and if patients are being saved at the eleventh hour it is usually from an infection the hospital itself gave them. Not that the medical profession doesn't do some good things, emergency medicine is worthy of praise, but most doctoring is very routine, quite boring and would make a terrible television show.

It isn't just the plots and action that mislead, but sometimes the very settings themselves. It is common now in TV shows to see what are portrayed as average, middle-class Americans living in homes that are way beyond the means of the real middle-class in this country. One can survey the kitchens alone and see top of the line built-in appliances, high end counter tops and hardwood cabinets that would cost many tens of thousands of dollars. To even think about appointing a small kitchen this way demands a cost that is simply not practical for most people. Yet room after sprawling room in these programs depict a lifestyle requiring a high six figure salary far beyond that even of most double earner households and really only accessible to those making up the professional middle class who comprise only about 15% of the American population. What does it mean to the average middle income earner and lower income working class person when they are constantly shown pictures of American life they cannot live up to?

For those few still holding pioneer values or those responding to the evolution of their consciousness they may simply disregard the comparison by being less materialistic and more interested in deeper experiences and spiritual values in their lives. But for those not quite there yet, for those struggling with their own ego's need for recognition and the validating regard of their peers, these shows must inspire a constant sense of inferiority. Just as they offer a false image of American life, they hide the failing fortunes of the working class behind a fantasy world. These unrepresentative images send the clear message to people that they're not winning the game, that they're not up with the crowd, that they're less than they should be inspiring anxiety and depression and shopping behavior that sends them constantly into debt in a futile attempt to "live the dream." But whose dream is it we must ask?

Pick any television show and what you are seeing is a misleading portrayal of life that is drunk down into the public unconscious to seed there the growth of all kinds of inaccurate beliefs about the world as it actually exists. When people are regularly misled as to the state of their civilization due to a steady diet of fantasy, they have little chance to raise their voices in the maintenance of democracy or in anger over the deterioration of the institutions that sustain a just and fair civilization.

On television everything is okay, sure there's a bad cop here and there, a tragic medical error, a lying attorney, as if to answer the doubts of viewers but in the end all the diseases are being defeated, all the bad guys are being arrested or killed, justice is served and the flag waves incessantly over it all as if to believe otherwise would be unpatriotic.

In interviews with Vietnam War veterans many cite John Wayne as the source of their misconceptions regarding war and heroism that led them to volunteer for combat, an experience that turned out to be much different than what the movies had suggested. During WWII John Wayne was actually booed out of a recovery ward in a Navy hospital he visited by men who had seen the true horror and tragedy of war and wanted nothing to do with the deceptive fantasy war heroes of the movie barons. [28] John Wayne has long since been replaced on the screen with a crowd of phony heroes even more deceptive in their glorification of killing and obedience to causes that are never evaluated from the mindset of a free and independent citizen of a democracy as described by Thomas Jefferson.

Jefferson believed that citizens have an absolute responsibility in the maintenance of democracy to scrutinize the agenda and directions of a federal government continually under the threat of cooptation by bankers and corporatists. The television heroes never seem to question who benefits from the dangerous adventures on which they are dispatched. There is this assumption that the killing they do and the death of their brothers-in-arms is always justified for some lofty and patriotic purpose that's never clearly delineated but much like the material status of the "average middleclass family" in television neighborhoods, simply hovers in the background as an unexamined mythos. These kinds of "givens" in television and film are the most subtle form of manipulation.

There are exceptions as always with occasional television and film works that seek not to manipulate but to inspire insight into the deeper forces of life, to evoke an appreciation for beauty and the true sources of happiness. But for the most part television and film are both products and tools of consumer capitalism. As such they seek to entice to purchase through any means possible and to reinforce in the viewer the pattern of striving that guarantees future purchases as it bolsters the dedication to the governing interests as a whole. The most dangerous thing about TV and film is not what it is obviously selling but what is beneath the surface of the stories in the assumptions of the characters regarding life and reality, the sort of world they believe in and are responding to. This is what the unwary viewer starts to take for granted as "normal," and thereby falls into habits that serve the needs of big money forces while departing from their own unique character and sources of wisdom.

When we examine the actual structure of film and television stories with regard to the presentation of violent action we find a consistent use of what is understood as "melodrama." This is a way of presenting conflict in which the sides are starkly dawn between a purely "good" hero against a purely "evil" bad guy. This chronic film and television mode of presentation tends to support a black and white interpretation of conflict in the public that works against any habit of seeking to understand the reasons behind conflict, the actual complex, human history, experience, and feelings that led the parties to the conflict in the first place.[29] This practiced viewpoint that sees one side as totally right and the other side as totally wrong then is likely to be transposed onto the public's assessment of real-world issues seen on other screens during news broadcasting. The whole world – other countries, religions, political parties – is then easily dismissed by a mind conditioned with melodrama, as *simply wrong*, without ever taking the time to try and understand the other side as anything but *stupid bad guys.*

The more sophisticated mode of storytelling known as *tragic drama* has always offered a healthier alternative to melodrama. In the tragic plot protagonists are pushed into destructive circumstances of their own making due to perfectly human issues that obscure their understanding-- egos led astray, a misplaced desire for retribution of past wrongs, a sincere belief that they are doing the right thing without understanding of the terrible consequences. In tragic drama the audience is led to sympathize with both sides recognizing the complexity of human struggles and thereby understanding the conflict and the terrible outcome as a human failing and therefore a tragedy, rather than as some ridiculously oversimplified heroic fight against a pure evil. In tragic drama the audience is educated, their insight into the human condition is deepened and they come away with compassion and a greater tendency to look for the misunderstandings and unknown history driving conflict. [30]

To not see the reason for the prevalence of melodrama and the rarity of tragic themes in the manufactured culture of America would be incredibly naive at this point in history. It is obviously essential for the maintenance of an American public easily maneuvered by corporate and political rhetoric that the culture machine pumps melodrama out in great volume. The public must absolutely be led away from any tendency to look beneath the surface and try to understand what motivates the "bad guys" targeted by a foreign policy driven by the needs of oil companies and the hegemonic corporate agenda overseas. Simplistic, black and white, good vs. evil, interpretations are encouraged in the public because this is exactly what you want in pliant masses under control. It is the basic stock and trade of all totalitarian systems, whether religious or political, that this kind of thinking is encouraged; Nazi, Stalinist, Maoist, Roman Catholic Empire, it is always the same. Seeing the other side as having some valid reasons for their actions is strongly discouraged. In the official doctrine no thinking is necessary. *We are good and they are bad.* No further analysis is required or tolerated. This aspect of the conditioning of the American public through entertainment is sustained by the erosion of the education system that then relieves people of the intellectual tools of critical thought necessary for deeper considerations. Thus, even if they wanted to look beneath the surface of events in the world the public finds it all too complicated. Not having the historical framework they soon become bored and turn away back to the movie version of events where the moral simplicity sooths away the angst.

PARADIGM MAINTENANCE

In order to keep the old toxic profit machine going in the face of ongoing studies the power structure employs what can be called, "the paradigm police." These are the men and women who spend their days looking for the truth pushing through the cracks in the edifice of materialism and do all that they can to debunk the information and ridicule the source. Some are specifically employed for this purpose by corporations. They cruise the Net looking for places to comment on new books and theories, products of all kinds, Youtube videos – whatever – in order to sow doubt and turn wondering minds away. Many others act as paradigm police simply out of their own desire to preserve the accumulated work in their fields of interest. Academics especially are often heavily invested in the long years of study, their place in the status quo of their fields and become easily provoked by anything that threatens to undermine their position. Still others are acting out of a psychological defense mechanism that automatically reject material that challenges the foundations of their belief system, an experience that causes fear, confusion, and a feeling of disempowerment that engages the ego to counterattack. And then there are the professional "skeptic" publications that are not actually skeptical at all, because to be a skeptic is to start with an open mind and proceed to seek evidence. But the people who run these publications start with a materialist prejudice and proceed from a belief that anything that challenges that doctrine has to be wrong. All of this is a rearguard action as the accumulating data challenging all the old theories presses ever harder on every institution and field of science. The idea is to try and keep as many minds tied to the mainstream as possible, to limit the numbers defecting to the rising integrated alternative culture. This is often approached through similar tactics as those employed in politics that seek to paint progressive information outside the mainstream as part of an undesirable culture of outsiders. This is seen regularly in television and movie scripts where vegetarianism, meditation, alternative medicine, and other such practices are presented in comical ways that make them look like the ridiculous choices of frivolous, wooly headed people, essentially: freaks, "weirdoes," and fools.

An excellent example of this tactic can be seen in the 2012 release, *Contagion* by Warner Bros. Pictures, where an infectious virus from China sweeps through world populations killing millions. The outsider alternative world is vilified in a character set-up to promote a false cure and do damage to many lives while he himself profits from the disaster. This popular Internet blogger is presented in the film giving interviews in which he states that "the pharmaceutical companies are in bed with the government," that vaccines are dangerous, and that natural herbal cures are being suppressed. He is ridiculed by one doctor he attempts to interview who says that he is not a "real journalist" and is generally shown to be a misguided opportunist, while the government employees are presented in a heroic light. One even gives her life for the cause. The film was made with the cooperation of the Center for Disease Control, a government agency.

Here we find a classic piece of propaganda disguised as commercial film work. A harrowing scenario is concocted where all the threats to the status-quo are set up and knocked down in one melodramatic blow. Both Internet journalism outside corporate control and herbal medicine, another threat to corporate profits, are portrayed as lacking veracity, and major revelations of the alternative media regarding government connections to *big pharma*, the AMA's long standing war against alternative medicine, and serious problems with vaccines are suggested to be ridiculous rumors coming from the mouth of a character designed to be discredited. This villain is given the name "Krumwiede," (crumb + weed) a moniker for a bad guy that is perhaps only slightly more subtle than calling him "Snidely Whiplash," but quite effective as a clandestine tool for manipulating audience perception at an unconscious level.

Anyone who does their homework on these issues will discover that it's not so much that the government is "in bed" with the pharmaceutical industry as that the pharmaceutical industry *has become the government*, in the reality that they pour money into political races and are rewarded with legislation that promotes their business and placement of their people in powerful positions within the CDC, the FDA, and Surgeon General's office, to name a few. Vaccines, as well, are a subject that requires a lot more scrutiny than this film suggests in that irrefutable evidence demonstrates that some have been tainted with mercury in the past as well as others having a number of bad side-effects for what turned out to be little to no benefit.[31] This isn't to say that all vaccines are bad, far from it, but this film promotes an unquestioning attitude that simply isn't justified given the history and the rabid *profit-above-all-else* policies of the pharmaceutical industry. As the tag line from the film suggests: *Nothing Spreads Like Fear*, this is exactly what this manipulative piece of propaganda counts on in suggesting that – *if you pay attention to those alternative sources of information you will die*.

The basic tactic of the old vested interests is to scare people into believing that harm will come to them if they stray from the official sources. This is the same game played by the Roman Church only now the devils and demons have been replaced by disease and financial ruin as the calamity that will be befall those who disregard the official sources. People have been conditioned to trust the stamp of approval from big organizations like the AMA and departments of Ivy League universities and such, but these "legitimizing" labels are often used to obscure the manipulative efforts of vested interests. For instance, nutritionists are licensed in many states and the boards that control those licensed have in some instances been influenced by big agri-business corporations and fast food companies.[32] So going to a licensed practitioner of any kind needs to be scrutinized to understand who is pulling the strings behind that particular "expert" opinion.

Keeping control of the paradigm is as important for industry and orthodox science now as it was for the Roman Church in the Middle-Ages. Every time a person discovers the work of the new pioneer scientists, like Rupert Sheldrake or Bruce Lipton, the edifice of materialism is weakened a bit more and the empire of greed is that much closer to defeat. So what they cannot debunk they ignore, what they cannot ignore they ridicule and that which cannot be ridiculed is simply subjected to well fashioned lies.

Dumbing Us Down

The "Reece Committee" formed by the U.S. Congress in 1954 to investigate the motives of highly influential foundations carrying on "social science" research at Harvard, Columbia, University of Chicago, and the University of California, was found to be directed towards what the committee called "oligarchical collectivism." These investigations uncovered that the Ford, Rockefeller, and Carnegie Foundations, were the primary benefactors to these researches into social engineering for the purpose of elite control of the working populace. The elite foundations goal was to find a way to move the American public away from traditions of individualism toward a more collective mentality so as to render the average person more amenable to group-think and top-down control. The primary strategy employed by the foundations uncovered in the Reece investigations was to use their influence to change the standards of public schooling. The conclusion was that these methods had been instituted and had in the years 1933 to 1936 precipitated a "revolution in education," that has resulted in "deterioration in the scholarship and techniques of teaching."[33]

When these findings were presented, a political block rose up to shut down the hearings and thwart any further probe into the issues revealed. Just the same, the evidence is clear and undeniable. Sharp and observant American teachers have been pointing out and protesting the planed decline in education standards ever since. One such teacher is John Taylor Gatto, who was a teacher in the New York City school system for over 30 years and was awarded New York City teacher of the Year, and New York State teacher of the Year. Mr. Gatto speaks quite frankly about the fact that what he and other teachers are forced to teach isn't really about the subject so much as it is actually about certain underlying lessons that all school children learn in the United States. These hidden lessons can be boiled down to seven basic messages imbued within the very structure of schooling itself.[34]

The first lesson is *confusion* that comes from the presentation of loads of information given piecemeal and disconnected from any larger understanding of the way things work. Everything is broken up into disparate chunks, dates and names, formulas and ideas without context. There is no logical sequence to the way classes proceed, one to the other, and no logical interconnections between the subject matter. Meaning is what human beings search for in patterns of information and it is the larger meaning of what's presented that is missing, hence the pervasive boredom and the persistent suspicion of students that beyond the basic skills the whole thing is irrelevant and has nothing to do with their real lives.

The second is *class position*, where children learn to be regimented into rows and numbered as to rank. They learn through this lesson how to think of themselves as represented by a grade that puts them above others to be scorned and below a different set of others to be envied so that this position within the ranks becomes the track on which the individual is conditioned to run. Progress is measured by passing others while moving toward a prescribed goal.

The third is *indifference*, which comes from throwing information at students, expecting their interest and then cutting the whole thing off in an instant when the bell rings. Nothing is ever brought to some logical conclusion. It is simply a chunk of time and a chunk of information. When the bell rings, then it doesn't matter anymore. Now the next thing matters and it will cease to matter too as soon as the next bell rings.

The forth is *emotional dependency*, which is fostered by a long regime of training wherein after completing the assigned task a child is acknowledged as "good" or maybe even "excellent" stars are awarded, treats are sometimes won, privileges granted. When the tasks are not completed correctly, then the student is dropped from favor. They now have a problem or maybe even *are a problem*. Students grow up seeking approval from arbitrary persons in their lives for completing arbitrary lessons.

The fifth is *intellectual dependency*, which comes from being conditioned to always defer to the teacher for what is true and not true. The teacher is the first of a never ending parade of "experts" who will be presented as having the right answers to everything, all the time. The lesson is that truth and answers come from official sources outside the individual. Those who resist, who demand to think for themselves, are subjected to a well-honed arsenal of techniques for breaking their will.

The sixth is *provisional self-esteem* that comes from being subjected to an environment wherein how the student is allowed to regard themselves has nothing to do with their own innate humanity, but comes from a prescribed performance consistently judged, rewarded or punished, like the way you train dogs or dolphins. "The lesson of report cards, grades, and tests, is that children should not trust themselves or their parents but instead should rely on the evaluation of certified officials."[35]

The seventh lesson is that *one can't hide*. Schools are run like totalitarian cities where constant surveillance is the rule, where free time and conversation is kept to a minimum, where hall passes are required and permission must be sought for even the most basic independent action such as going to the toilet. Students are conditioned to inform on each other when they observe anyone breaking the rules and parents are encouraged to inform the school of aberrant behavior at home. The monopolizing of time reaches into the child's home life where work must be completed each evening with the parents enlisted into the surveillance program. There is no place for privacy or personal reflection in this conception of school.

"School, as it was built," John Taylor Gatto informs us, "is an essential support system for a model of social engineering that condemns most people to be subordinate stones in a pyramid that narrows as it ascends toward a terminus of control. School is an artifice that makes such pyramidal social order seem inevitable, even though such a premise is a fundamental betrayal of the American Revolution."[36]

What is presented here is only the most cursory introduction to the subject of the true intent of public schooling. Those interested in all the facts should read the full text of John Taylor Gatto's *Dumbing Us Down*, and his *The Underground History of American Education*. The reality anyone who cares to enquire will find is that public schooling as it was conceived on a mass plan in America was inspired by a model developed in Prussia in the 19th century to convert rural farm laborers into factory workers. The Prussians divided their children up into three groups. The first was the leaders, the aristocrats and the new capitalist rich who's children would be given a full education with all the history, philosophy, literature and other subjects necessary to create understanding of the workings of the entire society, an education that taught them how to use their minds. The second was an education set up to train functionaries like engineers, architects, scientists and the managers needed to organize them. They were taught how to use their minds only in very narrow ways. The third was for the rest of the masses who would be trained as factory workers with their schooling focused on creating loyal workers and soldiers who would *never think for themselves*. These schools were literally designed like factories. This is the derivation of the bell system that was the way workers in early factories where signaled as to the starting and stopping of the massive machinery of production. The idea was to give these children the basic knowledge of numbers and letters to read gauges and understand the basic mechanics of factory work while conditioning them to a life of regimentation and discipline under the constant eye of an autocratic boss. This system was brought to America in the 19th Century by a man named Daniel Coit Gilman who studied the philosophy and techniques of the process in Germany and later became the president of Johns Hopkins University and of the Carnegie Institution itself.

Children raised on farms and ranches do not make good factory workers. They tended to stay in those communities from which their daily rhythms had been bred, an environment dictated by nature with the weather and livestock and lived in the open. Schools were designed to get children used to the regimentation of the systems they would find in factories, *to shift those rhythms*. Children have never been taught to think for themselves in public schools, but instead are drilled on the "right answers." In fact, independent thinking is just the sort of thing that is discouraged and any child who has their own opinion and insists on maintaining it will be labeled a "trouble maker" and be given bad grades or, in more contemporary times, drugged. Industry requires regimentation and narrow paths of behavior and individuality is confined only to the very top echelons of leadership. Industry as it has been classically conceived is the machine mind made manifest at its most ambitious and grandiose scale. People working within are seen as pieces of the machine and nothing more. They are to be efficient and so productive, all else is conceived as waste. The contemporary move by corporations to recognize their employee's broader human needs by incorporating gyms and such is all calculated to the same end of raising productivity. The structure of public school to this day remains one that encourages this ethic.

This is exactly what the elite captains of industry had in mind when they set to work to actualize long term plans through the power of their "charitable" endowments to take the responsibility for schooling away from families and individual communities and invest it solely in a centralized authority that would set the agenda for their own purposes.

The Reece committee investigation looked at the minutes of meetings in the big endowments and found some shocking things, such as the frank discussion at the Carnegie foundation in 1910 that *war was the best way of influencing people to change* and that a war should be encouraged. "We must control the diplomatic machinery of the United States by first gaining control of the State Department," was the suggestion by one trustee. The Reece committee found that the Carnegie foundation had become a "a powerful policy making force inside the State Department." After WWI the trustees discussed the idea that in order to prevent the country from returning to a way of life as it had been before the war that it would be essential to control education.[37] A cursory review of the true record of education programs and initiatives in the U.S. since that time shows quite clearly how successful they have been much to the sorrow of the American people.

> Mass education cannot work to produce a fair society because its daily practice is practice in rigged competition, suppression and intimidation. The schools we've allowed to develop can't work to teach nonmaterial values, the values which give meaning to everyone's life, rich or poor, because the structure of schooling is held together by a Byzantine tapestry of reward and threat, of carrots and sticks. Official favor, grades, or other trinkets of subordination have no connection with education; they are the paraphernalia of servitude, not of freedom.[38]

This Federal control and plan for creating "good workers" has continued through the years to our present time and the Bush administration's destructive "no child left behind," program, which teachers derisively refer to as "no child left with a mind." This "outcome based" program coerces teachers to teach to the test so that children are simply drilled in "answers" to questions rather than actually learning something. This process is exactly the opposite of how true learning takes place where subjects meaningful to the lives of students are explored and critically reviewed so that actual thinking, reasoning, and understanding is encouraged. This seems to be exactly what federal standards are seeking to eliminate. It is a rarity to find any critical thinking skills being taught in schools today.

The other major goal of the public school system in America was to forge a national identity. After the civil war an invigorated federal system proposed education standards with the goal of unifying the country under a single banner of ideology. Education had been under local control in the past and people resisted the compulsory kidnapping of their children with firearms at times and, ultimately, state militias were called in when needed to forcibly remove children from their homes to public schools. It was not long before the point of the education system became clear to parents.

For much of the early history of the United States individuals tended to think of themselves as belonging to a state first and the country second. Filling armies with conscripts is difficult when men believe their interests lay with their own land and region rather than what's going on in some foreign land far away. A new identity had to be constructed for children so that they began to think of themselves as *Americans* rather than belonging to their ethnic families and states first. To this end a nationalistic American history promoting our collective "destiny" as world leaders and torch carriers of democratic civilization was built into the lessons in a big way.

As a further incentive to a strict nationalism the pledge of allegiance was instituted in 1892 as a morning ritual for school children of all ages to include a hand salute much like that of the Roman military and that later adopted by the Nazi party in Germany. The arm would be outstretched with the palm down as they recited the oath, a salute later changed by Franklin Roosevelt when the Nazis made the whole point of such an exercise a bit too transparent for American tastes. The hand was then moved to the heart, (the second half of the Roman salute). The creator of the pledge, Francis Bellamy, intended the exercise to be a way of influencing immigrant and all less patriotic children to grow up to resist "subversion," and "radicalism," which is simply a way of negatively labeling independent thinking and the holding of opinions that do not coincide with the official line. It isn't that there is anything wrong with children celebrating "liberty and justice for all;" it is *the act itself* of compulsory compliance with a psychologically coercive method for binding individuals to a central authority in lockstep manner that flies in the face of *the actual practice of liberty*.

The "verbal" scores on SAT testing have plummeted since the 1960's, a direct indicator of the serious deterioration of reading, reasoning, and comprehension skills. A 2002 survey by the National Association of Scholars determined that in terms of general knowledge college graduates were found to have the same level as that of high school students fifty years earlier. In terms of cultural knowledge the college graduates scored far below college graduates of the mid-twentieth century. Even more dismal, 59% of graduate students in the U.S. were found by a federal study in 2003 to be incompetent in basic skills of literacy, unable to demonstrate any proficiency in reading and understanding information in short texts. Those in surveys across the academic spectrum that do score high on all measures are increasingly found to have been educated in Asia and Europe before entering college in the U.S.. The seminal study entitled, *A Nation at Risk*, stated flatly: "The educational foundations of our society are being eroded by a rising tide of mediocrity that threatens our very future as a nation and a people."[39]

The assault on the ability of Americans to use their minds for anything other than making money and creating and buying new products has also been aimed at the universities for decades. The reduction in the support for the humanities and liberal arts across the country means that fewer people are being exposed to those subjects that teach people *how to think* about values and choices from reviewing the historical record of humanity in all of its many socio-political and cultural creations. An historical tendency for anti-intellectualism, one of the lingering vestiges of America's not long gone pioneer past, has been revived and supercharged in recent decades as part of the dumbing down program. The current strategy is to turn people away from the very courses that would offer them the ability to decode and see through the propaganda and manipulation of the corporate and financial elite. So history and philosophy, the humanities that seek to understand the logic, symbols and systems of the Western tradition, have to be pushed into a corner or expunged entirely by "reforming" forces that want to focus students on more "practical" studies. In other words, eliminate those studies that will allow students to fill the ranks of the white collar industrial machine with no questions asked and without even the ability to formulate the right questions, even if they later come to resent their condition.

For centuries in the West the basic foundations of thinking and reasoning were taught in schools through what was termed since Medieval times, *the trivium*. The trivium is defined as the study of logic, grammar, and rhetoric. "Logic is the art of thinking; grammar, the art of inventing symbols and combining them to express thought; and rhetoric, the art of communicating thought from one mind to another, the adaptation of language to circumstance."[40] These studies were thought to be essential in being able to understand, acquire, and utilize knowledge. They also gave the student the ability to recognize false arguments and meaningless propositions, to separate the truly meaningful from the fallacious. This must have made this sort of study a target for those who would reconstruct American education to suit their need for a pliant work force.

The trivum largely disappeared from American schools in the early 20th Century, but was revived briefly by a Sister of the Holy Cross who held a doctorate from Columbia and taught at Saint Mary's College, from 1931 to 1960. Writing of the trivium as a key to a liberal arts education, Sister Miriam Joseph, stated:

> The utilitarian or servile arts enable one to be a servant – of another person, of the state, of a corporation, or of a business – and to earn a living. The liberal arts, in contrast, teach one how to live; they train the faculties and bring them to perfection; they enable a person to rise above his material environment to live an intellectual, a rational, and therefore a free life in gaining truth[41]

A study conducted by a sociologist at the University of California Riverside determined that from 1970 to 2000 degrees in the humanities and traditional arts and sciences had precipitously declined and that a sea change had occurred by 1998 where the old well-rounded undergraduate degrees with a mixture of courses meant to offer a broad education in the Western tradition, had been replaced by degrees meant to be immediately preparatory in pursuing a specific field. Traditional liberal arts colleges now only educate about 4% of graduates, which indicates that universities around the country have largely been turned into vocational schools.[42] So much for learning "how to live" or training the faculties, or enabling a person to acquire "a free life in gaining truth." Why bother when you can own a smart phone?

This purely utilitarian course of study is directly opposite of the sort of education thought by the founding fathers necessary for the average voter to understand the human condition and history well enough to exercise the judgment adequate to the maintenance of democracy. It is precisely what Thomas Jefferson feared in the power of concentrated wealth to turn the values and capacity of the American public to their own purposes and undermine freedom in the process.

In arguing for an amendment to the Constitution providing for education, Jefferson made his feelings clear:

> But of all the views of this law none is more important, none more legitimate, than that of rendering the people the safe, as they are the ultimate, guardians of their own liberty. For this purpose, the reading...is proposed to be chiefly historical. History by apprising them of the past will enable them to judge of the future; it will avail them of the experience of other times and other nations; It will qualify them as judges of the actions and designs of men; it will enable them to know ambition under every disguise it may assume; and knowing it, to defeat its views.[43]

The original American tradition of improvement in the conditions of life so as to offer a more nurturing medium for the expressions of the human spirit as it manifests in *every citizen* is no longer taught in America. The values cultivating higher truths and understanding that allows a person to "rise above their material environment," have been exchanged for a wallet full of credit cards. The largely unseen irony is that these higher truths are what allow for a deeper experience of the material environment, such that when they are missing the material is comprehended only superficially and so must be continually renewed. It is the same cultivation of the mind and spirit that allows the public to safeguard their liberties in understanding that liberty is more than access to a continual flow of products. The words of Jefferson, Hamilton, Franklin, Madison, Thomas Paine and the Enlightenment values that drove them have been neatly subordinated to consumer capitalism and the false promise of material riches as the one and only value in life. When Thomas Jefferson wrote, "Educate and inform the whole mass of the people, they are the only sure reliance for the preservation of our liberty," he was not thinking of technical expertise or marketing skills. "Enlighten the people generally and tyranny and oppressions of body and mind will vanish like evil spirits at the dawn of day." Jefferson was writing of reason and the life of the mind freed from the oppression of ignorance and the limiting beliefs instilled by despots of church or state. To this end, topics such as history and the humanities are absolutely central. Jefferson's own library is a model on which American universities would be based. Science and engineering are well represented on Jefferson's shelves, but history, literature, philosophy, and poetry well outweigh them.

In the rich and fervent philosophical debates in the Europe of the mid-eighteenth century the founding fathers had encountered the work of Jean-Jacques Rousseau who had posited that man in his natural state in following the dictates of nature was neither good nor bad but capable of either being plunged into a myriad of terrible behaviors or noble and good behavior, dependent on his education and the fairness of the social conditions his society thrust upon him. Rousseau believed that people were prone to the good if given a chance, due to the natural tendency toward the nurturance and protection of human life commonly demonstrated by human beings unencumbered by war or a competition for resources in an unfair society. Although Rousseau's ideas were only one of several important influences on the founding fathers, John Locke being perhaps primary among them, the source of much that is central to the constitution, including the self-evidence of the belief that "all men are created equal," come directly from Rousseau, who also championed a government of the people and by the people, the notion that the citizenry should be educated at public expense, the very thing Jefferson found to be essential to a fair society, as well as the conviction that "all men should be equal under the law." With this in mind the framers of the Constitution meant to enshrine in law an American state that would move the potential of citizens toward the good and noble possibilities of the human spirit. To do so, education and fairness was thought an absolute necessity for the maintenance of a society that would encourage the best in human nature.

Without an informed and educated citizenry the country is rapidly devolving into the class structure of the previous political form from which the democratic republic emerged. That is a new oligarchic aristocracy that looks different on the surface from historical forms, but underneath is essentially the same with a small middle class of narrowly educated professional functionaries that run the state apparatus and technical research and operations, a large standing army, and a broad peasant class of uneducated workers at the mercy of the rich and powerful. This condition is largely the outcome of the rise of corporate power, of business as new route to empire. In the past power was invested in aristocratic and military lines of authority that rose from the tribal stage of consciousness to the imperial emperors and kings of the mythological era. With the opening of the new world the merchant class that first rose to power in the Italian city states, now engorged itself with the windfall wealth of the Americas, exploding in political power that soon overtook the old nobility. These elder families had acquired their wealth as feudal lords who had been gathered under the banner of the Kings as vassals in the early period to noble aristocrats of the King's court in the later period, whose power arose from controlling the land. The rising of the mercantile class is the first power group in Western history to be simply based on wealth alone, without any claim to "noble" blood or rise via military might.

Through the philosophy of the British political philosopher, John Locke, the rising humanism and rational interest of the age gets wound up in the striving of new money to rid itself of the power of kings, their prejudices and arbitrary authority. Locke, as a representative of the rising upper class, is very interested in protecting private property and so aligns the interests of the new wealth with those of the common people in a theoretical alliance against the old powers. Minds start to change and a half a century later in France, Voltaire and Rousseau, further the philosophical enterprise with more emphasis on the common man and revolutions follow, first the American and then the French. The founding fathers, although mostly landed gentry and businessmen themselves, realized that concentrated wealth tended to replicate the rapacious tendencies of the old nobility. The Virginia Company, an early form of corporation in America, on their way to profit literally worked to death hundreds of indentured servants a year through neglect of adequate food, clothing and shelter. The East India Company, also served in the experience of the world as the most aggressively exploitive and downright murderous "business" ever known. Also, the early American colonies were not free from that same British "lust for profit" attitude that grew with the rising merchant class that would later be used by Karl Marx as his example of the depredations of capitalism. Therefore, Jefferson and his brethren expressed in the Declaration of Independence and built into the Constitution and the later Bill of Rights safeguards against the "moneyed interests" usurping the power of the people. America was not to end up in the same boat as the Indian people of the subcontinent sweating and dying under the sword of corporate power to enrich a new aristocracy. Although it would take nearly a century more for African slaves to receive the same consideration.

Unfortunately, the restraint of capital in the form of corporate power was not to be long lived. By the second half of the 19th Century wealth was being concentrated into massive holding companies that ultimately turned the political safeguards off. They did so first in what would become the water shed moment for the escalation of corporate power, the 1886 "Santa Clara decision" that created corporate personhood. In a number of successive Supreme Court decisions corporations outflanked democracy and came to overpower Jefferson and Lincoln's America in what Princeton University scholar of political science, Sheldon Wolin, has termed "inverted totalitarianism."

> The Nazi and Fascist regimes were powered by revolutionary movements whose aim was not only to capture, reconstitute, and monopolize state power but also to gain control over the economy. By controlling the state and the economy, the revolutionaries gained the leverage necessary to reconstruct, then mobilize society. In contrast, inverted totalitarianism is only in part a state-centered phenomenon. Primarily it represents the *political* coming of age of corporate power and the *political* demobilization of the citizenry.[44]

Totalitarian societies in the old context came from political movements that then dominated and utilized the economic sector for its own purposes; in inverted totalitarianism, the economic sector, big business, comes to dominate the political apparatus and absorb it into itself so that the ethos of corporate business culture becomes the controlling philosophy of the country – autocratic leadership in the service of a new financial aristocracy replaces the constitutional democracy of yesteryear. Professor Wolin does not believe this transformation is complete, but presents a substantial degree of evidence that it is very nearly there. This process represents the final triumph of the rise of the merchant class that began in the late middle-ages and came to push aside monarchies and emperors as it now has come to dominate the democratic and libertarian societies that replaced those royal overlords in a brief flowering of the untrammeled human spirit. This brief effervescence of liberty demonstrated in American history was purchased with blood and maintained by the education and proper laws of the people. With the diminishment of an educated and aware electorate the laws restraining corporate and financial empire building have been removed. Thus, the American public is finding itself swimming in a sea of information meant to maneuver their opinions to support the very forces that are progressively disenfranchising them from the wealth of the country.

THE MANAGEMENT OF SCIENCE AND INNOVATION

Although Thomas Edison is now featured in children's school books as the archetypal image of that fabled *American ingenuity*, the genius hero to the average man and woman, he was no hero to the scientific community of his time. Thomas Edison was an independent researcher, belonging to no university or industrial corporation. He went his own way, researching what he wanted to regardless of what the "experts" told him was possible. In short, to the establishment, Thomas Edison was a loose cannon and, unbeknownst to the America of his time, he would be the last of his kind. After Edison, scientific research would be carefully funneled into "acceptable" fields while other research would be managed so as to avoid rendering large capital investments obsolete.

When Edison strung up downtown Menlo Park, New Jersey, with his newly perfected electric lights, not only did the "experts" declare the whole idea a hoax, but flatly stated that it was impossible to wire anything in a series. The chief engineer for Britain's post office called the announcement of Edison's electric light and parallel circuit, "a completely idiotic idea." Another small minded electrical engineer stated for the press that Edison's claim was, "so manifestly absurd as to indicate a positive want of knowledge of the electric circuit..." The idea was so far beyond what the science of the age was willing to accept that no expert in the field would come to witness Edison's display even though hundreds of common people had come and seen the lights in Menlo Park and had written many letters to the press wondering why they had ignored it. Finally, the word got to the big money and they saw in it a new technology they could embrace; and so Edison's idea finally overcame all detractors.[45]

Such would not be the case when Thomas Edison teamed up with Henry Ford in the early years of the auto industry to create a true breakthrough in electric cars. It may come as a surprise to many that electric cars at the beginning of the 20th Century were quite popular for running about town on errands and were poised to leap into the larger market for heavier, longer range vehicles if a better battery could be devised. The public preferred electric cars to their gas driven cousins due to their relative quiet and lack of smoke. The gas models put out so much pollution they were commonly referred to as "stink pots," and with gasoline prices going up by 1910 electricity seemed like the better choice. By 1911 Edison had developed a better battery made of nickel and iron that showed it could hold a charge longer than the old lead models and quickly began to overtake the market leader powering electric cars and trucks all over the country. The problem for Henry Ford was that the market for electrics was confined to a few urban zones because the price of electrics was beyond the means of the common man. Although more and more electric vehicles were on the road each month, Ford was determined to do as he had with the Model T, to make an electric car for the "everyman." Having great confidence in Edison's ability, Ford went into partnership with him to bring the first open road affordable electric car to the masses. Edison and Ford's idea was that energy and transportation independence could be achieved for the average American by simply hooking a battery charger up to a windmill at night affording hours of driving time each day without cost.

Unfortunately, WWI shifted the lagging oil industry into high gear and the huge industrial build up for the war could not wait for electric vehicle development to come to the fore. Edison had experienced long delays in getting his improved batteries into new cars due to what seemed to be some kind of clandestine interference in Detroit. The batteries worked fine when tested in his West Orange facility but seemed to show problems at the auto factory. When Edison sent his own men to Detroit to supervise the operation, the batteries performed well, when they left, things reverted to problem status. And then there was the fire.

Edison went back to work determined to wait out the war boom and finally produce an efficient low priced electric automobile, but larger forces were just, if not more, determined to see that he didn't. On December 9th 1914, a huge explosion ripped through the air, then fires broke out all over the facility. The compound of laboratories and storage buildings were designed by Edison himself to be fireproof. They were made of concrete and no one could explain how the fire could spread so quickly. The only explanation was that something had ignited inside each separate structure almost simultaneously. In the end, Edison worked on, but was at that point at the end of his career and having lost the momentum in the early electric car boom, he lost the momentum in himself and never again brought the world a revolutionary invention. [46]

The battery has always been the lynch pin of the electric car problem and it remains so today. One hint as to why other industries like electronic communications have seen tremendous advances, but cars are still driving around with lead batteries first seen at the turn of the century, that power only their starters, can be found in the many reports of battery research being bought up by oil companies. Chevron, who owns the patents to the NiMH battery that showed great promise in the electric car field has chosen not to allow development in larger models suitable for cars. "Patent wars" are one of the typical maneuvers used to prevent competition by big money players. On another front, it has been proven possible to extract hydrogen, a flammable gas, from water on demand so that it can be used immediately to drive an internal combustion engine. The water car has been invented three separate times, at least, and each time it appears in some brief flash of news, working models are demonstrated for the public and then it suddenly disappears into the void of unknown status. To big capital knowledge is dangerous; new inventions are as much a threat to their economic territory as a nation developing a new weapon would be to the territory of a rival state.

It was precisely new weapons that drove the massive drive for innovation and progress during the Nazi era in Germany. Hitler was not concerned with the economic strategies of the Anglo-American alliance and took the lid off all scientific and engineering planned stagnation. Germany's amazing technological leap beyond the rest of the world during the Second World War is often marveled at like some kind of ancient mystery comparable to the building of the pyramids. The simple reality is that the Germans just stopped playing by the economic rules maintaining established markets against innovation that the rest of the West under the thumb of the English and American banking powers had been abiding by.

Think of the massive innovations that appeared in America in the late 19th and early 20th centuries. America virtually invented the modern world with electrical power grids, light bulbs, telephones, phonographs, radios, mass production of automobiles, airplanes, television, all manner of home appliances, the list goes on and on. This happened because

Americans were set free from European traditions and power structures and with the money and resources to fuel their unfettered visions of the future they set to work to make their dreams come true. Unfortunately, as Professor Quigley and others have pointed out, institutions develop and then slow change in order to protect an entrenched vested interest. By the 1930's the Thomas Edison's and Wright brothers are beginning to become scarce and the rate of innovation is slowing to a trickle. People who challenge the power of the Robber Barons with new ideas, like Nicola Tesla, are set up for ruin. When the Nazis come around they're not going to play that game. Britain and America were sure they had Germany in the bag after crushing it in WWI and began to build them up as an attack dog against the Soviets. Hitler didn't like communists any more than he liked Jews and the Americans were very enthusiastic about this, naming him Time Magazine's *Man of the Year*, in 1938. But Hitler would prove to be a big disappointment for the Western powers of the age when he broke off the leash and started making his own money and researching free energy and super weapons. By the end of the war it is discovered that the Germans have developed, not just unstoppable tanks and jet aircraft, but integrated circuits, laser beam technology, computers, synthetic fuel, Kevlar, and even atomic weapons. [47] After the war this technology that would have challenged markets was secreted away by American military intelligence and slowly doled out to companies like RCA and Bell Labs that released the innovations as their own years later when it suited their profit making picture.

What the German example demonstrates is not that their technological progress is proof that they are, indeed, *the master race*, but rather that when human beings are offered ample resources to carry on pure research and development without the interference of vested interests, great innovations can occur on a regular basis. There is no reason that all of the pressing problems in transportation, energy, and the pollution of the planet, can't be solved very, very quickly if the will was released and the way was open. The automobile industry in America serves as a perfect example of why it doesn't happen.

When in 1948 Preston Tucker went up against the big three automakers with a new car design full of innovations like the seat belt that would become standard equipment in the future, they reacted with every assault in their arsenal to shut him down and ultimately did so after a short production run. The Tucker far outpreformed the rival cars of its day requiring less maintenance and running smooth at high speeds, but this very point would have forced the other companies to spend a lot of money catching up and this is precisely what they didn't want to do.

Contrary to the advertising, innovation and efficiency has never been the driving force in the American automobile industry. Auto makers level the playing field between themselves with products of generally equal performance and then maintain this condition so as to create a stable market they all can profit from without need to change anything but the shape of the fenders every couple of years. Retooling plants to accommodate major innovation is expensive and cuts deeply into profits. It is simply not a part of the capitalist doctrine of growing returns on investment to do so at the pace of true human ingenuity and so that ingenuity must be blocked, bought up, sabotaged, debunked, crushed with criticism, and otherwise destroyed in order to insure that continuing long-term return on investment. The accelerating innovation technologists talk about is confined to industries that are open for development like computers and cell phones where true competition still exists and advances require only minimal manufacturing changes. Unfortunately, no matter how advanced these devices in the US may become they are hampered in their utility by the fact that the country has fallen far behind other nations in broadband deployment in both speed and cost, Americans typically paying much more for much less.

> The reason is that both the traditional telecommunications and TV industries are tight, powerful oligopolies deeply threatened by high speed internet services. A nationwide infrastructure of universal high-speed internet service would...render traditional telephone service, cable TV, and broadcast television totally obsolete.[48]

Buckminster Fuller, one of the greatest engineers, designers and innovators of all time, was the developer of the geodesic dome and the monumentally important concept of "synergy" in design. Fuller had a concept of engineering he termed "dymaxion," meaning a thing that had been designed to the maximum efficiency possible. When he presented his Dymaxion Car in 1933 it was a marvel of engineering, sleek and aerodynamic and getting three times the gas mileage of the common car of the day, it seated eleven, and was clocked at a top speed of ninety miles an hour. When he presented the vehicle for inclusion in the Detroit auto show he was shut out by the big producers. When Fuller pulled up in front of the exhibit hall and began giving people demonstration rides he was chased away by the police. At the 1933 Chicago World's Fair the Dymaxion Car suffered a catastrophic accident during a demonstration run when a mysterious vehicle following Fuller's car suddenly swerved around it cutting it off causing the Dymaxian car to roll over, killing the driver and injuring passengers. The potential investment capital for the new vehicle then dried up and the Dymaxian Car went the way the Tucker would go twenty years later.[49]

There are many things that are not allowed to be produced, regardless of the need – things like the invention of Dr. Royal Raymond Rife who created a new kind of microscope and a new method for killing diseased cells in the body using nothing but sound waves. His achievement was heralded as a new era in medicine after a demonstration before a group of 250 scientists testified to it in an article in the *Los Angeles Times* of December 27th 1931. The capacity of his microscope was first marveled at in an article in the *New York Times* of November 21st 1931"Dr. Rife's apparatus magnifying 17,000 times, shows germs never before seen!"[50] Regardless of the professional verification and support by numbers of medical researchers, Rife's breakthrough was opposed when he appeared before two leading doctors at Johns Hopkins medical school whose funding came from the Rockefeller foundation. Dr. Rife's discoveries happened at the same time the pharmaceutical industry was getting off the ground and Rockefeller and the other big bankers where pouring money into it. Rife's lab was thereafter sabotaged and his work viciously suppressed.

The United States has spent upwards of 200 billion dollars since 1971 on its "war on cancer," and yet cancer since then has done nothing but increase. The reason for this is simple economics – curing diseases destroys established markets and the cancer industry is a big one. On October 1st 2006 the *New York Times* reported that the world spent 24 billion dollars a year on cancer drugs in 2004 and this figure was expected to rise to 55 billion by 2009, it actually exceeded that figure. These numbers demonstrate that oncology drugs are the biggest category of pharmaceutical sales. Like all big money industries, "big pharma" protects itself and so many cancer cures have been suppressed.[51] One of the most interesting and well documented among them is that discovered, or actually *rediscovered*, at the Albert Einstein College of Medicine in 1990 by Doctors Kaali and Lyman. They demonstrated that pathogens in the blood, including cancerous cells, could be easily killed by the introduction of a weak electric current. In 1993 they received a patent on their work unfortunately it has never been adopted by conventional medicine. As it turns out, this effect has been understood for some time, being first noticed at the beginning of the 20th C. with previous patents being filed with the US Patent office. When Kaali and Lyman gave a presentation of their research and findings at a medical symposium for combination AIDS therapies showing that the AIDS virus when hit with electric current was unable to propagate, their work appeared in the *Houston Post* and *Science News,* but mysteriously all the information from their presentation was not included in the symposium catalog and all media coverage thereafter halted completely.

Perhaps the most infamous of episodes concerning the suppression of science in the name of big money is that of Nicola Tessla who brought the world alternating current and an array of breakthroughs in the understanding of electricity that rivaled those of Thomas Edison. It is said that Tessla was well on the way to creating free energy and being able to transmit that energy without wires for all to use when J.P. Morgan Jr. quickly withdrew his patronage and squashed any further work by the man who history remembers as one of the greatest minds of the twentieth century. Like Royal Rife after him, Tessla would die a broken man living in poverty.

Oil runs the world and is the greatest nongovernmental or military power block on earth. Exxon-Mobil is both the top money grossing corporation on the planet and the biggest polluter. The profits of the top oil companies far outstretch the gross national product of most nations on earth. In this light, it is not that hard to understand that all the usual tendencies commonly associated with the power of nations apply to big corporations like oil companies. Just as nations and empires have historically sought to enlarge and protect their territories through any means possible, regularly including organized murder as an instrument of state policy, so too do these major corporate interests do whatever it takes to ensure the continuation and growth of their power. This is precisely why the founding fathers of the American republic sought to strongly limit the concentration of wealth and power outside democratic structures. Power was to be kept in check through the "checks and balances" of a government that did not allow one group to have it all whether inside or outside the government. Only in this way could the needs of the people come first and the elevation of the human spirit throughout the population be championed. Tragically, this system has been neatly circumvented by power in the corporate form.

People generally have a hard time wrapping their minds around the notion that power at this scale has no problem killing people just because it's centered in a corporate business framework instead of a national or imperial framework. Concentrated power doesn't care how it is constituted in the particular historical instance and if a person may think power at the gargantuan scale seen in the oil industry has any compunction against disposing of innovative geniuses when their activities grow threatening to the trillions of dollars invested in drilling operations, refineries, shipping and transportation, not to mention the trillions upon billions of dollars in profit annually, then this person would be almost child-like in their naivety and innocents, indeed. Unfortunately, this describes a good part of the population.

The analogy between giant multi-national corporations and feudal states is a well-worn one by now. When feudal lords felt themselves threatened, they sent out the knights under their command to ride forth and destroy whatever it was that gave rise to their fears. Now the knights do not ride in the open for all to be intimidated by their gleaming armor. They set about at night and undercover, carrying out their missions in such a manner as to make them look like accidents and failures of health, random robberies gone bad.

On May 14th 2004, the champion of free energy, Eugene Mallove, was bludgeoned to death in what was to be written off as an interrupted robbery. Dr. Mallove was at the center of an ongoing controversy concerning the viability of a new type of nuclear power: cold fusion. Unlike the hot fission variety, cold fusion is pollution free, without radioactive waste, and so infinitely desirable over the old type. More importantly, cold fusion had been demonstrated to create "excess heat," meaning that it could produce more energy than what was needed to initiate the reaction. This is the golden ring of the energy sciences and the breakthrough that will release the world from bondage to energy monopolies. Present energy systems are a one to one bargain; so much fuel produces an equal amount of energy. "Free energy" has been long hypothesized by science and is achieved when what comes out is a sum greater than what goes in. This is precisely what cold fusion has been demonstrated to do, a monumental discovery first suppressed and now ignored.

Two University of Utah electro-chemists, by the name of Pons and Fleischmann, released their findings in 1989 that they had achieved cold fusion. This set off the expected running about in circles, ranting, name calling, and waving hands in the air of the scientific status-quo of the nuclear energy world. What particularly must have aggravated the nuclear physicists was the fact that a couple of chemists beat them at their own game. This, as well as the billons invested in hot fusion, along with the millions of dollars a year in grant money to nuclear scientists to work out all the obvious bugs, certainly sent the vested interests into a frantic tizzy. First, nuclear researchers at Cal Tech and then the Massachusetts Institute of Technology, set about madly trying to replicate Pons' and Fleischmann's results and in short order declared to the world that the whole thing was impossible. Dr. Richard Petrasso of MIT attributed the findings of the electro-chemists to what he called a "glitch" in instrumentation. Soon, the scientific press was replete with condemnations of cold fusion as having been the result of careless science, or even out and out fraud.

Eugene Mallove was the chief science writer for M.I.T. and so he began to investigate the science that sought to duplicate Pons and Fleischmann's results and discovered that the MIT team had purposely botched the experiment in order to give them the negative results they were after. MIT was part of the hot fission research world receiving part of the billions of dollars in grant money yearly handed out by the U.S. Department of Energy. Mallove discovered that the MIT scientists had actually confirmed the original research validating cold fusion but then "adjusted" their findings to their preferred conclusion. ,

Mallove quit MIT in protest. MIT, for its part, never admitted any deliberate wrong doing, but did concede that it may have made some minor error in adjusting the figures and quietly changed its original report from a negative finding to *"too sensitive to confirm."* Regardless, this made no difference to the majority of the reporting that sought to make sure the public forgot about the whole thing by calling it all fantasy and bad science. The major science journal, *Nature*, led the charge with a spree of the usual name calling and accusations. In the most transparent of political maneuvers for the preservation of the old energy order, the reviewing U.S. House Committee called the evidence for cold fusion, "not persuasive," and concluded that "no special programs to establish cold fusion research centers or to support new efforts to fund cold fusion are justified."[52]

All this, while four years later some 92 scientific groups in 10 countries around the world had demonstrated the Pons and Fleischmann cold fusion effect confirming its viability as a new power source. Not long after the House Committee declined to pursue the matter for the American people, the process was verified by the Stanford Research Institute, Oak Ridge Laboratory, US Naval Research Laboratory, Texas A & M University, and others. California Polytechnic soon produced kilowatt reactions with cold fusion that were 30 times greater than that accomplished with hot fission fuel rods without their accompanying deadly radiation. Cold fusion generators produce nothing but steam; regardless, the planning for new hot fission reactors goes on. Why? Probably because the drawbacks from hot fission keep it from becoming a major competitor to oil and gas power production and because a whole superstructure of big money has been institutionalized to "perfect" hot fission that depends on those billons in taxpayer funds to keep all those laboratory jobs going year after year.

Big egos, big money, vested interests, that is the way societies destroy themselves when the answers to their problems are right in front of them. Eugene Mallove went on to become a champion of cold fusion and new energy devices in general, started a magazine to that end and wrote a book about cold fusion, *Fire from Ice*, nominated for a Pulitzer Prize. He was to speak before a government panel demonstrating a new device the day before he was assassinated. His colleague in that endeavor was Dr. Brian O'Leary, a former Ivy League professor and NASA scientist who was once regarded as one of the top minds in energy science in the country. The energy advisor to the Carter administration, Dr. O'Leary was chosen in the planning stages for what would have been, if not for budget cuts, the first manned mission to Mars.

In his 2009 book, *The Energy Solution Revolution*, O'Leary chronicles in part the rough road traveled by new energy developers the last few decades. People have been physically attacked, threatened at gun point, arrested on trumped up charges, sued, had their research and devices confiscated by the government of the United States and Canada, and in the case of inventor Dennis Lee, was warned by agents of the US government to change careers, *or else*. Others have simply been murdered. Leading

European free energy scientist, Stephen Marinov, while a professor at the University of Graz, suddenly one day "jumped" from the roof of the university library. In March of 1998, Stanley Myers, another inventor of one of the infamous water cars, burst from the doors of a restaurant in his home town of Grove City, Ohio, screaming "They poisoned me!" and dropped dead on the concrete. In 2007, Arie DeGeus, the inventor of a highly promising self-powered battery technology was found dying in his car in the parking lot of the Charlotte airport in North Carolina. He died thereafter in the hospital of what appeared to be a heart attack, although the man had no history of heart problems and was in perfect health. He was on his way to a meeting of backers to demonstrate his battery and discuss going into production.

This is a very short list of individuals killed or intimidated to keep the world on oil and gas. The journalist and engineer, Gary Vesperman, had complied an extensive list of victims by 2006 that included 53 verified cases of new energy developers who had been attacked, threatened, or killed, and still others who died of mysterious, "natural causes."[53] Many individuals who find themselves challenging the big money in whatever field often seem to die of unexplained and "out of the blue" heart attacks. Researchers have revealed that there are various drugs and devices that can induce a heart attack in a healthy person. The 1975 Church Committee hearings of the US Senate investigating the CIA discovered they had developed a "heart attack gun" as a method for assassinations they wanted to appear as natural causes.

Dr. O'Leary wrote,

> Whether by "suicide," "accident," "natural causes," or "homicide by a lunatic," this carnage of our foremost unsung heroes seems to have a common cause: assassination by those who don't want break-through energy (or any other expression perceived as a significant threat to elite vested interests) to see the light of day[54]

Those living in Florida in the area of the British Petroleum oil spill in 2010 can tell endless stories of suppression of the facts, exclusion of all press from any effected areas, illnesses and death in animals and humans exposed to the spill and the intimidation and mysterious deaths of whistleblowers who came forward to report health impacts from the spill and chemical clean-up.[55]

Chitra Chaunhan, who worked for the USF Center for Biological Defense was poisoned with cyanide in a Florida motel. A cell biologist by the name of Joseph Morriessy, working on the toxic effects of the spill, was shot to death in his home. Senator Ted Stevens of Alaska died in a mysterious plane crash just after receiving inside information from a BP informant regarding defects in the "blow-out preventer" used by BP in the Gulf previously used in Alaska. Others died suddenly of "natural causes," while still others were jailed on out-of-the-blue charges. A top specialist in Swan health, Dr. Jeffery Gardner, after looking into the deteriorating condition of swans in the area after the spill suddenly, just before releasing his test results, was found to have problems with a prescription license and suddenly shut down his practice and left the area refusing to respond to any inquires. A news report had indicated that Dr. Gardner's tests would have wide ranging implications for all water fowl in the region.[56]

Mathew Simmons, an oil man himself and a public figure in the industry who had recently turned towards green energy solutions, was the only expert considered an insider to make critical statements regarding BP's conduct. Then he *accidently drowned* in his hot tub. The state medical examiner concluded that *heart disease was a contributing factor*. (How can anything other than water be a contributing factor to drowning in a hot tub?) Mr. Simmons met his end just after he made public statements saying that BP and the US government had lied to the people regarding the severity of the problem and that there were more leaks than what was being reported. He also stated that the disaster and its aftereffects might just lead to BP's ultimate bankruptcy, a situation that could not be tolerated by either the US or Britain because BP's oil is considered crucial for supplying the military. It was later confirmed by NOAA that other leaks did exist.[57]

It is suspiciously noted that British Petroleum had hired the infamous *Black Water Security* company of Iraq "over kill" fame to assist with security issues in the Gulf during the spill. There, of course, is no "smoking gun" linking oil companies with murder or any evidence a prosecutor could use to indict any BP executive for contracting for intimidation or assassination and there's plenty of disinformation pumped into the media claiming that all the above is simply a delusion. The aware public is left to weigh the evidence and decide for themselves who benefits from these unexplained deaths and sudden changes of status and who is most likely to be at the bottom of it all.

This is but a skim off the surface of a much deeper history of suppression and "mysterious death" that seems to ultimately follow any situation where big corporate profits are threatened. Again, all of this information is widely available to the public in Internet sites and books that go unnoticed in the eight inches of media below the mainstream whose subtext is always, "*everything is fine, go back to work*." British Petroleum perpetrated the worst environmental disaster in American history, pumping an "Exxon Valdez" tanker equivalent of oil into the Gulf every 3.5 days for 3 months and now, as of 2012 the Obama administration is getting ready to open up millions of acres of off-shore oil leases as if it never happened. Alternatives that are clean, safe and essentially free, sit unused while the planet and the common people continue to be sickened and robbed for the benefit of an elite corporate oligarchy.

The healthcare system in the United States at the time of this writing is a perfect example of an industry that is thriving at the cost of the people and offers a model through which to understand how obsolete systems maintain themselves through multiple avenues of manipulation. The health care debates and bills of 2009 are the setting for this sordid tale. What had been proposed was a "single payer" plan in which the delivery of services would remain private while one cost for everyone would be paid into a government system. This plan was polling well with the public so something had to be done.

The United States is the only industrialized country on earth that doesn't provide health coverage to all its citizens and it is the only one with a for profit system. The problem is perfectly obvious to anyone who wishes to examine the record: escalating pharmaceutical costs combined with the aggressive profit making strategies of the insurance industry. So the escape from blame becomes paramount in the strategies of the corporate offenders and their political allies, indeed, an entire sector of the corporate world went into overdrive in churning out propaganda to prevent forcing the insurance companies to roll back costs, to return the system to the purely non-profit status it started at, or to simply convert the whole thing to a national healthcare system, as Harry Truman proposed just after WWII.

What was done to prevent this was the production of one of the most massive propaganda efforts since WWI. The corporate news services began blasting the public with the message that American healthcare is the best in the world and this high level of lifesaving expertise and service would be jeopardized, if we allowed those evil politicians and misguided radicals to disturb one hair on insurance company heads. At the same time the mainstream news networks simply refused to cover any discussion on a single-payer plan. The media watch group "FAIR," *Fairness And Accuracy In Reporting*, investigated the black-out and determined that out of the major national papers only three columnists advocated for single payer on the public's behalf, while the other three mentions were all negative, otherwise not a word was spoken regarding single payer. On television, only three mentions of the single-payer plan appeared and two of those were negative, in all the hours and hours of national broadcast media leading up to the final crafting of the Obama health care bill. What the public did hear in a great torrent of never ending repetition was terms like, "government run," and "socialized medicine," that grossly mischaracterized in the public mind what was really being offered.[58]

The propagandists, or as they are currently called: public relations experts, assured Americans that there was a way to bring down premiums while keeping services high quality and the good old market was the way to make it happen. The "good old market" was what had driven the prices up to begin with and the reality was that American healthcare for the average citizen had been way short of the best in the world for several decades. As mentioned previously, "death by doctor" has become one of the top three leading causes of death in the country. It is also true that the AMA itself has reported that the overwhelming majority of complaints presented to doctors, some 96% can be neither identified nor treated and simply go away on their own, that out of the remaining 4% only 2% are accurately identified, and out of those that are, less than 1% are successfully treated. Added to this is the fact that most pharmaceuticals work less than half the time and in this any positive effect often coming at the cost of injurious side-effects. These facts paint a picture of American healthcare as a product with a bloated price tag that most often delivers nothing, which on the contrary if you don't watch out *may accidently kill you.*

The reality is that Americans are not the longest living people in the world, according to the U.N., sitting at 38th on the list of countries, and infant mortality rates in this country put 28 other countries ahead of us with lower numbers, some of them third world nations. The idea of an all-encompassing American superiority is a myth too many Americans are all too willing to believe and so the great propaganda machine won the day, seriously compromising support for any real efforts at

241

bringing down costs. No effort whatsoever went into how to improve the quality of the product. The final bill passed has been characterized by doctors and defenders of the public as a huge giveaway for insurance and pharmaceutical companies, exactly the two entities that are driving the problems, but seemingly have accrued such political power as to be untouchable. Here we find another perfect example of Professor Quigley's notion of "reaction" in vested interest groups defending their positions against the public's drive for a better accommodation of their dire needs leading to the further decline and fracturing of the society. "If the outcome is reaction then the decline becomes chronic." And the chronic decline is well underway in healthcare.

Propaganda or "Public Relations"

Corporate power has increasingly followed the strategies of Madison Avenue advertising groups who found out long ago that there were better ways to encourage the public to buy a product than simply listing the capabilities and good qualities of the thing. They went from ads that once said something like, *use Wonder Suds and your dishes will shine*, to a scene where a housewife is embarrassed by streaks on her glasses that then turns into a scene where the same woman is smiling with pride as guests ask her about her sparkling glassware. The advertising industry had taken lessons from the field of psychology introduced to them by a man named, Edward Bernays. Bernays, the nephew of Sigmund Freud, pioneered the application of psychology to propaganda efforts serving the allies during WWI. After the war Bernays found a willing audience for his ideas in the advertising industry. Under President Woodrow Wilson something that came to be known as the "Creel Commission," formally, "the Committee on Public Information," was put together to find a way to turn the American public from their pacifistic resistance to involvement in the European conflict. Berneys and his boss, George Creel, a master tactician of the art of propaganda, packaged concocted stories about horrendous German atrocities in Belgium provided by British Intelligence. In tactics not uncommon in European warfare, the German Army had burned a number of Belgian towns in response to guerrilla actions against their troops and this was used as the basis for all manner of exaggeration and false accounts of babies being dismembered and other enflaming outrages against humanity. American views on the war were flooded with very effective heart rending accounts in the papers, on news reels in the movie houses, on radio, and through a host of speakers who went into towns across the country reciting tales of the "terrible Hun!" Recruiting posters were prolific; one representative of the genre portrayed a murderous German as a raging ape with spiked helmet and club hauling away a damsel in distress. This emotionally manipulative campaign, pulling on the heart strings of Americans, persuaded men to see themselves in the roll of rescuers and the last hope of women and children brutalized by Germans portrayed as barbarous throw-backs to Attila's hoards. In point of fact, the Germanic tribal peoples had actually helped to defeat the Huns, stopping their advance into Europe, but the truth is no impediment to the seasoned propagandist and all stops were pulled out in portraying the Germans as drooling, depraved homicidal apes with more in common with Eurasian barbarians than polite and gentile Europeans.

The reality of the war in Europe was much closer to the original intuition of the American people as nothing but another round of power and land grabbing by the various empires of the region scrambling for position as the Ottoman Turks lost their grip on former possessions. The common people of Europe were once again being drummed up for slaughter to please the aristocratic and industrial leadership and Americans rightfully saw it as none of their business. This was not going to work for Wilson and his British allies who wanted very much to beat down the German Empire and its Naval build-up so as to take it out of the competition for world resources claimed by the British Empire and burgeoning American imperialist aspirations. The British had contrived a start to the war as a way of stopping the German effort to establish their own source of oil from the Middle East with a Berlin to Bagdad rail line which would have allowed the German economy to expand exponentially.[59] The British had mismanaged their own economy and were nearly bankrupt at the start of the war, giving American banks like J.P. Morgan the opportunity to make a fortune on massive loans for the British war build up. If the British lost the war then the bankers would lose their money, a fact not lost on the American people. So, American sentiments had to be manipulated and turned around with the application of deceptive and emotionally coercive techniques that were disguised as a straight forward effort to bring people information.[60]

After the war, Edward Bernays brought Freud's notion of unconscious motivating factors to the machinations of the ad men, and so advertising began to shift from ads addressing the logic of the buying public to ads that worked through psychologically manipulating the fears and desires of target populations. Since home products like dish or laundry soap were a female purchase, the ads began to play on the fear of being shamed by dirty dishes or clothing and thought a bad mother or housekeeper. They worked on women's desires for their families to be seen as immaculate examples of "good, clean living people," a strong underlying moray of post-puritanical American culture. So now we have tire ads with babies that suggest that if you don't buy the expensive all-weather safety tires you might kill your baby and cereal ads that suggest that if you don't eat that special cereal you could die of heart disease or colon cancer.

If the psychological manipulation techniques were confined to product ads it might not be such a dangerous problem. Unfortunately, Edward Bernays was primarily interested in using propaganda to shape society in much more profound ways.

> The conscious and intelligent manipulation of the organized habits and opinions of the masses is an important element in democratic society. Those who manipulate this unseen mechanism of society constitute an invisible government which is the true ruling power of our country…,

wrote Bernays.[61] After WWII the Nazis had given the term "propaganda" such a bad name that Bernays suggested that the entire field be renamed with the seemingly innocuous title: *public relations*. What could be more harmless than a government or corporation having good *public relations*? Certainly there's nothing wrong with passing out pens with your company name emblazoned. If the efforts of PR firms remained along those lines, then we could applaud their efforts. The problem is that psychological methods of coercion and manipulation have become standard techniques employed by PR firms for many years in an effort to keep the pubic ignorant regarding the true damage accruing from the civilization of side effects.

Much of the best advice from scientists and scholars is obscured and disempowered by the PR machine. The climate change issue is perhaps the most glaring example, but it goes way beyond this. People are sucking up huge quantities of toxic materials from water and soda bottles and food containers. They are bathing in toxins from shampoos and bath products. They are brushing their teeth with carcinogens and eating a myriad of food products containing toxins and carcinogens meant to improve shelf life, keep the color and consistency in place, or keep the calories down. The government has set limits on how much toxic material food products can contain and so, when questioned, producers – if they cannot question the science – will always shout that the quantity of bad stuff in their product is so low you'd have to eat 300 boxes a week to be affected.

What the government doesn't set as a limit, and what industry has fought hard to make sure they don't, is the cumulative amount of toxins a person should not exceed from the use of multiple products. When your shampoo, your lunch, your toothpaste, your drinks, the air you breath, including the pollutants from industry and automobiles and the outgassing of synthetic carpets and office products, are all putting toxins into your system; when you are taking medications and inoculations that sometimes contain toxins, when you are eating mercury in sea life, pesticides, herbicides, and fungicides on fruits and vegetables (the suffix *cides* from the Latin: *to kill*); when you are sleeping on a new mattress that is literally gassing you every night for months; if you are using feminine hygiene products or shaving cream or any number of things found in your average grocery store then – in short – *you are eating the 300 boxes a week and more*. This is precisely why the cumulative amount of toxins is not tracked or regulated; if this was done then it would be abundantly clear that everyone is being slowly poisoned. This doesn't even get into the other forms of attack on the human system coming from the radiation from cell phone equipment and other sources, as well as magnetic fields from all kinds of electronic equipment that disrupt cell function.

As these products, designed as they were by the reductionist, disconnected conceptions of the machine mind, multiplied in our society, so too did a continual flow of revelations pointing out to the public that each had carried with it into our homes and bodies a little toxicity. Each time this happened the public relations people got a little more work. The tricks of the trade used by PR firms to fool the public are a study unto itself, so a few quick examples will have to suffice here.

Say evidence begins to proliferate that suggests that eating a certain type of packaged food will cause health problems. The manufacturers of that product will hire a PR firm to do something to halt the lagging product sales. One of the common methods used is to bring together a group of medical "experts," paid large sums of money to form a group with a name like "the American Healthy Families Counsel." Then, they will design a piece of research that is purposely skewed to provide the conclusions they are looking for. This group will prepare a press release that will be sent out to hundreds of local news stations in major metropolitan areas throughout the country. On some slow news day, the news director will reach over to his pile of such submissions and, since the PR people have considerately made his job easier by including all the script and video material he will need to turn it into a report, it will go on the air. The folks at home will see a news announcer tell them that a new study has been released by the *American Healthy Families Counsel* that contradicts reports of bad things from a certain food; in fact, not only did the study find that the product wasn't bad for you, but on the contrary, some people showed health improvements! People hearing this report will conclude that a group that is on their side has reviewed the evidence and found that it was a false alarm. They don't need to cut back on eating that stuff they love so much after all. Even if some members of the public don't completely trust the positive findings they will most likely decide that there is contradictory evidence and this will slow down any decision they make about stopping their intake of that food. This may lead to their early death through some form of cancer or congestive heart failure or some other malady, but the corporation in question really doesn't care about that. They take no more responsibility for that than do the companies and legislators who pulled the rug out on the steel industry so long ago. The side effects of their actions and products are not their concern. The food companies didn't tell those people to eat themselves to death and so when faced with the results of their work they shrug their shoulders and think, *those people should have made better choices*. The problem is that people make the best choices they can given the information they have to go on and PR firms often make sure the information they have is either clouded with doubt or just plain wrong.[62]

These "dummy" public welfare organizations are not confined to those supporting food producers, of course, but dot the landscape as political "think tanks" with names that reveal nothing of their true prejudices as they provide "experts" to move your opinion on news shows. There are medical and dental health groups that are funded by the pharmaceutical industry and toothpaste companies that pretend to be objective providers of information to the public, as there are "alternative energy" organizations secretly funded by the oil industry to slow down the move to a nonpolluting energy future by promoting the solutions that will take the very longest to produce, while downplaying real threats to continued oil company profits. There are front groups paid for by chemical producers releasing "studies" disputing the bad news on their products, and even employees of weapons manufacturers masquerading as experts on foreign relations.

Another tactic is to produce magazines or websites that pretend to be on your side as unbiased sources of information that in actuality are there to promote a particular industry. For example, there has been a women's "health" magazine that appeared on grocery store checkout stands that presented itself as on the side of the American woman searching for the best advice on diet and exercise that was actually funded by the dairy industry. Inside you will find articles extolling the virtues of eating yogurt and cottage cheese and drinking milk, disputing the growing research findings that suggest that cutting down on dairy products may be essential for good health.[63]

Our information systems, especially "news" programing have been seriously compromised by the forces of manipulation. As the side effects of our machine mind way of doing things and the status quo's hanging onto outmoded methods have become more and more evident, as the mercury has built up in fish, as the leaching of carcinogenic styrene and estrogenic alkylphenols from styrofoam food containers has come to the public's attention – and the list goes on and on – industry simply goes into evasive maneuvers through disinformation campaigns, phony studies, and by paying "experts" to argue their case on news programs.

PATRIOTISM AND GOVERNMENT CORRUPTION

In the history of the West there has been two major methods for raising public support. The two topics most effective in generating a fever for action in the average mind are: religion, and patriotism – God and country. It was this that the humanist author, Sinclair Lewis, was thinking of when he predicted that when fascism came to America it would be "wrapped in the flag and carrying the Cross."

The language and mythological imagery of American "freedom"

has been used time and time again as a method for disguising the actual withdrawing of true liberty and justice for all. This premier tool engineering the society of manipulation is perfectly displayed in its more recent manifestation in the deceptively titled "Patriot Act" that wraps itself in the red, white, and blue, while actually cancelling an entire section of the Constitution of the United States on which our right to privacy, and so liberty, was guaranteed. Now security forces can enter your home with or without your knowledge and rifle through your belongings, not being libel for any damage, tap your phone, intercept your post and e-mail, review your purchases, bank records and library withdrawals, and there is nothing you can do about it, because you no longer have a right to privacy in the United States. If you are an American citizen your liberty has been curtailed, pledge of allegiance or not. The 2012 *Defense Authorization Act* went further and made indefinite detention an option so that if they find anything the FBI doesn't like while spying on you they can now throw you in jail without trial for as long as they want. These are the hallmarks of dictatorships not democracies. You would think this would provoke riots in the streets. Instead, many Americans with the flag firmly tied around their eyes have no idea two of the major pillars of American liberty have been kicked out from beneath them. This is how manipulation works best. The mark thinks he or she is getting one thing when they're really getting the opposite.

It was Niccolo Machiavelli in the 16th Century who wrote the archetypal work on political manipulation, a book later entitled, *The Prince*. In it he explained that in order to take over a state that has "been accustomed to live under their own laws and in freedom," without raising the opposition of the populace you must leave all of the traditional institutions in place while you hollow them out from the inside so that they appear to be working as they always have but have actually come under your control.

> Establishing within it an oligarchy which will keep it friendly to you…such a government, being created by the prince, knows that it cannot stand without his friendship and interest and does its utmost to support him; and therefore, he who would keep a city accustomed to freedom will hold it more easily by the means of its own citizens, than by any other way.[64]

This is precisely what has been going on in the United States for some time as the big wealthy interests in the form of corporate power and the major banks behind them have slowly usurped democracy for their own purposes by filling the government at all levels with what are essentially their retainers and gradually changing the laws and regulations to favor their profits and power, often at the growing expense of the average citizen. This is most obvious in how campaign support from corporate and financial groups has become essential for coming to power in the first place, thus creating dependencies that, "cannot stand without his friendship and interest," and operationally in what has come to be called the "revolving door" situation in the regulatory offices of Washington. Individuals go from being leaders of industry to positions in regulatory departments, like the Food and Drug Administration or the Environmental Protection Agency, that oversee those same industries, then back to those industries when they are done being "regulators." Airplanes crash and pilot wages have been driven downward, because the FAA is in bed with the airline industry.[65] Pollution continues unabated because the EPA is run by a former polluting executive who, when his government service is done, will again be a polluting executive. The pharmaceutical companies continue to market dangerous drugs because the FDA is led by a drug company man, etc., etc. When a regulator does try to do their job, as in the 2008 financial scandal when the head of the Securities and Exchange Commission did try to blow the whistle on phony financial products, they are preempted in their efforts by higher political forces, as she was by the Bush administration.[66]

In this way and simply by reducing the operating budgets of the regulatory offices to skeleton crews to render them largely incapable of doing their jobs, the patrons of the government become the government itself. The removing of protections for the populace from the side effects of a deteriorating system is completed in favor of increasing profits, thus driving the civilization ever downward while appearances are preserved. Machiavelli would be proud.

Mind Control

Mind control in America has largely been carried out on two fronts: first, as a technique aimed at direct manipulation of the human mind via an intense conditioning program delivered to individuals in confined and controlled environments; and second, as subliminal advertising that attempts to access and influence the subconscious mind of the public through the general media environment.

Direct mind control programs grew out of the Korean War when an infamous group of American POW's fell victim to new Chinese methods of coercive indoctrination that turned their sympathies and beliefs in support of communism. These 21 men elected to abandon their families and homes and stay in North Korea and China when the armistice was signed in 1953 and all other POW's came home. The men made statements to the effect that they had rejected the Western capitalist system in favor of the communist. This sent a shockwave through the American government, military, and social science nerve centers. It was clear from the condition and testimony of other returning POW's that something had been done to these men to produce this turnaround. That something came to be understood as "brainwashing."

Long before this episode spurred American power toward its own frantic effort to perfect brainwashing techniques so as not to be outdone by the communists, American psychologists following the work of Wilhelm Wundt in Germany had late in the 19th century begun to look upon human behavior and belief as something purely learned and without basis in any intrinsic humanity. Wundt was the psychologist of the age, a complete materialist and promoter of the machine model of life. From this basis the theory arose that the human mind was simply a mechanism and therefore ultimately malleable and so those in the seats of power sought to develop methods to mold the average American citizen into a perfect instrument of an orderly society and efficient industry. *Efficiency* was the byword of the age. The industrial revolution had become a technical dynamo that promised to remake the world in the image of a Jules Verne novel where science and technical knowhow would conquer all limitations and erect a fantastic civilization of machine wizardry. A man named Frederick Winslow Taylor had applied what he called "scientific management" to human activities with the intent to make factory workers more efficient by closely analyzing the most economical way of completing their tasks. The intent was to meld workers with the machine so as to increase output, but Taylor's methods tended to also increase the stress on workers to a point of rebellion. A congressional hearing found the application of Taylor's methods to the work at the Watertown Arsenal so disruptive that they banned them from any further application there. This didn't discourage managers elsewhere from pushing forward with the general idea of ever increasing methods of efficiency and Taylor's methods persisted becoming the starting place of a whole new field of management theory.[67]

There was in this era the rising spirit of a new consciousness as well as the older spiritual view that human beings could in no way be compared to machines, being complex creatures of deep, even metaphysical layers of motivation, identity, and desire. The confluence of the old spirituality and the rising consciousness of the integral was well displayed by the work of individuals like Theroux, and Walt Whitman, "...I contain multitudes," he declared in, *Leaves of Grass*, but this rising current of expanding consciousness was not accepted by the lords of industry who were blind to the work of more humane psychologists like William James. Their more complex views of the human psyche made consciousness a grand mystery of ultimate depth and so were not useful to industrialists who needed to see workers as one dimensional creatures to be prodded into ultimate efficiency and cowed into minimal wages, more a pack of animals than complete human beings. In remarking on the sort of person suitable for handling pig iron, for instance, Taylor noted in 1911, "He shall be so stupid and so phlegmatic he more nearly resembles in his mental make-up the ox more than any other type." The owners of industry began looking for a way to see every worker as pieces of their mechanical world, if not stupid, then of whatever sort of constitution trainable to carry out the tasks required with the sort of one mindedness seen in draft animals or army ants, all without complaint or demand. To this end, the Rockefeller Trusts and the Carnegie Corporation, along with the Ford Foundation, and other industrialist fortunes, began pouring money into what came to be called, "human engineering." It was the start of social science in America and its direction and goals would be shaped by big money as noted in Rockefeller Foundation policy documents that spoke of bringing order to the chaos of social life in the form of, "social regulation," and set the goal as: "Social understanding and social control in the public interest."[68]

This early social science was billed in the press of the day as a great hope for mankind in creating a better world. The industrialists saw the rising tide of public criticism evidenced in greater concern for the poor and the drive toward freedom and respect in the ranks of the working public in union agitation and they weren't going to have it. The alternative to industrial reform was found in the idea that human beings could be made happy under any circumstances if the proper methods could be deduced from the application of science to human affairs. The idea of stretching the human mind and body to meet the needs of industry rather than changing society and industry to meet the needs of human beings was the steady drone of elitist foundation ideology production. The elitist structure of society and industrial work was promoted as simply the natural evolution of things and as such trying to change the course of civilization in this regard was conveyed to the public as an impossibility, a course against nature. The "scientific" social science created by the wealthy foundations suggested all answers to the problems of industrialization accommodate the status quo. If the workers were unhappy, then adjustments were to be made to the workers and the established order was not to be questioned.

Industrialism can indeed be understood within the evolution of consciousness, the materialization of a mechanical vision that was a working out in time and space of the mental/rational structure. The power relations within society were more a result of a lack of moral development in elite individuals that simply reserved true human attributes for members of their own class and aspirants to it, seeing the average worker as another sort of creature altogether, a kind of empty headed drone, born to be commanded by *the captains of industry*, and that had no value to the future of humanity other than their labor potential.

And this is one of the main elements of the running down of the primacy of the mental/rational structure in Western Civilization: the element of time as an arrow with destiny being projected into the future where the imagined utopia of a materialist vision finds its inspiration for the present. Workers are harnessed to the yoke of tomorrow's dreams of faster, farther and better, where "better" is never really defined, other than as *more powerful*. The "*Why?*" and the, "*Where are we going with our power and speed?*" is never really considered. The mental/rational mind pushed out of balance with other structures of consciousness can't see the value of anything that doesn't propel the materialist agenda forward, can't find the value of the present in and of itself *that is life*, but sees in the unworked moment only stagnation, in the "undeveloped" wilderness only a wasteland. So, the population is ordered from "stupid" to "smart" based on a criteria of ability to move the machine into the "better" future, that is the degree of contribution to the development and marketing of more elaborate products. Those people on the stupid end are to be used as brute force, as oxen for the pulling, and the smart end for the various tasks of planning, designing, and managing industry's project into the glorious tomorrow. With this value spectrum in mind elite interests at the top of the money and power pyramids in America and Britain sought to shape a new human animal out of the creatures below they saw as nothing more than soulless pods to be filled with whatever directives they found most helpful for their agenda.

It was the research of Ivan Pavlov that really got their attention. Here science had demonstrated with dogs and bells that creatures could be programmed to associate something good with anything the scientist cared to insert into their experience. The bell was rung every time the dog was fed and so the sound of the bell alone soon became capable of producing salivation in the dog. What had begun as a natural response to the smell of food had been transferred to the bell and from this power interests saw the hope of transferring the natural responses of human beings onto whatever they required of them as *good workers*. This was the beginning of the field of Behaviorism in American psychology and due to the huge sums of money poured into this search for the controls of behavioral mechanisms Behaviorism soon became the dominant force in social science. This model of psychology completely pushes aside any notion of a unique individual nature, a human spirit, or any sort of central organizing characteralogical element within people that could be called an authentic self, replacing it with a radically environmental model that finds the source of the individual personality and behavioral tendencies in an arbitrary experiential history. The idea that emerges from this model is that human beings have no core of humanity to be tended and developed by a society, but rather can be programmed through control of the environment to attach pleasure and pain to anything. Everything a person may feel in themselves as individuality is understood by Behaviorism to be nothing more than the sum total of what has been impressed on them by their culture and families. In other words, personal identity is an illusion, and most importantly for industry, an illusion that can be molded and manipulated for profit.

John B. Watson was the founder of Behaviorism in America, a student of Wundt and Pavlov, Watson carried out experiments on children to produce evidence he believed supported the conclusion that people could be conditioned to love or fear anything. One such experiment began with a young boy who was given a docile white rat to play with. As the boy at first had fun with the animal, Watson demonstrated that the boy could be made to fear the rat if he slammed a steel bar with a hammer producing an unnerving clanging every time the rat was brought into the room. Indeed, after a period of conditioning the boy would cry each time he saw the rat brought in, thus Watson proved to his colleagues that a child could be made to fear anything when an unscrupulous scientist accompanies the event with something entirely shocking and terrifying. Watson was overjoyed at the possibilities suggested by his cruel investigations. "Give me the baby...and I'll make it a thief, a gunman, or a dope fiend. The possibilities of shaping in any direction are almost endless...Men are built, not born."[69] Watson dreamed of having "an experimental farm for babies" to further demonstrate his science but, mercifully, he was never able to achieve his dream. What he did do was go to work for Madison Avenue as an advertising executive where he brought his manipulative arts to the American people through another route. Regardless, John Watson's foundational work had a strong effect on an increasing number of persons in the field, including, oddly enough, his child care doctrines that warned against an excess of coddling and motherly love, aimed at creating out of the morally ambiguous American melting pot culture a well-disciplined society. "Social and moral drift was to be replaced by control mechanisms that replaced tradition with order and purpose." [70]

But the new science of social engineering was put to work not just to program babies or sell products but to make them, all billed as an attempt to create a "better world" as defined by big money. John Rockefeller Jr. was on the board of directors of the Colorado Fuel and Iron Company his family owned, where in 1914 what came to be known as the "Ludlow Massacre" was perpetrated on striking workers and their families. The Colorado National Guard aided by company guards attacked a tent camp full of men, women, and children eventually killing 25 people, including the strike leader who was captured and later found shot in the back. Thereafter, a stream of Rockefeller money went to fund research into "deradicalizing" workers through a regime of psychological programing. A plan researched and carried out by a psychologist named Elton Mayo who believed that social radicals, leftists, and all manner of "agitators" on the job were, rather than carriers of legitimate protest against exploitation, simply mentally ill. This was an idea that appealed to big money and Mayo subsequently became a big name in American social science, securing a position at Harvard in the business school rather than the social science department where he carried out the infamous "Hawthorn experiments."

Mayo took his theories to the Hawthorn works factory of Western Electric where he found a way into the minds of the workers on the line through their interpersonal relationships, which he believed were more important than wages or working conditions. Mayo's theory said that if an employer could manipulate the sentiments of workers toward each other, they could ignore compensation and improving conditions because the workers would find work satisfaction as part of their social programing within a group bond. Employers needed to enlist the workers feelings of being in it together with each other and ultimately with management. To this end Mayo discovered that people like to be listened to and felt a part of the operation so he suggested that managers interview employees from time to time in order to instill this feeling of importance to the overall effort.

This was primarily a response to growing union agitation that was meant to give workers the feeling that their needs were known and important to management without having to actually increase wages or change anything. Mayo's experiments showed that animosity toward management could be reduced by this technique of allowing workers to vent. Managers were instructed not to interrupt or argue but to simply listen and appear to take note of the worker's feelings and ideas. In other words, it was a kind of deception meant to drain off the rage generated by working as a cog in a machine in depressing conditions while it engendered a false feeling of unity with management, thus allowing the company to avoid incurring any real costs. Mayo's techniques are still found in management doctrine today even though a strident voice of criticism followed his work as it established itself, often being accused of "adjusting men to machines," and "substituting therapy for democracy." [71]

These kinds of deceptive techniques meant to manipulate the feelings of working people proliferated, but were really only a prelude to more invasive tactics yet to come. In 1939 the Rockefeller funded, Yale Institute, published a book called, *Frustration and Aggression*, which was an American response to the theories of Sigmund Freud and was really a kind of accommodation of European depth psychology to American behaviorism. What the Yale institute did was take Freud and reduce his drive theory to a mechanical model meant to simply enlarge the Behaviorist scheme; what was essentially a vast oversimplification and misinterpretation. In this way thought was again removed from the formula so that drives were not responded to by the individual as choices within the consciousness of a unique human character, but simply more automated programing. From this the human engineering was off and running once again, determined to modify people like robots with an eye toward the creation of an ultimate order. To this end rat mazes became all the rage as the work of the Yale Institute began to test the limits of instinct. Their approach invaded research departments in universities across the nation making rat and animal testing a staple of American psychology departments. Human life was now reducible to that of rat behavior. The influence of rat studies in America became profound and has served as inspiration for policy at all levels of society, everything from industry, to education, to civic planning. When people say they are tired of the "rat race" there is a very good reason for it.

In a more direct way the Yale Institute research formed the basis of what would become a clandestine brainwashing program run by military intelligence and the CIA during the cold war and perhaps to this day.[72] What had become clear from the Yale studies is that subjects could be psychologically coerced into changing deeply engrained or even instinctual behaviors; things like the basic drive to preserve life.

In programs with secretive code names like Bluebird and MKULTRA, the CIA used experimental psychologists at a number of universities to carry out abusive research on unwitting patients and volunteers who were put through regimes of sleep deprivation or dossed with high levels of drugs like LSD and other strong psychoactive agents, for sometimes weeks on end, given hundreds of hours of post hypnotic suggestion, termed "psychic driving," and released in states of almost total amnesia. In actual events that became the basis for James Bond movie scenarios thought by the public to be purely fiction, the CIA brainwashing specialists proved that a person could be broken down and remade to become an assassin on command.

It has long been a truism of hypnosis theory that a person cannot be made to do something strongly against their moral beliefs that they would not do in a normal waking state. This has been proven to be simply wrong in documented experimentation. Dr. George Estabrooks, chairman of the Department of Psychology at Colgate University during and after WWII, and key researcher in mind control for the CIA and military intelligence once said, "I can hypnotize a man without his knowledge or consent into committing treason against the United States." His colleague, J.G. Watkins demonstrated the thesis in one of several experiments on Army privates, which showed that they could be made to attack a superior officer, a thing they had been strongly conditioned against, simply by suggesting under hypnosis that the officer was an enemy infiltrator and was preparing to kill them. In all cases the men attacked the officer with intense violence, one soldier producing a knife from his pocket and nearly killing him. Subsequent CIA sponsored research demonstrated that certain subjects could be conditioned to carry out a range of complex actions including those necessary for assassinations through rigorous hypnotic programing, emerge from the ordeal with no memory of what they had been through, to be "activated" later through the administration of a command by telephone. Dr. Estabrooks was interviewed by the *Providence Evening Bulletin* in 1968 and stated for the paper: "The key to creating an effective spy or assassin rests in...creating a multiple personality with the aid of hypnosis." The doctor went on to suggest that such things were "child's play," and that Lee Harvey Oswald and Jack Ruby, "could very well have been performing through hypnosis."[73] Anyone who has lingering doubts about the power of hypnosis, even in brief sessions, to motivate people to act in deadly ways can witness the experiment done by master hypnotist, Darren Brown, chronicled at: (mindcontrolwiki.com/assassin-protocol/). There is no doubt regarding the power of hypnosis as an espionage tool utilized by American intelligence services against foreign and domestic targets. The FBI files show domestic targets to be everything from peace groups, to Black empowerment groups, to environmental organizations. The infamous FBI program termed, COINTELPRO, aimed at spying on and violating the civil rights of Americans was uncovered in the 1970's plus numerous other reports on both the CIA and FBI to this day confirm this long term intent to use the most aggressive and abusive methods for controlling dissent against a government that has ceased to uphold the tenants of a free society.[74]

There is abundant evidence for anyone willing to do the research, but again, this isn't something you are going to find broadcast by the corporate controlled media. This wasn't always the case. After the Senate Church Committee probed allegations of CIA and FBI abuses against American citizens and released their findings in 1979, an ABC television special talked all about it. You can still see this on YouTube: (CIA Mind

Control Techniques: Mk-Ultra Program Brainwashing Experiments Documentary (1979).) Since that time these organizations have become much more vigilant in keeping their dirty laundry out of the news and the news itself has become almost completely sewed up by the power interests. Just the same, people do emerge from the darkness to tell their stories and the Internet is swimming with individuals with excellent credentials blowing the whistle on continued abuses of power.

As a final example the story of Susan Lindauer is illustrative of what happens when a person of good conscience tries to do the right thing for the American people. Ms. Lindauer was a CIA asset on Iraq and Lybia, she was with the United Nations and had direct contact with sources in the Middle East who warned her of the attacks planned on the World Trade Center, which she reported to her handlers. After 9/11 she went to members of Congress and told them of this prior knowledge; within weeks she was arrested on the Patriot Act and incarcerated, heavily drugged, and subjected to long hours of psychological torture in an effort to get her to change her story. She was kept in prison without trial on completely bogus charges for five years and the FBI now claims she is mentally ill, although independent evaluations indicate she is not.[75]

If direct assaults on the minds of Americans were confined to mind control victims within institutions it would amount to a small minority, but unfortunately there are also a number of other more clandestine technologies. Miniature radio controlled devices that are implanted directly into the brain and sinuses have been around for some time; it is a technology developed by Yale professor, Dr. Jose Delgado in the 1970's with the direct intent of controlling people's behavior. These devices have been greatly improved since then, but may have been superseded by energy broadcasting technologies that don't need any kind of hardware in the individual to receive their message. A thing called HARRP broadcasts on a frequency that matches that of the human brain and information can be piggybacked on signals that blanket a population area.[76] A suggestive newspaper article published in the *Oregon Journal* in 1978 was titled, "Mysterious Radio Signals Causing Concern." The FCC investigated and had found that microwave radiation was the cause of a range of symptoms, from skin rashes and headaches to hearing clicking in the head. In 1985 members of a British peace group protesting outside the gates of an American air base at Greenham Commons, began to experience similar and more extreme symptoms including memory loss, depression, and disorientation. A former radar engineer with the group took readings of electromagnetic levels in the area and confirmed they were 100 times stronger than in surrounding areas. [77]

The well-known story of the American embassy in Moscow in the 1960's being bombarded by microwave radiation causing illness and agitation is another piece of evidence that energy weapons have long been used to manipulate people. Since then various articles appeared in defense journals that indicated that Americans were behind in the development of "radio frequency weapons," citing the need for more research and development.[78] Since that time a number of reports have surfaced regarding mind control energy weapons designed to stimulate aberrant behavior and hallucinations in human targets and even give audio commands.[79]

The most potent form of "mind control" in America is, of course, without a doubt the media – mostly in the form of television that carries out broad scale manipulation of the American people daily. Besides the content of stories meant to shape belief discussed above, the technology itself can produce a mild altered state of consciousness designated "alpha" in the science of brain wave patterns. Alpha consciousness is the same as that experienced in light hypnosis. This means that the normal waking "beta" state that engages experience with discernment and critical assessment is lost making viewers highly susceptible to suggestion. This explains the experience regularly described as "vegging out" in front of the TV. This state can be highly addicting due to its relaxed and yet stimulating nature. Studies show that endorphins, the brain's natural "feel good" drug are released when in Alpha and people slip into Alpha states within one minute of watching television.[80]

The psychologist Eldon Taylor has made a study of subliminal advertising and suggestion in sound production. Dr. Taylor presents a long list of studies demonstrating the reality of subliminal suggestion and its ability to create intended effects in human behavior. He has used subliminal suggestion in his work as a psychologist for many years and has served as an expert witness on the subject. Despite this fact after giving testimony in a hearing in Utah for what would have been the first law in the nation against subliminal messaging in media representatives of the advertising and other industries were able to cloud the issue to the point that the legislation was eventually voted down. The ad men and producers claimed that a law wasn't necessary because the technology wasn't used, was too expensive, and didn't work anyway. It was curious that they had flown in from New York to a small city in Utah to fight off local legislation against something they weren't using and didn't work. To date no law prohibits the use of subliminal messages in advertising or music productions. This, even in the face of a number of teen suicides and attempts that have been directly linked to suggestions found at subliminal levels in music they were listening to at the time. In a well-publicized case in 1984 two young men shot themselves with a shotgun, one fatally, after listening to a Judas Priest album for hours. The attorneys for CBS Records argued that subliminal messaging was unproven and didn't work, while CBS claimed they "lost" the master to the recording so it could not be analyzed; the suit was eventually dismissed. Regardless of the claims of industry, the US Patent Office has issued over 100 patents on subliminal technologies, some of which have as a stated purpose the insertion of subliminal messages in ambient music for shopping centers and department stores. Others are specifically for use in television and other video production.[81]

Dr. Taylor was contacted after the Utah hearing by an anonymous whistle blower inside the advertising industry that sent him an actual manual on subliminal advertising techniques that he partially reproduces in his book *Mind Programing*. The approach outlined uses a number of devious manipulations of repressed fear and sexual desire, as well as the use of archetypal symbols long known by depth psychologists to stimulate unconscious emotional reactions.

In recent years a movement known as "transhumanism" has become a popular topic in tech circles and in the occasional human interest story in the Sunday paper. Basically, transhumanism is simply the augmenting of human ability through the addition of technological hardware to the human body. The director of engineering at Google, Ray Kurzweil, has become famous as the champion of this movement. Ray wants to live forever, he tells us, so he's betting on the merger of man and machine so he can have his consciousness downloaded into a cybernetic being.

In an article for *Futurist Magazine*[82] Mr. Kurzweil has predicted,

> The implementation of artificial intelligence in our biological systems will mark an evolutionary leap forward for humanity but it also implies we will indeed become more "machine" than "human." Billions of nanobots will travel through the

bloodstream in our bodies and brains. In our bodies, they will destroy pathogens, correct DNA errors, eliminate toxins, and perform many other tasks to enhance our physical well-being. As a result, we will be able to live indefinitely without aging.

The most disturbing thing about this sort of thinking is not the obvious over-population issue (because this technology would probably be reserved for an elite minority), but the idea that to enter a "post-human" world would be a good thing. What kind of mind conceives of a situation that transforms people into things "more machine than human" as constituting an improvement? It is the mind of the hyper-materialist technologist, looking through the iron clad exclusivity of the deficient mental/rational structure of consciousness now seeking to defeat Nature once and for all. Ray Kurzweil, and those that share his enthusiasm for replacing biology with technology, have drunk the KoolAid of Darwinian random evolutionary theory that sees humanity's path as simply representing a series of meaningless random events pushed by weather and cosmic circumstance. To this ideology, there is no guiding intelligence, intrinsic pattern, or any such *natural* path of evolution. Ours is simply a story marked by accident. What transhumanism suggests is that we take control of evolution rather than allow these cosmic random accidents to guide our future. This is, of course, a grave and terrible overstepping of the human mandate for improvement that fails to recognize that we have emerged from a system that is much, much, older than we are and quite a bit more organized, and it is that larger organization, pattern, and yes, *consciousness*, that holds the larger framework for our advancement. It is through that ultimate organization that we have slowly gained independence – not from, but *within* Nature – and it is this organization that we must advance in harmony with as we gain more consciousness and so choice.

We need only turn to the *anthropic principle* as a singular example that tells us that life on Earth arose within very, very narrow parameters. If the temperature of the planet had been even slightly in variance for millions upon millions of years then life could not have arisen. The same goes for gravity and great numbers of other conditions and this gives biophysicists the feeling that the universe is set up for creating life, that it wasn't a convergence of happy errors that brought us here but simply part of the pattern that is intrinsic to the way the universe works. Neo-Darwinists, of course, hate this idea but there is so much evidence in support of the principle that only a willful blindness prevents a person from admitting it. Not just physics but biology itself offers support for guiding principles in Nature. Convergent evolution demonstrates that many organisms in totally disconnected lines of evolution develop the same structures. This could not happen if random mutation was operating. The Nobel Lauriat biochemist and cytologist, Christian de Duve, has stated categorically that, "life is the product of deterministic forces."[83]

If this is true, and the evidence is overwhelming, then there is a deep guiding principle within biology and the subatomic fields that interact with it that should not be violated. The fossil record shows us all kinds of evolutionary dead ends that branched off the main road and ended in total extinction. I believe it is consciousness in harmony with what the anthropic principle represents in Nature that allows us to make decisions about our future that avoids these extinction traps. Turning human beings into cybernetic entities more machine than human represents an extinction trap of monumental proportions, because it is a radical veering away from the main core of nature that perpetuates the universe and all life within it. We can improve ourselves and our society in a myriad of ways, but we must do it within Nature not in opposition to it. This opposition that resides in materialist science is an unconscious influence that was carried over from the deficient mythological mind that preceded it. The old patriarchal religion split the universe in two pitting the bloodless sky god against the "sinful" feminine earth with all its lust and carnage. Orthodox science in its transhumanist agenda has continued the tradition of "inferior biology vs. superior disembodied intellect," even as they pursue their war against religion for the greatest of ironies.

In 2004 doctors at Brown University implanted a device in the brain of a paralyzed patient who was then able to move a computer curser with his mind. This research is always framed with the stated intent to use it to help people like this so as to avoid the discussion of the possible negative implications such a technology poses. History is clear that technology is power and power to manipulate the human mind at will being available to an increasingly autocratic corporatized government should be a major topic of debate. The reality is that the population of physically impaired people doesn't offer a big enough market for the billions of research funds being expended. The real goal is to provide a mind/computer interface for the general public that will allow people to make calls in their head and send and receive information. The computer chip giant Intel Corporation has teamed up with Carnegie Melon University and the University of Pittsburg to map the human brain for neuronal activity so they can develop a chip to be inserted in the human brain with the goal of allowing mental control of computers and communication devices. In probably one of the most dangerous developments in human history, the transhumanists can now interface technology mind to mind. Researchers at Duke University recently demonstrated how two rats could influence each other's behavior by connecting their brains through a computer interface. It doesn't seem too farfetched to assume that before long whoever is programming the brain chips will be influencing people's behavior. If getting a virus in your lap top seems a major upset, consider what it would be like to get a virus in your brain chip! If the medium is really the message, as the great media scholar, Marshall McLuhan, insisted, then what sort of message does this medium carry? How would it change our society even if the privacy issues could be solved? Google Glass is going to bring smart phone technology to eyeglasses so that media can be overlaid on the world. Then the medium not only becomes the message, it shapes what's left of actual *unmediated* human experience. In the place of personal reflection people will get provided content. The last bastion of the human spirit, already battered by a thousand forms of mediated influence, will be breached and challenged in its own domain by these physical invasions.

As corporate controlled media become more pervasive and invasive and as the content becomes more subtle and sophisticated in its persuasions, we must ask exactly what is being done to people on a steady diet of commercial and political propaganda? For much of the public staring in an altered state into the many screens of their lives the mind simply sucks in all the advertising, aggression and sexually suggestive programming, stimulating the most primitive structures of the human mind and body. The result of a steady diet of this is to keep viewers in a state of continual retarded development. As long as a person is focused on basic matters of safety, competition, acquiring sex, luxury and ego aggrandizement, the standard fare of media, they are reinforcing these primitive functions at the expense of the development of higher order thinking and feeling. Problem solving beyond the use of violence, non-material values, and more mature relational patterns that explore deeper character and intellect are neglected. Romance on television, for instance, perpetuates a juvenile "boy meets girl" syndrome where the usual comedy of errors ensues and it doesn't seem to matter whether the pair are 16 or 60. The same is true of the "good guys vs. bad guys," scenarios where completely unrealistic stories reinforce a reactionary syndrome in human relations where those who do not cooperate with the social order are *bad* and *must be punished or killed*. This nicely keeps the public away from the more sophisticated "system questioning" plot where individuals are not only held accountable for their choices but their choices are traced back to conditions within the status quo society. It is never a problem for popular culture to identify the early victim of neglect and abuse who becomes a criminal. What is never explored is how this so called "healthy" society stimulates criminal behavior. Ken Lay and the other corporate criminals that looted and ultimately destroyed the ENRON corporation didn't have bad childhoods. Their behavior was a product of regular mainstream and corporate culture that encourages "winner take all" egotism and daring business strategies that play fast and loose with the law and show zero concern for the damage done to the lives of employees. As societies show increasing strain in maintaining the status-quo at the expense of the people, it becomes essential to blame criminal behavior on failures within the individual alone, found either crazy, evil, or weak; not to confine criticism there would lead speculation back to the system and that's not allowed. This is one of the major media's main functions: to reinforce the status quo, while directing the public to find any problems created by it within the individual's inability to "properly" adjust. With a brain chip the adjustment will now be downloaded.

Controlling Stories

It is the content of these increasingly invasive media productions we must turn back to now as we attempt to understand exactly what effects are being created as corporate media furthers its encroachment on human life. There is a need for human beings to have healthy egos and basic material goods, as well as working defense mechanisms to defend themselves from physical attack and most would agree that regular sex is a prerequisite to a healthy life but there is a larger world beyond these basic needs that television and film spends little time exploring. The result is a society of sexually frustrated, emotional retards waving their fists at the *bad people*. A population of this sort is much more highly tractable for purposes of both military engagement abroad and the maintenance of a police state at home where suspicion, alienation, competition and envy aids the controllers and where those who have been abandoned by prosperity or refuse to conform can be housed in prison facilities when they act up.

A more sophisticated society interprets social phenomena like the over representation of African-American men in the criminal justice system, for instance, as a symptom that something is wrong within the social fabric of the country, but this would mean shifting some economic priorities toward social programs and job creation with something in mind besides massive profits. This is something that corporate control will not tolerate, so it promotes the "every man for himself" society that plays on racism by reinforcing the image of ghettoized people as lazy and stupid and simply living off other people's hard earned money. Never is mentioned the millions upon billions annually paid out in corporate welfare in the form of government subsidies, but none of this is seen on television nor in the movies or anywhere in the mainstream media. What we do see is a perpetual conditioning for fear, suspicion, sexual obsession, childish ego fantasy, materialist addiction, and violence as the heroic method for dealing with problems. A typical movie or television drama includes a violent hero who laughs at the attempts to talk and work out disagreements, who at some crisis point in the story pulls out his or her big gun and blows the demons back to hell, chiding the "do-gooders" as they blow the smoke off their pistol. This is the perpetual error that chains the public to a never ending struggle against a vision of "encroaching evil forces." This represents the misapplication of a mythological mindset that brands people as agents of an evil force to be exterminated rather than complex human beings to be understood. This is a form of mind control because it actively seeks to keep the human mind from evolving to higher levels of social sophistication. A healthy society produces art and culture that seeks to uplift their populations though depicting, not the simple answers, but the difficult dilemmas. Traditional warrior cultures everywhere have stories of their most accomplished heroes eventually transcending violence, like Myamoto Mushashi, the greatest Samurai of feudal Japan who laid down his sword at the height of his prowess. The story of how a person goes from champion of death to enlightened sage is one well overdue in American story telling. Instead, what has been offered is the "High Noon" scenario.

In the 1952 classic western, Gary Cooper, has taken off his star and hung up his guns after marrying pacifist Quaker, Grace Kelly, but trouble comes to town and Cooper must make a choice between peace and killing. He chooses the latter, of course, and confronts the bad guys all on his own, vanquishing the evil that wouldn't be satisfied any other way. This American cultural trope is seen over and over throughout television and film to this day. The hero tries to find peace, even in some stories becoming a priest or monk, but eventually he must pick up the gun, sword, or phaser once again and take it to the "evil doers" with fire and blood. The underlying message here is simply that *there is no higher path*; violence is the only way to confront negative forces. Those who think they can escape this reality are shown the folly of their ways.

This is an absolutely insidious form of cultural programming that arose from the earliest American moral dilemma of the Christian pilgrims encounter with Native Americans and their struggle to square the Bible with the gun.[84] This is a story that should have come to a resolution in American culture a century ago, if not more. There should be an instructive story of an American hero who transcends deadly violence, that learns the ultimate ignorance of it, that all young people learn and live by, but this story was never allowed to arise because the culture was taken out of a condition of natural growth and evolution into that of "the desert of the real," and the artificial productions and manipulations of the big money. It isn't that intelligent, probing films aren't made (see: *Syriana*, or *The East*, as examples), and the rare television show at one time did demonstrate occasional insight and inspiration (see: *Northern Exposure*), but they are the exception to the rule and aren't enough to penetrate the mainstream conditioning. Independent film is never shown in corporate theaters and so is limited to a tiny distribution.

The millions it takes to make a movie come from banks that regularly include in their contracts "script review" rights, which give them leverage to insist on editing anything they don't like before access to funds is authorized. In this way stories are generally dumbed down so as to make the production accessible to a broader market, as well as having anything challenging to corporate interests removed. In this kind of financing milieu filmmakers have become clear on what sort of film is likely to get backing and what isn't and so a great amount of self-censoring goes on. Television has always been more about selling commercial time than anything else and as such anything that might cause viewers to think is avoided in favor of "feel good" pabulum and exciting fare that holds viewers in their seats to find out what will happen next. Anything that might not conform to audience prejudices, might cause discomfort and channel-changing is avoided. On top of this system of mediocrity is simply the fact that the major media companies that produce television and the big films are financially intertwined with the major corporate interests, who are themselves linked to the big banks. It's all part of one big system of interlocking interests that depends on growth in the global market. Those whose investments require a docile electorate and an aggressive military stance abroad cannot have the public indulging in higher consciousness if there is going to be enough young men to feed into the slaughter the next time some obstreperous foreign leader has the temerity to attempt to control his own economy and natural resources. A large, expansive standing military is essential for the maintenance of empire even when not engaged in direct combat, so the population must be conditioned to fill the ranks and cultural mind control through the stagnation of a certain primitive marshal masculinity becomes essential. But the staunch defender of violence as tool of the righteous will shout: "Pearl harbor! September 11th! What else could we do?" This question leads us to the topic of the next section.

If direct manipulation of the human mind is the most personally invasive form of methodology for the control of the public, the most audacious tool of manipulation has to be the actual orchestrating of large scale news events to serve as fulcrums for the shifting of public opinion. This has been described as "the tail wagging the dog," and is an old American favorite. Ever since greedy white men in the course of Westward migration wanting to get their hands on land ceded to Native American tribes dressed up like Indians and attacked their own people to cause an "outrage" cunning elements within the country have planned and initiated *fake events* as a method to move the public in line with their plans. In the next chapter you will find no conspiracy theories but well documented events from American history illustrating these effective and deadly theatrics.

NOTES

1. Peter Seybold, "The Ford Foundation and the Triumph of Behaviorism in American Political Science," in: Arnove, *Philanthropy and Cultural Imperialism* (Bloomington: Indiana University Press, 1982), p. 275.
2. Ibid., p.277.
3. Arnove (1982), p. 13.
4. Ibid, p.13.
5. Ron Suskind, Faith, Certainty, and the Presidency of George W. Bush (*New York Times Magazine*. October 17, 2004).
6. Robert W. McChesney, *The Problem with the Media: US Communication Politics in the 21st Century* (New York: Monthly Review Press, 2004). See: www.fair.org; www.projectcensored.org
7. Nicholas Carr, *The Shallows, What the Internet is Doing to Our Brains* (New York: Norton, 2010).
8. Michael Hastings, The Afghanistan Report the Pentagon Doesn't Want You to Read (www.rollingstone.com, posted: February 10, 2012).
9. Pagels (2003) p. 54.
10. Robert and Michele Root-Bernstein, *Sparks of Genius, The 13 Thinking Tools of the World's Most Creative People* (Boston: Mariner Books, 2001) p. 23.
11. Hugh Wilford, *The Mighty Wurlitzer: How the CIA Played America* (Cambridge: Harvard University Press, 2009).
12. Noam Chomsky, *Deterring Democracy* (New York: Hill & Wang, 1992).
13. Chris Hedges, *Empire of Illusion, The End of Literacy and the Triumph of Spectacle* (New York: Nation Books, 2009), p. 142, 143.
14. According to The Center for Media and Democracy, sourcewatch.org, this was originally reported in the French publication: Minutes, June 19, 1991; also: Lectures Francaises, July/August, 1991; Hilaire du Berrier Report, September 1991.
15. This is an argument that both Noam Chomsky and Chris Hedges have made repeatedly.
16. Black (2006).
17. John S. Friedman, editor, *The Secret Histories, An Anthology* (New York: Picador, 2005).
18. F. William Engdahl, *A Century of War, Anglo-American Oil Politics and the New World Order* (Wiesbaden Germany: edition.engdahl, 1992, 2011); Engdahl, (2009).
19. Engdahl (2011); (2009), p. 153.
20. James Bradley, *The Imperial Cruise, A Secret History of Empire and War* (New York: Back Bay Books, 2009).
21. Jules Archer, *The Plot to Seize the White House: The Shocking True Story of the Conspiracy to Overthrow FDR* (New York: Skyhorse Publishing, 1973).
22. Lemov (2005), p.5.
23. Thomas De Zengotita, *Mediated, How the Media Shapes Your World and the Way You Live in It* (New York: Bloomsbury, 2005).
24. Marshall McLuhan, *The Medium is the Message, An Inventory of Effects*

(Berkeley: Ginko Press Inc., 1967). Neil Postman, *Amusing Ourselves to Death, Public Discourse in the Age of Show Business* (New York: Penguin, 1985). De Zengotita (2005).
25. One of the best works on Disney culture is William Irwin Thompson's: *The American Replacement of Nature, The Everyday Acts and Outrageous Evolution of Economic Life* (New York: Doubleday Currency 1991).
26. Quigley (1979), p. 144.
27. dailytech.com/Monsanto defeats small farmers, 3-1-12.
28. William Manchester, The Bloodiest Battle of All (*New York Times Magazine*, June 14, 1987).
29. Gregory Desilet, *Our Faith in Evil, Melodrama and the Effects of Entertainment Violence* (Jefferson, North Carolina: McFarland & Company Inc., 2006).
30. Ibid.
31. Louise Kuo Habakus, Mary Holland, & Kim Mack Rosenberg, editors, *Vaccine Epidemic, How Corporate Greed, Biased Science, and Coercive Government Threaten Our Human Rights, Our Heath, and Our Children* (New York: Skyhorse Publishing, 2012).
32. Marion Nestle, *Food Politics, How the Food Industry Influences Nutrition and Health* (Berkeley: University of California Press, 2013).
33. The Dodd report to the Reece Committee on Foundations, 1954.
34. John Taylor Gatto, *Dumbing Us Down, The Hidden Curriculum of Compulsory Schooling* (Canada: New Society Publishers, 2005).
35. Ibid., p. 10.
36. Ibid., p. 13.
37. The Dodd report to the Reece Committee on Foundations, 1954.
38. Gatto (2005), p. 69.
39. David S. Mason, *The End of the American Century* (New York: Rowman & Littlefield, 2009).
40. Sister Miriam Joseph, CSC, PhD, *The Trivium, The Liberal Arts of Logic, Grammar, And Rhetoric* (Philadelphia: Paul Dry Books, 1937, 2002).
41. Ibid., p. 5.
42. Washburn (2006).
43. Thomas Jefferson, "Notes on the State of Virginia," Jefferson (New York: The Library of America, 1984), p. 274.
44. Wolin (2008), p. xvii.
45. Milton (1996), p. 18.
46. Black (2006).
47. Henry Stevens, *Hitler's Suppressed and Still Secret Weapons, Science, and Technology* (Kempton IL: Adventures Unlimited Press, 2005).
48. Ferguson (2012), p. 292.
49. R. Buckminster Fuller and Robert Marks, *The Dymaxion World of Buckminster Fuller* (New York: Anchor Books, 1978).
50. Eisen (1999), p. 138.
51. Ellen Hodgson Brown, *Forbidden Medicine* (Baton Rouge: Third Millennium Press, 2008).

52. Milton (1996).
53. Gary Vesperman, History of New Energy Suppression Cases (http://rense.com/general72/oinvent.htm June 19, 2006).
54. Brian O'Leary, *The Energy Solution Revolution* (Hayden ID: Bridger House, 2009), p. 33.
55. www.bpwhisleblowers.blogspot.com
56. Fox News, YouTube: All Kinds of Sea birds Paralyzed and Dead Around Sarasota.
57. Maryann Tobin, Matt Simmons: BP, CIA Conspiracy Theory Suggested Behind His Unexpected Death (www.examiner.com Aug. 11, 2010).
58. Media Black-Out on Single-Payer Healthcare (http://fair.org/take-action/media-advisories/fair-study-media-blackout-on-single-payer-healthcare/ March 6, 2009).
59. Engdahl (2011).
60. Chris Hedges, *Death of the Liberal Class* (New York: Nation Books, 2010).
61. Edward Bernays, *Propaganda* (New York: Ig Publishing, 1928, 2005).
62. Sheldon Rampton and John Stauber, *Trust Us, We're Experts! How Industry Manipulates Science and Gambles with your Future* (New York: Tarcher/Putnam, 2002).
63. T. Colin Campbell, PhD and Thomas M. Campbell II, *The China Study, The Most Comprehensive Study Ever Conducted* (Dallas TX: Benbella Books, 2006).
64. Niccolo Machiavelli, *The Prince* (New York: Dutton, Every Man's Library edition, 1958), p. 25.
65. PBS, "Flying Cheap," Frontline.
66. See the documentary: Inside Job, Charles Ferguson producer.
67. James Hoopes, *False Prophets* (New York: Basic Books, 2003).
68. Lemov (2005), p.51.
69. Vance Packard, *The People Shapers* (Boston: Little, Brown & Company, 1977).
70. Lemov, Rebecca, 2005, World as Laboratory, p. 61.
71. Hoopes (2003).
72. John Marks, *In Search for the Manchurian Candidate* (New York: Norton, 1991).
73. Walter Bowart, *Operation Mind Control* (New York: Dell, 1977).
74. Alex Constantine, *Virtual Government, CIA Mind Control Operations in America*. (Los Angeles: Feral House, 1997).
75. The account of her ordeal in her own words can be viewed on YouTube: CIA Whistleblower exposes everything.
76. Nick Begich and Jeane Manning, *Angles Don't Play this HAARP* (Eagle River AK: Earthpulse Press, 1995).
77. The Zapping of Greenham and Seneca (*Peace and Freedom Magazine*, Jan./Feb. 1989).
78. *Executive Intelligence Review*, July 3, 1987.
79. "America Behind in Radio Frequency Weapons," Defense Electronics (July 1993).

80. Eldon Taylor, *Mind Programing* (New York: Hay House, 2009).
81. Ibid.
82. Reinventing Humanity: The Future of Machine-Human Intelligence (www.singularity.com, March 4, 2006).
83. As quoted in: Lynn Picknett & Clive Prince, *The Forbidden Universe, The Occult Origins of Science and the Search for the Mind of God* (London: Constable and Robinson, Ltd, 2011), p. 241.
84. Richard Slotkin, *Regeneration Through Violence* (Hanover NH: Wesleyan, 1973).

CHAPTER 6

ORCHESTRATING HISTORY AND THE THEATER OF CONSENT

For many, one of the most startling and hard to accept aspects of the program to control American citizens is the discovery that much of what has been understood regarding major events of American history is simply wrong or so incomplete as to be generally misleading. The history taught in high schools and seen in the movies is one completely sanitized so as to serve more as an official mythology than as an actual analysis of the people's struggle to build a nation with all of the stresses and weaknesses of the human condition revealed. This short review of major events in American History of the 20th Century is essential in completing the task of the last chapter in coming to understand the strategies employed by the power elite to shape history in its inception and thereby the future to their ends. Theirs is a worldview shaped by a philosophy of elite dominance as a carrier of ultimate human value, a view entirely at odds with the rising human spirit embodied in the population as a whole. The individual, awakening to the stresses produced by the ideals of their spirit in dissonance to the manufactured culture of manipulation and who would seek to liberate their spirit, must make themselves aware of the true basis of American history, if they are to fully free their minds from the machinery of control. This chapter should serve as a mere beginning to this project.

America is the story of two competing social trends; one is the story of the triumph of the common man and woman finding open space to finally live free of despots and exploiting aristocrats, to have their labors benefit themselves and their kind rather than the descendants of some ancient warlord; the other is the story of an elite class, an importation of gentry from the old world who sought to extend their culture of position and rank above the common populace. The founding fathers built into the Constitution a democracy for the masses and a republic for the gentry who did not want their high sensibilities and property to be overwhelmed by mob rule. There is wisdom in this, of course, and it remained a system that served high ideals, protecting human dignity and freedom as a genuine goal of public life for most of the first century of its existence. The new experiment in freedom did not include Native Americans or Africans and the role of women was highly circumscribed, but it was the start of something with great potential for humanity on its journey of civilization.

What arose was eventually a parting of the ways between the two groups as to the future path of the country. What was imagined by the elite gentry and the common people began at the end of the 19th Century and the closing of the frontier to be two different things. Average Americans were quite happy with their farms, ranches, and small businesses, raising their families in moderate abundance and a certain measure of peace, freedom, and justice but the elite, with their sights set on an ever expanding American empire would not be happy to simply enjoy the fruits of the land, work within its borders to bring small improvements by the generation and drink lemonade on the porch in the summer time. The masters of the "gilded age" were hooked on a literal myth of progress, where the common people saw progress as largely a spiritual task in the building of "God's country." They had captured the land from both pagan savages and a daunting force of nature, as they saw it, and were in the process of reaping the benefits of this "land of milk and honey," promised by the Lord of their prayers. The average man or woman aimed to make themselves worthy with hard work and diligence at home and found nothing to be excited about in the calls for a spreading American power emanating from mansions in Manhattan and Washington. The Pacific Ocean provided a natural stopping point and calls to cross the Rio Grande and push the border farther into Mexico fell flat in Congress. "Manifest destiny," was played out as far as the people were concerned, but elites like Theodore Roosevelt weren't even half done with the idea.

Roosevelt and his ilk were taken with a certain "frontier thesis" that warned that with the close of the frontier all that made the great Anglo-Saxon American male great was fading from history. The result would be a weakened people that had lost their "barbarian vigor" a natural core of the masculine spirit that needed to be constantly exercised to survive within the breast of the evolving white man as he spread his superior culture around the world. A fear of "over-civilization" clutched at the stomach of the wealthy urban elites and academics, a softening that would make the country vulnerable to those adversaries still in touch with their primitive fighting spirit. The frontier was both that which tempered the will of men and the "safety valve" for the settled rejoins that would be threatened by the bottling up of the more aggressive of the succeeding generations of young men with no *West* to go to. Additionally, for the industrialists, it was clear that American wealth could not sustain its incredible growth that had come from the massive windfall profits possible from a continent of untouched resources without taking the show on the road. At the same time the worst depression in American history hit the economy in 1893 blowing some of the mightiest names in American business, like the Union Pacific Railway, right off the stock exchange.

James Bradley sums it up.

> Overseas expansion was seen as a cure-all for the triple whammy of over civilization, economic depression, and the end of the frontier. Battling others for their land would enhance the American male's barbarian virtues and secure profitable markets, and the United States would once again have a frontier in which to hone its Teutonic blade. For many, the sun was not setting on America but rising on a new ocean of opportunities.[1]

The problem was that this was a thesis confined to a handful of intellectuals, politicians, and big business people, along with an urban population of rightwing armchair intellectuals consuming the books and newspapers of the expansionist elite. The common man toiling on the ranches and farms and factories was not too prone to feeling a bit light in the jockstrap, nor was he concerned about expanding his wealth overseas; it was a certain element within the urbanized middle-class and elites like Roosevelt that felt their manhood challenged by the frontier thesis and their bank accounts threatened by an end to plunder.

Roosevelt, who was one of the most ardent supporters of empire and continual war, was a member of the New York aristocracy of multigenerational wealth and had grown up literally with a silver spoon in his mouth. After being accused of appearing a bit too feminine before the

New York State assembly to which he was elected at the age of 23 (where he had appeared in a purple satin suit and spoke in a squeaky voice), Teddy decided to set out West to the Dakota territory to make himself a man. He basically bought some ranchland and spent several years trundling back and forth between Manhattan and the West in a luxury Pullman train car while he created an image for himself as a frontiersman that was largely a façade erected for political purposes. T.R. spent more time in coat and tails and tennis whites then he ever did in buckskins and riding boots, but he published three books on his adventures and philosophies garnered in the West, spinning tales from pure buffalo chips about facing off with outlaws, renegade Indians, and mammoth grizzly bears charging into his blazing guns. Roosevelt had pictures taken in New York photo studios for public consumption that showed him stalking prey dressed in buck skins and fur hat like a latter day Daniel Boone before a faux forest in painted backdrop.

The problem comes when men of this type try to convince the men whose world is neither theoretical nor theatrical that they should leave their families and go to another land overseas to take on, as Kipling put it, "the white man's burden," the spreading of the *light and cleanliness of civilization in the savage lands of filth and darkness*. A notion that was a thin cover story for the economic gain and lordly power that would bolster the egos and pocket books of the wealthy class, an angle not lost on the common man either.

There is always a minority of young men who will sign up for imperial enterprise in an attempt to recreate the heroic mythology of their forebears and a number of others that will go to escape poverty or the drudgery of the factory, but most Americans have always felt war required a damn good reason – one that satisfies the moral necessity that is required of the Christian mentality that will kill only to preserve one's home and family, "mom and apple pie," as the old saying goes. This being the case, the sellers of empire have had this job on their hands that required the ditching of *the shrinking testicle theory* and the *mandate for conquest due to race superiority theory*, and even *the economic necessity theory*, in favor of what is now an old standard: rescuing women and children, which is the only story that will get the boys off the farm.

This is the classic American heroic motivation, one honed in the Western migration on real tales of women and children taken by Indians in what historians have called the "captivity narrative." Stories were written by women who escaped or otherwise found their way to freedom and these tales helped drive a heroic mythology that was both genuine in conception and archetypal in its capacity to be deeply disturbing to the male psyche. Nothing could be more horrifying than the defilement of a genteel feminine purity by a dark and filthy savagery. This image penetrates to the core of the Christianized containment of women within a virgin/whore dichotomy that sees the line between the two as a point of no return, a fate worse than death. Something similar by association and helplessness applies to children who undergo such depredations. The call for heroic action is almost beyond the capacity to resist in any "red blooded American male."

Rescuing women and children from abusive captivity is, of course, something that anyone can justify on the simple grounds of morality and compassion, but this story in the American mind has taken on the ability to enflame passions to the degree that it becomes a perfect tool for manipulation in the hands of forces wishing to evoke a response that circumvents any rational consideration or even fact checking. Hence, when Teddy Roosevelt and his chums decided to pump up their barbarian vigor in snatching some colonial possessions from a weakened Spain, they evoked the "captivity narrative" in concocting stories for the papers that described the molestation of innocent young Cuban women at the hands of their Spanish overlords. The Cubans were depicted as white for the papers, but when the troops got there and found them to be quite brown and even black they refused to have their pictures taken with the people they came to rescue.

The other major method for manipulating Americans into war has always been the "they hit us first" scenario. It has been always the case that Americans have an isolationist tendency that pressures against going abroad in military involvement with other people's problems. Antiwar sentiment was very high before the Spanish-American War, WWI, and WWII. This comes as something of a surprise to people schooled on the "heroic rescue" tales of especially WWII, but the reality was that Americans didn't accept the idea of empire at all and going to assist the Europeans, who had been at each other's throats for centuries, wasn't much of a winning argument with the average man or woman either. What has, in the end, been always necessary, is an "unprovoked attack" on Americans by the intended enemy.

The Spanish-American War

The Spanish-American War was largely the brain child of Theodore Roosevelt, who was willing to use all the influence of his office of the Assistant Secretary of the Navy to make it happen. A letter to a West Point friend, reads: "In strict confidence...I should welcome almost any war, for I think this country needs one." The waning Spanish mission in the Caribbean and Eastern Pacific was to serve as the perfect opportunity. Both places had armed resistance fighters giving the Spanish a run for their money and both would be packaged for sale to the American people as venues for a demonstration of American dedication to liberty. Roosevelt and his supporters began talking up the plan to attack Spanish holdings, but Americans were unmoved, having a strong aversion to European style colonialism.

Then, out of the blue, a mysterious letter arrives in the warmongering office of the newspaper magnate, William Randolph Hearst, which purports to have been written by the Spanish Minister to the United States in Cuba to a friend, supposedly stolen by a supporter of the revolution in the post office there. The letter basically casts dispersions on the manhood of President McKinley, calling him weak, and "catering to the rabble...a low politician."

What's interesting about this letter is how it mirrors Roosevelt's own reservations about the President, who he felt was unresponsive to his campaign for war due to a lack of "backbone." McKinley had been an officer during the Civil War, had witnessed much carnage, unlike Roosevelt whose confrontations with death were largely fantasy. McKinley had been marked by real blood and death on a massive scale and would have rather spared Americans another such episode, but Roosevelt was backed by powerful interests and he would have his war one way or another. The Hearst papers declared the rather timely letter, "the worst insult to the United States in history!"[2]

The next event in the build-up to war would be decisive. The battleship Maine, while at anchorage in Havana harbor, suddenly blew up. Without any evidence whatsoever the Hearst papers declared in banner headlines the explosion to be the work of the enemy. Before any investigation by the government could be done, Congress rushed through a 50 million dollar war appropriations bill to prepare the nation for immediate attack. When McKinley voiced his feelings that he would like to avoid war, he was ridiculed in the papers as a "goody-goody," as they called for a "declaration of American virility," saying that this was the time for a "real man" to be at the helm in Washington.³

It came out later that the explosion on the Maine was said by the surviving captain to have been most likely the result of an accident. The timing certainly does suggest an accident that someone arranged, but none of this mattered at the time. The sabotage of an American ship and the death of its crew at the hands of a hostile force, proven or otherwise, whose spokesman had called the President "a sissy" and whose men were busily "molesting fair maidens," was more than American manhood could take sitting down. Roosevelt and the imperialists got their war – a war that lasted a month in Cuba, said to be a "splendid little war," by Teddy Roosevelt and 14 years in the Philippines, that was not so splendid. In a political maneuver that would be repeated by George Bush on the deck of an aircraft carrier in the Persian Gulf a century later, the U.S. President declared "mission accomplished" after the Spanish surrendered, but the war would go on, and on, and on, plaguing future administrations and costing the Philippine people, much like the Iraqis, hundreds of thousands dead. It seemed they weren't interested in having the Americans take over for the Spanish as their new overlords.⁴

WORLD WAR I

The run up to WWI is equally instructive as to the role of manipulation and "arranged" disasters to motivate a reluctant American public into giving up its sons. The sinking ship that really threw it over the edge into war this time was the British passenger liner, "Lusitania" sunk by a German U-boat in 1915 with 128 Americans aboard. The British were transporting munitions and other war supplies on the liner and the Germans knew it. The Germans warned the U.S. that they would take action if they did not stop this activity, since the U.S. had not declared war on Germany. The Germans did everything they could to warn the U.S. and Britain. Knowing that the sinking of a passenger liner would be used for propaganda purposes, the German consulate actually took out newspaper ads all across the country trying to warn Americans that they were being set-up and that Germany could not overlook this violation of their neutrality forever. All but a few of the ads were censored, but some did make it into print. With no change in the policy the Germans eventually sank the Lusitania and, as expected, it was set upon by the imperialist "mouthorgan" papers as an outrage against America, starting a groundswell of public sentiment that eventually forced Woodrow Wilson into the war. It was a war that saw human carnage at levels previously unseen in the history of human stupidity, 400,000 and even half a million men dying in a single day of combat. It was a war that so challenged previous ideas of human progress that numbers of people simply committed suicide out of despair for the human condition.

The reality was that the overwhelming majority of men in the war were not craven killers demonstrating a human condition forever mired in savagery. Rather, what moved them to fight was a simple loyalty to what had been sold to them as the "higher ideals" of manhood and patriotism by the manipulative propaganda emanating from papers who's owners sat in industry board rooms and aristocrats, new and old, who saw common soldiers as simply pawns in a game of world strategy for power and resources. The Great War, as WWI came to be known in its day, was entirely avoidable if not for the grandiose egos and land grabbing schemes of the powerful who didn't mind shedding their people's blood in the game. The European elite and aristocrats alike, quite nervous in an age of escalating democracy and human rights, were relieved by the numbers of workers being drained from their populations that otherwise might have overwhelmed available employment and come knocking on their door for a bigger piece of the economy. War serves many purposes for the rulers of a nation and death is among them.

At the end of the 18th Century and into the 19th, Thomas Robert Malthus produced his highly influential studies and theories on population control. Malthus proposed that unchecked expanding populations tend to outstrip their available resources for food and other essentials and that this reality would work against the popular utopian dreams of improving society toward a higher goal. He noted that populations had been kept in check by "positive" means – hunger, disease, and war – and "preventative" means, which centered on birth control, which in those days meant abstinence. Since human beings have never been too good at the preventative approach, it was widely held that the "positive" approach was the only solution. Disease and poor sanitary conditions among the poor kept the infant mortality rate high in Europe for centuries, but later in the 19th Century and into the 20th sanitary conditions began to improve causing an uplift in population numbers. This trend was of great concern to the elite who saw their plans for a scientific, modern utopia threatened by the swelling masses. This concern was mixed with popular social Darwinist theories on improving bloodlines in human populations, usually around racial and elite ideals, to make war seem a natural "cleansing and honing" force in human civilization. The people, for their part, as they contemplated the building tensions before the Great War, were blinded by trumpeting nationalism and had no idea what they were getting into. There hadn't been a major war in Europe for generations, their minds filled with gallant fantasies from the Napoleonic period. Perhaps no one was ready for the machine guns and mustard gas, but the inability to pull back and reassess strategy in the face of such horrendous casualties was more than simply stubborn generals. It was tolerated, even embraced, by the elite as a fulfillment of a natural social destiny. Bertrand Russell, considered one of the brightest scientific minds of the 20th Century and a member of the British aristocracy, voiced their general concern regarding the overpopulation of the "lower orders" and was disappointed in the war's capacity to reduce their numbers. "War has hitherto been disappointing in this respect," he stated in his 1951 book, *The Impact of Science on Society,* "but perhaps bacteriological war might prove more effective."

WORLD WAR II

World War II is understood popularly in America as, "the good war." It has become mythologized as a great crusade of American freedom against tyranny. The literary scholar, Paul Fussell, who served in the war in Europe as an infantry platoon leader, has written of the contrast between the actual experience of the men in battle and what was being spun back home. "They knew that in its representation to the laity what was happening to them was systematically sanitized and Norman Rockwellized, not to mention Disneyfied."[5] The way the war has been treated as national myth and heroic legend constitutes a misuse of the mythological structure of consciousness as a means of stunting the cultural progress that would have led to the "transcendence of warfare" story discussed above. Fussell states it well, "America has not yet understood what the Second World War was like and has thus been unable to use such understanding to re-interpret and re-define the national reality and to arrive at something like public maturity."[6] Rather than the stuff of children's story books, of knights now in tanks and Davey Crocket in army green, what the war was really like, Fussell and other men as honest have portrayed, is conveyed in images of men driven mad on a Pacific beach after spending the night in a pile of corpses and body parts pinned down by bunkers missed in hasty planning; bomber crews psychologically disintegrating into madness while flying suicide runs where their friends are blown out of the sky one after another by enemy guns; an infantrymen weeping beside the body of a German solider he has killed looking no more than 14 and much like his little brother. It is the necessity of sponging this all away, of replacing it with "solemn sacrifice on the altar of freedom," with marching parades, cinematic adventure, daring, and even comedy, in order to set up the next bunch for the following war, that is the technique of the manipulator, the exploiter of honor and honest fidelity. Americans have been convinced by the mythology that they were simply responding as a representative of human decency against threats in the Pacific and Europe that were positively indecent, as if these foes rose up out of hell, suddenly and without pretext.

Few Americans understand the true story of the build-up and the fabrication of the war as an instrument of deliberate policy of the American financial elite. Hitler's Germany, as mentioned above, was well supplied from American corporations, including war materiel such as tanks and trucks build in Ford and G. M. Opel plants, but the most important gift to the Nazis came in the form of a great financial boost from Rockefeller, JP Morgan, Warburg, and other American banking powers. It was their loans and the transfer of technology that was absolutely essential in the build-up of the I.G. Farben corporation in Germany. In records seized after the war an order was discovered transferring 400,000 Reichs Marks, a substantial sum at the time, to a secret Nazi slush fund that financed Hitler's seizure of power in 1933. Farben had become the largest chemical company in the world by the opening of the war and was the central industry behind the German war machine with Wall Street representatives sitting on its board of directors even as the Third Reich tooled up for war. I.G. Farben produced the infamous Zyclon B gas used in the concentration camps as well as explosives, gun powder, plastics, synthetic fuel and numerous other essential war materials. [7]

The war in the Pacific was the result of a much more long term project for American hegemony in the Pacific basin and Far East. James Bradley's fine book, *The Imperial Cruise,* lays out the historical evidence for what really led to the war, a story that started again with Teddy Roosevelt and President William Howard Taft early in the 20th Century. The Japanese were built into a modern industrial nation almost overnight and their men sent to American and British engineering and military schools in order to create a proxy force for American imperialism in the East. Unfortunately, the Japanese "got off the leash" as another American benefactor in Hitler's Germany would. The Imperial Japanese Army decided that if anyone was going to reap the rewards of empire in the East it was going to be them. They had already kicked the Russian army and navy around the block in the largest land and sea battles in history, had brushed the Chinese army aside like insects and were no longer intimidated by the round eyed Western imperialists who gave them their start on world conquest.

So, suddenly it became essential to convince the American public that the Japanese needed to be taken down a peg or two, not an easy task when facing an isolationist public who really didn't give a damn if the former protégé' was out terrorizing Chinese people on the other side of the world. It hadn't been too long since the infamous "Chinese exclusion act," had attempted to push Asians out of America after they'd finished building the railroad and had become a target of racist paranoia. No, Americans needed another *Maine*, another *Lusitania*, to feel they were directly threatened. This time the ship would be an old obsolete "battle wagon," known as the *Arizona*, right there in home port in American territory.

There has been much scholarly argument over the years as to how much President Franklin D. Roosevelt knew before the Japanese Imperial Navy bombed Perl Harbor. Freedom of information act disclosures in recent decades and other deep probes by investigative authors on the question have revealed a wealth of information that makes any argument claiming the Roosevelt administration didn't have prior knowledge of the Japanese attack positively ridiculous. There now exists a significant degree of evidence available to anyone who can read showing that, not only did Roosevelt and his top advisors know the Japanese were planning to attack Hawaii for many months prior, but it was very much a part of the administration's plan for getting America into the war in both the Pacific and Europe.[8]

Franklin D. Roosevelt had won his seat in the oval office by convincing the people that he would not lead them to war. Polls showed that approximately 80% of the American population was against any involvement in a foreign war. Having been coaxed into WWI and having seen how it had not turned out to be "the war to end all wars" as advertised, and having paid a dear price in blood for Wilson to sit at the table of winners and concoct his "League of Nations" that had gone nowhere in preventing another war, the people were not interested in world war act II. This did not discourage F.D.R. who, like a true politician, simply lied to the people assuring them he would, never, ever, take them to war, and then immediately turned around and started making plans with the British to come to their defense once again. "If the isolationists had known the full extent of the secret alliance between the United States and Britain, their demands for impeachment would have rumbled like thunder throughout the land," wrote, Robert Sherwood, the President's biographer.

The idea was that two birds could be provoked with one stone. If F.D.R. could push the Japanese into attacking, then the Germans would have to declare war on the United States, as well, due to the pact that existed between Germany and Japan. Roosevelt's Secretary of War, Henry Stimson, wrote in his diary for October 1, 1941, "We face the delicate question of the diplomatic fencing to be done so as to be sure Japan is put into the wrong and makes the first bad move – overt move." He later mused, "The question is how we should maneuver them into firing the first shot." The Roosevelt administration had done everything they could to antagonize the Japanese: cutting off trade of vital imports, closing the Panama Canal to them, freezing their assets in American banks, just to start. Naval Intelligence had recommended to Roosevelt eight different acts that might provoke the Japanese into an act of war. The President enacted all of them. Then he ordered the Pacific Fleet to be stationed in Hawaii, an act bitterly resisted by naval commanders who felt they were way too exposed to attack on an island where the enemy could approach from any direction. The U.S. had succeeded in cracking the Japanese diplomatic code that gave the administration a wide open window on communications between Tokyo and all their embassies abroad as well as naval dispatches. These communiqué's show a rather unmistakable march toward war, including the mapping out of ships in Pearl harbor, and a clear statement of intention to attack the same. On November 26, 1941, a message from Admiral Yamamoto to Japanese forces in the Pacific stated: "The task force, keeping its movements strictly secret and maintaining close guard against submarines and aircraft, shall advance into Hawaiian waters, and upon the very opening of hostilities shall attack the main force of the United States fleet and deal it a mortal blow."

Strangely, although the U.S. Government had issued Japanese decoding machines to their British allies, they refused to send any to Hawaii, so all decoded messages had to be relayed from Washington. Those authors who continue to propagate the myth that Roosevelt didn't know, after tying all the facts in knots to avoid the obvious conclusion, as a final act of denial ask people to believe that somehow the President, or his commanders, never saw the above intercept from Admiral Yamamoto launching the attack. How such an obviously vital report would not end up in the hands of someone in-charge stretches credulity to the breaking point. Government documents that might clear up the matter remain classified to this very day.

This is a small portion of the overall evidence implicating the Roosevelt administration in secretly maneuvering both the Japanese and the American people into war. Over 2000 service men were killed in the attack and 16 vessels including 8 battleships where sunk or heavily damaged. The crew of the USS Arizona remains entombed in the oil leaking monument that continues to enshrine this "day of infamy," for the American public. The problem is, most of the public still believes the fairy tale about Pearl Harbor: how military commanders were caught unprepared. This version of events has been immortalized in several Hollywood films, including the latest 2001 Disney release starring Ben Affleck that is so ridiculously historically inaccurate it should have come with a warning label stating that it is "FICTION: loosely based on historical events," but this would never happen because the whole purpose of these type of films is to serve as "history" lessons for a gullible public that has lost the ability to know when they are being manipulated. Although critics saw the flaws, the public loved the film, which went on to gross over 449 million dollars. Lamentingly, the "maturity" Paul Fussell spoke of will have to wait.

THE KOREAN WAR

The Korean War was the next conflict that seems to have been largely a creation of American foreign policy maneuvering with an eye to increasing power abroad at the expense of both the Koreans and American troops. The celebrated investigative reporter, I.F. Stone, put together a comparison of sources in a book he produced early in the war showing that European news reports didn't match what was being told the American public. The background is this. At the end of WWII the victorious Russian and American governments split Korea in two, after having liberated it from long term Japanese rule. The American government had given the Japanese the nod to annex Korea early in 1910, when the Japanese were still the trusted Western protégé and the Koreans were viewed as easy pickings. Now that the "obstreperous Japs" had been put back in their place, the American government put in power in South Korea a man that would serve their interests in escalating the Cold War. War was necessary as an ongoing excuse for empowering the continuing war economy American industrialists had become addicted to and expanding American *interests* (empire) overseas depended on. "American leadership was still gripped by dread of the consequences of peace upon the economy," wrote I.F. Stone. [9]

Through continued agitation along the border and raids into the North, including a massacre at Mungyeong where the South Korean Army killed 88 people and blamed it on marauding bands of communists, the American puppet regime managed to provoke an attack. The Soviet supplied North stated as their goal the arresting and executing of the mischievous Southern leader. The North drove deep into the South overrunning American and Korean forces alike and bottling up Southern forces in a small region on the Southern tip, as well as a UN force at Pusan on the East coast. The Northern forces also murdered numbers of Southern people identified as enemies of communism just as the Sothern leader had been killing off people he thought were communist supporters. The valiant defense of the Pusan harbor area was enough to give the American forces in Japan a landing zone from which they poured support into the South resulting in pushing the North almost out of the Korean peninsula entirely. With their backs to the wall, the communist forces convinced the Chinese to give them a hand and with this assistance they pushed the Southern and UN/American armies back to the middle of the peninsula where they had started. This should have been the end of the war but that was not the way it would be.[10]

The war had begun in May of 1950 and by January of 51 it was over. The Chinese largely withdrew support and the North generally ceased operations in the border region. This was very frustrating for American forces that wanted to overtake all of Korea and were afraid that peace was going to break out before they could accomplish their task. This is when, I.F. Stone began to notice the propaganda machine shifting into high gear.

Reporters on the ground were finding little if any action going on, usually only the clashing of small patrols, but the American military dispatches that ended up in the US news told of major battles and characterized the lulls as periods of building enemy forces for imminent attack. The inflating of the occasional small actions grew to the point where American military sources were reporting huge enemy casualties that rivaled the most costly battles of WWII, an absolute impossibility given the time frame and the scale of men and supplies in the area. "Enemy troops in almost full division strength fell before the UN onslaught each day this week," said a February 10, 1951 dispatch from 8th Army headquarters. That's four to six thousand enemy dead a day, a rate unprecedented in the history of warfare. General MacArthur's headquarters reported that between February of 1951 and the previous October that his forces had killed 134,616 Chinese soldiers, about 36,000 a month, and this during a period when foreign correspondents were reporting that most of the time MacArthur's army had been in full retreat and out of engagement with the enemy.[11]

It had become essential to convince the American people that the Chinese were still in the war and that an absolute escalation and all-out effort would be necessary to save Korea from communist aggression. President Truman compared the communist forces to "Mongol hoards" and called for a "moral mobilization," by the American people to meet the challenge. I.F. Stone's account says that there was no questioning of any of these wild numbers in the mainstream U.S. press. The people were being fed stories of massed assaults of Chinese troops and it all seemed expected.

> "These figures did not seem so strange to a newspaper reading public in America," Stone explained, which had been led to picture Chinese hoards 'marching abreast' and 'in human waves' against American guns in supposed 'Oriental' disregard of their own lives. Belief in fairy tales is not limited to children. The experts paused to wonder but expert analysis does not make headlines.[12]

American air power at the same time was prosecuting its own unilateral war against the uncooperative enemy who was barely showing up for the party. The Air force literally ran out of industrial targets in the North and started bombing any village in areas where enemy troops had been spotted. Using napalm without discretion for the lives and property of noncombatants the jets strafed and fire bombed with DuPont's flaming gel everything with a structure on it. Stone quoted a reporter from the *New York Times*, George Barrett, traveling with an armored unit who wrote how entire villages were given the "saturation treatment" in response to the presence of a few enemy soldiers in the area. Telling of one village he entered after an attack, Barrett wrote,

> The inhabitants throughout the village were caught and killed and kept the exact postures they had when the napalm struck – a man about to get on his bicycle, fifty boys and girls playing in an orphanage, a housewife strangely unmarked holding in her hand a page from a Sears-Roebuck catalogue...there must be almost two hundred dead in the tiny hamlet.

These missions would be reported to the American people as huge victories against massive Chinese and North Korean communist forces. When I.F. Stone published his, *The Hidden History of the Korean War* in 1952, John Friedman reports, "it met with an almost complete press black-out and boycott." Stone came to learn that in Mexico the U.S. embassy had "bought up and junked all the copies it could lay its hands on of the Spanish translation of *Hidden History*."[13] I.F. Stone was blackballed as a communist sympathizer and was later rumored to be a Soviet agent, an accusation that boiled down to him having lunch with the Soviet Attaché' in Washington, as many reporters did regularly during the cold war. Although released Soviet records show that Stalin had a plan to invade the South, when the North Koreans were pressed to near defeat in the early part of the war, it was not the Soviets who came to their rescue, but the Chinese. The Chinese were perfectly happy to let the border between North and South return to the middle of the country where it had started. No major effort to move into the South supported by the Chinese or Soviets was launched after the battle lines returned to the original border zone, the fighting for the next three years all raged in that central region around the 38th parallel and mostly along the Northern side.

As the war bled on there were terrible battles with colorful names, like Heartbreak Ridge, and Pork Chop Hill, that cost dearly in American blood and all of it was essentially for nothing once the border was returned to the 38th parallel at the armistice in the summer of 1953. There were over

33 thousand American men killed in action and over 8 thousand missing. Korean casualties numbered in the millions and most of this happened in the second part of the war after the Chinese pushed the fighting back to the middle of the country when the war should have ended. There was a call to exchange prisoners at that point, but MacArthur couldn't let that happen. So as to justify pressing the war onward, he cooked up outrageous stories of massive battles rivaling Verdun and D-day, while reporters on the ground were observing American forces fighting ghosts. I.F. Stone attempted to alert the American people and for his efforts he was nearly destroyed as a journalist.

The Vietnam War

The start of hostilities in Vietnam offers another classic instance of an intention to set up a situation that would serve to escalate a war from American advising and support to all out military intervention. Although scholars may continue to argue over Pearl Harbor and the vagaries of Korea, the Tonkin Gulf incident has been so thoroughly revealed as deception that there really is no way to twist the evidence into something else.

The basic story is that the "Tonkin Gulf Resolution" was rushed into Congress as an official go-ahead for President Lyndon Johnson to bomb North Vietnam and send into action American service members in whatever numbers he saw fit after two American ships of war were reported "attacked" in the Gulf of Tonkin in the South China Sea off the coast of North Vietnam. It was 1964 and American advisors had been "in country" since 1955 assisting a corrupt government that by 1963 had proven incompetent in pursuing the war, so a new government was then "assisted" into power by the CIA. The former French Imperialists had been at long last booted out of the country a few years earlier by a revolutionary army and the U.S. was afraid the whole place was going to go communist. The revolutionary leader, Ho Chi Min, had praised the United States in earlier years and petitioned the US to help against the French, seeing Vietnam in the role of revolutionary America with the French as their England and mistakenly thinking that Americans, who had such high praise for democracy, would want to come to their aid. American power had other ideas and immediately began to attempt to reinstitute French rule in South East Asia after the Japanese were defeated at the end of WWII. With no one left to turn to Ho Chi Min made friends with the Chinese, the Vietnamese traditional enemy, by adopting communism as a way of garnering the military support they needed to defeat the French. The American military planners even contemplated using nuclear weapons to soundly repel the Vietnamese revolutionaries, but President Eisenhower and the British government rejected the plan. Nobody wanted to start a land war with the Chinese. After the French defeat in 1954, the country was divided at the 17th parallel and a contest of systems of government ensued, communist vs. capitalist, much like that which had blown-up Korea.

The American government had become increasingly concerned with the Vietnamese leadership's continuing inability to defeat the communist guerilla activity in the South, was sure they would never get the job done on their own and was looking for any way to sell the war to a reluctant American public. Lyndon Johnson in 1964, after having become president through the Kennedy assassination, was now campaigning for the Presidency on the assurance to the American people that he would not broaden American involvement with the war. Polls had shown that most Americans had no taste for another war in Asia, so invading Vietnam was not a winning position. "I am not about to send American boys to Asia to fight the battles that Asian boys should fight," Johnson had flatly stated in his Texas drawl.

The answer to the President's dilemma was to pull out the old, tried and true, American, star spangled, red, white, and blue *goad the enemy into attacking plan*; it had always worked before, so why not again? This time it would be a combination of "*Remember the Maine!*" and the Korean *War* method of, "blasting away at an imaginary enemy while you claim to be under siege." The Navy of South Vietnam had been given a couple of old American gun boats that were sent to stir up the North by shelling two islands off the coast of North Vietnam. They were also dropping commando teams on the mainland to carry out sabotage missions. The American Destroyer *Maddox* was sent into the very same area on August 2nd and in darkness was met by 3 North Vietnamese patrol boats said to be armed with torpedoes. The *Maddox*, after issuing warnings to the oncoming vessels, opens fire. The Vietnamese PT boats retreat and the destroyer resumes its patrol, issuing a report that states that torpedoes were fired at them that missed while sustaining one hit by a machine gun round. The North Vietnamese reported that an American destroyer had invaded their waters and was chased out. Two nights later the *Maddox* is sent again into the same area with the destroyer *Turner Joy* and this time they report being attacked by as many as 5 or 6 torpedo boats firing a total of 22 torpedoes at them. No damage or any evidence of a battle is sustained by either ship, although they do fire their guns into the darkness for 3 hours and report that by midnight they have sunk 2 of the PT boats and the others have broken contact. The North Vietnamese respond later that they had not been in the area that night, but no one is listening.

The ploy works perfectly and the American Congress and people are led to believe that our forces have been wantonly attacked by godless communists in international waters. The same day, Washington time, President Johnson goes on television just before midnight to tell the American people from his own lips that they have been attacked and announces his intention to bomb North Vietnam in retaliation. Two days later Congress passes the "Tonkin Gulf Resolution," a document meant to get the Congress on board for immediate escalation of the war. The resolution had been prepared months in advance.

By 1970 things are not going so well in Vietnam and people have discovered that things were a bit uncertain on that dark night in the South China Sea back in '64. A committee in the US Senate is convened, led by Senator William Fulbright, to investigate the incident that opened the way for the deployment of American troops. What they are told by the Navy is that the *Maddox* had been fitted with a "special device" that could intercept enemy transmissions and that these reports verified that North Vietnamese patrol boats had been sunk and sustained damage on the night in question. The committee was not convinced by the "black box intercepts" and in their examination of reports found that there had been bad weather and much confusion that night. They heard many stories from sailors, but nothing convincing or actual proof.

The committee was never able to come to any clear conclusion regarding the reality of the reported attack on August 4th and the investigation was halted, but Congress did vote to repeal the Tonkin Gulf Resolution, thereafter. By that time the war was winding down as the American government realized they could not overcome the North without the sort of all-out escalation that might provoke the Chinese. It was also clear the American people were no longer willing to back the effort. By the time of the Fulbright Committee in 1970 over 44 thousand Americans were dead and over 300,000 wounded and more were on the way, little could be said to have been gained by their sacrifice. It was later discovered that the Navy had only passed on to the committee those statements from sailors on the two destroyers who believed there had been an attack, all those that doubted they had ever been under attack were suppressed. One report withheld from the committee but discovered later was believed by Senator Fulbright to have been of such magnitude that it would have given the committee the evidence it was looking for to launch a full scale investigation. It was a report by Captain Herrick of the *Maddox:* "Review of action makes many recorded contacts and torpedoes fired appeared doubtful. Freak weather effects, and overeager sonar man may have accounted for many reports. No actual visual sightings by *Maddox.* Suggest complete evaluation before any further actions."

After the Vietnam War ended, the American people were left confused and dejected regarding what they had been led to believe about their country's role as the "defender of the free world." Vietnam veterans painted a picture of the war as a commitment gone mad, of a deadly machine that had gone off the tracks causing immense suffering, death and destruction on an industrial scale, whose leadership had become detached from the actual conditions on the ground so that orders from above began to make no sense whatsoever to the people actually fighting the war.

The fall of Saigon and the capitulation of the South to the North Vietnamese communist forces was a tragedy for the people of Vietnam as a whole. The communists went about murdering thousands of people in a political cleansing campaign, including the dropping of Soviet made "yellow rain" chemical weapons on the mountain tribes that had fought loyally with the American Special Forces throughout the war. The President of South Vietnam just before the fall made a broadcast to the people telling them they had been betrayed by America, abandoned to their fate under the North. There was rioting in the streets with people frantically trying to get on the last helicopters, iconic images of the final day show people clawing over one another to get on that last chopper leaving the roof of the U.S. Embassy. In 2005 the NSA declassified documents from the period revealing an analysis that found no evidence for any Vietnamese attack on the second night.

Former generals and government employees with connections and off-shore bank accounts ended up in plush homes in Hawaii and California, but the rest of the people who worked with Americans, who had no such luck ended up in labor camps and just plain dead. To the people of America the war represented a shattering of the old mythology of the righteous American hero who uses violence for good and in the service of freedom and humane progress. The soldiers and marines and all those who saw the war up close knew no such naïve principle could be applied. The people of Vietnam had been treated like expendable tokens in a game of geo-political hegemony between two economic systems that cared no more about the human life that happens to be scrambling around the surface of a contested region than did the East India Company centuries before. In 2003 the Secretary of Defense during the war, Robert S. McNamara, admitted in the documentary, *The Fog of War*, that the August 4th attack never happened.

THE PROGRAM OF EMPIRE

It's about the resources, that's what a myopic focus on material economics and the worship of profit amounts to. People are simply a "labor force" or they are *in the way* and it doesn't matter whether that system was inspired by Adam Smith or Marx and Lenin. When it comes to places like Korea and Vietnam, Iraq or Afghanistan, it's about dominating the ground—the oil, the bananas, the opium poppies, whatever. Much is different between Marxist/Leninism and Smith's free market philosophies, but they are essentially the same in one crucial way: they are both products of the mental/rational mind, which is hyper materialist, mechanistic, and prone to mathematical and spatial metaphors in their conceptions of the world and its meanings and values.

The map is a perfect example of a mental/rational conception – a highly useful thing for navigation, but lacking much as a representation of reality in all its living attributes. Power dominated by an exclusive mental/rational perspective will tend to discount everything not delineated on the map. Medieval maps were illuminated with little paintings of beasts and striking features of the environment lending them a visceral quality, but on the modern socio-economic map the "illumination" has been transformed to statistics. Everything is reduced to number and volume – population size, mineral deposits, agricultural products – bloodless digits of computation lacking human and earthly dimension, these are the spoils of modern economically inspired warfare. The communist systems have generally tended to be even more inhuman and dictatorial than most capitalist states and so they've had to build walls around them to keep people from running away. But the "freedom" cherished at the center of the capitalist empires is never what is promoted at the peripheries. In the "client states" (a telling business metaphor) the people are subjected to whatever tactics are deemed necessary to ensure the flow of resources and capital back to the center of the empire. This is the way it's always worked, from the Romans to the British, and this is the very thing that most Americans have never been quite able to figure out, seeing the spread of *freedom* where really only subjugation in the service of economic exploitation exists.[14]

The reason for their quandary lies in the split that arose as America began to pursue an imperial agenda at the close of the frontier. To clarify the matter once again: On one side were the people who simply wanted to live their lives in honest work that garnered a fair share with freedom to raise their children in peace and adequate prosperity, to go to whatever church they wanted, or not at all, to build lives with their own two hands and never at the mercy of some exploiting overlord or imperious king. On the other side was the elite who had every desire to continue the economic boom times provided by the windfall riches of the unspoiled continent on which their families had won their fortunes. For the rich a simple life of spiritual virtues was not enough, they measured their success in material capital alone and were determined to continue *their* American enterprise right into the Pacific and around the world. The people who just happen to be occupying those potential lands of opportunity would be treated just as the Native Americans had been treated.

The average American had no desire to indulge in empire. Empires were for kings and emperors, for the bloody British and the old world pompous aristocrats they had left behind. So, right from the beginning the elite had a problem. In their own rhetoric amongst their own set they spoke of empire openly and without reservation, but the people would not be moved by such grandiose visions. Hence, the necessity of the American mythic hero – who goes forth into the badlands of this world to fight for freedom and to keep the dark powers of the earth at bay, to *fight them over there so we don't have to fight them here*! A grand mythology was constructed out of Daniel Boon and Davey Crockett. Part George Washington and part Wild Bill Hickok, it would be nourished through the 20th Century with Wild West Shows, movie heroes, and then television cowboys and cavalry charges. Each war would be fought by the men in that mold for those grand and godly reasons, not for imperial economic gain, but for "mom and apple pie," for *freedom and to protect the innocent*.

Vietnam would be the death of all that. Vietnam would show it all to be a lie, a deception, a manipulation so painful and disorienting in its realization that most of the country would simply turn away and go back to their TVs where the world made sense. In the streets the hollow-eyed veterans in their tattered field jackets kept up their endless march home, the defeated warriors having seen the myth explode before them leaving only murder and mayhem as their deeds. Without cover of mythic valor so wounded in their hearts and spirits they never really return. And the public just brushes them aside as they don't fit the profile of the hero they expect. But even on the mythic screen the hero had grown increasingly cynical.

Dirty Harry, with his 44 magnum in the face of a young black man, "go ahead...make my day," was the Old West *gunfighter for justice* locked in a world of corruption and insanity, blasting his manly weapon at all the creeps and freaks and perverts this new out-of-control world could dish up. This was the myth to save a myth. This was the myth of the violent male hero now turning on the forces that had corrupted his myth of cleanliness, and goodness, and freedom. It wasn't the corporate elite who the specially constructed new hero turned on as the true violators of his sacred trust in movies and television; it was *those damn hippies and politicians* that pulled the rug out on the mythic hero in battle. In this way the elite would now turn the culture machine toward pitting its soldiers against its political opponents and it worked perfectly. No one ever blamed the corporate fear of losing another "client" for the senseless slaughter of Vietnam or the voice that turned away Ho Chi Min when he asked for help in order to back French colonial rule. No one looked to the money made, to the military-industrial-complex that Eisenhower warned of engorging itself for a decade or more while the hero's blood flowed freely. The mainstream culture matrix is not allowed to go there, to go to the truth it can't see, because the corporate and banking elite that have stood behind this military backed economic imperialism for a century have become experts at camouflaging themselves behind the political apparatus and through media dominance making sure that mainstream eyes remain firmly glued to their chosen patsies.

Economic Imperialism

After the "Vietnam debacle," the empire continued to need new territory, but the war had really left a bad taste in everyone's mouth and so it put the military machine into low gear for a couple decades. In this climate of heroic confusion the big money had to confine it's depredations to "economic hit-men" working through the IMF and World Bank, destroying the livelihoods of populations in third world nations around the globe through deceptive, predatory loan packages. The World Bank was established after WWII to help rebuild countries after the war and to assist in the development of third world nations. John Perkins, who was selected by the NSA (National Security Agency), to become an EHM (economic hit man) worked in conjunction with the World Bank and explains that in fulfilling its role it established very "cozy" relationships with multi-national corporations:

> This opened the door for me and other EHM's to mount a multitrillion dollar scam. We channeled funds from the Bank and its sister organizations into schemes that appeared to serve the poor while primarily benefiting a few wealthy people. Under the most common of these, we would identify a developing country that possessed resources our corporations coveted (such as oil), arrange a huge loan for that country, and then direct most of the money to our own engineering and construction companies – and a few collaborators in the developing country. Infrastructure projects, such as power plants, airports, and industrial parks, sprang up; however, they seldom helped the poor, who were not connected to electrical grids, never used airports, and lacked the skills required for employment in industrial parks. At some point we EHM's returned to the indebted country and demanded our pound of flesh, cheap oil, votes on critical United Nations issues...[15]

Perkins explains that these loans become impossible to pay when the projects never bring in the advertised revenue they were supposed to produce. So this gives the World Bank and American operatives the leverage to extract concessions from the country. The burden for paying off the loans ends up on the back of the common people, while the elite within the country grow extravagantly rich doing favors for American corporations who plunder the country thereafter.

In 1971 John Perkins was sent to Indonesia to help develop an infrastructure for oil exportation. A few years earlier, then *General* Suharto, in order to keep his people in line, responded to a communist coup attempt by slaughtering 300,000 to 500,000 citizens and then promptly took over the presidency. Perkins states that the people had turned to the Chinese for assistance in their guerilla war against their oppressive government only when it became clear they could not win on their own against the American backed Indonesian Army. In the 70's American companies became interested in substantial oil and gas deposits on the island of East Timor and when the islanders declared independence from Portugal in 1975 this gave President Suharto the opening he needed to carry out an American devised and backed invasion, murdering some 200,000 people, fully one third of the population, in the process. The complicity of the U.S. government has been substantiated in this matter by a release of records from the National Security Archive.[16] Of course, the government was only working for the oil companies.

The striking thing about all the atrocities and horrors of Indonesia over the years is that it has been well hidden from the American public. The obvious oil/military/government conjunction of power displayed by the Indonesian situation has never had to be explained, because it has been nicely blocked by corporate media from entering public conversation. In this way, the American Corporate Empire rolled onward without having to face the Vietnam malaise.

No one was going to tolerate a draft again, that was for sure, so overt exercises of brute force were limited to a few days in Grenada and Panama, missions that have their own dirty little secrets behind them, as well. The story of the split between the public's need to pin military adventures to a moral backdrop and the corporatocracy's need to simply secure access to resources abroad that inconveniently happen to have *little brown people* running around on top of them, was not a dilemma needing to be faced again until the Gulf War seemingly appeared out of nowhere in the early 1990's.

The First Iraq War

The Iraqi dictator, Saddam Hussein, had asked his American friends in the *Bush the First* administration if it was alright to invade his neighbor, the sovereign nation of Kuwait. Saddam was a bit peeved at them for driving down the price of oil and slant drilling oil out of his territory. Saddam met with the American ambassador in Baghdad, April Glaspie, who told him, "We have no opinion on Arab-Arab conflicts," thus giving him tacit approval that he may proceed as he saw fit. So, knowing that all the borders of the Middle East were put in place by the British a century earlier and feeling that Kuwait really was a part of Iraq proper, anyway, he sent in his tanks.

Bush the First reacted with great dramatic outrage, *This aggression will not stand!* The President trumpeted from his televised pulpit in Washington, suitably indignant as if the whole thing were a surprise. The corporate news began to spew inflammatory comparisons between Adolf Hitler and Saddam Hussein, a comparison that was apt for reasons other than intended, seeing as both men were good friends and clients of American power before their respective demonizing. Of course, it wasn't hard to cast shadows over either figure. Saddam, although hardly a Hitler, was a terrible tyrant and mass murderer long before the Gulf War and certainly deserved all the mud thrown at him, but while the Iraqi dictator had previously been up to various crimes against humanity he had been fully funded and encouraged by the U.S. Government. During that earlier phase, when U.S. weapons dealers were soaking up billions in oil money from Iraq selling them every weapon on the market, the corporate news was silent about Saddam's crimes. It must be understood that Saddam Hussein was thought necessary for the continued harassment of Iran after the fall of the Shah. Reza Shah Pahlevi had been whisked into power by the CIA and British Intelligence as the Western replacement for the pesky democratically elected president of the country who had the audacity to take back his oil fields from the British. Now those fields were in the hands of the dreaded Ayatollahs and Saddam's army had been built-up in order to create a counter force against Islamic fundamentalism, that popular trend in the Middle East that wasn't good for Western business. Religious fundamentalism is the natural response of a people under siege who find the basic, black and white, moralizing and advocated violence of primitive stages of religious thought to be perfectly suited to their fight against what seems a monstrous demonic force oppressing them. The religious leaders of Iran had been the only people who spoke up who weren't murdered or imprisoned by the Shah's secret police and so they were the only alternative to the Western puppet regime.

Why *Bush the First* gave Saddam the green light to invade Kuwait and then acted as though he was the worst thing since Genghis Khan is not clear. It very well might have been about creating a major American military foothold in the Middle East in preparation for the larger strategy of direct military dominance across that oil region now in effect. In any case, the response by *President Bush the Frist* was quite melodramatic, evoking all the major metaphors of American heroic, "mom and apple pie" patriotism in order to get the war drums pounding in the hearts of the citizenry. It had to be made clear, by the usual rhetorical manipulations, that this was not about controlling foreign oil—*my heavens no*—this was about "protecting the innocent and stopping a new Hitler" who, this time—*by God*—would not be appeased. *Bush the First* read from a letter supposedly from an Army private saying how proud he was of his country's "firm stance against inhumane aggression." (Does that sound like an army private?)

But oil was not entirely absent from the rhetoric. President Bush also spoke in terms that were part of the new lexicon of American political-speak, referring to oil as "our national interests abroad" in his speech to the Congress on September 11, 1990. He suggested that if Saddam was allowed to control the oil of Iraq and Kuwait he would be able to mass an army so powerful he could threaten the world with oil blackmail, "We cannot permit a resource so vital to be dominated by one so ruthless." Bush then went on to encourage Congress to move swiftly ahead with developing domestic oil interests, including drilling in the Alaskan wilderness, so as to be free of this sort of foreign dependence.

The Gulf War serves as a perfect display of the typical two pronged maneuvering that goes on when the corporate run government decides to engage in a military operation abroad for the purposes of solidifying its power over a resource. First, the "enemy" is set-up to provide the proper villain for the political theater to come. Second, the public must be rallied behind the flag with stories of how this action threatens everything that is sacred to American feeling: rightness violated, innocence endangered, threats to "our way of life."

In President Bush's speech announcing the opening of American military action against Iraq he flat out lied to the American people, saying that everything had been done to avert war, that "months of constant and virtually endless diplomatic activity," had been employed to get Saddam to back down, but to no avail. The truth was exactly the opposite, Saddam was willing to leave Kuwait, State Department officials had admitted to several offers by Iraq they termed, "serious," and "negotiable," but the script called for military action and Bush and Company were not going to let Saddam's backing down spoil their plan. A *Washington Post*/CBS poll had shown that people two to one would be in favor of Saddam's withdrawal from Kuwait in exchange for U.N. Security Council consideration of the Arab-Israeli conflict, which, as it turned out, was exactly what Saddam was asking for. So, all of this had to be kept from the public at the time. The results of the poll were not widely reported nor were Saddam's offers. Noam Chomsky asks us to consider,

> Suppose that people had known that the offer was actually on the table and that it was widely supported and that in fact it's exactly the kind of thing that any rational person would do if they were interested in peace...Supposed that it had been known...I would assume that two- thirds would have risen to 98 percent of the population. Here you have the great successes of propaganda.[17]

Chomsky suggests that the people who answered the poll, never seeing any result, must have thought they were alone in their feeling that such a deal should be struck to avoid war. Seeing all the reporting in the major media saying what Bush would later tell the American people, that no offers existed, they must have thought the whole poll an exercise in hypotheticals. The reality was that Saddam had made just such an offer eight days before the poll was taken.

Just to make sure the American public had the right idea about why they were sending their sons and daughters into a killing zone, President Bush in his speech at the opening of hostilities said, "While the world waited, Saddam Hussein systematically raped, pillaged, and plundered a tiny nation, no threat to his own. He subjected the people of Kuwait to unspeakable atrocities – and among those maimed and murdered, innocent children." He then went on to list all the terrible things that happened "while the world waited," repeating the phrase over and over as if to say that all the attempts at negotiation were foolish, even invoking the plight of third world countries whose "fragile" economies were damaged by the unabated action of the tyrant. But the greatest stroke of manipulation came with the bit about "maimed and murdered, innocent children." In a now infamous piece of deception the Bush administration paraded a Kuwaiti girl in front of Congress who told the story of how Iraqi troops had *ripped babies out of incubators and threw them on the floor* as they ransacked a Kuwaiti hospital. The story played broadly and loudly in the mainstream news outlets. Later, it was learned that the girl was the daughter of the Kuwaiti ambassador to Washington, had not been in the country during the invasion and had been coached to present the bogus tale with heart rending feeling.

The speech is a masterpiece of rhetorical deception and simple falsehoods. "The terrible crimes and tortures committed by Saddam's henchmen against the innocent people of Kuwait are an affront to mankind and a challenge to the freedom of all." Strange the murder of one third of the population of East Timor didn't seem to affront mankind or challenge freedom when Suharto was securing oil fields for American companies. When South Africa was invading its neighbors and murdering people en mass it was handled with quiet prolonged diplomacy and concessions, a policy denied for Iraq.[18] "Saddam Hussein met every overture of peace with open contempt." Iraqi diplomats had been begging for a compromise, but they were rebuffed over and over. Of course they knew they couldn't stand up to the U.S. military. This wasn't Vietnam. There was no jungle to hide in, no China to back them up. Saddam's military might, *his terrible threat to the world*, was a propaganda paper tiger pasted together by the Bush administration. When the American military machine moved in, it went through Saddam's forces like a hot knife through butter. At the wars end it was admitted by military experts that the Iraqi Army had been highly overrated, the threat grossly inflated, that in reality most of it was composed of unmotivated, poorly trained and equipped conscripts who simply threw up their hands or ran away when the fighting started. Many of them never got the chance. They were men who just wanted to live their lives, not storm troopers from some movie set, but simple human beings who were pushed out into the desert by a maniacal dictator to be incinerated by the overwhelming weaponry of the latest empire in a geopolitical game for dominance. Their lives didn't matter to this game anymore than the Americans or Kuwaitis who died there mattered.

At the end of the war, they had a parade, the parade they couldn't have for Vietnam. Everyone cheered and threw streamers. There were marching bands and row after row of smiling troops. President Bush gave a speech in which he declared that the country had "finally kicked the Vietnam syndrome!" By this he must have meant that the people were ready for more war.

One of the more bizarre but telling "quotes" included in Bush's speech at the opening of the "war" was this one, supposedly from a Master Sergeant from the 82nd Airborne: "We're here for more than just the price of a gallon of gas. What we're doing is going to chart the future of the world for the next 100 years. It's better to deal with this guy now than 5 years from now." What? Chart the history of the world? How, one wonders, does that happen? Unless the message is that the war was a demonstration of exactly what the American corporate state had in mind for the rest of the world for the next century. The next war in Iraq, orchestrated by the next Bush, would answer that question and the "next 100 years" would be laid out for them by the Neo Conservative advocacy group, "Project for the New American Century."

The stated goal of *The Project for the New American Century*, or PNAC, which began in 1997, was: "to promote American global leadership... through a Reaganite policy of military strength and moral clarity." Among the rhetoric of this organization was the idea that America must insure its security and "greatness" for the next 100 years by dominating the world militarily. (As fascism goes this is really quite modest when you compare it to Hitler's call for a *thousand year Reich*; they probably figured they'd conquer the next century when they got to it.) In the service of this glorious vision of a new American century PNAC advocated a massive arms build-up. The United States already had at the time the most capable military in the world, but they wanted it to be virtually unstoppable, capable of carrying out multiple engagements around the world at the same time, increasing troop strength to 1.6 million. The guiding light of this titanic military presence in the world would show the way to "extending an international order friendly to our security, our prosperity, and our principles." In other words – to remake the world in our image; to ensure that our corporate investment in any resource on the globe proceeds without hindrance and that our "principles," our "Reaganite moral clarity," is forcibly inserted everywhere into the cultures of the world. The principles of the corporate state are simply those of commerce alone. That's it – to increase the bottom line at any cost to the environment, workers, or long term viability of societies. That is what John Perkins as an *economic hit man* has revealed the strategy to be and that is what the history in places like Guatemala, Iran, Chile, Nicaragua, Indonesia, others and even within the U.S. itself tells us. The moral clarity of Ronald Reagan was that which allowed 1.5 million people to be killed by South African forces in surrounding countries by way of maintaining their racist regime, and that responded to this scorched-earth policy with casual diplomacy and in the end allowed the invaders to annex a chunk of Namibia without outrage, without humane concern, and certainly without any military response. Americans knew little of this at the time since the corporate media allowed little coverage. [19]

If there was anything more ominous in the PNAC declaration than its call for regime change in Iraq in 1997 and, frankly, the fascistic undertone of what was outlined in the whole thing, it was this particular line: "Further, the process of transformation, even if it brings revolutionary change, is likely to be a long one, absent some catastrophic and catalyzing event—like a new Pearl Harbor."[20]

BUSH II AND 9/11

When George W. Bush took office through ballet blocking in Florida and what was probably electronic vote manipulation in Ohio, (exit polls radically differed from the ballot count in this state that used the new Diebold computerized voting machines), appointed by right wing partisans on the Supreme Court, he brought with him a number of PNAC members into key positions in his administration, including Donald Rumsfeld, Eliot Abrams, Dick Chaney, Paul Wolfowitz, and many others, a total of 18 people from the PNAC camp. The record shows they immediately began planning for an invasion of the Middle East.[21] Then, the "new Pearl Harbor" came to fruition. September 11 brings the attacks on the World Trade Center and the Pentagon. The Bush administration and the *Project for the New American Century* team have just what they were hoping for, a "catastrophic and catalyzing event." The door is then open for the 100 years of American dominance now achievable through public support for the massive military build-up as a response to this new "war on terror." This new kind of war Dick Chaney and George W. Bush began to immediately warn the public, *would be a long, long, war, not easily winnable, one the American public would have to get used to fighting.* (This is what it takes, apparently, when you make war on a noun.) The case the Bush administration made to get into Iraq has now been clearly shown to be largely fabricated. They lied and got away with it, a sign of just how far the consolidation of a totalizing control of the population has gone.[22]

The question of whether the 9/11 attacks were orchestrated by a cabal within the U.S. government and military has become a quiet but furious debate in the U.S. and around the world. The sheer complexity and magnitude of the various arguments and evidence involved in the differing theories, official and otherwise, goes way beyond what can be reasonably summarized in a work of this sort. On one side is the 9/11 Commission Report that lays out the government position and on the other are the increasing pieces of evidence that suggest that the buildings were brought down by demolition explosives, or perhaps other classified weapons, as well as problems with the events at the Pentagon and the crash of Flight 93. There are so many things wrong with the official version of events that, if it wasn't a conspiracy, then it has to be the most botched investigation in the history of the country. On the "9/11 truth" side are growing numbers, thousands of architects, structural engineers, demolition experts, pilots, and many others who deliver fact after fact as to why the official explanation is simply wrong. These are not wild-eyed "conspiracy theories" promoted by untrained armchair speculators; these are expert opinions with hard, scientific arguments that have never been given a response from official sources.[23] The government experts refuse to debate any outside body of experts saying that it would only give support to ridiculous theories. This is, of course, all very convenient. If the official version is right then they should be able to explain why these buildings are the first steel frame structures in the history of architecture to be weakened by fire. This alone is a baffling situation. Steel frame buildings have been hit by aircraft and many have burned all over the world and not one melted structural steel or ever collapsed. They just burn up all the combustibles and the steel frame remains standing when the fires are out. The fact is that the temperatures generated by office fires never reach those necessary to melt structural steel and the idea that jet fuel allowed for this is impossible since all of it ignited and burned in less than a second leaving nothing but flaming office furniture. In fact, there are so many "firsts" just in the architectural aspects of the day that if 9/11 was just as reported then, as some have suggested, it constitutes a kind of miracle, a sort of *dark divine intervention* where the laws of physics and material science simply cease to function. Interested readers are directed to the works of David Ray Griffin, for a scholarly discussion of fact-based errors in the official reports. Many former high ranking military officers, intelligence professionals, scientists, structural engineers and even a majority of those who served on the government's 9/11 commission, now say the official story is a lie.[24]

This catastrophic event is still so raw in American feeling that it cannot be debated without bringing up a torrent of emotion and outrage that stems from a response that recoils from the idea that some element within the country could be evil enough to carry out such a horrendous act of mass murder. The idea simply jams up in the corridors of people's minds. They become unable to contemplate such a thing as this and they turn away without consideration of the many facts that suggest something other than the work of religious extremists with a few hours of simulated flight training and some box cutters.

In 2009 a study of ground zero dust particles was published by Dr. Stephan Jones of Brigham Young University along with a team of 9 scientists in the peer reviewed *Bentham Chemical Physics Journal.* The paper was strenuously reviewed and vetted for accuracy, due to the highly inflammatory nature of the findings. What the study demonstrated beyond a shadow of a doubt was that an explosive known as *nano-thermite*, or "super thermite" was discovered in the dust samples from all three buildings of the World Trade Center. Thermite is the typical compound used in demolitions work, but super-thermite is a special variety only available to *special ops* military units. It is highly controlled even within the military.

The fact this startling finding was not blazoned across the headlines of the *New York Times* or leading the evening broadcast on CNN and FOX is simply another blatant sign to the aware public that the media has been coopted by the same people who have benefitted so grossly from the 9/11 attacks. And what has been the benefit? Bills rushed through Congress initiated mammoth funding packages for a period of war on two and sometimes three fronts that continues to this day, pouring billions monthly into the coffers of the *military-industrial-complex* and expanding the military toward the PNAC goal stated above. Oil company access to the immense virtually untapped Caspian Basin oil

305

field in Turkmenistan with its essential pipeline through Afghanistan to the Pakistani coast on the Arabian Sea has been assured and the constructing of the pipeline has been well protected by the American military, an aspect of the war few Americans have ever heard of. The folks at the *Project for the New American Century* closed their doors, stating in 2006 that *their goals had been achieved*, "our view has been adopted," said former executive director, Gary Schmitt in his closing statement. These are the winners, the losers are the Iraqis and Afghanis and the American people, who have experienced an escalating trend of general financial decline during the same period, a frightening erosion of their civil rights in the name of "security," and rising military suicides from the war zones that now exceed those from WWII, Korea, and Vietnam, combined, another fact kept quiet.

There is a thread that travels through American history from the Spanish-American war right through to 9/11. It is the story of manipulation of the masses for the purposes of expanding the power and economic empire of an oligarchy of the ultra- wealthy banking and corporate controllers and the "best and the brightest" they recruit to their cause. The idea that these people are not capable of mass murder in the name of furthering their ends is, unfortunately, not tenable. This is the same malignant spirit that enslaved millions of Africans, that depopulated the Scottish Highlands and sent the people to be worked to death in the colonies as indentured servants. This is the same dark spirit that wiped off the face of the earth entire societies of Native Americans. This is the same spirit that depopulated whole provinces of the Philippines. This is the same spirit that arranged the massive obscenity of killing at Verdun and the Somme, the same sick spirit that fire bombed residential areas of Japan killing millions of women and children and the elderly and then obliterated not one but two cities with the most horrific inhumane weapon ever devised by mankind – *the atom bombs were not dropped on military targets, but people; they wanted to see what would happen to lots of people at different ranges.* This is the same twisted, "aristocratic" spirit that swaggered through the streets of European cities for centuries kicking the "riff raff" to the curb. These people who send Americans to die in wars of conquest wrapped up in red, white, and blue, and sold as rescue missions for heroes are quite capable of murdering a thousand or so people in three airliners and a couple of big buildings in New York and Virginia – no problem, no problem at all.

It would not be the first time that elements within the country had conceived of a rationale for killing fellow Americans for the purposes of igniting a war. It is known that in 1962 a plan was devised for orchestrating a false attack on the United States in the guise of Cuban communist forces in order to push public opinion toward an invasion of Castro's Cuba. The plan, Operation Northwoods, "which had been written with the approval of the Chairman and every member of the Joint Chiefs of Staff, called for innocent people to be shot on American streets."[25]

It was revealed by Seymour Hersh, the New Yorker's Pulitzer Prize winning journalist, that in the summer of 2008 a source within the White House told him that Vice-President Dick Chaney had considered a number of plans to incite a war with Iran using false flag tactics. One of these ideas called for Navy Seals to dress up like Iranian sailors and attack American ships in the Straits of Hormuz on specially constructed fake Iranian gun boats.

Many people harbored a great hope that the presidency of Barak Obama would change all of this, but the terrible truth is that nothing has changed at all. In fact, the war in Afghanistan escalated and Obama has long ago beat his predecessor's record for targeted killings by way of drone aircraft and the other conventional methods. The continuity between the Bush presidency and the Obama presidency should be ample evidence that certain policies do not originate with elected administrations. What the American people need to come to grips with is the fact that the President is working for the Empire and it is the Empire who groomed Barack Obama as an "alternative" candidate since his days at Columbia University as a protégé of Zbigniew Brzezinski. The one time National Security Advisor to Jimmy Carter, Brzezinski was a founding member of the Rockefeller's Trilateral Commission, a coordinating body of the American Imperium. Brzezinski has long been an advocate for American domination of central Asia.

THE LOGIC OF EMPIRE

Taking a good hard look at all this with eyes wide open, the question arises as to how such people live with themselves as they carry out the extermination of their fellow human beings without regard for the suffering and sorrow that follows, without conscience. The answer is twofold. First, you have the ego development that encourages the elitist self-image, that which divides groups and allows one to see the other as something less than human, an ethnocentric prejudice that favors those of like quality. Secondly, you add to this the mental/rational structure of consciousness that encourages a cold mathematical logic in understanding a problem, and this gives the necessary element of a moral refuge in that the individual can perform the appropriate calculation that always ends in their having chosen the "greater good." It goes like this: *"Well, we may be murdering thousands but in the end many more will benefit from their sacrifice."* It's always about the future. In Mao's China or Stalin's Soviet Union this was all quite in the open, the idea that people had to sacrifice now to create the "worker's paradise" later. In the West the idea always has had to be wrapped up in some grand crusade and sold as a *mission from God*. War is still sold to Americans in this package and it certainly is true that once you have invested heavily in developing monsters like the Nazis, the Imperial Japanese Army, and Saddam Hussein, when they get off the leash and start to break things and murder people then there is virtue in the sacrifice of those who go out to stop them. This is not in question, but the real issue is: should they have had to make that sacrifice to begin with if those in power had not carelessly set-up the situation in the first place? And this is the point, this game of geopolitical power-play that uses human beings as expendable pawns. This is about ego and numbers, the desire for "grandeur" and the count of dollars. and this game is played within the machine mind that sees the replacement of parts as no problem at all. The people think of themselves as unique and their loved ones and friends as irreplaceable, but the machine doesn't. It thinks of them as units in an investment game, *ten now for thirty later*.

So, "worker/buyer" units, that is: the average person, as civilians or soldiers, are expendable. You can use them up, throw them on the world table like poker chips and gamble their lives away and it means nothing to the calculating minds at the top of the pyramids of power, because one chip is just like another. There are always more pyramid laborers being born every day, more worker/buyer units replacing the old on a regular basis. They serve their purpose and then they conveniently die, although apparently, not always in the numbers the elite would like to see. This is the end phase of the dissipation of empire where the society has grown to the point where prosperity is dying due to the obsolescence of major institutions and the population has split between those who exploit their positions at the top of those institutions to gather in more and more wealth as the rest of the population gives up more and more. This is a phase that historically has always been accompanied by imperial overreach abroad – the Romans, the French, the British, all tried to shore up the status quo power base at home by acquiring and exploiting more foreign resources.

Although oil has been at the basis of geopolitical maneuver throughout the 20th Century, America entered the overt phase of "oil wars" with the Gulf War in 1991 – oil being the premier basis of power in the country: electric, automotive, political and financial. Through the 1990's the U.S. had expanded military bases throughout the oil rich lands of the old Soviet states of Central Asia around the Caspian Sea and beyond, including: Kyrgyzstan, Pakistan, Uzbekistan, and Afghanistan. "In these cases the government has produced elaborate cover stories for what amounts to the use of public resources and the Armed Forces to advance private capitalist interests," wrote the scholar Chalmers Johnson.[26] Here we find one of the greatest single sources of oil and natural gas in the world: the Caspian basin, the real reason a war in the region was inevitable. This was the rationale behind the backing of Islamic extremist groups to hasten the Soviet withdrawal during the 1980's, the backing of the oppressive Taliban during the 1990's, and the failure to list Afghanistan as a terrorist state when Al Qaeda was using it as a training area and base striking American embassies in Africa long before 9/11. Everything was being done to promote the pipeline that Unocal and their partners wanted to build through Afghanistan. When the Taliban proved a final obstacle after the Soviets left then their demise had to be arranged as well. The attacks of September 11th came with perfect timing to provide massive American military intervention and the pipeline has been proceeding with great vigor since the first day of combat operations.[27]

Oil should have been replaced as a source of power decades ago, but it is being held in place by sheer viciousness and an absolute, all-encompassing determination. Oil is a commodity that is heavily tied to banking; all of the big 3 banking powers are heavily invested in oil, as well as making substantial profits through the handing of oil company accounts: *petrodollars*. (The Rothschild banking empire specifically owes much to oil investments at the opening of Middle Eastern markets.) It is the great windfall of petrodollars that has been recycled in third world loan packages that has allowed American power to convert those rejoins to vassal states through debt. This is explained to the public as something third world people brought on themselves, always reported with a lot of phony concern for the *third world debt crisis*. [28]

This managed history has brought us to the point where the banking/finance and petrochemical/energy power group seeks to extend its life through the Neo Con, (neo-fascist) corporate front in government. A ploy that has disguised itself as a patriotic movement for continued American "greatness" and prosperity and now a bulwark against the "Islamic threat," is a scary story for children that any educated teenager could unmask with a little careful research. As the veteran CIA Middle East analyst, Michael Scheuer, has pointed out in exacting detail, the violent stance of Islamic people is a direct response to specific American foreign policy actions in the Middle East and has nothing whatsoever to do with any animosity to Western lifestyles, democracy, or Christianity.[29] These ideas have been wholly concocted by government propaganda experts for the consumption of the dumbed-down masses who have to be kept away from the truth so they will continue to support the war and volunteer for combat while believing they are saving the world for democracy and their homes from the sword of Islam.

Few Americans will volunteer their lives for securing oil, as the quote from the Master Sergeant from Bush I's speech goes, "We're here for more than just the price of a gallon of gas..." That's the whole deal, right there; you have to have something *more*. Here we see the strategy that encourages the public to link oil with a legitimate reason to go to war, but there has to be the moral element to square it with American culture – *we're here for more* – otherwise men look in the mirror and they see an *enforcer*, a kind of armed accountant, not a hero, and the moral cover fades. In the Francis Ford Coppola film about Vietnam, *Apocalypse Now*, there is a scene that perfectly portrays this condition. The Army Captain sent up river to eliminate the rouge Colonel Kurtz has been captured and brought before Kurtz. They have a discussion and Kurtz asks Willard if he is an assassin. Willard replies that he is a soldier. Kurtz scoffs, "You're neither...you're an errand boy, sent by grocery clerks, to collect a bill."

Most Americans have come forward to fight with the wholehearted intent of serving their country out of the highest ideals of the defense of freedom and this is recognized, in any context, as worthy of respect. This being so, it makes it even more disgusting how this faithful dedication to the cause of freedom has been manipulated and used within the cynical calculations of geopolitical gamesmanship perpetrated by those in the seats of power. The light of truth shown on the military today can only serve to strengthen those sacred ideals of the republic so many have suffered and died for, so that, as Abraham Lincoln put it on the tragic fields of Gettysburg, "– these dead shall not have died in vain; that the nation, shall have a new birth of freedom, and that government of the people by the people for the people, shall not perish from the earth."

Having drug the reader through this bloody review of American history one may ask what this all has to do with the evolution of consciousness and the coming of the integral structure of mind? The answer is that these events are not separate from our psychology. Our history and the corrupt government we've come to are all wound up in what we are as citizens of the modern age. We are integrated with the world as it is. It is us and we are it. It is not valid to claim that one lives separate from all this in some progressive culture drifting above it all. We are all children of the empire, it is in the food we eat, the electronics we use, the clothes on our backs and the stories recited in the deep recesses of our minds that govern our tastes, our desires and the moments when we laugh or shed a tear. The empire is now American, but in a certain sense it's just been traveling around since Mesopotamia, the same bloody passion we are now poised to overcome. The structures of consciousness are filled with the history of the world. To move into a new world means we have to become aware of this, all that we are, and transform it in a new integration.

Notes

1. James Bradley, *The Imperial Cruise* (New York: Back Bay Books, 2009), p. 68.
2. Ibid.
3. Ibid., p.79.
4. Ibid.
5. Paul Fussell, *Wartime, Understanding and Behavior in the Second World War* (New York: Oxford, 1989), p.268.
6. Ibid. p. 268.
7. Sutton, (2002).
8. Interested readers should check out: John Toland's Infamy: Perl Harbor and its Aftermath. Toland is a highly respected Pulitzer Prize winning historian who carefully documents every conclusion; and: Day of Deceit: The Truth About F.D.R. and Perl Harbor, written by the retired WWII Navy veteran, Robert Stinnett, who uncovered still more documentary evidence.

9. I.F. Stone, "The Secret History of the Korean War," in: Friedman, (2005).
10. Ibid.
11. Ibid.
12. Ibid., p. 41.
13. Ibid., p. 31.
14. John Perkins, *The Secret History of the American Empire* (New York: Dutton, 2007).
15. Ibid. p. 2.
16. Ibid., p.46.
17. Noam Chomsky, *Media Control* (New York: Seven Stories Press, 2002), p. 59.
18. Ibid.
19. Ibid.
20. Wikipedia: Project for a New American Century.
21. Neil Mackay, *The War on Truth* (Drexel Hill PA: Casemate, 2006).
22. Ibid.
23. David Ray Griffin, *9/11 Ten Years Later, When State Crimes Against Democracy Succeed* (Northhampton, MA: Olive Branch Press, 2011).
24. Go to www.investigate911.org
25. James Bamford, as quoted in: Peter Scott Dale, *The Road to 9/11* (Berkeley: Universtiy of California Press, 2008), p. 14
26. Chalmers Johnson, *The Sorrows of Empire* (New York: Metropolitan Books, 2004), p. 168.
27. Ibid., Johnson, (2004); Dale, (2008).
28. Engdahl, (2011).
29. Michael Scheuer, Imperial Hubris, *Why the West is losing the War on Terror* (Dulles VI: Potomac Books, 2007).

Chapter 7

The Integral Structure

Previous eras of consciousness have tended to leave behind and even demonize the preferences and focus of the prior stage, so that as the high mythological stage reigned supreme in the form of the Roman church it hunted down and put to death all those practicing spiritual arts from the previous magic stage of consciousness. Where shamans and "witches" were once the interpreters and workers of spiritual interactions for the people in healing and prophesy, they then became "consorts of the devil" in the eyes of the next stage of consciousness. When the mental stage took hold, then the degradation of the mythological stage began with science's war against religion that continues to this day.

The problem with discarding the focus of previous levels of consciousness is that one ends up discarding pieces of the makeup of the complete human being. We build on what has come before and transcend each stage in turn—as an exclusive focus—but we can't get rid of our evolutionary heritage any more than we can get rid of the primitive organisms in our digestive track just because their existence predates our own, we depend on them and they on us. Human beings retain a need for the level of awareness in consciousness prominent in each previous stage. There are virtues to each stage from the archaic to the mental; each has something to offer a complete life. It is the task of the integral structure of consciousness to which we are now evolving to assure that these previous stages be recovered in a conscious way and integrated so as to create a powerful synthesis of mind, body, and spirit.

Historically, the rejection of the previous stages came by way of the degeneration of what was something healthy in its inception, but had become deficient at the end of its evolutionary run. So, the "magic" of the tribal consciousness degenerated in some quarters to black magic and curses. As the mythological stage ran down, the church degenerated into murderous corruption and doctrinal manipulation in the pursuit of power, rendering it easy prey for the criticisms of materialist science as the mental/rational structure ensued. We are now at the end of the mental/rational stage and we have been discovering the limitations of the purely rational perspective that peaked in the 1950's, but continues to generate absurdities to the present day. Extreme rationalism produces odd contradictions, like the classic Vietnam War admission, "we had to destroy the village to save it." Rationalism taken too far comes up against the boundaries of common sense where a numerical reason seems to discount the human factor. The auto industry, for instance, will calculate the loss from a recall and decide it makes more sense to simply pay the lawsuits off from any deaths or injuries as they arise, rather than initiate a recall, because they believe it will cost less in the end. This is a purely rational decision that misses the point: allowing people to die and be injured to save money is not just an economic decision, but a moral one. It is one of the terrible truths of our era that too many leaders make decisions based on this cold hearted rationalism believing they are "making the tough calls," and other such self-justifying rhetoric when a wider focus reveals such logic to be tragically flawed.

It was morality after all, that was the justification for raising reason above faith and tradition in the first place. When the new scientific perspective was adopted by the leaders of European society it was to help bring an end to the Thirty Years War that had ravaged the population of the continent in an attempt to fill the religious power vacuum as Protestant and Catholic struggled for supremacy.[1] Simple facts could be attained by the scientific method that all could agree on in defining a new guiding spirit for the rule of earthly affairs – regardless of religious loyalties; heaven would take care of itself. Voltaire, the French philosopher and champion of reason, took this new approach to truth finding and found reason as a route to defeat the arbitrary abuse of power by the elite of his day. It was this vision that helped bring on the collapse of the system that allowed any and all abuses of common people by aristocrats. Their former rights as members of the nobility simply became "unreasonable," the aura of grandeur having evaporated under the bright light of reason. Reason led to the notion that common people had "rights" as well, simply by virtue of their humanity. "Human rights" were a direct challenge to the age old social systems that placed some individuals above others as either "relatives" or favorites of the gods, or god, with "superior" blood lines. John Locke, Voltaire, Jean-Jacques Rousseau and others, including those that conceived of a republic of the people in North America, were guided by a spiritual morality broken free from the dictates of any particular religion. Now, nobility would be found in life itself, placed there by the Creator as a function of granting that life. To oppress any person was an affront to the Creator and the potential he placed in each life. It was this potential that the framers of the American Constitution believed, if placed within the right framework, would create the illumined "city on the hill," that Augustine spoke of. God's creation unfettered by corrupt power would, in time, if properly nurtured, produce the ultimate social order.

That potential, whether granted by deity or some vast order beyond our simple knowing, is a very real thing, but has been cut short in America due to the rise of a reason detached from its original guidance by morality. As the scholar John Ralston Saul has aptly pointed out in his deep exploration of the subject, *reason without morality is simply structure*, and structure is a tool that tends to be shaped and controlled for the interests of whoever holds the keys to power.

> What's more, the renewed and intense concentration on the rational element which started in the seventeenth century had an unexpected effect. Reason began, abruptly, to separate itself from and to outdistance the more or less recognized human characteristics – spirit, appetite, faith and emotion, but also intuition, will and, most important, experience. This gradual encroachment on the foreground continues today. It has reached a degree of imbalance so extreme that the mythological importance of reason obscures all else and has driven the other elements into the marginal frontiers of doubtful respectability.[2]

This is why the ultimately rational Germans could believe the dictates of National Socialism in the rise of the Third Reich to be perfectly reasonable: they saw a problem in the Jews and set out to solve it in the most efficient manner. This was no more unreasonable than the slaughter of Native Americans who were seen as "savages" incapable of "properly" utilizing the territory, despite the treaties. It was all perfectly reasonable. Napalm is a perfectly reasonable way of incinerating soldiers in holes in the ground, as are chemical agents and nuclear weapons that efficiently kill masses of people without firing a shot. Never mind that these methods erode the humanity of those using them as they eradicate people in the most gruesome manner possible; pure reason dictates their use. Super penetrating uranium tipped tank rounds used in Iraq have left radioactive contamination all over embattled cities like Fallujah, resulting in masses of grossly deformed infants being born. Yet, they were seen as perfectly reasonable by American military planners, because *they get the job done*. And that is how reason detached from humanity and ethics works: it concentrates on the job and solves the problem with masterful efficiency through a calculation that does not include any immediate moral concern. If asked, the generals would offer a calculation of current death vs. later lives saved. (As if extreme tactics were necessary to defeat a rag tag guerrilla force in a third world city.) This is the favorite excuse of reason in the hands of power unrestrained by any human compassion. When pressed, there is always a pleading that terrible things must be done to accommodate a greater good. This is the same calculation that makes it all very reasonable to plunge entire regions of the United States into poverty when shifting capital to foreign markets, or moving operations over the border, or buying steel elsewhere – *don't fret, you may be poor but everything is cheaper at Walmart.* The question is always – whose greater good?

It's a lie, of course, an obfuscation designed to conceal the ruthlessness of power. Reason utilized in this way divides people from their humanity and then asks others to excuse them because, *"I was only following orders; I was just doing my job; you can't argue with the numbers."* As the mental/rational stage of human development has reached its deficient end phase, we are left looking at the barren wasteland of reason that has simply been used as any other mythology or metaphysical principal has been used in history to serve as a justifying framework for an imposed order favoring an in-group whose desires are presented to the people as an inarguable logic. *It just can't be any other way,* a sentiment worthy of Sargon of Akkad. The truth is, of course, that it can be another way and it has many times. Terrible things do not have to be done to accommodate a future good; sacrifices, if necessary, have been made without those involved becoming monsters, where humanity and compassion have been applied. People do it all the time.

Humanity has over the ages gained ground on ruthless power and elitism as it has resisted the heartless calculations of power in its misuse of reason for hundreds of years now. The resistance rises and falls back over and over, from William Blake, who's work stands as warning to those who would surrender their spirits to the material world, from the romantic poetry of Keats and Shelly lamenting the despoiling of the world by a rising industrialism, to Emerson and Theroux whose transcendental musings pointed back at nature as a curative to the frenetic obsessions of urban culture. The road leads form Elisabeth Cady Stanton, Abe Lincoln, Frederick Douglas, John Muir, Gandhi, Chief Seattle, Martin Luther King and Jack and Bobby Kennedy, and now Vandana Shiva, fighting the corporate conquest of Indian agriculture, among countless others, who remind ruthless power often at their own peril that the people on the ground matter. Indeed, *the ground itself* matters.

From our distance in history looking back it is clear that this march of humanity can't be stopped by ridicule or assassination. The human spirit is an indomitable force that recedes like the tide in some periods but rises up again in great waves in others to erode the foundations of despotism bit by bit. Now the human spirit is in rebellion once again and is gathering its forces and this time a new plateau in the evolution of consciousness is coming within reach.

With the current entrance into the integral stage we have entered the age of redemption where we are now asked to bring back into our experience and values direct acknowledgement of the original healthy expression of each of the previous stages. Of course, we cannot experience the magical stage with its aural focus in the same way people did in the Paleolithic. We simply do not have the mind generated from an exclusive oral culture living in partnership with nature. What we can do is resurrect the sense of being that corresponds to that structure of consciousness and give it expression in our own way in our own time. All of the structures of consciousness that have been successively displaced by the growing sophistication of the mind never really left. They simply were downgraded in human experience. Often made suspicious, things as innocent as a sneeze arising from an involuntary spasm of the body, were thought to be vaguely "dark" in origin and so a "bless you" began to be offered as a talisman against the body's primitive and so "sinful" challenge to conscious control. As the mind has expanded in the Western world it has grown more remote from its origins and many capacities have been lost that can be recovered so as to create a new synergy, an emergent view that uses everything we have been and have come to be.

As we review the makeup of the previous structures of consciousness it is good to remember that, although each of the stages may have come before and can be seen as a progression, it is an error to suggest that one structure is superior to another. Each is necessary and contains its own world of experience and power. Evolution grows through expanding complexity, but earlier stages in time are not inferior stages in the present, that is, unless they are practiced in the degraded "deficient" mode that typified their end stage in history. As an example, the end stage of the exclusive reign of the mythological structure during the Reissuance used the mythic mind as a weapon to coerce and terrorize – *do as the Pope says or burn in hell* – as well as to inhibit the rise of rational thinking in its healthy inception. It is possible to find many people and groups still suffering from this inferior mythic mind today and unfortunately still invoking terror, but this shouldn't characterize the mythic structure in its entirety, which also has a healthy expression. With this warning in mind let us proceed to outline the basic content of the structures as it pertains to humanity's current evolution and then go on to show how each can be incorporated into an integrated life capable of delivering a fuller experience and greater satisfaction, as well as a deeper and broader understanding of what human life actually is.

The Archaic Structure of Consciousness

In the place of being from which humanity began, from a place before all that which differentiates the experience of human beings from the animal kingdom, there was the first human consciousness. It was a consciousness of pure presence, where neither yesterday nor any tomorrow existed. It was a place without judgment, without reason, without stories, only instinct to live, to eat, to breed, and to protect one's kind just as all warm blooded creatures do. This consciousness structure is one in which all that humanity can be lies dormant and in potential, but according to the view taken by Jean Gebser, is *there* in its origins. Gebser believed that here humanity was closest to the totality of the human potential, because in this state men and women were completely without the ego consciousness that separates the individual out from the whole of their nature. Therefore, human beings were, in a manner of speaking, *swimming in the sea of the origin of all things.*

This idea is rooted in the physics that suggests that everything comes into being at once, that time reveals a path through a field of infinite possibilities, all latent at the beginning, the "super position of all super positions," in terms of quantum wave form probabilities. Of course, such a concept is not entirely intelligible. It boggles the mind and is really just another story we've told ourselves to explain something we can't entirely grasp at our current level of mental development. What Jean Gebser was suggesting through applying this quantum understanding to his theory of origin is that what humanity actually is, what human growth and evolution is informed by, is this force which gave rise to the universe in the first place and continues to express itself in this dimensional field through our experience over time. It's as if that force is all on one side of the divide, this non-material energetic potential, and we are on the other side in this ego conscious, material world of human actualities. In the deep unconscious, in the place of the archaic mind, that totality is feeding into the mind as consciousness evolves over time.

Archaic humanity could not know this totality. It only felt at home in it, like a cell in a body or like any animal ensconced in its native ecosystem. This was Eden, not as a perfect place without hardship, pain, or fear, but as a place of perfect repose. Most people have noticed the calm stature of cats sitting or walking through the grass, with a kind of smooth balance and keen concentration, ever ready and yet without the slightest hint of tension. The cat may be suddenly brought to alert by an advancing dog, but after the chase is over and the cat is safely on the other side of the fence, he returns to his perfect sense of calm, almost instantly, because animals know only the reality of what's absolutely true in the moment. The cat has no place to be, no job to complete, no identity to construct, no ego to protect, nothing competes for his attention, but the ever present sense of being exactly what he is, in a life he was born to live just as he is. This sense is the archaic structure of consciousness, functioning as a quantum of life, but undivided from the universe that gave rise to it, both particle and wave, at one with creation itself.

The greatest accomplishment of humanity will be *to know this consciously* in whatever amalgam of the structures of consciousness are possible and to turn this meta-conception into a society, or what will most likely be *societies*, as different cultural approaches render different styles of origin. This, of course, is a never ending project of expression. Archaic human beings did not have an ego conscious understanding of origin but, as the title of Gebser's magnum opus tells us – we live with *the ever-present origin*. That which gave rise to the universe and us is always with us in its totality just on the other side of consciousness. Our job is to make it conscious in our own way, any way we can. This is to express the onrushing totality of what it is to be the universe in human form.

It's not as if we haven't been doing this all the way along, that is, expressing impetus from origin. But the human race has been doing it in a somewhat out of balance form, full of painful mistakes and wild detours to dead ends. This has been driven by the growth of ego consciousness and the competition that it seems to have generated. This growing sense of individuality that is the undeniable order of evolving organic life has offered much that is positive for human experience and yet has come with a heavy price. We are now at a point on the evolutionary road that this troubling adolescent phase of humanity's childhood can end. This is exactly what children do as they experiment with their new lives. As a healthy person develops and grows up there comes a time when they achieve a capacity for balance within their environment, a kind of functional repose in their work and relationships that allows them to get on with life. In a like manner the human race is moving toward a new balance, a maturity that will be informed by a direct expression of our originating energies without so much ego related dissonance. The result will be more freedom to be fully human without shame or needless limitation, to have more joy and less pain, more cooperation and less injustice and strife.

There are ways to return to the archaic structure of consciousness for some moments, to take a dip in that sea of eternal life and return with new eyes to see the world with fresh thoughts to carry a new society into being. The origin of the universe and humanity is accessible through the archaic mind in meditation or what in the West has been more often termed *contemplation*. It simply takes a return to presence with a focus that leaves behind all that civilization and social interplay has poured into the mind – to be like the cat for a short time, to watch and wait in perfect repose with nothing but the present in mind, waiting without concern for time. This leads through detached diligence to what the mythological mind has termed *the well of truth*, the spring from which the *waters of life* emerge, the *voice of God*, and so on. If one prefers a more scientific label then it can be called *interfacing with originating life parameters*, or perhaps, *cerebral downloading the universal constant*. What seems to be the case is that this *first source* is not so much a dictator but a point of balance, a stream of basic code that informs the growth of the universe, a base rhythm to write our music by, a true North by which to navigate. It doesn't make style choices. It simply presents a flow, a harmony, and people can move with the flow and harmonize with the basic heartbeat of the universe and live in grace or they can swim against the current and clash with the tone and live in strife. Life will always present its challenges, but it makes no sense to work against the grain, to essentially *take on God*, or if you like, to try to work outside the basic format of the universal operating system.

Trees look like trees because they grow within the natural parameters offered, they can do nothing else. Crystals form in geometric shapes because that is what their basic formatting compels them to do. In a like manner human beings are subject to what are essentially invisible fields of influence, but because we have free will – individual ego consciousness – unlike trees and crystals, we can deviate. There are endless choices for free will and culture to operate within the universal parameters that emerge from the foundations of existence. A regular habit of return to the archaic mind, the well of truth, is essential to align those choices with this flow. Archaic humanity could only rest in repose within the flow and follow the course, but Integral humanity will be able to utilize the realization of harmony to its origin to build this repose into a technologically advancing civilization.

THE MAGIC STRUCTURE OF CONSCIOUSNESS

In the magic stage of development, or what some theorists have called the "tribal" stage, there existed in its original flowering a mind just emerging from its immersion in nature. It was a fresh ego consciousness newly aware of itself as an individual being with a unique life, but still very much living enmeshed within an ecosystem, hunting and gathering much like their hominid ancestors, but now with the aid of rudimentary tools. It is impossible to really know how people in the magic stages of human history actually thought, but we can gain some evidence from tribal peoples today, although the comparison can only be taken so far. They, too, have evolved.

Regardless, it is a fair guess that this new sense of reflexive consciousness, where a person can mentally "see" themselves as a separate being, brought forth individuality, but an individuality still greatly connected to others and the natural environment – a personal sense of being that also included the sky and earth and animals they hunted and lived in awe of. This state would have been sensed very much as we navigate through a dream. The interwoven motifs of Celtic and Old Norse art where animals and humans and trees and dragons are all strung together offer some evidence of this worldview, mind as a "web of life."

In that first human world the inside was on a continuum with the outside, the subjective to the objective – all part of one thing, the line between the two not yet developed. This is the basis of shamanic spirituality to this day, the belief that by altering consciousness through the magic structure travel into a dream world can be accomplished where the inside mingles with the outside, allowing for direct alterations of physical ailments and conditions in the physical through the manipulation of the dream. Glimpses into the future through a *spiritual interface* are also part of the shamanic art. The physical and the "non-material" *interior* phenomena, the "spiritual" are, indeed, within the magic structure of consciousness experienced as one thing. The spiritual architecture becomes visible and a living energy that surrounds and permeates everything is acknowledged in all considerations. This level of awareness has not changed due to our evolution and it is possible to partake of this old capacity for personal edification and healing.

It is clear that our ancestors at this stage carried out rituals of concentrated mental activity that they recognized as having an effect on the future course of events. The hunt was assured by rituals beforehand that aligned the future with the intentions of the hunters showing them where they and the game would cross paths within the visions of ecstatic trance and the land itself.

As evidence from physics, parapsychology, and anthropology suggests, these ancient practitioners of magic were not just silly savages screaming at the moon for a favor, (as some ignorant ethnocentric viewpoints still maintain). They understood something about the way the invisible world works, probably because they carried with them from their previous immersion in the archaic mind sensitivities to the vast fields of energy that coordinate ecosystems, tapping information that increases survivability. The view the shaman obtains through ecstatic trance may have been easily accessible to the animal mind in the previous archaic stage of development where hominids had little self-awareness but much "eco-awareness." This interwoven one-pointed worldview, where all time was *right now*, allowed for the development of rituals that sought to manipulate the future through this connectivity. Gebser gives the example of a tribal hunting ritual where an outline of an antelope *is* drawn on the ground and an arrow shot into it. In this instant the future is brought into the present. The drawing is the antelope, not a representation, but a spiritual impression of the actual creature in a coalescence of time so that the kill becomes a *fait accompli*.

As anthropologists have reported this seems to work, so it can be assumed that ritual constitutes a kind of conscious manipulation of the entangled particles of ecological fields, or some such nonlocal coordination of event processing, or some other dynamic that conventional science has simply not deciphered. It is our first thought as "mental/rational" beings to look for a *mechanism*, but this machine model is completely inadequate to the task of deciphering the way this phenomenon operates. In any case, the magic structure of consciousness can still be used in this way. Most people are doing it without even knowing it, because it doesn't require a deliberate ritual but only seems to take prolonged attention or a short but structured intentional effort to make effects. Strong emotion seems to be a factor. This could all be done in a completely unconscious way and this is where problems can start.

First of all, this doesn't mean that everything ancestral humans did through this method was effective or that we can, through developing and utilizing this part of the human endowment, simply wish our lives into any form we like. We have no evidence to support that radical view, but it does suggest that as individuals we must be aware of the power of our minds, that our strong intentions do have an effect. We can refer back to the hundred years of parapsychology findings and *The Intention Experiment* organized by Lynne McTaggart[3] that offers a convincing demonstration, but although we have confirmed the reality of the effect, how much of an effect we live with daily we really don't know. It seems that these effects can be increased by well-practiced rituals carried on by individuals or groups of some deep conviction. Certainly the records of historical societies and current magical oriented cultures around the world would attest to such a possibility.

Instead of thinking of this part of the human endowment as "primitive" or "tribal" or some other label pulled from an attitude of condescension or some colonial frame of reference (even using the term "magic" brings to mind something childish and illusionary), we simply need to reorient ourselves to this capacity from our current evolutionary position in time. Which is to say – we need new language. We can call it "entangled mental reactivity," or anything more "scientific" sounding if it makes people more comfortable, but if you are not aware you are creating effects when you are concentrating on certain expected outcomes in your life then you may be blindly driving yourself into obstacles and ignorantly chalking it up to *bad luck*. We see this all the time when we meet very negative people who have their beliefs constantly confirmed as they encounter one disappointing event after another in their lives. Even to those unaware of this subtle mind/matter connection it is often so obvious that such negative people would do so much better with a serious "attitude adjustment."

There is a terrible *downward spiral effect* well known to mental health professionals where bad events create bad attitudes which foster more bad events, on and on, to the inevitable "crash and burn." What these ignorant individuals simply don't understand is that their intense concentration on negative outcomes actually helps to bring those events into reality. The victim makes the mistake of believing that their "luck" and their attitude are not connected, when it can be absolutely demonstrated that they most assuredly are. (This doesn't mean that all those treated badly in history had victimized themselves; it seems that sometimes the collective will of larger populations outmatch the conscious intention of individuals. Actions that harm are the responsibility of the perpetrators, because ultimately human beings are conscious actors regardless of what sort of potentiating forces may be unconsciously operating in the background.)

Athletes certainly have learned the advantage of visualizing their goals and proceeding with a strong, focused intention. Military commanders throughout history have known that morale and belief in the final victory of one's cause is everything, so one battle lost is not allowed to set the tone for the rest of the war. The great commanders and coaches of history all knew how to reverse a defeat by changing the outlook of their men, by lifting their spirits and concentrating their belief in victory. So, in this period of the emerging new consciousness we have to be alert to the effects of our attitudes, beliefs and emotions. We don't know how these mental connections work exactly. We don't know how strong they are in the given individual, but we do know that they are there. Any person capable of wresting control of their personal beliefs away from the declining status quo and their obsolete Newtonian view of the world should begin to remind themselves daily that *what you believe and concentrate on matters*.

What is suggested here is not a radical "create your own reality" philosophy as if all people lived in their own independent worlds. The planet was here before we got here. We obviously create reality together and that means everyone involved in a given event, which may very well extend to the environment itself, even animals and all living things. Certainly many tribal traditions assert that even the ocean and the mountains themselves exert a particular intelligence and power. This may sound fanciful to the person accustomed to the boundaries of materialist science, but the truth is that once you realize that these old boundaries have been ruptured long ago then we have to be open to a definition of life that flows from something *prior to matter*. The atomic particles that make up a tree or a rock are just the same as those that make up the human body, all emerging from the same energetic field, and so we have to ask where life starts? Is it only on the organic level? Only in animals or is the organic boundary simply another early arbitrary judgment become habit? Is it an anthropocentric bias perhaps: things that look more like us are alive and those that don't aren't?

We may discover in the future of a new, broader scientific view that "life" or "intelligence" is something much more complex than what we have previously considered. It may very well be that consciousness, or the essence of it, is something that takes a different form in different structures, organic and inorganic, but it is there all the same. This is precisely what the old tribal cultures tell us – the consciousness of natural objects, an ancient redwood tree, or a massive granite bolder formed in the primordial past, may not be like ours but there is something "there." Modern, Western people are only beginning to understand what a true communion with Nature really is when encountering arresting natural environments. There is a certain enlivening of spirit, even a sense of sacredness about certain moments when in touch with the beauty of nature and in those silences within there is often a yearning for greater contact with some pure source of life that seems tantalizingly just beyond the surface. The awakening mind wonders how this contact is made.

Rousseau may have sensed a lost kinship with nature and pointed Western humanity back in that direction in pursuit of a deeper morality, but Rousseau and his nature redeeming brethren of the late Renaissance looked at Nature as a kind of grand spectacle to be admired and studied in the classic Western tradition of detached observation from outside "the subject." Much of the Western tradition celebrating nature, for all its enthusiasm, is stuck in this external observing mode. Nature in this way only provides what can be empirically measured and "inspiration" that can be the source of esthetic reverie and joy, but it is an entirely different thing to go beyond the barrier of the constructed Western, formal operational mind and allow a return to the magic, primal mind of deep structure that can actually connect directly to the energetic currents within Nature itself. In this mode the surviving tribal cultures have much to teach the "advanced" cultures of the world. In this work we will not become more like them; there is no going back, but we will integrate this level of mind in a way that will expand our culture using our own terms. We will not find the "Great White Buffalo" on the plains of North America, but we will find something. It will be understood using our own language and it will enrich our culture.

We don't really know what these "intelligences" or sentient energy patterns are, but they exist at a level accessible to the magic structure of consciousness. We can learn from them just as we learn from material objects and animals at our more "ordinary" focus of attention. It may very well be that these energy patterns don't "speak" as we speak, but that within the right structure of consciousness our minds retain the primordial ability to read these patterns and translate them into images and even words. This would make sense as part of an evolutionary capacity for survival that simply taps into the subatomic field energies that hold the world together. The Australian aboriginal peoples speak of this communication as a form of dreaming, a dream that emerges from the land one steps into.

Sandra Ingerman is a psychotherapist and long-time practitioner and teacher of shamanism. She has written the following:

> Shamanism teaches that there are doorways into other realms of reality where helping spirits reside who can share guidance,

insight, and healing, not just for ourselves but for the world in which we live...since we are part of Nature, Nature itself becomes a helping spirit that has much to share with us about how to bring our lives back into harmony and balance.[4]

Modern minded people tend to hear this language with a sense of cynicism, regarding such things as "helping spirits" as primitive superstition, but if such people would simply recognize the possibility that such *autonomous energy constructs* may well exist in dimensions outside that of gross matter, dimensions well demonstrated by particle physics, then with this updated language they might reconsider the possibilities. An effort has to be made to realize that tribal peoples of the world were not, and are not, stupid savages who know nothing. They are simply people who engage reality in a different language, a different frame of mind that was discarded and disparaged by developing civilizations but valid just the same.

In retrieving the magic structure of consciousness and including it once again in our way of living in the world we will begin to heal a great wound that has slowly opened as our modern cultures have split themselves off from their core connections to the nature that gives form and substance to humanity. The mythological structure as it evolved in the West finally took the form of a celestial monotheism that put Nature in the role of the unredeemed, the wild source of all sinful impulses, and as such the home of the demonic element that it held in strict opposition to the pure goodness and holiness of heaven it found in the clean, airy realms of the sky.

This split between heaven and earth was heavily impressed on European consciousness during the reign of the Popes. Then the Enlightenment, as it was articulated by Rene Descartes, subjected the Western mind to the same split into a different form – this time as a split between mind and matter. The human mind swallowed whole the archetypal powers of what previously were thought to belong to gods and goddesses. The world of matter was now rid of demons, but condemned to the level of a dumb, soulless machine. This cultural foundation went on to push humanity toward a radical split from Nature to the detriment of the environment and a healthy balance of the human mind.

There is a longing in modern man and woman, a painful void that is the broken connection with Nature. It manifests as depression and a vague feeling of a *paradise lost* that has been misunderstood by psychoanalysis as a remembrance of an idyllic childhood. In part it underlies the drive to war so potent in many young men. War is the great adventure and decent into the *heart of darkness* that has been shut out from modernity, but calls to us with its wild intensity. War is the return of the repressed and the magic structure in its most deficient mode. In bringing the magic structure back into alignment with the sources of human sanity the consequences of the heaven/earth split can be healed in individuals and in time our entire civilization and as it happens war will lose its fascination.

What this means for the individual is the necessity of spending time in Nature – not a park, but areas where natural processes have alone been allowed to shape the land. This is done in order to find the external equivalent of the original face of Nature within. Only by immersing oneself in a purely wild environment can a person hope to reinvigorate the vital connection with Nature that is the original human experience that provides the foundations for all healthy human existence. The wilderness is the original foundation on which all civilization is built, and as such, contains the basic primal sources for, what Ken Wilber calls, "the big three," that are Plato's the good, the true, and the beautiful, or in other words: morals, logic, and art.

In the wilderness we find the primordial definitions and in the magic structure of consciousness we find a method for interpreting them. It is not a mental/rational reduction of the thing to primary pieces and then erecting a theory from tracing the physical relationship of the parts. The magic structure interpretation emerges from taking the thing on as a whole, through the guts and the subtle level feeling states therein which provide a knowing unknown to mathematical reasoning. The person does not come away with an "answer" to a "problem." They come away with something out there having been provided and something within having responded and in so doing a kind of *sacred marriage* has occurred that doesn't connect the inside to the outside so much as it demonstrates a resonance between the two awaking what is common to all. This remembrance of the origin in Nature grounds the individual in the basics of life on earth. Without this grounding we cannot know what is truly good for us or what morality really means. We lose touch with beauty as an experience when it becomes a judgment. The big three become muddled and end up in abstractions so remote from life that experts must be educated for years just to explain it to everybody else. Civilizations trace a departure from Nature. They begin as derivative structures based on Nature, but after thousands of years find, as we have in the West, that the original source of life has been lost. This does not indicate a necessity to return to the society of a former era but does necessitate a bringing forward something left behind. When civilizations are crashing, a return to source is the first step in getting back on track to creating healthy structures for the continued advance of the creative impulse that is evolution.

As the magic stage of historical development ran down and became deficient in the face of a rising mythological mind, this sort of activity was deemed improper. The social program has always been to break free from the previous stage of consciousness when a new stage was arising, so at this juncture in the evolution of consciousness we find the shamanic trance interaction with nonmaterial intelligences condemned for the average person as a specialized priest class took over the relationship with the invisible world. After all, it was a source of power in the information gained. In the early civilizations Nature continued to have a place in the expanding mind and heart of humanity, but in time the crucial connection was lost as the priests carried on their rituals in a rote manner that became empty gestures to powers now remote and unknown. The evolving mind became awakened to the stars, sought to understand their influence and so discovered mathematical patterns. Gods took up residence in the high places, on mountain tops and in the clouds. Urbanized societies began to think of the powers of nature as something external to the city walls and the walls of their own skin. The gods and goddesses of the earth became the stuff of tales of a magical time long ago when super beings walked the earth. Certain cults arose in Greece that spread throughout the ancient world to offer the populace a way to maintain a connection with the waning original powers of nature, to understand the forces of creation within the individual through cults of wild ecstasy in intoxication and lust.

What we are now attempting is to return to this reservoir of evolutionary power and reconnect with its capacities on new terms. Most, in integrating the magic structure, will only use the potential of the magic mind to access their own deeper wisdom for health and life guidance, but some will carry on the shamanic enterprise in investigating the esoteric capacities within the world of what the yogic tradition in India calls the "subtle" realm, and what shamanism calls, the spirit world. The subtle is simply that level of life that is closest to us, but beyond our senses, nature under the surface.

The magic structure of consciousness gives special attention to the sense of hearing and so is also the home of music. It is the strings of our hearts and souls that are played by the musician through tones that resonate with psycho/emotional structures in our bodies. The sound of the world was the first music: wind in the trees, the cry of birds, the howl of wolfs on the hunt, game animals crunching through the underbrush, the trickle and crash of water in the river and creek, the booming voice of the sky as the thunder heads loomed out of the distance. These sorts of sounds made up the repertoire of the earth in its primal song and humanity was exquisitely attuned to its melodies. Human beings then learned to make their own thunder to send signals over distances through pounding on a hollow log, no doubt, and in time found a myriad of ways to mimic the sounds of nature. It all led to music, from chant to song to symphony, humanity has created its own sound track since the early days of consciousness.

Music is not intellectual. When sound is made with an intellectual intent it ceases to be music, because music is the evocation of love and fear, anticipation, ecstasy and longing, excitement and wonder. It is the sound of human feeling in all its colors and temperatures, fire in the belly and joy in the heart forming the foundations of an appreciation for life itself. Emotion is the body's way of interpreting life. Without this vital connection to this basic structure of consciousness we become "all up in our heads." The man or woman who surrenders to this extreme cerebral dominance becomes as cold as a list of numbers, all axioms and rules and formulas for life. These people who have lost touch with the magic are always failures at anything but official business, or academic relationships. They make excellent bureaucrats, engineers and officials of one sort or another but they are terrible spouses or parents. The degree to which they are split off from the understanding of their own emotional level of feeling in the magic structure will be the degree to which they will be unable to relate effectively to others on a "human" level. It is now clear that intelligence is not just intellect, but includes an "emotional I.Q." that is essential for a complete life.[5]

Our emotions act not only as barometers to our own reactions to personal matters, but also can be used as a sense organ. Just like our skin can sense temperature, emotion can alert a person to conditions on the invisible subtle level in any environment they may enter. It is not unusual for a sensitive person to notice that "something heavy" has gone on in a particular place, perhaps an intense argument just previous to their arrival. People notice that they feel good in some places and bad in others regardless of the physical attributes in how the room is decorated or other cues. Some people can sense dishonesty in others, as well as sincerity. Being able to attune oneself to the subtle level can be extremely helpful.

This basic, foundational structure also allows for the ability to be lost in a story, to fall into the created reality of a novel or a film. Anthropologists call this tendency when applied to their study of human cultures the participation mystique. This tendency to fall into entrainment to a piece of music, a story, dance or ritual, also applies to whole cultures where the mind falls into the pattern of life created by the routines and rituals of that society. In its strongest form this tendency can be exploited by advertisers to put people into mild trance states that are more susceptible to suggestions to buy certain products or simply associate certain brands with good things, so that when the person is next in the grocery store they get a good feeling about a certain laundry soap and they really don't know why. In this example the person is reacting to a suggestion loaded into their subconscious that is triggered by the image of the product. This trick is a mild form of brain washing that seeks to supplant the person's own deeper sense as discussed above with a suggestion from the advertiser. To be well versed in this level of consciousness allows a person to know the difference and to avoid the commercial conditioning in the first place.

The use of the magic structure of the mind to manipulate entire crowds is most poignantly illustrated in Adolf Hitler's speeches on the zeppelin field where the films reveal a wide eyed trance state across a sea of faces. The Nazis were very good at the manipulation of symbols and environments in order to create high drama and the deep stimulation of root structures in the mind by setting up giant ritual spaces in which to pull the participants into mental entrainment with the leader's words. One can see this effect occurring in our own time when people become overly emotional about the flag and find themselves spouting a kind of irrational, blind patriotism that amounts to an unthinking "blood oath" to the country in what is essentially a tribal response completely out of place in a modern society with pretentions to a democracy requiring critical thinking on the part of its citizens. Politics is not an area where the tribal, or magic, structure of consciousness is appropriate. When you find yourself slipping into this level of cognition during ads or political events you are in danger of being manipulated. The half-time show at the Super Bowl or the opening and closing *ceremonies* at the Olympics also offer examples of mass rituals that make powerful suggestions to viewers. It can be quite interesting to review the video from some of these events with an eye towards spotting the ritual and the symbolic message.

This is the level of mind where Carl Jung came to understand archetypal symbols to have their most potent reception.[6] The archetypes as Jung theorized are the images of primordial experience, the way that the unconscious has stored the basic categories of thought that both shaped and were filled out by evolutionary experience and that are the psychological heritage of humanity residing in what he termed the "collective unconscious." Jung equated the basic structure of archetypes on the psychological level to physical elements within the body that inform structure on the biological level. The crucial thing to understand about archetypes is that these root psychological image complexes can be "activated" from the outside and when this happens the associated feelings and impulses can have an unconscious effect on conscious control, (and this is where the magic starts to blend into the mythic). Most people know the obvious effects of common symbols like the cross or the skull and cross bones, but few understand the subtle psychology of the image of the rising sun, or a coiled serpent, or a mountain. Anyone truly interested in how their unconscious mind can be stimulated through imagery to invoke feelings and thoughts for purposes other than their own should begin at least a cursory review of symbols and begin looking for them in their environment. Many are greatly surprised to discover the large number of corporate logos that include ancient symbols of power. Most people are completely ignorant as to how these symbols operate on their unconscious, believing erroneously that they are aware of all influences and always in control.

In a like manner, it has been shown in popular reviews of subliminal advertising the degree to which sexual imagery is utilized in an attempt to link sexual desire with a given product, usually alcohol. Sex is one of the most powerful ways to manipulate people as it is also part of the most basic instinctual level of consciousness where the body takes president over the mind. Sex is a great human mystery, a joy that is part of any healthy lifestyle, but because its functioning borders on unconsciousness it is also a way into a person's subconscious. Any kind of imagery where sexual figures are combined with other things must be carefully inspected for exactly what the creator of the image is trying to sell you, exactly what string they are trying to pull. Sex is also a doorway to higher states of consciousness and has been used for thousands of years in the East as a yoga to access illumination experiences, which is to say, more information from a higher/broader view of existence.[7] To move into the higher mysteries of sex one has to be able to give oneself completely over to the deeper energies that start in the archaic structure of consciousness, but quickly move into the depths of the human body/mind to the energetic core where the underlying connection with the source of existence lies. These terms may sound mystical because they are, ecstatic sex being one of those areas where language fails and the mind experiences something that, like all higher states of consciousness, cannot be explained to others; only personal experience will do.

To truly discover all that the magic structure of consciousness has to offer one needs to learn to open up a relationship with that world in all its many facets. A person doesn't have to be an expert traveler of the emotional currents or a yogic adept, but simply needs to become conversant with their own emotional and physical being. To do so allows for the solidifying of the first foundational structure of consciousness. Although there is no absolute order, the redeeming of the magic structure can then allow more progress in what was the next "higher" development in our historical progression.

The Mythic Structure of Consciousness

Imagination finds its home in myth. Where sound and emotion were at the center of the magic mind, image and psyche are primary in the mythic structure of consciousness. These take form in story, the stories humanity has always created to explain reality are the imagination at work creating culture and order out of chaos. The archetypes become elaborated and extended from primordial image complexes to narrative structure seen in the world in the form of heroic events. Archetypes have no exact form or story and so they are endlessly developed through time. The "great mother" archetype appears in many different guises from earth mother goddess, pregnant with the life of the entire world, to individualized tales of feminine figures bestowing food, like the corn goddess of the Southwestern Native American tribes, to figures of deadly enticement, like the Greek Diana the huntress, to goddesses of ultimate sexual desire, like Aphrodite, to Mary, mother of the living, dying, and resurrected Christ.

In the mythic mind time is a circle where seasons follow one another in an eternal round. Light and dark flow one into the other and everything in life is seen in this polarity. The yin and yang circular symbol of the East is the classic model. In this world life has a certain fatalistic pull, nothing can stop the tide, or the night, or the winter and nothing can stop what will become of the heroic ego that in the end must succumb to death. This polar dynamic within the mythic structure allows for a certain relaxed acceptance of the ultimate processes in life that go on forever, around and around, without need of human exertion. A celebration of human participation in the greater round of universal forces is part of the mythic experience and forms the basis of the environment through which the exploits of the emerging heroic ego moves. This mythic landscape is a good place to allow the center of mind to rest while taking on the rational exploits of the modern hero who finds him or herself often stressed and daunted by the need to out race death with constant achievement. As the mythic circle spins there is a still point at the center where peace resides in the midst of tumult. The circle of life is the beginning and the foundation of everyone's story and there is a rhythm that is achieved in a life in harmony with its flow that allows for an unhurried accomplishment proceeding from the authentic structure of a person's life rather than as an assignment from the accelerating mental/rational machine.

Everybody needs a story and all stories are provisional. They are provisional in that all explanations are dependent on a person's developmental capacity. The degree to which their mind has developed allows for the sort of story they can conceive of. When the mind develops further, the stories become more involved reflecting that development. Somewhere in the misty annals of time the magic structure of consciousness began to break open to allow a broader view. The human mind began to comprehend larger possibilities. What was before a worldview dominated by a reverence for the animal powers on which the tribe depended for their sustenance became a world view that saw a more intricate plan behind it all. So were born the gods and goddesses, the super beings that shaped human destiny as parents shape the lives of their children, and so was born the heroic human ego that challenged those gods for the right to guide the people's destiny.

It appears that the first great mythological stories began with the conception of the mother goddess as the source from which all life sprang. A "Great Mother," who stood behind all the birth of the world, inseminated by the male aspect in the rain clouds, who was a secondary figure to the mother goddess. The Goddess seemed to have reigned supreme for thousands of years to the point where a new male dominated conception of worldly and heavenly power arose somewhere between 3000 to 2000 BCE. Where women were associated with the earth goddess, men were associated most often with sky gods and the source of rain and thunder. As the mind expanded this male aspect came to be linked with the struggle to wrest consciousness away from immersion in Nature, the sky god seemed to be revolting against the dominance of the earth goddess. This struggle can be understood as the rise of the next phase of ego development and consciousness. Where the goddess focused on nurturance of the community that demanded strict adherence to her requirements, the growing individuality of the ego pushed against these demands in planting edible plants where human beings wanted rather than where Nature had put them. Later, the growing heroic ego would cease carrying skins of water from the river to irrigate the crops, but would divert the river itself in canals that bent the goddess to the designs of humanity, rather than humanity taking what was offered without question. On this path great stone cities came to be built.

More room to move was allotted to humanity as we progressed, but as we have seen previously this progress carried with it hazards such as the type that arose with Sargon of Akkad and his ilk. The ego unleashed from natural restrictions can become predatory and elitist. The human mind as it grew more independent from instinct and the nature-embedded consciousness of the magic mind began to identify the body and its instinctual fears and desires as an enemy to this burgeoning free will. In the evolution of the great mythologies of the world we see the first gods and goddesses being earth based in their authority. The mother goddess was primary and the moon bull, her consort, was the secondary element that waxed and waned, came and went while the Great Mother was perpetual. Then in a great shift toward the high mythological stage the evolving mind produced a second set of gods and goddesses of the sky, the Asir of the Teutonic/Norse pantheon is exemplary: Odin, Thor, Freya, and the rest rose beyond the earth to live across the rainbow bridge on the celestial throne of Asgard. Just as Zeus and his retune on Mt.

Olympus conquered the Titans of the earth, these deities gave power to men in their quest to move beyond the basic dictates of a life in thrall to nature and set history on the course of adventure. Homer's *Odyssey* is one classic tale of the opening of the Western mind to a world populated by mythological friends and foes that is the melding of the world of that which is inside to that which is outside.

Joseph Campbell quotes Novalis to this end: "The seat of the soul is there, where the inner and the outer worlds meet." Campbell further tells us that, "From the outer world the senses carry images to the mind, which do not become myth, however, until there transformed by fusion with accordant insights, awakened as imagination from the inner world of the body." This realized connection of the subjective life world of humanity to the objects of this world as a process starts with the first limited horizons of the people of the tribe, the extended clan groups that often saw themselves as the only "real" or "true" people with their tribal name often simply translated as "the human beings," and the land they inhabited seen as the sacred land, the only "real" place. A modern day example of this tribal mind in action was seen in the Vietnam War where it was common among soldiers to refer to the U.S. as "the world," as in: "When I get leave, I'm going back to *the world*." Vietnam, a land without movie theaters and hamburger joints, of water buffalo and rice paddies, was a lesser place, not quite "real," to the provincial mindset of the average American soldier.

Historically, as humanity moved into the high mythological stage within the imperial stone cities that brought different peoples together as they were dominated by the new warrior kings, the horizon of the mythic human mind broadened. At the time of these first cosmopolitan megalithic civilizations the human mind shifted its focus from the land and the earth gods to the stars as the most significant sacred mystery to be studied and revered. The stars and planets ruled over everyone, no matter where you first grew up on the land. The emperors and pharos of these ancient times sought to synchronize their world with the heavenly bodies associating themselves with different celestial objects becoming, "the son of the sun," and such things, as well as building their structures to reflect the sky. We find, for instance, thanks to the work of Egyptologist, Robert Bauval, that the pyramids are aligned according to the stars on Orion's belt.

The pitfall for the mythological structure of mind for the individual now is to fail to recognize that the significance of these outward objects invested as they are with human imagination is not absolutely tied to the object itself. The sun is a celestial object that is a quantifiable material source of power and is also the symbol of an archetype of psychological "light" or realization, and so the sun is also within us. That aspect that is within is portable. The "enlightenment" provided by that inner sun need not be tied to a religious reverence for the *actual* sun. This, people figured out quite a while ago. Unfortunately many have yet to figure out that other "power" objects in their lives are equally invested with imagination that is portable so that, for instance, a person's dignity does not have to reside in the magical robes of designer label clothing or a glowing luxury car. Equally so, such things as "the promised land," and "the holy land," and "God's country" are not actual places on earth to the exclusion of all other places, but are anywhere the individual chooses to place their own sacred judgment on the land. This revelation that says, "home is where the heart is," represents another step in the expansion and evolution of consciousness, but we are living in an age where many are still prone to the error of the literal mythological reading, while still another group is prone to the error of the literal materialist reading. The first fails to understand metaphor – that the realization of a power in the earth or sky is a realization of a power within humanity. The second fails to understand that just because an analysis of the dirt in some mythological holy land renders nothing special this doesn't mean that the original revelation of power and glory there was nonsense.

The integral view knows that both are right in their specific expertise, but wrong in their extended judgments that violate the boundaries of their vision. Materialistic science knows nothing of the "seat of the soul," this place, "where the inner and the outer worlds meet." And tribal religious views can't quite get high enough on the mountain to see beyond their limited worldview where they're convinced there really is something special about certain patches of dirt that make them more holy. This isn't to say that real differences don't exist in various locations on Earth. Of course they do, not only in climate, terrain, flora and fauna and such things, but in energetic subatomic phenomenon such as magnetic fields and other forces discernible to human physical and psychic perception. However, these differences should not make a place any more "holy" than any other, in the larger sense of the term. The view that transcends this limited "holy ground" view is well conveyed by the Medieval Hermetic text, *The Book of the Twenty-Four Philosophers*, which tells us, "God is an infinite sphere, whose center is everywhere and circumference is nowhere."[8]

Another complicating reality that hinders this larger understanding of mythology is that often mythological stories are bound up with actual, material world references to actual historical figures, real places and events. This is how the mythological structure of mind works, as Joseph Campbell has explained: the outside objects and action of the world are met and colored by the imagination, which gives meaning and order to experience. Of course we find real places and people in the *Bible* and the city of Troy, long thought to be a "myth," turns out to be a real place, but this doesn't mean that all elements of these stories are *literally, materially, true*. Being not "materially true" doesn't mean they cannot be true in a different way.

This is the conundrum of the mental/rational structure applied deficiently – it mistakenly leads to erroneous conceptions regarding the nature of truth, which it insists must be demonstrated by matter and observed objectively. But the lives of history have not been made up of simple material. They have been driven by the truths of human conceptions, cultural formations, and psyche, and these things are without end and impossible to climb out of through any amount of "scientific objectivity." The philosopher Emanuel Kant spent hundreds of pages in his *Critique of Pure Reason* demonstrating in painstaking detail why no final objectivity can ever be reached. Science may deliver certain facts about the world, but the approach for deriving those findings and how they are interpreted are both subject to imagination, which is always and forever a product of culture and evolutionary development. At the same time, as discussed earlier, it is clear that mind and matter and the course of events on earth are mysteriously bound up together, thus the idea of "objectivity" itself suggests a theory of reality that has been supplanted by a "participatory" model.

So we see the progress of humanity carried by the rise of the mythological view, the great stories of gods and heroic people who shaped the future according to their will, a will patterned on the powers of the earth and heavens. This was an evolving mythology that transcended, first the local sphere of the tribe, then the greater sphere of the stars, then to adopt a view of an entirely abstract god whose home is beyond the stars and finally everywhere at once. Women, unfortunately, in many societies did not fare so well in this new system where human power apart from the earth gods came to be exclusively associated with masculinity. The male sky god ceased to have a body and rejected all that came with one in favor of a "higher mind." Women were left in the instinctual "inferior" role as they were tied to the act of birth as representatives of the great mother. With the rise of rationalism this would change. Women could successfully argue this prejudice that cast them as irrational, instinctual creatures was associated with arbitrary, discredited, mythological thinking. Such thinking that illustrates the dark side of the mythological mind – that is the human tendency to institutionalize early revelations so that once a story is laid down and associated with some "divine" source then great wrongs can be perpetrated in the name of "heaven" or "tradition," or established "truths." It must be remembered that the revelation is portable, so that women, once the goddess incarnate, need not be representatives of birth, sexual attraction, milk and sustenance indelibly. Biology need not be destiny for the liberated mind. The Goddess can appear when appropriate for those who know; just as the "holy land" can follow you beneath your feet. Stories carry great power. In investigating the mythological structure of our minds on our way to the integral view we must examine all the stories our lives are based on and use discernment as to their current value in the light of a broadening human freedom. In doing so we should not lose our "sacred" way of seeing, only the tribal taboos that limit it.

We have family stories and neighborhood, community stories. We have regional stories, and national stories and stories as a civilization and as a species. They all are true in the effects they create. They all are partial and they all will be replaced by a greater wisdom in the future. This is the paradox of story: it is a temporary explanatory model, it is order out of chaos, a way of reassuring ourselves that we have a handle on life. What is "right" in one era becomes "wrong" in the next, but when it was right, it was very, very right, and a whole world sprung from that conviction. Take the world of the flat earth at the center of God's galaxy of stars and planets. The universe had order in what was known as *the Great Chain of Being*, from the highest regions of heaven through legions of angelic hosts down to humans and animals below them and at the bottom a hell. It was a fantastic tale, a magnificent story that ordered the universe and as such gave great solace to people everywhere; it's nice to know where you are. Some version of the great chain appeared in all the high cultures of the world, East and West.

Then along came Copernicus and Galileo and the chain was shattered. The story gave way, after many battles, to a new story rendered by a new method of obtaining knowledge. In actuality it wasn't totally new. People had been reasoning things out for a long time, since Mesopotamia, the Indus River civilizations, Egypt and the Greeks, but now reason took on a weight and thrust unseen in history. A method was developed by Galileo, Newton, Descartes, and then Francis Bacon that would narrow the scope of human myth making quite a bit. Now we live in the West primarily by the stories provided by science and we believe them just as fervently as our ancestors believed the stories provided by earlier mythological conceptions of the universe. We are just as sure that our stories are true and the earlier stories were wrong as the mythic mind was sure it was right and the old magic cultures were wrong before them. The Greeks referred to those outside their cultural realm still living in the magic mind as "troglodytes" a disparaging term that meant something like: cave men, or morons. The scientific mind sees those holding religious views as troglodytes today and fails to differentiate the tribal prejudices of some religious views from the higher spirituality that actually subsumes science itself within its integral multi-dimensional, transpersonal sphere.

Are our stories true? They are as true as any one person's can be, because all stories are true within a limited perspective. Some stories may be true only in a personal perspective, but they all have their range of authority depending on the disposition of the reader or the one hearing them. The literalness of a story as a marker of truth is a recent and very narrow way to understand those truths most crucial to humanity. Joseph Campbell put it like this:

> The distinguishing first function of a properly read mythology is to release the mind from its native fixation on such false ideas, which are of material things as things-in-themselves. Hence, the figurations of myth are metaphorical...in two senses simultaneously, as bearing (1) *psychological*, but at the same time (2) *metaphysical*, connotations. By way of this dual focus the psychologically significant features of any local social order, environment, or supposed history, can become transformed through myth into transparencies revelatory of transcendence.[9]

By this definition fantasies sometimes contain the greatest truths, as the work of James Joyce suggest, or even in our contemporary mythology in something like the *Star Wars* movies, where the hero goes into the dark cave to fight his nemesis and discovers that it is himself. Some novels, like Steinbeck's *The Grapes of Wrath*, were not true as if reporting on known people, but represented *a truth* in the lives of real people and so had a powerful effect on the public of his day. It didn't matter that it was fiction; it was a story that told a hidden truth that moved an entire society. Even though the ruthless powers that were exposed by it called him a liar, the public knew truth when they read it and he won the Nobel Prize in literature for it. Science has always claimed that its stories were different, but as discussed earlier, its stories turn out to be limited to perspective as well, as the "laws" of universal motion laid down by Sir Isaac Newton have, too, turned out to cease to matter at the quantum level of particle physics where a new story takes over. The more we grow and evolve the more our stories grow with us.

In integrating the mythological structure of our minds it is important to closely examine the stories that shape our lives. A person may discover stories they carry about themselves that do not serve their desire for a full, meaningful life, full of love and accomplishment. People carry stories created while growing up that may limit them unnecessarily. We all carry a "personal mythology," that often needs revision, if we are to reach our potential as individuals for ourselves and for what we can contribute to our families and communities, which is where the most important stories are written. "Your personal mythology acts as a lens that colors your perceptions according to its own assumptions and values. It highlights certain possibilities and shadows others. Through it you view the ever-changing panorama of your experiences in the world."[10]

We carry myths around our race and myths about our nations; all of it is up for revision. We can't change the past, but this is the crucial point: *stories provide the format for the future* – if you want to change course, you must change the guiding principle within the story you live by. The great scholar of mythology, Joseph Campbell, once said that he could tell immediately the mythology by which anyone lived simply by asking them for their description of reality. Simply by hearing what a person believes is true, the stories they are using to guide their lives are revealed. The prime lesson of the mythological structure is that truth is not a static concept when it comes to human belief and destiny. So many people are not defeated by life, as they believe, but are defeated by what they believe to be true about their life.

The mental/rational structure of consciousness epitomized in the scientific endeavor is fixated on establishing truth, once and for all. Although we can be fairly sure that gravity is a truth that will generally operate as expected, most of what we have identified as "truth" will one day be scrapped. A thousand years from now our carefully collected "facts" will be a source of humor to our distant progeny. We will be the troglodytes then, the primitives who battled their own shadows and saw solidity where there was only vapor. All this will not matter, because life is not measured by the "facts" but rather by the progress of our souls, the soul of humanity as it journeys through the evolutionary experience. Today's "facts" whether eternal or not, produce the substance of our culture and with this human beings look deeper into the grand possibilities for life. Cultures are momentary experiments in creative function seeking greater life, joy and beauty, achieved through a particular perspective and belief. Cultures are at their most vibrant when exploring an unbounded perspective free from false judgments based on "final truths." As societies progress their founding beliefs begin to close in on them as the limits of their vision become apparent. When this happens the society begins to live by these self-imposed limits they have mistaken for final truths that in actuality are really only yesterday's dogmas projected into the heavens. This historical moment opens an age of anxiety and signals the beginning of the next developmental, evolutionary step toward a new society.

The gods of science condemn humanity just as readily as the old punishing god of the desert fathers. The old time religion has their apocalypse and orthodox science has their meaningless universe destine to collapse into "heat death," as entropy delivers the final blow to us all. These self-defeating nihilistic stories do nothing but rob the individual of the drive to create a better future. It is a constant task at hand in staying healthy at the mythological structure of our consciousness not to fall prey to this tendency to shackle ourselves to absolutes. The multitude of spurious myths spewed out by popular culture with regard to "human nature" is a major area for review in this work. Violence and greed so often attributed to human nature will be found to be largely a function of culture and poverty, material and or spiritual.

The entire existentialist movement ran the Western philosophical tradition into a dark room from which it has never completely emerged due to the idea, following the scientific doctrine, that all of life is a meaningless accident and as such human striving itself can be nothing but absurd. No wonder Jean-Paul Sartre entitled one of his works, *Nausea*. There are so few absolute ideas we can depend on and those we can, like death and change, are easily fit into a myriad of stories, some will favor us and others will lead us to nothing. The story, the myth, is the map we make for the territory we will discover. We make worlds through our endless creativity and industry and so we must pick our myths carefully, personally and as a people, because they allow us to see the possibilities and they blind us to everything a story does not include and cannot name.

THE MENTAL/RATIONAL STRUCTURE OF CONSCIOUSNESS

To refresh the reader's memory the terms are here again defined. The mental/rational mode of consciousness is made up of two major structures: the "mental" aspect is experienced in the perception of space as a three dimensional field the modern observer believes themselves to be inhabiting, a space that goes on to infinity, as well as the tendency to quantify that space, as in measurement of distance, volume, and weight, and in time as hours and days going into a limitless future. The "rational" aspect then applies this quantified spatial model to everything as an abstraction that renders an understanding, such as when a person says "I'm carrying a heavy load," even when their work is entirely digital and weighs nothing at all. They might equally say, "I've got a long way to go to finish," where there actually is no distance involved. Everything is understood in this spatial measurement frame of reference and this way of thinking produces, like all the structures of consciousness, a certain psychology and experience. To be *rational* is to perceive and utilize this quantified structure in planning and decision making.

Human beings have probably always used the mental capacity for reason to solve small problems for themselves. Certainly making the first stone tools and weapons required some logical reasoning skills, but the world and life itself did not begin to be scrutinized with reason it seems until the pre-Socratic philosophers began to apply reason and logic to the larger questions of life that had previously been answered through mythological scenarios. This was but the first glimpse of mental reasoning that would not come into its own as a full blown, systematic method for describing and working with the material world in the West until the Enlightenment in the 17th Century. The East has had its own relationship with reason that reaches far back into antiquity, but reason and mythology in the East became bound up with one another in a way they did not in the West – where one was pitted against the other and where reason finally triumphed as an exclusive world view.

What happened with the Western way during the rise of the mental/rational structure of consciousness was that, in Gebser's terms, the mythological circle was broken and perception expanded out into a limitless space. Human beings began to see themselves as living, not in a vital, feeling eco-scape, as in the magic mode, nor within the imaginative story land of heavens, hells, and middle-earth, as in the mythological mode, but suddenly thrust out into the vast, endless, void of space itself. This space, devoid of quality, was to be comprehended through abstract numbers alone and those numbers would become preeminent as the greatest path to knowledge. In time this engineering of space would break out of its proper technological role to take over the way people live and so introduce the deficiency that would lead to the chronic anxiety of our age. It will be the goal of this section to work through that deficiency.

It isn't as though the mythological or magical minds have disappeared. They have not, but the rational has been held up as the only true road to knowledge for centuries. Western humanity has grown slowly trapped by the narrow confines of this one, lone faculty. Rationality is, of course, a necessity. Without it we would be in sad shape with regard to solving all the simple, material challenges our lives present and the greater technical accomplishments our civilization continues to solve broadens the possibilities for everyone. There are many instances where a purely rational approach is best, such as fixing a car or building a bridge. We need not spend time here going over what is abundantly illustrated all over the modern world. It is, after all, a giant exercise in the mental/rational structure of consciousness. This being true, that reason has given us so much, it is also equally true that reason, improperly applied, can also take away so much more. In the current decline of Western Civilization we can trace many eroding influences to the end of the functional application of reason, the economic system being the most glaring recent example.

Within the personal realm of a single mind it is a necessity to take inventory of all the ways we approach the challenges of our time with an eye to discovering where reason should be applied and where it should not. Reason is simply the logical application of a mental strategy for understanding and utilizing structure to accomplish a given goal. Understanding the structure and dynamics of electricity allows a person to utilize its power to accomplish a creative end, say, moving an object. Reason thinks in terms of linear causality, one thing leads to another, and so we can use our reason to plot a course for ourselves. It is simply foolish to live a life devoid of reason.

This being so, it is also essential to realize that it is equally foolish to live a life dominated by reason. This tendency has led to frustrating dead ends for Western thought; reason is a tool, but does not reveal purpose in anything under its lens. If a person looks for purpose with reason they will be forever thwarted, because purpose cannot be divined from a mechanistic analysis of parts within the structure of things. Reason leads to odd assumptions about the meaning of life in that it only reveals what something does as a matter of basic physical operation. So, we end up with strange declarations by scientists that say, for instance, people are simply complicated systems for digesting proteins and passing on genes. This obviously has nothing to do with purpose or meaning. Maintaining physiology and reproduction are simply the base level of creation that make higher level functions like creativity and culture possible. To conclude that physiological functions are somehow the point is to make certain errors of logic that seem to result from looking in the wrong end of the telescope. Regardless, this peculiar reason that science maintains in following functions back to their beginnings and finding purpose there alone is the official doctrine. A doctrine to be avoided in one's personal life.

Given everything we know about physics and the course of history it seems a more cogent understanding that the physical body is a vehicle that allows for the human spirit, or *conscious energy complex*, to operate in the density of our three dimensional space/time condition that came into existence with the Big Bang (which is where mythology meets reason). Certainly, it is true the purpose of a boat is to do more than float and the purpose of a human life is to do more than exist and reproduce. Reason only reveals structure, not purpose.

We cannot know the ultimate purpose for human existence, as frustrating as this might be to the old scientific or philosophic view. Purpose is revealed through us as we develop and carry on the creative impulse that has been present from the beginning of time and continues to push evolution and human activity forward. What is being revealed is not finished revealing itself, so obviously, it is a bit premature to talk about final purposes.

If we can say anything with complete confidence about the purpose of the universe we can only say that it is a system for endless creation. The individual human life is part of that revelation and reason is properly applied as the tool for making dreams actual. When it replaces the dream, in a life or a society, then the life and society grows sullen. It is the dream, the creative source within humanity, that is the proper subject for evaluating purpose and that is something for each person to consider, rather than a subject for scientific enquiry, which is simply a study of structure from a very narrow, materialistic, linear and mechanistic perspective. Asking a traditional scientist the purpose for human existence or life in general is like asking an auto mechanic for their opinion on the purpose of a car. They could tell you many things about how the car operates, but the only answer they could possibly give as to purpose would be *to take you from one place to another*. Unfortunately, orthodox science, in its effort to replace the role of the church in human affairs, has often mistaken its method as an unlimited tool for divining truth. This it is not. Without making any errors in logic and in all sincerity the honest scientist could only answer that human life seems to be for providing a means of greater creation, like a car, it seems to be going someplace. Where you choose to go in your human vehicle is very much in your own hands. Where we choose to go as a people is very much in the hands of society as a whole and reason and intellect will be an important but not the sole mode of getting "there."

The main limit of the mental/rational mode as applied to existence is that it prescribes a method for observation in understanding anything that places the observer, he or she who considers, *outside actual experience*. That is, intellect applied rationally positions itself separately from the thing being observed or subject considered so that all ideas derived from this mode of inquiry do not take into consideration any feeling, intuitive, esthetic, or relational information regarding the subject. It is viewed the way old naturalist studies viewed butterflies pinned to a board. This creates a detached, non-experiential, understanding that seeks to uncover mechanism at the expense of comprehending the subjective whole. This presents big problems to those who limit their considerations of life and the world to this purely rational view due to the fact that it is entirely partial, superficial and, taken alone, turns the world into a mathematical formula devoid of quality. It is the "tour bus" view of the world, the museum understanding, that is set apart from the living experience of a thing. A person can study Italian culture for many years, for instance, go to museums and look at artifacts and view films and pictures of Italy, even take a tour and see the external structure of Italian architecture and society, but until they actually go and live in an Italian village, learn to speak some of the language, interact with the people and take part in their customs and routines, they will never really begin to understand the living, breathing, vital nature of Italian culture. This is a destination to which reason's bus will not take you. The same is true of any aspect of life on earth. Unfortunately, the standard of our age has been to stay aloof from the subject so as to examine. This sort of participation in life processes is precisely what has been distained in anthropology, for instance, as "going native," a mistake thought to destroy the researcher's scientific "objectivity."

Jean Gebser saw this gathering alienating systematizing tendency in Western civilization as an element of the deficient end phase of the current reign of the mental/rational structure. Gebser drew attention back to the fact that the term "rational" is derived from "ratio," which speaks to the "dividing" aspect, seeking, from the classic orthodoxy of the scientific view to examine pieces of something in an effort to understand the function of the whole. As discussed previously, this view has value, but a value that is limited. Once a society takes this method beyond its functional range then it begins, in Gebser's terms, to "denature" its experience and begins a track toward greater and greater isolation. It is against nature, because this way of interpreting life takes no account of living process and it is process, in the joy and sweat of experience that forms the stuff of a full life in a body, not just in a mind. It is isolating, because this form of intense mental speculation puts the individual always outside the subject, looking down or in. This kind of view tends to keep people apart, always analyzing each other and their interactions, rather than immersing themselves fully in experience with others and the world. Lives are led according to theories and concepts about others.

People create lists of accomplishments and attributes for themselves that seem to add up to some significant sum in the mind, but often lack the vital element of the magic structure that has no need of abstractions but lives in the vibrancy of the moment experienced with the heart and soul. This view of life requires intimacy and relational openness, qualities lost to the over rationalized life always at a calculating and judging distance. This condition, where life is made into ideas that bounce around in the mind between the idea about the thing observed and the idea the individual observing has about themselves, creates what Gebser referred to as "a kind of shadow boxing before a mirror whose reflection occurs against the blind surface." The blindness is due to the distortion created by a purely speculative appraisal of the world which leads to an often equally superficially constructed view of the self. "This negative link to the psyche, usurping the place of the genuine mental relation, destroys the very thing achieved by the authentic relation: the ability to gain insight into the psyche."[11] Without genuine, open relationships an individual cannot hope to gain insight into themselves. In echoes of Rousseau, Gebser reminds us of the deep truth that we move into experience of our own true humanity in authentic relationship to the humanity of others.

We find this denatured isolating tendency showing up everywhere. In political ideologies, consumerist market culture, in the development of technologies, as well as personal psychologies, it typifies the modern world. The atomizing effect of our constantly objective perspective isolates individuals from nature and society and societies from other societies. It drives the engines of war in an age when humanity should be evolving beyond their primitive warrior ruthlessness. This isolating complex of the mind makes it all too easy to turn foreigners into loathsome enemies through a strategic application of propaganda. It is the spawn of authoritarian ideologies that seek to file people away in social systems bent on a rational, systematic, machine-like structure that optimizes efficiency at the expense of being fully human. We find this in the Chinese factory complexes where workers live on the premises and are fed into the manufacturing process like just another commodity and in the capitalist West epitomized by corporate speech, the cubical and the bland voice on the phone reading pre-prepared responses to your pleas for help.

If there is one great virtue in European culture, wherever it has landed, especially the Americas, setting aside for a moment all the destructive effects, it is in the fact that the wild element outside all the attempts at machine-like efficiency continues to find its quarter and from there disseminate a renewed connection with the archaic, magical and mythical structures of the human body/mind. We find this in new artistic and socio-spiritual expressions and movements emanating from these corners of "free" societies. Transcendentalism, impressionism, jazz and rock and roll, were all break-out expressions of the repressed spirit that led to revitalizations of culture required by humanity. Eventually, even the Soviets couldn't keep out blue jeans and rock and roll.

Despite the emphasis on workers, the Marxist totalitarian states followed Marx and Lenin's unfortunate modernist proclivity against nature and spirituality toward the strict systemization of all human activity and in doing so drained the life out of all of it. In this it shared a similar desire with industrialism everywhere, as the sociologist, C. Wright Mills, once said, to create "cheerful robots" out of everyone outside the elite circles of power. But in the democratic nations the human spirit always had a place to retreat and regroup and plan its counterattack against such dehumanizing forces, efforts which then blossomed forth in the form of music, theater, literature, new philosophies, progressive research, and spiritual movements. It is an unbounded human ingenuity at work within the spirit in evolution that will not halt unless forcibly contained and even then, like the countless drops of rain that turn mountains into gravel, it will eventually break through as it did in Poland and Romania and now in the Middle East. Here too, Americans are breaking free as well from their own gathering oppression.

The Integral Structure of Consciousness

The main function of the integral stage in the evolving mind is as the name suggests: to integrate – to bring together the whole of human perception in all its structural modes so as to create the platform for a new multidimensional way of life. This way of life is profoundly experiential in its orientation to the world in that it seeks to break out of the detached analytic view of life so as to encounter the world with the whole being. The "whole being" is simply all the structures of consciousness that awoke in historical progression and remain an ongoing part of human life and experience. The habits of modern life have drastically restricted the use of previous modes of perception placing the mental/rational mode at the forefront of the public mind and so individuals have a task before them in bringing back on-line the archaic, magic, and mythic structures of consciousness in a much more deliberate and integrated way than is commonly experienced.

With the dawning of the integral stage in the evolution of human consciousness we have the transcendence of the singular identity of the mental/rational structure marked by the end of the insular ego consciousness that perceives itself as an isolated personality requiring constant vigilance in repelling threats and building prestige and power of one sort or another. In this progression humanity grew out of the archaic structure as an animal totally enmeshed within the eco-consciousness of Nature, awakening first to the rudimentary individuality of the magic tribal stage of development, where the self-sense was mainly focused through the identity as a member of a tribe, with little individuality, each person seen as woven into the tapestry of Nature. Moving next to the mythic structure of consciousness where the ego becomes an autonomous agent on the world stage, what was unconscious connection within becomes projected outward and the individual feels now apart from the world. Here we find the sense of individuality growing into a fullness that allowed for an identity as a unique, separate personality, with Nature in the form of "the gods," receding to the status of autonomous forces working for and against the individual. With the coming of the mental/rational consciousness we have a further step away from the original embedded status within Nature to a point of complete separation. The individual ego consciousness is experienced as being in opposition to a nature that threatens a strict control with instinct and sensuality, which are kept at bay by a devotion to an absolute mental "clarity" that is understood as a totally emotionless, unfeeling, analytic perspective where the mind sits outside the frame of nature and the "objective" world *looking in*.

This development of the autonomous ego seems to have been to the purpose of all evolution, as the model of Nature shows us, and that is to move to greater and greater forms of complexity. The growth of ego consciousness in separating from Nature creates an individuality capable of far greater ranges of creativity than was available to that bound by instinct. But this development of unique individual personality and creative function through separation then reaches a point of maximum effectiveness in the early mental stage and thereafter begins to dissipate its energies in the pathological obsessions of alienated ego maniacal projects. These obsessions are disconnected from the health of the environment and society, on the external level, and disconnected from a genuine relationship to other persons on the personal level. Thus, the bonds of humanity fray and competition and rivalry reign supreme. The world deteriorates in war and economies fail that have been rigged by the rich to make them richer in a culture driven by materialist elitism where everyone's ego competes with everyone else's for a chance at winning a game of wealth and power, where power can be anything from running the corporation to running the dump. This is a culture where passion has been annexed by a machine efficiency and anxiety about social position and achievement run rampant as boredom, frustration, and insecurity drive a compensatory consumerism that stuffs bodies, homes, and storage lockers full of junk.

When systems become unstable they move into crisis and the deteriorating order makes a reformation possible. Out of the chaos a new order arises and in reference to the evolution of consciousness it is the integral that is rising to prominence at this time. We know this because the evidence has been rising, slowly but surely, for a century or more. But what does it mean for the ego and the human sense of individuality to move into the integral consciousness? The main point of the integral, as stated above, is to integrate, and in integrating all structures of human consciousness into one meta-system of thought and feeling the individual gains what Jean Gebser referred to as "ego freedom." In ego-freedom the ego is understood to have gone through an evolution of separation from total immersion in nature in the archaic consciousness, to a total isolation within the individual in the late stage of the mental/rational structure of consciousness. In moving into the integral consciousness this deficient ego condition is transcended by way of incorporating all previous structures so that the individual, rather than being unconsciously embedded in the world, *is consciously connected.* Here, for instance, the sense of a highly developed individuality remains, but the connectedness to Nature and the human body, what might be termed the "ecosystem of humanity," is reestablished through the incorporation of the magic structure of consciousness resulting in an easing of the isolation of the alienated modern consciousness wherein the person doesn't lose the finely honed mind developed through millennia of evolution, but rather now feels in communion with Nature, inside and out.

The mythological structure is incorporated, as well, and in doing so the temporal nature of the universe is reestablished in the individual so that the polarity of forces circling from night to day and season to season, around and around, and oppositions from sweet to sour, tragedy and comedy, present a living flow in which a person's life gracefully resides.

The deficient mental/rational mind has attempted to escape from this natural flow of forces, perpetually fleeing from one side of the polarity in avoidance of what it has labeled "bad," so that people seek a never ending summer, light and never darkness, a perpetual sweetness never giving sorrow its due, a youth that fears age, and a crumbling in personal apocalyptic defeat when the other side of the polarities of life ultimately close in, as they must. The integral mind can see the virtue in return to the mythic structure in what Joseph Campbell called, "the night sea journey" that appears in the mythology at times when the hero must go into the darkness and spend time in brooding metamorphosis to emerge a new being. This is an initiatory experience, a confrontation with death and eternity that modern people have done everything to escape from; so when overcome by a dark episode they simply anesthetize it away with drugs or alcohol, thereby missing the call to greater consciousness. Returning to an efficient relationship with the mythological mind relieves a great stress on modern humanity while reestablishing the power in the darkness and the sublime beauty of the winter. We ride this wave or we are ultimately crushed by it. And so mythic polarity is incorporated into the integral mind without the limiting "anti-progressive" frame of its original inception, which is to say the eternal round is not a closed circle but an upward evolving spiral.

In bringing in the magic structure the sounds of the world also rise to significance, rather than as background to mental dramas. The resonant nature of music and song are now understood as forces that move, shape, and infiltrate the emotional body, and so a world opens up to be more than "listened to." Sounds, natural or made by human intent, form part of the environment in which we live. As such, when we reincorporate a conscious approach to sound, we begin to master an aspect of our being in the world that was previously undeveloped and so a route through which forces could influence the individual in a manner that circumvented awareness. Movie soundtracks are the most obvious use of sound as an emotion inspiring tool, but most are unaware of how sound enters their lives in so many other ways that are equally causing effects in their experience, but without their conscious notice.

The imagery that is the currency of the mythological structure is also brought back under the power of the individual within the integral mind. Symbol, sign, and image are powers that affect this deep structure of consciousness. Just as with sound, those who are ignorant of their power to move consciousness put themselves at risk for unconscious manipulations. What has been termed, "symbol literacy," must be undertaken as part of the initiation into the integral structure of consciousness so that the individual masters the imagistic element within their environment so that they can be in charge of themselves. They know when they are being assaulted by imagery and can make healthier decisions as to what they allow to populate and motivate their deeper mind. *Awareness in consciousness conquers all.* Most people, for instance, have their minds daily filled with imagery of violence from television and film and then wonder why they don't always sleep well or carry a level of perpetual worry or guardedness that goes largely unnoticed, but continually wears on the person, contributing to the exhaustion so endemic to modern society.

Closely bonded community, family and friends, who are more than mere companions, but form interwoven systems of mutual trusting support, are another element of ego-freedom within the magic structure. Without a "tribe" the stress and challenge of modern existence all is laid at the feet of the individual ego and it often proves to be too much. The life of the competitive egocentric being of today, especially in metropolitan areas, experiences the "lonely in a crowd," effect noted by sociologists. The person that is constantly worried about dignity, prestige, accomplishment, and such without sincere acceptance for who they are as a unique individual, is always at risk of falling to pathological addictions and the abandoning of their genuine nature to became a "mass man or woman." This is one of the greatest cultural maladies of our age, conforming to the mass in rejection of the authentic self is a regression to an unconscious tribalism, a deficient magic structure effect mistakenly taken as a route back to the lost community. But unlike genuine community the mass offers only egos in lockstep, reflecting each other's style in a society of mutual fear and desire. People become stuck between giving up themselves to conform to the masses or living in psychological isolation. Gebser suggests that there is only one way out of this central dilemma of modern existence and that is to achieve ego-freedom. This is done by incorporating the integral mind that sees through material forms and social conventions to see with all the structures at once, which means that human "origin," the entirety of the universe from which all things arise, that envelops the individual in the archaic structure and dominates the body in the magic structure, and is projected onto the world in the mythic structure, and reduced to abstraction and number in the mental structure, now becomes conscious in the realization of the multi-dimensional nature of the universe realized in the integral structure. In this epiphany ego-freedom is achieved through *making the whole conscious* where one is neither alone in disconnected autonomy nor swamped by the homogenous masses. Ego-freedom comes both from liberating the self from the mass through shedding the need for mass acceptance and by the escape from the mirrored isolation of the alienated interior life by seeing beyond the self to find *oneself* in others in a refined individuality in communion with humanity, nature, and the cosmos from which all arose. This is the prize of evolving consciousness.

Through the mythic structure of consciousness ego freedom is advanced by incorporating the aforementioned underdeveloped relationship to image. Contemporary life is flooded with imagery and yet the average person knows little about how images, symbols and signs, suggest narratives that deeply affect their minds and bodies. This vast mythic ignorance once relieved allows a level of comprehension that can result in the shattering of the manipulative cultural matrix that constantly tugs at, pushes, and shouts orders at the ego demanding compliance to the mass by inspiring a myriad of stresses and insecurities. This condition leads the unaware individual to don a public mask that seeks to project the "right" image in response to this cultural expectation. The schism between the genuine personality behind the mask and that artificial creation of the forced outward expression breeds a terrible sense of constant hiding. Ego-freedom sees through the artificial culture of manipulation and allows the individual to relax into a deeper valuing of themselves based on *human criteria* rather than commercial. In this way the genuine personality emerges, rather than one in phony "adult" compliance to the mass, or equally bogus extended adolescent "rebellion" against the mass, the individual finds their authentic voice and begins to speak out in all forms of self-expression. In doing so, the authentic tribe comes together. Those with real affinity and shared values and interests will gravitate to one another in natural creation of a new community based on genuine depth and not just surface. Here is the origin of humanity that is the energetic push behind evolution seeking expression through unique human collaborations as consciousness achieves a more intense, richer field of experience. This cannot happen as long as individuals allow themselves to be suppressed and their life-force hijacked to add strength to the empire building of centralized power.

Through integral vision the image becomes transparent to all its connections, past, present, and future, so that the image's mystic capacity for unconscious suggestion is neutralized and the intent of the suggestion laid bare before the efficient mental structure that understands where this image is trying to lead the public and whether that place offers something in harmony with personal integrity or is simply another phony myth of perfection and glory in support of exploiting political and/or financial power. In this vein, general cultural myths that form the instructions for life are also seen through in an integral consciousness so that ego-freedom is achieved by a matching of what is deeply authentic and right for the individual with the vocation that blends that person's life with the life of the community in a manner that enhances the health of both. Through this creed new business structures that are both innovative and respectful of people and the environment in its magic, mythic, and mental dimensions, will be built.

In actualizing ego-freedom it is essential to consider the experience of time. Jean Gebser speaks of the creation of "time freedom" as one of the major tasks before the person moving into the integral consciousness. The general public in the West is suffering from a rationalized deficient mental structure relationship to time. Time becomes the "avenger" the ultimate "destroyer" in Western literature, where time waits for everyone like the grim reaper at the end of their days to nullify their lives. This is an expression that comes to a mind that experiences space as a void, a meaningless expanse of distance that time moves into, day after day, toward a never ending nothingness. The mental/rational way of seeing the world as a quantity to be divided into sections of measure that is counted off into the distance when applied to time becomes deficient as a way of comprehending the progress of a life, because it robs the individual of meaning. This is due to the idea that meaning is to be bestowed by goals, while within the same frame of reference those goals are ultimately dust, as "time the destroyer," returns all to nothing. The meaning lost in this over-determined rationalism is recovered through achieving time-freedom where all of the experiences of time in its magic "now only" orientation, its mythic circularity, and its efficient mental progression, are comprehended at once. This is to say they are constituents of an overall attitude toward time that allows for their efficient use in the given instance and for a general understanding that time is not one thing but at our disposal in each orientation's appropriate application. With this is the overarching sense of what Gebser calls the "achronon," which is experience without time where the origin of all life and matter shines through everything experienced in the timeless now. This is not a regression to magic unconscious timelessness, but rather a fully conscious recognition of origin in the present.

"Wherever man becomes conscious of the pre-given, pre-conscious, originary pre-timelessness, he is in time-freedom, consciously recovering its presence. Where this is accomplished, origin and the present are integrated by the intensified consciousness."[12] Gebser speaks of consciousness as an "intensity" that increases over the course of evolution. In the current stage of development that intensity is blowing through the old mental conception of time as a march into the void. The relief of the time anxiety of the current era is achieved through realization of "the ever-present origin."

In comprehending this riddle one must remember that the psychological connection to the whole of nature and the origin of life and the universe from which humanity came was slowly broken as individualized ego-consciousness developed. This gave rise to the mythology of "the fall from Eden" and a feeling of having left behind "God's grace," and is the unconscious source of the scientific obsession with reductive reasoning that searches for meaning in smaller and smaller pieces of reality looking ever backward for the secret of the first starting point of it all. The only solution to the dilemma of quantified endless empty space where meaning is always ahead or behind and in the end futile is in the fully conscious realization of the power of origin *expressing itself through everything right now*. This is to hear the voice of, "God" if you prefer religious terms, or "the energetic source of creation," if you prefer something more technical, every moment one looks at the world, seeing through all the projections and theories to the actual living reality. God's grace was never withdrawn and the power of life has never been remote from us. It takes only a leap in consciousness to realize that it was always here waiting for the human race to notice. Again, this is not magic structure "oneness" that is achieved through a regressive consciousness in an "altered state", but is akin to what spiritual doctrines call "non-dual" in what is a fully conscious realization of a collapsing of the past and the future to this moment where spirit, origin, and matter in the space of time are perceived as being one thing, an experience that is sometimes described as "one taste." All the myriad teachings of Buddhism are said finally to be of *one taste* and that is the taste of Nirvana, or paradise, in Western terms – what the psychological approach might call a state of perfect emotional poise where nothing is impinging on a person's calm sense of momentary perfection, the fruition of existence.

As described in an earlier chapter, this integral worldview has been bursting through the old mental/rational structure for some time now. It is seen in many cultural creations and in the science of particle physics where every moment is the beginning and the end of the universe, where the quantum wave function representing all of the probabilities of creation are collapsed to the one reality we perceive – a collection of light particles that form the world and us – and in the next moment happening all over again. Creation didn't happen a long time ago in a big bang. It happens every moment. Thus, the creator, the force of life we seek, is "ever present." Once we know this thoroughly then the world becomes "diaphanous," which is the translucent quality of matter when creation shines through to our deep feeling, our knowing within the cycles of nature, while illuminating our concepts of progress in every moment.

It is of course true that these previous sentences seem quite mystical and out of reach of the average person not long acquainted with these ideas, but it must be remembered that when the mental perspectives of science were first widely introduced to the people of the 17th Century they seemed entirely strange and counter to "common sense," as well. When people first were told the Earth is round, they must have looked about themselves and laughed at the utter *nonsense* of the idea. What is being suggested here is not something mystical in terms of actually seeing some glowing world of divine energy emanating from everything. What is meant by "non-dual," or Gebser's term "diaphanous," is more a kind of deep certitude and "knowing" that informs the individual's experience of material reality so that they look at everything with the conviction and constant realization that what they are seeing is the presence of its "origin" manifesting within the myriad forms of material reality and doing it with a "time neutral presence." It is this notion – that time is not stealing anything from us, that time does not push life out in front of us like a carrot on a stick for us to perpetually run towards – that is central to this new way of perception. It is a way that assures us that the "paradise lost" is not lost at all but right in front of us. What is most profound in life is our connection to the origin of all things that is present in every moment. And, of course, these are just words on a page and not the experience itself, which is the only real way to comprehend this shift. But these words are offered here as an initial approach to this *knowing* that will become a constant way of seeing and living in the world. Once the philosophy is understood the experience will become real in sudden moments of illumination that will in time become normal. For a certain subset of the population these moments of illumination have come first and the theory and philosophy has been sought to explain them.

This is a way of perceiving that is commensurate with the dawning realization of the integral mind that is showing up increasingly in science and culture everywhere. It will slowly take over the world the way the mental/rational structure did during the "enlightenment" and the other structures did in their own eras. But we are only now in the early middle stages of that transition. So, although paradox in the study of physics has become common, time is understood as relative to the individual and capable of retroactive effects, and each moment is known to be a quantum event where causality is not found in the previous moment in time but is somehow strangely contained within itself, time lines spread out from each moment in every direction. These ideas seem like nonsense. Our minds can't quite follow and so they will remain "counter intuitive" until our intuition adjusts.

Jean Gebser had this to say about the way of knowing that is particular to the integral structure:

> It can be fathomed only dimly in vital, magic life, and is realizable through imagination and experience, as in myth and mysticism, only in a twilight of consciousness. It is approached in thought, but thought immediately closes itself off since in its process of deduction discursive thought always excludes any openness in its compulsion to system.[13]

The idea is essentially that the whole of creation is perceived, not with the eye, but with the spirit or "meta-mind," one could say. The whole, that is "origin" cannot be modeled in a three dimensional picture and so it will forever escape a mental "perspectival" thought that always seeks to stand at a distance and measure height, width, and depth and their changes through sequential time. This way of knowing is the mental/

rational structure that is simply inadequate for comprehending the new phenomena entering human awareness as consciousness has evolved to a new plateau allowing for a multi-dimensional realization. Non-Euclidian geometry creates mathematical formulas for "shapes" that cannot be three-dimensionally modeled, this, along with things like Eisenstein's relativity, and even attempts by artists like Pablo Picasso to render multi-dimensional figures on a flat canvas, are all responses that enter into the capacities of this new rising consciousness.

Just as in the growth of a child's mind as they mature, in the evolution of consciousness within humanity as a whole there are certain developmental tasks that must be attended to, if the individual is to find their way to the more sophisticated understanding. In the current transitional age many people have come to suspect that the old materialist "positivist" perspective on life is simply inadequate to describe the grander multidimensional realities being demonstrated by the progressive edges of science, as well as from the evidence of their own contemplations and experience. Mechanistic materialist perspectives are useful within a certain limited range, but it has become increasingly clear they simply do not describe the whole of reality. With this fact looming large, many people have now set out to piece together new ideas and models of reality on their own in their desire to make sense of their intuitions and experience.

The realization of the "diaphanous" nature of "time neutral" reality is one developmental task. The utilization of each structure of consciousness in their efficient modes is another task. In moving into the integral we must give each realm of experience its due. Each realm is not reducible to another realm. When someone takes music and reduces it to symbolic category, which is a mythic response, or sound engineering, which is a mental response, then they do violence to what music is in its own right – rightfully a magic mind, feeling art. In essence, they replace the vital power of music with something else. At the same time, there is an undeniable relationship between the realms of the Magic structure, the Mythic structure, and the Mental/Rational structure. They are approaching the same things from differing "angles," one might say (another spatial metaphor—see how they're everywhere). When the magic structure moved into the mythic mind, then the magic did not go away. It simply was transcended as a primary mode of comprehension. In poetry we find a link between the mythic mind and the magic

359

mind, where the mythic symbolic representation of happenings and environments, words as such, are utilized to paint moods within the experience of the reader. As cultures progress these moods have been woven into grand themes in heroic action, love, and accomplishment, from ancient tragedy and comedy, down to our day where we find all the categories and subcategories of our modern mythos laid out as movie genres: family drama, political thriller, espionage suspense, romantic comedy, psychological mystery, etc. When a person goes to watch a movie they ask themselves, "What am I in the mood for?" When one seeks a mood the story and the meaning become secondary. There is an ambiance that is the primary thing sought. In seeking a Western where "wide open spaces" and a simple morality is played out there is one kind of experience and mood offered, and when a sophisticated, urban drama is set in Park Avenue penthouses and chic' night spots, another kind of mood and experience is offered. There is a sense of '"being" that is evoked from these films that often is the main draw. In making a choice based on mood, the movie viewer is paying homage to the magic structure of their consciousness. Humans like to evoke moods as curatives as well and may choose a comedy as a remedy for a low mood. Our mythology has become a kind of smorgasbord of moods and ego fantasies of power and desire fulfilled.

In the mythic structure we find the first systems of thought that sought to order the universe and human experience within it. In the tribal magic stage it seems people were simply reacting to the overwhelming power of the environment they struggled to survive in. Not story, but simply images of raw power were sketched on cave walls in the form of animals, lightning and such. It was as if by picturing the main forces of their world, early humans began the process of coming to terms with these powers and through reverence stay on good terms with the forces they depended on. This is all speculation, of course, but it is clear that today the relationship with the mythic mind is one of archetypal powers at the service of heroic types moving through landscapes of experience. What is important to the mythic structure of consciousness is not merely the feeling of riding the range or of sailing a tropical sea but to where the rider or the boat is going and what for? The "where to" and "what for" is the stuff of myth and the answer is usually summed up by the word "discovery." Myth and story, a subcategory of myth, is all about the seeking of answers. This is why adolescents and young people in general are driven to adventures of one sort or another. The mythic mind seeks new experience as a means of defining the self – I am this, I am not that – as the world is tested for a resonant feeling response, usually defined as "having fun," or something wild or intense, simply interesting, or the confrontation that tests personal truth.

Mythic systems are formulas for ordering reality. Where is heaven? Where is earth? Where am I in relation to the two? People read books and watch movies, fiction and nonfiction alike, in search of answers. Even entertainment is a search for something, a meditation on the transient trivia of the day waiting for anomalies in the story we already know the ending of. We watch because we like to see evil vanquished and the hero win again, or two lonely souls find each other in true love. In time, of course, the same old trivia and the same old stories will lose their attractive quality and the viewer will seek something more. So the hero wins, perhaps that's the easy part, what does the hero do now? How does the hero find meaning, day to day? What sort of society does the hero go on to build? These are the more sophisticated questions and the more difficult stories to write. These are the stories that each must write for themselves, but before people attempt such a daunting task they consult the ten thousand stories already written and scour them for answers, searching for a mood and a meaning. Then they go into the world and attempt to act out the mythic model of their choice and therein the lessons begin.

An Inner Voice

As the rational mind has done its best to break the world down into pieces from its lofty position outside the subject, imposing the machine mind template on the world for better and worse, another voice within Western humanity began to sing a siren's song from a vital region not recognized in the schematic, disembodied charting of the overly rational mind. People have responded to this inner voice with romantic reveries looking back to search for something their feeling tells them was left behind. There is a deep connectedness with the body of Nature that speaks to us from tales of tribal peoples; images of Native American or South Sea Island life fill the fantasies of urban dwellers. The image of a lusty life in a perpetual camp site, ensconced in the arms of a giant family, seems to hold the promise of some kind of vital tonic for modern humanity's anxiety. This longing draws them in to try to recreate their romantic vision in camping trips, "adventure travel" and island vacations in a tropical paradise, while the more intrepid reach father in bold quests for the lost experience in expeditions into uncharted terrain, vast ocean crossings in sail boats, and ordeals climbing mountains into the clouds. They seem to be hoping for some magic change within, a transmission of some essential wisdom they'll feel in their bones and hear the song of their soul for the very first time, something that will cure their longing and stay with them forever.

The problem is just this: that it is the specialist that goes on the adventure – the top scientist, the rare artist, the professional athlete or academic – that takes on the quest while most of the population sits waiting for the results, watching it all unfold on television or in film. But watching will not cut it when only personal experience and the seeking of the authentic within each self will do. The languishing masses sit before the endless dramas, the legends of our time, tales of lost maps that speak of riches buried on remote islands or on the New York Stock Exchange. In the lost cities of the artificial jungles of suburbia people gather in the cinematic temples to watch the same stories unfold, over and over again in unrecognized hopes that this time one will deliver what they need to know. One will cause the laugh that releases all grief, reveal the secret to true love or the missing piece of information required to solve the riddle and open the door to a beautiful reality beyond the stifling work houses and road crews, beyond the hum, drum, routines of modern existence, out of a life that has been sanitized and optimized so that everything flows along predetermined lines where hope and dreams have no column on the digital accounting books that seem to favor fewer and fewer with the transient satisfactions of monetary reward.

Our stories always hold out the promise of transcendence, a sacred path beyond the struggle. They sweep us away to the land of *never, never* and *what could be if only*. There in these mythological realms, (and myth can be set even in "realistic" modern times or the future) we watch the heroes solve the puzzles, fight through the obstacles and come away with the prize of life and love and grace under the gaze of some eternal force. But this public ritual rarely offers the true art that renders insight. Rather, it presents more often a mirage, an opiate masking symptoms, the *soma* of a consumer culture reinforcing itself. Without the individual leaving the novel, the net, the TV, video game and the cinema behind, they will never be able to discover their true path through their own "real time" adventure, engaged with the forces of life directly encountered in the flesh. Only then is the individual able to grapple with the force of creation that is life and evolution itself that is working through them in confrontation with our deficient reality as it exists. Stuck in "story time," the deficient mythic mind, a person will be swept along into a job and life out of sync with themselves and experience an uninspiring life as a result of the mass story they have bought into but never questioned. In the classic materialist predicament previously discussed, the individual stuck in the provided myth will say to themselves, "My life sucks, because I don't make enough money and so I cannot purchase the objects that will endow me with power, fun, sexiness, etc." This race toward a materialist nirvana and ego victory has replaced the real adventure that is found in the challenges of saving democracy and creating an increasingly fair and fulfilling society. The great adventure of restoring true freedom in the midst of a civilization deteriorating into a police state awaits those with the courage to wrest control of their minds and bodies away from the dark spells of a manipulating centralized power.

This is the deficient end phase of a mental/rational materialism as an exclusive world view, i.e., "story." To escape this trap the individual must now integrate the magic and mythic structures of mind in their own experience to create their own story to find the proper balance of forces on their way to a fulfilling life determined by solid contact with their own genuine being as a representative of the true human spirit.

This force that is coming through us that we call "evolution" can't be stalled permanently. That inscrutable intelligence that some call God and others might term *the ultimate logic of the universe*, that is not a god made in man's image, but a complexity of being so far beyond our mental grasp that all attempts at description fail. Its story is renewed continually according to the human developmental capacity that allows a greater view from an intensified consciousness. That which gave birth and growth to the universe is in us, always, as we watch our stories in the theaters and on the TVs, read the papers and on-line commentaries as we examine ourselves. As humanity appraises their idealized and demonized reflections in the stories they create, a way of pondering the possibilities of our imaginations is provided. All of history and the future become the place for our current stage in the evolution of consciousness. We do not see the past in our tales, or the future. We see ourselves right now, projecting our images backwards and forwards into realms that fascinate and appall so that we can lay out our fantasies for inspection, for vicarious experience, educating and "entertaining" ourselves.

Entertainment had its beginnings in religious ritual. The Greek theater was a place for the populace to process its emotional baggage, so to speak. Life was full of tragedy and comedy and the plays helped to move people in line with these emotional forces, so that they could express their grief and laughter together, in a group setting that helped to keep the populace on the same road through life. The plays gave meaning to it all, as the gods looked on and even intervened from time to time. As Western civilization developed theater took on the role of social commentary so that people could examine the endless moral dilemmas their societies found their way into. Today film largely serves this same purpose and as such is both a definer of culture and a reflection of it. The defining aspect is often utilized by the power structure to reinforce the social outlook that supports their profits and position. This attempt to control the defining aspects of mainstream culture has produced a disconnect with evolving minds. As these older structures of Western civilization fail, their story begins to ring hollow. The same old violent heroes and *innocence rescued from the clutches of evil*, and the worshiping of fame and riches, has become a comic book version of reality that few but children find compelling as a reflection of anything actually relevant to their daily lives.

Every story matters, even the ones that are just for fun or are presented to manipulate. Every story tells us something about what we're struggling with. If we enter into them *consciously*, they tell us what we crave, but can't admit that we do, like violence, conflict, and sorrow. These things we are fascinated with reveal in some often adulterated form a piece of the human puzzle at this stage of history and evolution, the neglected and denied parts. As we enter the integral stage of development, we need to pay very careful attention to the stories we are attracted to. A person can find there signs on the trail back to themselves, because the integral is about reconstituting ourselves from the ground up so that we reconnect with the deepest impulses of our humanity with awareness. In doing so we come together to bring to fruition the new rising society whose story will move beyond the rationalizations of ego and fear – injustice, destruction, and greed – to a place where human potential can bloom.

There is a way to build a society that optimizes life and potential, but it is a system that must optimize all life, not just human. This healthier society has a structure we can discover and establish through attention to the structures of consciousness in their efficient expression and our ability to mold the elements of this world through collective will and action into a new culture in harmony with those structures. In this we must recognize our embedded status within the natural world. Regardless of the human ability to create artificial habitats for itself, it cannot be denied that Nature is an extension of our bodies. What we do to it, we do to ourselves. It's not just the air and the water we need from the environment, but the healthy fields of life that form the home of the rudimentary structures of our consciousness – the place where mind and body meet. A healthy spirit requires wilderness untouched and sacrosanct. Through the realization of the deep structures of consciousness within humanity we reestablish the human ability to consciously sense this *original* matrix of life. This is the starting place for a new world.

THE CONSCIOUS LIFE

So how are we to live? This is the central question of existence that every society has faced once simple survival has been assured. How *are* we to live? Certainly, the integral vision is not another utopian dream of perfection. Neither Jean Gebser, nor the contemporary champion of the cause, Ken Wilber, have attempted to couch the integral movement as the last word in human development or promote it as a route to utopia. Scholars realized some time ago, perhaps starting with Fredrick Nietzsche, who said, "To define me is to limit me," that every utopian dream contains a hidden totalitarianism. It is impossible to create the perfect human community and life philosophy, because to attempt to do so would necessarily limit the ever expanding nature of human life and creativity. Any utopia suggests a steady state society that reproduces itself in perfect form, which means, *the last form*. This is not what human beings, nor evolution itself is all about. Rather, as the great scientist/engineer, Buckminster Fuller, once suggested, the human being is not a noun but a verb, it's always in action.

Healthy human society always contains an element of *wildness*, of unaccountable creative friction. We expand like the universe that gave birth to us and in consideration of this the average life must allow for spontaneous creative flexibility. The new life in harmony with the whole of the human endowment as it now stands is one which gives space to all the structures – archaic, magic, mythic, mental – within the integral whole that *transcends and includes*, allows each to come forward in the appropriate moment, blends and creates new (not in synthesis, which blends the former out of existence in favor of the new, but rather respects the former on its own terms), and uses it as a source of inspiration for creative combinations within an ever renewing approach to life.

As has been covered above there are many opportunities to recognize the efficient expression of each structure: the vital feeling, aural, musical, lustful living, communal dancing, moments of the magic structure; the imagery, narrative, polar revolving living forces in the human experiential adventure of the mythic structure; and the conceptual, abstract, and rational formulas within the mental structure. Even the total loss of ego with immersion in the totality of the origin of all things in the archaic structure can be experienced to great benefit during deep meditation and contemplation. Most people pay some homage to each of these. It's hard not to, but the mental/rational has over-determined the others to a crippling extent. The real challenge of our time is to bring each structure into conscious relationship so that one renews and develops the structure, bringing it out of the shadows or, "play time," to become a regular constituent of a healthy life. All of this is achieved with the integral mind that sees origin expressed in all things within the timeless living present, an open field of experience without stress, without anxiety in authentic expression of a self that is humanity in singular form.

In establishing ego-freedom the individual must examine all the ways they have been affected by the artificial culture of manipulation to become a mass person seeking external acceptance, on one side, and a fragile, isolated ego hiding their authentic identity, on the other side. So many people are so used to repressing their genuine feelings and unique character that it takes some deep contemplation and active effort to bring their true self out of the darkness. It is in releasing the unique spirit within each person that allows the real life to begin, that which will fulfill the individual while it brings forth the genuine community of deep interest, values, and belief. The formula for this freeing of the repressed human spirit is simply stated by Joseph Campbell as "Follow your bliss." This does not mean, "follow your reactionary ego," which has been described by C.G. Jung as, "the shadow," and which contains all the refuse from the abuse and lack of respect for each person's unique spirit that has built up in the unconscious of the average individual during their life. Everyone has to do their shadow work – the purging of all the animosities, the hatreds, the competitive habits and subtle put-downs people throw out onto the public as a regular part of the game of ego competition. Maintaining one's "superiority" or nursing the wounds that fuel all kinds of ugly behavior is like a great stone hung around the neck that calls for a massive expenditure of energy just to keep from being drug to the bottom of the "ego pool." When this battle is given up then a wonderful feeling of freedom, a lightness of being, is achieved. Once the off-loading of shadow material is substantially underway, the authentic Self rises to consciousness. When it does, it seems very familiar, like a long lost friend from childhood, a vitality of interest, a view and a voice that never really left, but had been distorted, pushed to the back in favor of a public persona constructed for the purposes of the ego competition out of various heroic models provided by the artificial culture.

The individualizing trend in the evolution of human consciousness should have been better dealt with through a progressive culture and a more compassionate community but, unfortunately, the power dynamics of a declining Western Civilization came into play and harnessed the growing autonomy of the ego for its own purposes. On one side is the whole consumer capitalist machine that has accelerated beyond any healthy human limits that requires competition and ego striving for its propulsion. On the other side is the deliberate pitting of the public against itself in a myriad of "culture war" arguments generated and inflamed by the commercial media for the purposes of preventing any large scale political coalition from uniting average citizens against their true adversaries. The banking and corporate elite who have been busy disenfranchising a growing portion of American citizens from the prosperity of the country since the 1970's can only maintain this game if they prevent the public from thinking about the real division between people. The right/left culture conflict is constantly fueled and focused on in a frantic effort to prevent people from looking up and down the financial class scale, which is where the real problem is. This artificially induced dynamic has created an increasingly vitriolic society of squabbling dissension that permeates the social environment in a way that clouds the recognition of the fact that the United States and much of the Western world are dismantling democracy in favor of the return of the old system of aristocracy and privilege camouflaged in a new corporate globalist costume.

Understanding that we are all living in the midst of this highly orchestrated contentious social scene can allow an individual to recognize the game and simply opt out of being manipulated. Doing so allows a level of peace to be developed that is necessary to build a new society of trust, cooperation, and civic action that transcends cultural differences in favor of deeper shared values. Things like returning jobs to the country that pay a living wage, respect for workers and the natural world, a safe and low, or *no cost* medical system that offers the best of all approaches, rather than just drugs and surgery, a court system that doesn't run on money, a representative democracy that actually represents the people instead of the corporate powers that fund the elections. The integral mind moves towards cooperative efforts to collectively work for an economic system that works for everyone, not just those inhabiting the top of the pyramids of power. Capitalism is a tool that can be made to serve the people or it can be bent into a system of oppression by an elite few who have distorted their sense of morality and ethics to the point where they are the only ones contained within it.

Withdrawing the shadow of ego projections happens through the security and self-acceptance that comes from cultivating the genuine self through the rejection of the "mass man or woman," and the release of the unique human spirit. The integral way forward is one of cooperation and compassion where power is largely decentralized and put in the hands of the people. The centralizing of power under an elite minority who maintain their authority through manipulation and coercion is now being transcended as a growing percentage of the public wakes up to the "intensification" of consciousness that is bringing forward the next phase in the growth of democracy. People are waking up, but action is required to move new feelings and views into new ways of living that will support a just and truly free society.

In moving into the integral consciousness it is essential to create a format for daily life which moves allegiance away from the crumbling culture of manipulation and exploitation. This means withdrawing from old patterns that include the consumption of toxic food stuffs and poisoned products of all kinds – not just those that are harmful to consumers and the environment, but those that are produced in exploitive circumstances of virtual slavery. If a person could walk into a department store and see signs hanging everywhere that told the truth, something like "this product made by starving Indonesians who live in shanty towns with open sewers, who make barely enough to survive and who's children die regularly from infections and exposure to toxins put out by the factory that made this product," then people would have an easier time deciding what not to buy, but of course it isn't that way. There are no signs on the electronics that tell you, for instance, that people regularly commit suicide in the Chinese plant where this smart phone was assembled. There is no sign that tells you about the rising cancer rates, birth defects, and general illness in the communities within a perfect ring around the chemical plant that produced the elements that went into the other twenty products you buy. There are no signs so each person must do their own homework. The information is available on the Internet and it is only a matter of a few short hours of work to figure out a person's whole life in terms of those products that support the world they want to live in and those that do not. Further, all services, especially medical care, and everything else a person supports with their money must undergo this process of scrutiny and discernment. This is crucial as the first step in the individual's withdrawal from their role as a "worker/buyer unit" in the declining civilization.

The bringing of power back to the integrated individual in harmony with the human spirit within themselves, within their unique community of interest, and within the greater community of human values happens through this process of withdrawing support from the old system of exploitation. The freeing of the ego and the freeing of society go hand in hand, you cannot have one without the other. The integral mind experiencing ego-freedom doesn't have to wait for the world to be free, but they do have to free their world.

Once this is well underway, further work to encourage global freedom can be pursued with health and grace, but the first crucial step is one's own life. This is where the inside, the subjective world, hooks into the objective world out there. The subjective must be free to pursue a life practice that includes all structures of consciousness, and that practice is done individually and in community. As individuals change, communities change. Through the awakening richness of the integral experience the grip of materialism weakens as a deeper value begins to inform life.

Life Practice

The subjective practice starts with the slowing of the mind and the withdrawing from the imagery and ideas inserted into the mind through the artificial culture that creates a never ending circus of anxiety. This is achieved through a meditation practice that can be done in Eastern style, or Western style, moving or sitting. There are many ways and each must find a way that works for them, but all must do this "mental cleansing" work. What is achieved by this is a moving toward the *calm center* that allows the unique human spirit, the "true self" to emerge more easily. It also will very much help with the removing of the toxic garbage that has built up in the mind as a result of living in the society of ego competition, which fills the memory with fear and argument and aggravation.

This is the foundation of the archaic structure practice and with some dedication it can help to bring back the intuitive skills that were normal for people living in the original magic structure societies. Psychic knowing, an ability to "read" the fields of information available all around the individual, and the "field of probabilities" spreading out from the moment, is one of the archaic/magic structure capacities that is a natural, human birthright. Each person will be as good at this as their native talents allow, but everyone has some intuitive capacity that can be reactivated. Once this starts to happen a new value system automatically emerges in the mind that begins to feel the lost connections to the fields of life that connect their own bodies with the body of the world.

The magic structure is one of vital activity so a person has to take care of their body. This means healthy food, joy in vigorous physical activity, as well as subtle physical experiences, which is the sensual world of feeling exemplified by things like massage or the feeling of water smoothly flowing over the skin. The body once freed from mental garbage, food garbage, and sensual depravation, will reward the individual with a new vitality that often surprises by opening a dimension to life the value of which many could not of previously understood. The body and the magic structure of consciousness is not "primitive." It has its own intelligence, a way of perceiving the world that offers vital information. A relationship to Nature is, as discussed above, a vital aspect of the reactivation of these deep human capacities.

The magic structure includes the world of sound as a phenomenon that penetrates into the feeling body. Music is one element of this, singing and chanting another, but in a larger sense it includes all sounds of the natural world of wind and water and animals, of the living web of life whose rich sounds carry a power hard to describe. A person simply must sit quietly and allow them to speak to them. The magic structure is about many things and each person will discover what gems it has to deliver through attending to its needs and avenues of expression in their own way. In this, we must also, "follow our bliss."

The mythic mind must have its daily fare as well. It must be freed from the mythic narrative and imagery that supports the old elitist society of greed and power, war and domination. The mythic mind must be cleansed. The symbol literate individual must adopt a mythic structure for themselves that serves the human spirit coming through the unique self and into the community. We must change the story we live by, first by deconstructing and thoroughly understanding how the old story makes us easy prey for manipulation. The "good people vs. the bad people" is an example of one such story that requires reconsideration. The "violent hero to the rescue," is another story we must examine to determine how such narratives can lead to exploitation of the youth. By examining carefully all the stories we live by we can better know when they are appropriate and when they are not. There is a meta story above all others in the integral mind and it is the story of "knowing about stories." This "master story" allows for the understanding of what our mythology does, how it operates in a field of consciousness. It shines a light on the array of possibilities to avoid being captured by the archetypal powers of stories that urge unconscious reactions so a person can make more aware choices.

It takes time to adopt a new mythic structure, but the evolving consciousness walks the path every day. Every day we work on ego-freedom that is to disconnect the tethers of our self-respect from the commercial machine that manipulates. Every day we break free from the disempowering narrative that allows us to move beyond our status as worker/buyer units in the empire of consumption by looking for our values and inspiration within the deep core of our own human spirit. Every day we further our education in the mythic structure so we can become symbol literate and understand the way imagery is used to control and cajole, and so take back our aesthetic life creating a place of beauty and adventure suitable for our creative truth. Every day we indulge our bodies in music, dance, motion. We run. We swim and feel the sensuous currents of life, the thick air rushing past our limbs, the sun on our faces.

We embrace our friends, our loved ones. We share the healing loving touch of human warmth. Every day we bring community back through reaching out to the tribe of kindred spirits pulling together the bonds of shared values. Every day we hear the voice of Nature singing the song of primal life resonating with our embodied spirits. Everyday our freed minds employ a rational understanding that is *based in life*, a life that is more than matter. Shaped by a mythos informed by the human spirit, it is integral culture that is born from that spirit. Whether one applies an expanded multi-dimensional scientific perspective or a metaphysical or spiritual perspective, it is equally valid to assert that what we have termed "the human spirit" is that energetic pulse that gives rise to matter and therein expresses itself through an escalating complexity of life forms. In time, as the platform for consciousness evolves in the human species, that spirit has the potential to guide civilization as an originating creative impulse for life.

As more and more people awaken to their evolving consciousness during what some are calling "the shift," the dedication to the old system of domination will become rarer and people will respond more readily to the urgings of the human spirit that is the driving force of our humanity. The primitive unfeeling "reptiles" that inhabit the board rooms of the big banks and corporate headquarters and their government employees at the top of the pyramids of power will find it harder and harder to manipulate the masses to support their dirty work and in time even their own children will refuse to carry on business as usual.

Conclusion

The desire to acquire money and status rises in an ego dislodged from a healthy course of development having been captured by the artificial culture of consumer capitalism that feeds an elitist trend in both social relations and economics. American society has been derailed from the course set by the founding fathers and their original vision of a people set free from the values of monarchy and aristocracy. Instead of a self-sufficient people ruling themselves, allowed to develop free from the malignant forces of depravation, cultural and political oppression, we have seen a great reversal that has thwarted this noble experiment in human freedom and true democracy and that leaves "*we the people*" in a condition of increasing oppression under the heel of a new aristocracy.

This new form of totalitarian control growing in the U.S. is not obvious to the casual observer. On the surface all seems to be proceeding as usual, they say our problems have arrived out of the blue from unaccountable economic variables, but there is more than meets the eye firmly glued to the corporate owned media. The British author of the classic novel: *Brave New World*, Aldous Huxley, spelled it out quite succinctly in 1958:

> It is perfectly possible for a man to be out of prison, and yet not be free—to be under no physical constraint and yet to be a psychological captive, compelled to think, feel, and act, as the representatives of the national State, or of some private interests within the nation, want him to think, feel, and act.
>
> The nature of psychological compulsion is such that those who act under constraint remain under the impression that they are acting under their own initiative. The victim of mind-manipulation does not know that he is a victim. To him, the walls of his prison are invisible...
>
> All the traditional names, all the hallowed slogans will remain exactly what they were in the good old days. Democracy and freedom will be the theme of every broadcast and editorial... Meanwhile, the ruling oligarchy and its highly trained elite of soldiers, policemen, thought manufacturers and mind-manipulators will quietly run the show as they see fit.[14]

Powers rose in the United States that set out to return the public to a state of servitude under a centralized authority. The original decentralized socio-political condition of America set in motion by Jefferson, Franklin and the framers of the Constitution, where individuals, regions, and states, were meant to be architects of their own destinies, could not be tolerated by those whose growing financial power needed cooperative working people for the building of a new empire. The rise of democracy in North America and Europe, driven by the evolution of consciousness, in throwing out the old monarchies created opportunities for the freeing of the human spirit where new avenues of expression came to prominence. Human creativity thus released was in time coopted by the mercantile class that rose to dominance through a financial power driven by colonial exploitation abroad. The "moneyed interests," as Jefferson derisively referred to the early corporate factions whose influence he saw as a threat to democracy, would actively work to reverse Jefferson's vision of an American citizen thoroughly educated in history and critical thinking and independent of mind and spirit. This would be pursued through the "dumbing down" of the education system in implementation of a program of national identity as "Americans," rather than as individual loyal citizens of regions within a republic. It would include the gradual coopting of the major media outlets that has allowed a cementing of these changes within an artificial culture that champions and reinforces an elitist materialism and unquestioning patriotism ever at the ready to go to arms in pursuit of economic goals abroad thinly disguised as *the defense of freedom and democracy.*

All of this has been at the service of the trends explicated by historians like, Carol Quigley, who outlined the factors that accompany the rise and fall of civilizations. The "instruments of civilization," what Quigley identified as those businesses and government structures that help to build a vital, healthy cooperative enterprise within the populace, have become "institutionalized" as bureaucratic systems that support their own power and profits at the expense of the overall society and the welfare of those within it. This has been the intended consequence of a society run on elitism – a dynamic that tends to consolidate wealth and power in fewer and fewer hands over time. The major institutions of the United States in their present form, be it law, medicine, banking, media – whatever – have become wealth generating machines as their primary function in direct contradiction to the actual purpose of their creation. The American people are now a "prey species" for oligarchic predators that have a huge vested interest in stopping any reform or transition to a healthier system. As a consequence this civilization is sick and exhibiting regular breakdowns.

It is the evolution of consciousness that has opened new vistas of understanding and that created the impetus for the new form of government that was the United States in its inception. That consciousness is still pushing and moving forward and is breaking into the lives of greater and greater numbers of individuals all over the world. It is driving liberation movements everywhere, because it is a force for a new individual not interested in either being a collectivized mass person under the thumb of dictators, nor is satisfied with following their own way in an isolated private life out of view. The political power player and advisor to presidents, Zbigniew Brzezinski, has called it, "the global political awakening." Dr. Brzezinski wrote in an editorial in the *New York Times* on December 16, 2008: "For the first time in history almost all of humanity is politically activated, politically conscious and politically interactive. Global activism is generating a surge in the quest for cultural respect and economic opportunity in a world scarred by memories of colonial or imperial domination."

The new way is individual freedom in cooperation with a thriving community of people with a unique creativity within a nation of mutual interdependence. The individualizing growth of the human ego over the ages has reached a point where it has intensified the unique features and creative intelligence of each person in a broad spread throughout humanity. This dynamic represents a kind of democratization of consciousness in contrast to the ancient past where an intensity of consciousness was concentrated in fewer individuals who filled the leading roles within early civilizations.

This is the original source of elitism. The differences between those who had the dawning light of intensifying consciousness shinning a bit brighter demonstrated creative abilities that made them naturally superior to their fellows who seemed more of a herd. Some moved into the magic structure of consciousness sooner than others and became chiefs. In the next age those who moved into the mythic structure sooner became kings and architects and astronomers, while the masses filled the rank and file of laborers and soldiers. Those who distinguished themselves must have been easily spotted and moved into roles where their brighter minds could be utilized, but in time this system fell victim to the tendency for "institutionalization." Instead of the brighter minds rising to lead, a hereditary system of privilege rose up and the various structures of civilization became bogged down in mediocrity, leading to unhappy citizens and the intrigues and revolutions that punctuate history.

In our present age the evolving mind of humanity has reached the sort of broad spread development that nearly the entire population of the earth has some capacity for the mental activities that distinguish the mental/rational structure of consciousness. It is true that fewer have moved into the latest development in the integral structure as it has been opening in the last century or so, but this juncture in the evolution of consciousness is somewhat different than the others in that it represents a plateau stage where the previous structures are all consolidated and integrated into one multivalent structure. That being the case, *all people have the makings of the new integral structure*; it is only a matter of desire, learning, and practice that separates those who live integrally from those who don't. This being the case, those making this shift into the integral are not *superior*, to others, in the sense of being "more evolved human beings," as if others are incapable like small children asked to interpret quantum physics but rather are capable yet not utilizing the capacity. This means that although those moving into the integral consciousness can't rightfully say, "I'm better than you," they may quite truthfully say that they are more content, more fulfilled, having more fun, experiencing less stress, and are more alive than others still stuck in the alienated, repressed, artificial culture as worker/buyer units.

Many people have been moving into the integral structure and they simply don't have a term for it or simply haven't put it all together. But they know that they don't fit into the old rational materialist "machine mind," civilization any longer. They're looking at our civilization as it has been created and realizing that some major fundamental changes need to occur to get society back in alignment with that ever advancing human spirit.

In opposition to this rising drive are the institutionalized powers that have an elitist identity even though they are not really "elite," at all. What they are is an in-group of power mongers who mostly inherited fortunes from ruthless people like the robber barons of an earlier America and who are stuck in a deficient mental/rational consciousness that has mistaken material wealth for superiority. The silly "elite" of today are not superior by any lasting human measure, but are simply playing roles in a tired old story with their costumes and shiny baubles pretending they're truly special when in reality they're very ordinary and terrified of others finding this out. Others within the so-called "power elite" simply have certain skills that match the technical challenges of the age that have brought them to positions of wealth and influence, while in spiritual and moral maturity they remain terribly underdeveloped. Unfortunately, the philosophy that motivates much of this group is simply a very primitive materialism, the desire to move as many digits into their column as possible. Due to their devotion to this primitive religion they will do whatever they can get away with to accomplish the task. As public agitation grows with the decaying system, as wealth is moved into fewer hands at the expense of everyone else, the big power players have to increase their propaganda efforts through their media control to insure the public misjudges who is at fault for their increasing hardships. As outlined earlier the major power centers private and public have sponsored efforts to find ways of controlling public reaction by increasing tactics of mind control, culture control, information control, manipulation through the staging of public "events," sabotage, and, if all else fails, by assassination of key individuals who are pursuing avenues that challenge their interests. These efforts have escalated over time as the stress has increased on the public from the increasing failure of institutions to meet common needs as well as the wrenching economic shift the globalist corporate agenda has perpetrated on American workers.

A major strategy of power in our time has been to promote division in the public so as to prevent large political blocks from developing that would allow those of single interest to effectively fight back against corporate control. This has been achieved through a media that shifts focus from the issues that unite those of similar economic class to "culture war" issues that pit progressives against traditionalists, left against right, democrat against republican, red state against blue, on and on and on, all displayed in an exaggerated, provocative, and histrionic mode specifically designed to enflame emotions and raise the ire of the public. Critical thinking is not encouraged in these witch hunts. Any calm and thoughtful analysis of the truth of the positions is never seen. A meaningful discussion of the merits within each issue is impossible to reach when this is the stance taken at the outset, which is precisely what the manipulators had in mind.

The only way to combat this tactic is to realize that these terms: right, left, conservative, liberal, etc. have been completely drained of all meaning and are no longer useful as identifiers for individual positions or for topics. All thinking people who don't want to be manipulated must get used to ignoring all inflammatory rhetoric in the media, brush aside all labels that seek to make-up minds before they've even heard the merits of the issue, and approach each topic with an open mind toward understanding all sides of the issue as well as all the corresponding data, making sure that information is coming from reliable sources. All mainstream media must never be taken on face value alone. Any topic a person seeking their own freedom of mind assesses must go far beyond the mainstream in order to get all the pertinent information necessary to fill in the picture. It must be always remembered that the mainstream media is largely a tool of the status quo, and it must never be forgotten that: *the status quo always seeks to reinforce itself.* What this means at this particular point in history is the reinforcement of an embattled banking and corporate elite that is seeking to further enrich and protect their own positions while transitioning the rest of the populace to the role of a support class of compliant workers and technocrats at their service.

People often simply don't understand what is oppressing them and so in their confusion and frustration they become prey for mass movements against invented enemies: devils, heretics, rival political systems, religions and nations, other races. It becomes easier to give up on reconfiguring life and simply turn yourself over to the crusade, to the simple answer that plays into the hands of authoritarian ideologies that promise to set things right again and vanquish the "bad" things. Americans are seriously at risk for this type of manipulation and a final big push in this direction by the corrupting powers of the corporatocracy is still quite possible.

The public could be even more at risk for major manipulation through a manufactured event at this time due to the increasing pressures during the current stage of declining empire that Carol Quigley's historical analysis terms: "the age of conflict." The age of conflict is an age of class rivalry and is accompanied by the rise in imperial wars abroad in an attempt to shore up the economy, as well as divert the young unemployed into the military.

> At the same time they turn to irrationality to compensate for the growing insecurity of life, for the chronic economic depression, for the growing bitterness and dangers of class struggles, for the social disruption and insecurity from imperialist wars. This is generally a period of gambling, use of narcotics and intoxicants, obsession with sex (frequently as perversion), increasing crime, growing numbers of neurotics and psychotics, growing obsession with death and the Hereafter.[15]

In our own time we could add: chronic shopping, over eating, and video addictions.

Quigley goes on to tell us that, "The vested interests encourage the growth of imperialist wars and irrationality because both serve to divert the discontent of the masses away from their vested interests..."[16] These maneuvers are growing more tenuous as the crusade against Islam as a cover for operations to gain control of the oil and mineral rich Eurasian heartland seems to be stalling. As the economic factors don't add up anymore, the machine is starting to sputter. More and more people are leaving the ranks of the mainstream population controlled by the artificial culture of corporate media. The younger generations are not interested in television and the old newspapers, magazines and radio and the population that remains firmly in the ranks backing the status quo elite are being slowly cannibalized by their manipulators who produce a toxic mainstream system that generates disease, obesity and poverty.

The intensified consciousness sees through the games and subterfuge of the false culture of materialism, because it understands that life is lived on many levels simultaneously. It is not about rejecting the material world or possessions. Rather, it is about understanding their place in our lives. It is the play we write not the props we use that ultimately matter. The materialist elite are not the enemy, but "elitism" and the cruelties it produces. At the same time true freedom insists that individuals will create and acquire according to their unique talents and focus. An integral society isn't an economic flat land, but simply one where compassion for the human spirit is built into the very structures of civic life, where people have a place simply by virtue of their humanity and where humanity is given every chance to blossom. This means a society that leaves no slums in its shadow, which truly educates its people and encourages ultimate creativity in the individual without blocking anything on the basis of maintaining the prestige and advantages of those whose creations came first. What this requires is a people who trust human value above empire, that see the deep human impulse as a source of greater life rather than a source of sin or anarchy. Our current culture gives lip service to this idea while it does everything to promote the opposite. As the integral structure of consciousness rises to prominence in the world, humanity will live out this promise without reservation as the values of a fully embodied and connected adventure of multi-dimensional experience replace the fleeting joys of the disconnected ego.

The spirit is in revolt against all that confines, nullifies, and manipulates its thrust toward greater life and you are its insurgent. Every life, human and animal are part of a great logic that defines the orbit of planets, the structure of crystals and sea shells, and the complexity of the human hand and heart. There are those who have asserted that we are born alone and die alone and in between we struggle to find love, intimacy, connection.

Nothing could be further from the truth. We are not born alone and we do not die alone. This is the delusion of an alienated spirit caught in the darkness of the mental/rational structure. Children are born literally as a piece of their mothers and in full, albeit unconscious, connection to the origin of all things, God, the Logos, whatever term you like, they come completely at home in the world. They will learn loneliness, but no child is born with it. We do not need to struggle thereafter because we are literally built into connection with others and the world. We need only open ourselves to this truth within the very structure of our beings. And death must be a great opening as well, as the spirit, the personal energy configuration, if you like, is released from the limitations of the body into the limitless whole of its origin. This must truly be the opposite of alone, rather a great embrace than a solitary farewell.

We are faced with the end of time as we know it – time as an arrow with a beginning shooting off into eternity. This time scheme is a developmental artifact whose hold on us we are overcoming in the intensifying brilliance of our evolving minds. Time is exploding to include timelessness, endless cycles of seasons in time, mythic time as set in motion by culture heroes, and subatomic time that expands from the moment creating the past necessary for its present and spreading out in a fan of probabilities into a future that already exists in multiplicity. Clearly time is a field malleable by the scope of our understanding and the focus we choose. We are particles, individuals in the stream of our origin, and we are waves on that stream fully integrated with the whole as it flows, both still at the center and raging at the periphery.

There is a powerful voice hidden at the center of each life and only cultural delusion and deliberate disinformation can render it mute. That part of us that is tied to the old egocentric materialist culture will go down as it falls and those parts that are expressions of the new culture of the integrated human spirit will flourish as it rises. It isn't about beating an enemy it's about releasing a prisoner. Civilizations grow corrupt as they move to wall off the human spirit in a vain attempt to make eternal that which is transitory. It's time once again to storm the prison gates, the uprising is eternal and the uprising has just begun.

Notes

1. Stephen Toulmin, Cosmopolis, The Hidden Agenda of Modernity (Chicago: University of Chicago Press, 1992).
2. John Ralston Saul, Voltaire's Bastards, The Dictatorship of Reason in the West (New York: Vintage Books, 1993).
3. Lynne McTaggart, The Intention Experiment (New York: Free Press, 2007).
4. Sandra Ingerman & Hank Wesselman, Awakening to the Spirit World, The Shamanic Path of Direct Revelation (Boulder CO: Sounds True, 2010), p. ix.
5. Daniel Goleman, Emotional Intelligence (New York: Bantam Books, 1995).
6. Carl Jung, The Archetypes and the Collective Unconscious, Collected Works, 2nd Ed., vol. 9., part one (Princeton: Bollingen, 1959).
7. Jenny Wade, Transcendent Sex (New York: Paraview, 2004).
8. As quoted in: Joseph Campbell, The Inner Reaches of Outer Space (New York: Alfred Van Der Mack Editions, 1986), p. 44.
9. Campbell, (1986), p. 56.
10. David Feinstein and Stanley Krippner, Personal Mythology (Los Angles: Tarcher, 1988), p.1.
11. Gebser, (1985), p.97.
12. Ibid., p. 289.
13. Ibid., p. 541.
14. Aldous Huxley, Brave New World Revisited (New York: Harper Perennial, 1958, 2005), p. 333.
15. Quigley, (1979), p. 152.
16. Ibid., p. 152.

Appendix

Suggestions for an Integral Uprising

1. We must reclaim the territory of our own minds and bodies. This means wresting control of all structures of consciousness away from the matrix of the machine mind and its socio-political apparatus: the archaic/magic physical vital life, the mythic symbolic narrative of life, and the logic and rationale of the mental life. We are helping to create the dysfunction through deep programing in the egocentric materialist doctrine. A complete review and appraisal of beliefs, habits, activities, feelings and addictions must be undertaken. The future emerges from you.

2. Opt out of being a worker/buyer unit. Work towards the immediate withdrawal of all support for the civilization of side-effects. Reevaluate the role of material things in your life. Undertake a complete review of all buying habits to uncover the lies that sustain the slavery and poisoning of the environment you may be unwittingly supporting. Make plans to reform or withdraw from any employment that in any way perpetuates exploitation, slavery, war, and the pollution of the body and nature.

3. Educate yourself. Most people have not been truly educated but really only indoctrinated and trained to do a job. This is true of even people with advanced degrees. Learning *how* to think is a different task than learning *what* to think. Consult the Trivium, and go on to learn the true history of your world beneath the top inch of managed information. Never accept any mainstream news reporting without cross checking in the alternative press and the foreign media. Utilize fact checking websites like fair.org. The body must be

reeducated as well through the purging of all imperial programing such as that which is perpetuated in action films where physical excitation is coupled with violence and killing.

4. Create an integral life. Review what you fill your time with and replace all that does not support the revitalization of the structures of consciousness. A meditation practice of some kind is vital, be it moving or sitting. The body and its emotional vibratory life must be invigorated with daily action of some sort. Open the senses during activities to broaden a multisensory experience. Build a personal mythology that supports poise and the adventure of creative development where the personal touches the communal. Replace as much isolating "entertainment" with community as you can. Work to withdraw the mental/rational mind from where it doesn't belong. Trust your intuition and allow it to develop. Cultivate ego and time freedom through study and practice.

5. Protect the natural world, wilderness, and ecosystems worldwide. Get out into these environments as often as you can. Consciously open to the field of nature as an extension of your body and mind. It is an originating source for a renewed civilization.

6. Oppose tyranny at every turn and let power know you are watching and are not deceived.

BIBLIOGRAPHY

Arnove, Robert F., editor. *Philanthropy and Cultural Imperialism, The Foundations at Home and Abroad.* Bloomington: Indiana University Press, 1980.
Anti-Imperialist League. www.Wikipedia.com.
Archer, Jules. *The Plot to Seize the White House: The Shocking True Story of the Conspiracy to Overthrow FDR.* New York: Skyhorse Publishing, 1973.
Aurobindo, Sri. *Letters on Yoga.* Pondicherry: Lotus Press, 1995.
Bakan, Joel. *The Corporation, The Pathological Pursuit of Profit and Power.* New York: Free Press, 2004.
Begich, Nick and Jeane Manning. *Angles Don't Play this HAARP.* Eagle River AK: Earthpulse Press, 1995.
Berman, Morris. *Why America Failed.* Hoboken: John Wiley & Sons, Inc. 2012.
Bernays, Edward. *Propaganda.* New York: Ig Publishing, (1928), 2005.
Black, Edwin. *Internal Combustion.* New York: St. Martin's Griffin, 2006.
Bohm, David. *Wholeness and the Implicate Order.* New York: Routledge, 1995.
Bowart, Walter. *Operation Mind Control.* New York: Dell, 1977. bpwhisleblowers.blogspot.com
Bradley, James. *The Imperial Cruise, A Secret History of Empire and War.* New York: Back Bay Books, 2009.
Braud, William. *Distant Mental Influence.* Charlottesville: Hampton Roads, 2003.
Brown, Ellen Hodgson, J.D. *The Web of Debt, The Shocking Truth About Our Money System and How We Can Break Fee.* Baton Rouge: Third Millennium Press, 2010.
Brown, Ellen Hodgson. *Forbidden Medicine.* Baton Rouge: Third Millennium Press, 2008.
Butler, Smedley. *War is a Racket.* Los Angeles: Feral House, (1936), 2012.
Campbell, Joseph. *Oriental Mythology, The Masks of God.* New York: Penguin, 1984.
Campbell, Joseph. *The Inner Reaches of Outer Space.* New York: Alfred Van Der Mack Editions, 1986.
Campbell, T. Colin, PhD and Thomas M. Campbell II. *The China Study, The Most Comprehensive Study of Nutrition Ever Conducted.* Dallas TX: Benbella Books, 2006.
Cardena, Etzel, Steven Jay Lynn, & Stanley Krippner, editors. *Varieties of Anomalous Experience, Examining the Scientific Evidence.* Washington: American Psychological Assoc., 2001.
Carr, Nicholas. *The Shallows, What the Internet is Doing to Our Brains.* New York: Norton, 2010.

Chandogya Upanishad, 3. 18. 1.
Chomsky, Noam. *Deterring Democracy.* New York: Hill & Wang, 1992.
Chomsky, Noam. Media *Control.* New York: Seven Stories Press, 2002.
Constantine, Alex. *Virtual Government, CIA Mind Control Operations in America.* Los Angeles: Feral House, 1997.
Cultural Creatives. www.worldforum.org/creatives-overview.htm
dailytech.com/Monsanto defeats small farmers, 3-1-12.
Dalal A. S. *An Introduction to the Psychological Thought of Sri Aurobindo.* New York: Tarcher/Putnam, 2001.
Dale, Peter Scott. *The Road to 9/11.* Berkeley: Universtiy of California Press, 2008.
De Zengotita, Thomas. *Mediated, How the Media Shapes Your World and the Way You Live in It.* New York: Bloomsbury, 2005.
Desilet, Gregory. *Our Faith in Evil, Melodrama and the Effects of Entertainment Violence.* Jefferson, North Carolina: McFarland & Company Inc., 2006.
Dodd, Norman. Report to the Reece Committee on Foundations. New York: Long House, 1954. http://archive.org/details/DoddReportToTheReeceCommitteeOnFoundations-1954-RobberBaron
Eisen, Jonathan. *Suppressed Inventions & Other Discoveries.* New York: Avery Publishing Group, 1999.
Elgin, Duane. *Awakening Earth, Exploring the Evolution of Human Culture and Consciousness.* New York: William Morrow and Company, Inc., 1993.
Eliade, Mircea. *Shamanism, Archaic Techniques of Ecstasy.* New York: Penguin Arkana, 1964.
Eliot, T.S. *The Hollow Men.* 1925.
Engdahl, F. William. *A Century of War, Anglo-American Oil Politics and the New World Order.* Wiesbaden Germany: edition.engdahl, (1992), 2011.
Engdahl, F. William. *Seeds of Destruction, The Hidden Agenda of Genetic Manipulation.* Montreal: Global Research, 2007.
Engdal, F. William. *Gods of Money, Wall Street and the Death of the American Century.* Joshua Tree: Progressive Press, 2009.
fair.org.
Feinstein, David and Stanley Krippner. *Personal Mythology.* Los Angles: Tarcher, 1988.
Ferguson, Charles H. *Predator Nation: Corporate Criminals, Political Corruption, and the Hijacking of America.* New York: Crown Business, 2013.
Ferguson, Charles, producer. *Inside Job.* Sony Pictures Classics, 2010.
Feuerstein, Georg. *Structures of Consciousness.* Santa Rosa: Integral Publishing, 1987.
Fox News. All Kinds of Sea birds Paralyzed and Dead Around Sarasota. www.YouTube.com .
Frankl, Viktor E. *Man's Search For Meaning.* New York: Washing Square Books, (1946) 1984.
Freeland, Chrystia. *Plutocrats, The Rise of the New Global Superrich and the Fall of Everyone Else.* New York: Penguin Books, 2012.

Freeland, Chrystia. "The Rise of the New Ruling Class, How the Global Elite is Leaving You Behind." *The Atlantic*. January/February, vol. 307, No. 1, 2011.

Freke, Timothy & Peter Gandy. *Jesus and the Lost Goddess*. New York: Three Rivers Press, 2001.

Freke, Timothy & Peter Gandy. *The Jesus Mysteries*. New York: Three Rivers Press, 1999.

Friedman, John S. editor. *The Secret Histories*, An Anthology. New York: Picador, 2005.

Fuller, R. Buckminster and Robert Marks. *The Dymaxion World of Buckminster Fuller*. New York: Anchor Books, 1978.

Fussell, Paul. *Wartime, Understanding and Behavior in the Second World War*. New York: Oxford, 1989.

Gabriel, Richard. *No More Heroes, Madness and Psychiatry in War*. New York: Hill & Wang, 1988.

Gatto, John Taylor. *Dumbing Us Down, The Hidden Curriculum of Compulsory Schooling*. Canada: New Society Publishers, 2005.

Gebser, Jean. *The Ever Present Origin*. Athens: Ohio University Press. 1985.

Goleman, Daniel. *Emotional Intelligence*. New York: Bantam Books, 1995.

Green, Michael. *Theories of Human Development, A Comparative Approach*. Englewood Cliffs: Prentice Hall, 1989.

Greenwald, Glen. *With Liberty and Justice For Some*. New York: Metropolitan Books, 2011.

Griffin, David Ray. *9/11 Ten Years Later, When State Crimes Against Democracy Succeed*. Northhampton, MA: Olive Branch Press, 2011.

Habakus, Louise Kuo, Mary Holland, & Kim Mack Rosenberg, editors. *Vaccine Epidemic, How Corporate Greed, Biased Science, and Coercive Government Threaten Our Human Rights, Our Heath, and Our Children*. New York: Skyhorse Publishing, 2012.

Handcock, Graham & Robert Bauval. *The Master Game*. New York: The Disinformation Company, Ltd., 2011.

Harman, Willis W. and Elisabet Sahtouris. *Biology Revisioned*. Berkeley: North Atlantic Books, 1998.

Harner, Michael. *The Way of the Shaman*. San Francisco: Harper, 1980.

Hart, Tobin, Peter L. Nelson, & Kaisa Puhakka. *Transpersonal Knowing, Exploring the Horizon of Consciousness*. Albany: Suny, 2000.

Hastings, Michael. The Afghanistan Report the Pentagon Doesn't Want You to Read. www.rollingstone.com, posted: February 10, 2012.

Hawks, John. www.johnhawks.net

Hedges, Chris. *American Fascists*. New York: Free Press, 2007.

Hedges, Chris. *Death of the Liberal Class*. New York: Nation Books, 2010.

Hedges, Chris. *Empire of Illusion, The End of Literacy and the Triumph of Spectacle*. New York: Nation Books, 2009.

Hoopes, James. *False Prophets*. New York: Basic Books, 2003.

Huntington, Tom. www.americanwwii.com/stories/audiemurphy.

Huxley, Aldous. *Brave New World Revisited*. New York: Harper Perennial, (1958), 2005.

Ingerman, Sandra & Hank Wesselman. *Awakening to the Spirit World, The Shamanic Path of Direct Revelation.* Boulder CO: Sounds True, 2010.
investigate911.org
Jefferson, Thomas. "Notes on the State of Virginia," Jefferson. New York: The Library of America, 1984.
Johnson, Chalmers. *The Sorrows of Empire, Militarism, Secrecy, and the End of the Republic.* New York: Metropolitan Books, 2004.
Johnson, Simon and James Kwak. *13 Bankers, The Wall Street Takeover and the Next Financial Meltdown.* New York: Vintage Books, 2011.
Jones, Gerard. *Killing Monsters, Why Children Need Fantasy, Super Heroes, and Make-Believe Violence.* New York: Basic Books, 2002.
Joseph, Sister Miriam, CSC, PhD. *The Trivium, The Liberal Arts of Logic, Grammar, And Rhetoric.* Philadelphia: Paul Dry Books, (1937), 2002.
Josephson, Matthew. *The Robber Barons.* New York: Harcourt, Brace, & Co., (1933) 1962.
Jung, Carl. The Archetypes and the Collective Unconscious. *Collected Works,* 2nd Ed., vol. 9., part one, Princeton: Bollingen, 1959.
Jung, Carl. *The Structure and Dynamics of the Psyche.* Princeton: Bollingen, Princeton University Press, 1960.
Kaku, Michio. *Parallel Worlds.* New York: Anchor Books, 2005.
Kasser, Tim. *The High Price of Materialism.* Cambridge: MIT Press, 2002.
Kauffman, Stuart A. *Reinventing the Sacred, A New Vision of Science, Reason, and Religion.* New York: Basic Books, 2008.
Kurzwell, Ray. *Reinventing Humanity: The Future of Machine-Human Intelligence.* www.singularity.com, March 4, 2006.
Lane, Robert E. *The Loss of Happiness in Market Democracies.* New Haven: Yale University Press, 2000.
Leach, William. *Land of Desire, Merchants, Power and the Rise of a New American Culture.* New York: Vintage Books, 1994.
Lemov, Rebecca. *World as Laboratory, Experiments with Mice, Mazes, and Men.* New York: Hill & Wang, 2005.
Lindauer, Susan. CIA Whistleblower exposes everything. www.YouTube.
Lipton, Bruce H. & Steve Bhaerman. *Spontaneous Evolution, Our Positive Future.* New York: Hay House, 2009.
Machiavelli, Niccolo. *The Prince.* New York: Dutton, Every Man's Library edition, 1958.
Mackay, Neil. *The War on Truth.* Drexel Hill PA: Casemate, 2006.
Manchester, William. The Bloodiest Battle of All. *New York Times Magazine,* June 14, 1987.
Mangan, Katherine. Today's Students are More Globally Aware, Less Materialistic, Leading Pollster Says. http://chronicle.com/article/Today-s-Students-Are-More/47701, posted: June 7, 2009.
Marks, John. *In Search for the Manchurian Candidate.* New York: Norton, 1991.
Mason, David S. *The End of the American Century.* New York: Rowman & Littlefield, 2009.

McChesney, Robert W. *The Problem with the Media: US Communication Politics in the 21st Century.* New York: Monthly Review Press, 2004.

McLuhan, Marshall. *The Medium is the Message, An Inventory of Effects.* Berkeley: Ginko Press Inc., 1967.

McTaggart, Lynne. *The Intention Experiment.* New York: Free Press, 2007.

Media Black-Out on Single-Payer Healthcare. http://fair.org/take-action/media-advisories/fair-study-media-blackout-on-single-payer-healthcare/, posted: March 6, 2009.

Mills, C. Wright. *The Power Elite.* New York: Oxford, (1956), 2000.

Milton, Richard. *Alternative Science, Challenging the Myths of the Scientific Establishment.* Rochester: Park Street Press,1996.

Mindell, Arnold. *Dream Body.* Boston: Sigo Press, 1982.

Mindell, Arnold. *Quantum Mind.* Portland: Lao Tse Press, 2000.

Moyers, Bill. The Secret Government. www.YouTube.com.

Murolo, Priscilla & A. B. Chitty. *From the Folks Who Brought You the Weekend* .New York: The New Press, 2001.

Nestle, Marion. *Food Politics, How the Food Industry Influences Nutrition and Health.* Berkeley: University of California Press, 2013.

newscientist.com. Revealed: The Capitalist Network that Runs the World.

Nichols, John & Robert W. McChesney. *Tragedy & Farce, How the American Media Sell Wars, Spin Elections, and destroy Democracy.* New York: The New Press, 2005.

O'Leary, Brian. *The Energy Solution Revolution.* Hayden ID: Bridger House, 2009.

Packard, Vance. *The People Shapers.* Boston: Little, Brown & Company, 1977.

Pagels, Elaine. *Beyond Belief, The Secret Gospel of Thomas.* New York: Random House, 2003.

Pagels, Elaine. *The Gnostic Gospels.* New York: Vintage Books, 1989.

PBS. "Flying Cheap," *Frontline.*

Perkins, John. *The Secret History of the American Empire.* New York: Dutton, 2007.

Petersen, Melody. *Our Daily Meds.* New York: Picador, 2008.

Picknett, Lynn & Clive Prince. *The Forbidden Universe, The Occult Origins of Science and the Search for the Mind of God.* London: Constable and Robinson, Ltd, 2011.

Postman, Neil. *Amusing Ourselves to Death, Public Discourse in the Age of Show Business.* New York: Penguin, 1985.

projectcensored.org

Project for a New American Century. www.Wikipedia.com

Quigley, Carroll. *The Evolution of Civilizations, An Introduction To Historical Analysis.* Indianapolis: Liberty Fund, 1979.

Radin, Dean. *Entangled Minds.* New York: Paraview Pocket Books, 2006.

Radin, Dean. *The Conscious Universe.* San Francisco: Harper Edge, 1997.

Rampton, Sheldon and John Stauber. *Trust Us, We're Experts! How Industry Manipulates Science and Gambles with your Future.* New York: Tarcher/Putnam, 2002.

Riesman, David, Nathan Glazer, & Reuel Denney. *The Lonely Crowd*. New Haven: Yale University Press, (1950), 2001.

Root-Bernstein, Robert and Michele. *Sparks of Genius,The 13 Thinking Tools of the World's Most Creative People*. Boston: Mariner Books, 2001.

Rosenblum, Bruce and Fred Kuttner. *Quantum Enigma*. New York: Oxford, 2006.

Rousseau, Jean-Jacques. *Reveries of the Solitary Walker*. New York: Oxford, (1778), 2011.

Saul, John Ralston. *The Collapse of Globalism and the Reinvention of the World*. New York: Penguine, 2006.

Saul, John Ralston. *Voltaire's Bastards, The Dictatorship of Reason in the West*. New York: Vintage Books, 1993.

Scheuer, Michael. *Imperial Hubris, Why the West is Losing the War on Terror*. Dulles VI: Potomac Books, 2007.

shadowstats.com

Shakespeare William, *As You Like It*.

Sheldrake, Rupert. *Science Set Free, 10 Paths to New Discovery*. New York: Crown Publishing, 2012.

Slotkin, Richard. *Regeneration Through Violence*. Hanover NH: Wesleyan, 1973.

Stevens, Henry. *Hitler's Suppressed and Still Secret Weapons, Science, and Technology*. Kempton IL: Adventures Unlimited Press, 2005.

Suskind, Ron. *Faith, Certainty, and the Presidency of George W. Bush*. New York Times Magazine. October 17, 2004.

Sutton, Antony C. *Wall Street and the Rise of Hitler*. San Pedro, CA: GSG & Associates, 2002.

Swanson, Claude. *The Synchronized Universe, New Science of the Paranormal*. Tucson: Poseidia Press, 2003.

Taylor, Charles. *The Ethics of Authenticity*. Cambridge: Harvard University Press, 1991.

Taylor, Eldon. *Mind Programing*. New York: Hay House, 2009.

The 2007& 2008 Shift Reports. Petaluma: The Institute of Noetic Sciences, 2007 and 2008.

The Center for Media and Democracy: www. sourcewatch.org.

The Zapping of Greenham and Seneca. *Peace and Freedom Magazine*, Jan./Feb. 1989.

Thompson William Irwin. *Self and Society, Studies in the Evolution of Culture*. Charlottesville: Imprint Academic, 2009.

Thompson, William Irwin. *The American Replacement of Nature, The Everyday Acts and Outrageous Evolution of Economic Life*. New York: Doubleday Currency 1991.

Three Initiates. *The Kybalion, Hermetic Philosophy*. Chicago: Yoga Publications, (1912), 1940.

Tobin, Maryann. Matt Simmons: BP, CIA Conspiracy Theory Suggested Behind His Unexpected Death. www.examiner.com Aug. 11, 2010.

Toulmin, Stephen. *Cosmopolis, The Hidden Agenda of Modernity*. Chicago: University of Chicago Press, 1992.

Towle, Eric W. *An Exploration of the Experience of Paradigm Change in the Individual*. Ann Arbor: ProQuest LLC, 2010.
Valenstein, Eliot S. *Blaming the Brain, The Truth About Drugs and Mental Health*. New York: Free Press, 1998.
Vesperman, Gary. History of New Energy Suppression Cases. http://rense.com/general72/oinvent.htm, posted: June 19, 2006.
Wade, Jenny. *Transcendent Sex*. New York: Paraview, 2004.
Washburn, Jennifer. *University Inc., The Corporate Corruption Of Higher Education*. New York: Basic Books, 2005.
Wilber, Ken. *Sex, Ecology, Spirituality*. Boston: Shambhala, 1995.
Wilber, Ken. *The Marriage of Sense and Soul*. New York: Broadway Books, 1998.
Wilford, Hugh. *The Mighty Wurlitzer: How the CIA Played America*. Cambridge: Harvard University Press, 2009.
Wolin, Sheldon S. *Democracy Inc. Managed Democracy and the Spector of Inverted Totalitarianism*. Princeton: Princeton University Press, 2008.
Yale Journal of Medicine and Law, October 2010, Vol. VII, issue I.

Index

2008 financial crisis 117

Afghanistan 124, 187, 188, 200, 268, 293, 306, 307, 309, 387

alternative energy 122, 247

American Empire 312, 389

Anti-Imperialist League 19, 52, 385

archaic structure of consciousness 43, 319, 320, 333

Aurobindo, Sri 36, 53, 385, 386

automobile industry 7, 231, 232

banking 6, 7, 20, 22, 175, 185, 197, 198, 199, 230, 282, 295, 306, 309, 310, 367, 374, 378

Berman, Morris 53, 385

Bernays, Edward 242, 244, 270
Propaganda 242, 270, 385

biology xxviii, xxx, 29, 32, 41, 67, 146, 147, 150, 261, 262

Biology 90, 146, 339, 387

Bohm, David 65, 90, 385

British Petroleum oil spill 238

Bush, George W. 184, 268, 303, 304, 390

Bush the First 298, 299

Campbell, Joseph 118, 135, 336, 338, 340, 341, 352, 366, 381, 385

Capitalist Network that Runs the World 52, 389

Chandogya Upanishad 89, 386

Chomsky, Noam 268, 269, 300, 312, 386

Christianity xiii, xxii, 71, 74, 77, 78, 80, 84, 86, 88, 191, 310

CIA 169, 170, 172, 195, 238, 256, 257, 258, 268, 270, 289, 298, 310, 386, 388, 390, 391

consciousness structures 45, 109

corporate xx, xxv, xxxi, xxxv, xxxvii, 6, 7, 14–16, 18, 20, 22, 23, 26, 30, 53, 72, 87, 107, 108, 112, 130, 140, 163, 167–173, 177, 180, 185, 186, 193, 204, 207, 208, 212, 213, 214, 222, 225, 227, 228, 234, 235, 240, 242, 249, 257, 263–267, 269, 295, 297–299, 302, 303, 306, 310, 317, 332, 348, 367, 368, 372–374, 377–379, 386, 387, 391

corruption xx, 182, 295, 314

Creel Commission 242

cultural creatives 23, 386

Democracy 52, 268, 312, 373, 386, 387, 389, 390, 391

De Zengotita, Thomas 268, 386

dumbing 180, 222, 374

education xxvi, xxxv, xxxvi, 10, 86, 121, 133, 153, 156, 175, 178, 180, 182, 189, 205, 213, 216, 218–221, 223–225, 228, 256, 371, 374, 391

Duane Elgin 52, 58, 386

energy weapons 259

Engdahl, F. William 198, 268

393

eugenics 198

evolution ix–xiii, xv, xvi, xix, xxii, xxiii, xxv, xxvi, xxviii, xxix, xxxiv, xxxvii, 2, 21, 23–27, 30, 32, 34, 35, 37, 39, 41, 42, 51, 58, 63, 68, 70, 72, 74, 76–79, 81, 83, 87, 88, 95, 100, 109–111, 116, 119–121, 129, 131, 132, 146, 147, 150, 174, 193, 203, 210, 252, 261, 262, 266, 311, 317– 319, 322, 329, 335, 337, 345, 349–351, 354, 356, 359, 363–365, 367, 373, 374, 375, 386, 388, 389, 390

false flag 181, 307

Federal Reserve 131, 199

Food Politics 269, 389

foundations xiii, xix, xxxi, xxxviii, 22, 40, 82, 178, 181, 182, 183, 184, 213, 216, 222, 252, 317, 321, 328, 330, 385, 386

Freeland, Chrystia xxxix, 52, 386, 387
  Plutocrats xliv, 386

French revolution 84, 85

frontier thesis 274, 275

Fuller, R. Buckminster 269, 387

Gatto, John Taylor 216, 218, 269, 387

Gebser, Jean xv, xxxiv, xxxviii, xxxix, 24, 32, 35, 36, 37, 39, 41, 52, 63, 79, 85, 128, 135, 225, 315, 318, 319, 343, 347, 351, 355, 358, 365, 387, 390

genetics 104

Germany 20, 196, 198, 200, 219, 221, 230, 231, 250, 268, 279, 282, 283, 284, 386

globalism 21, 167, 174, 390

Gnostics 75, 77, 83, 85, 86

Hawks, John 9, 24, 44, 52, 53, 56, 100, 107, 126, 148, 174, 181, 205, 211, 216, 218, 225, 226, 253, 254, 268, 269, 270, 288, 296, 297, 303, 311, 312, 315, 317, 381, 385, 387, 388, 389, 390

health care 6, 139, 154, 240, 241

Hedges, Chris 90, 195, 268, 270, 387

Hermetic wisdom 55, 84

Huxley, Aldous 373, 381, 387

Imperialism xxxviii, 181, 268, 296, 385
  American 181, 268, 296, 385
  British 181, 268, 296, 385

institutionalization 5, 375

Intention Experiment 323, 381, 389

Internet 174, 186, 202, 203, 214, 240, 258, 268, 369, 385

Iraq war 198

Japan 168, 265, 284, 286, 306

Jefferson, Thomas xxx, 10, 27, 45, 53, 90, 103, 117, 178, 191, 197, 211, 224, 228, 231, 234, 268, 269, 270, 280, 385, 386, 388, 389

Jesus 74, 76, 88, 90, 387

Johnson, Simon and James Kwak 51
  13 Bankers 388

Jung, Carl 33, 34, 40, 53, 61, 62, 101, 104, 134, 194, 332, 381, 388

Kauffman, Stuart A. xxxviii, 388

Kurzwell, Ray. 388

labor xxxvi, 10, 11, 21, 30, 83, 89, 127, 162, 169, 170, 177, 195, 199, 200, 252, 292

Leach, William 10, 14, 52, 61, 69, 82, 89, 90, 194, 198, 251, 268, 269, 278, 283, 291, 317, 385, 386, 388, 390,

Lemov, Rebecca 90, 201, 270, 388

Machiavelli, Niccolo 248, 270, 388

magic structure of consciousness 34, 322, 323, 326, 327, 328, 330, 333, 334, 351, 370, 375

management theory 251

materialism xix, xx, xxii, xxiv, xxv, xxxiv,

25, 30, 42, 46, 49, 53, 56, 59, 69, 73, 89, 94, 95, 99, 102, 103, 109, 113, 114, 117, 122, 125, 126, 128, 142, 144, 174, 177, 193, 213, 216, 363, 369, 374, 376, 379, 388

McLuhan, Marshall 263, 268, 389

media xxv, xxvi, xxxv, xxxvi, 6, 8, 14, 48, 52, 72, 94, 101, 172, 180, 184, 185, 186, 187, 188, 189, 190, 193, 194, 195, 196, 203, 214, 234, 239, 240, 241, 250, 257, 259, 263, 264, 265, 267, 268, 270, 295, 297, 300, 303, 305, 312, 367, 373, 374, 377, 378, 379, 383, 389

media manipulation 52, 180

melodrama 212, 269, 386

mental/rational structure of consciousness 57, 128, 141, 159, 166, 168, 193, 261, 308, 342, 344, 351, 375

Mills, C. Wright 48, 53, 349, 389

mind control xxxv, xxxvi, 51, 79, 181, 201, 249, 250, 256–259, 265, 267, 270, 377, 385, 386

Moyers, Bill 175

The Secret Government 175, 389

Murphy, Audie 44

mythological structure of consciousness 34, 281

mythology xxxvii, 3, 9, 17, 34, 74, 75, 76, 80, 82, 94, 105, 118, 135, 144, 273, 276, 277, 282, 293, 294, 316, 338, 340, 341, 344, 345, 352, 356, 360, 371, 384–386

Nazi xxvi, 20, 198, 201, 213, 221, 227, 230, 282

non-material reality 100

oil xxxii, 6, 7, 20, 22, 94, 169, 170, 171, 172, 180, 182, 197, 198, 201, 213, 229, 230, 234, 235, 237, 238, 239, 240, 243, 247, 285, 293, 296, 297, 298, 299, 301, 305, 309, 310, 379, 386

O'Leary, Brian 237, 270, 389

Operation Northwoods 307

paradigm xxx, 57, 59, 213, 216

parapsychology 59, 61, 322, 323

Perkins, John 296, 297, 303, 312, 389

Postman, Neil 269, 389

power elite 21, 27, 73, 183, 273, 376

Project for a New American Century 312, 389

psychology xxxiv, xxxv, xxxvii, 13, 62, 63, 82, 83, 97, 101, 104, 116, 182, 183, 190, 242, 253, 255, 256, 311, 332, 343

public relations xxxv, 15, 16, 180, 241, 244, 245

quantum physics 56, 57, 64, 65, 376

Quigley, Carroll 4, 52, 389

The Evolution of Civilizations 389

Reece Committee on Foundations 269, 386

Riesman, David, Nathan Glazer, & Reuel Denney 134

The Lonely Crowd 107, 108, 134, 390

Robber Barons 231, 388

Roman Empire xxvi, 13, 74, 84

Rousseau, Jean-Jacques 85, 135, 225, 315, 390

Rupert Sheldrake 53, 104, 216

Saul, John Ralston 52, 315, 381, 390

Scheuer, Michael 310, 312, 390

Science xviii, xxxviii, 7, 53, 56, 60, 90, 156, 183, 225, 228, 234, 268, 269, 270, 271, 281, 338, 341, 387, 388, 389, 390

Shakespeare, William 69, 90, 194

Shamanism 53, 326, 386

Sheldrake, Rupert 53, 104, 216

social engineering 216, 218, 254

395

students 164, 174, 217, 220, 222

Suppressed Inventions 53, 386

Taylor, Charles 130, 135
  The Ethics of Authenticity 130, 135, 390

Taylor, Eldon 259, 271
  Mind Programing 260, 271, 390

Thompson, William Irwin 14, 52, 269, 390

tragic drama 212

transhumanism 181, 260, 261

Transpersonal Knowing 90, 387

Trivium 269, 388

university xxxi, 7, 30, 153, 154, 228, 238

unwarranted power 117

vaccines 214, 215

Wilber, Ken xxxviii, 53, 158, 171, 264, 328, 365, 391

Wolin, Sheldon S. 391

World Trade Center 258, 303, 305

www.ingramcontent.com/pod-product-compliance
Lightning Source LLC
Chambersburg PA
CBHW022056150426
43195CB00008B/157